The Book of
Daniel

Writings and Prophecies

G. Erik Brandt

The Book of
Daniel

Writings and Prophecies

G. Erik Brandt

Copyright © 2018

Published by: Independent Publisher

Lehi, Utah, USA

First edition produced by Independent Publisher, August 2018

First Printing August 2018, First Edition (Electronic) August 2018

Version 1.12 - 12.04.2018

Cover designed by: Erik Brandt

Cover art: "Daniel Answers to the King" Manchester Museum of Art by Briton Riviere 1892, © 2018, Used with Permission

Printed in the United States of America

ISBN 13: 978-0-692-16672-7

ISBN-10: 0-692-16672-6

Acknowledgements:

To my good wife, Shari and my wonderful children who have always kept me grounded and centered in what is really important. To my parents, Edward and Carol Brandt, who have ever been supportive and helped build my love for the Gospel of Jesus Christ.

Special thanks to the Chief Editors: Cal Stephens, Susan Schauerhamer, Shari Brandt, Carol Brandt

Special thanks to the reviewers Ed and Carol Brandt, David Brandt, Brad Probst, Susan Schauerhamer and other evaluators who offered clarifying points and invaluable insights and corrections.

Special Note

All efforts were made to be accurate and in accordance with the doctrines and teachings of The Church of Jesus Christ of Latter-day Saints. However, the author is solely responsible for the contents of this book.

You will also note that to properly address the subject matter of the visions a significant amount of historical exposition is required. So enjoy it!

5

Table of Contents

Table of Pictures, Maps and Illustrations

PREFACE

The Book of Daniel is comprised of six historical events or stories and four visions. The histories and prophetic visions of the prophet are among the most compelling found in scripture. His well-known stories of his faithfulness in the courts of the kings have inspired generations. His visions depict the rise and fall of the gentile kingdoms from his day to the latter-days and the conflicts that befall the competing nations are detailed with impressive accuracy (Chapters 7-12). They serve as a guide to foretell God's dealings with the gentiles and the chosen people. Each chapter contains important lessons, panoramic details and messages. Perhaps the most quoted among Latter-day Saints is the prophecy of the kingdom of God, "the stone cut without hands," that rolls forth to become a mountain and break the nations of the world. Daniel saw that the mountain would eventually fill the whole earth (Dan. 2:44; 7:18).

A key and relatively unknown prophecy from Daniel's record is the account of the Seventy Sevens, which speaks of the return of the Jews to rebuild the temple and Jerusalem and the prophetic announcement of the coming of the Messiah (Dan. 9:25-26). What makes this prophecy so impressive is how Gabriel presents the vision using a coded timeline (Dan. 9:23-26). The nature of the revealed clues and the precision with which they are fulfilled demonstrates God's great care in planning future events relative to His people and the mission of the Messiah.

Daniel's prophecies are as profound as John's Revelation or Isaiah's writings. They are as detailed as Nephi's visions of His people in the

Promised Land (1 Ne. 11-14, 22). The Lord used them as He taught the twelve on the Mount of Olives. He specifically referred to Daniel's vision of the "abomination of desolation" (Matt. 24:15; see also Dan. 9:27; Dan. 8:11-13), which predicts the desecration of the temple by Rome and the scattering of the Jews. A similar abomination of desolation is prophesied to come again in the latter-days when the saints come under great persecution and the world is engulfed in battles and consumed in conflict. His writings are rich in prophetic substance and provide insight, not only of what is to come, but how to prepare and endure well.

Associated with the turbulent events leading to the Second Coming, Daniel was shown the Ancient of Days (Adam), who, with his heavenly hosts, will come to defend the Saints in a time of great tribulation (Dan. 12:1). He will "sit" (or preside) at a great council at Adam-ondi-Ahman, declaring the end of the kingdoms of the world and pronouncing the downfall of the kingdom of the devil. The council will consist of the great dispensational leaders and the faithful saints from all ages who will meet the Lord and give an account of their earthly stewardships.[1] The record declares: "a thousand thousands ministered unto him, and ten thousand times ten thousand stood before him: the judgment was set, and the books were opened" (Dan. 7:10). The great congregation will then sustain the Lord as the Messiah, the King of kings and Lord over the earth. (Doctrine and Covenants 116).

Daniel's visions are remarkable, together with the stories of faithfulness and devotion to God, his record provides great insights and teaching to be both studied and pondered.

Daniel: A Man of Wisdom and a Prophet

The Hebrew name Daniel means "God is judge." Very little is known of his parentage or background prior to his arrival into Babylon. We understand that he was born and lived in Judah during the reign of king Josiah. In those days, the king exerted great effort to reform the Jews and turn them again to the Law of Moses (2 Kgs. 22:1-10). While Daniel was still young, Josiah was killed in battle with the Egyptians near Megiddo and was succeeded by his second son Jehoiakim (also known as Elkiam) (2 Kgs. 23:29), a wicked and brutal man. Jehoiakim ruled when the Babylonians first besieged the land and Jerusalem. After three years, Judah was forced to surrender and pay tribute to the Babylonian empire. In subsequent years, especially during Babylon's second siege, Jehoiakim became

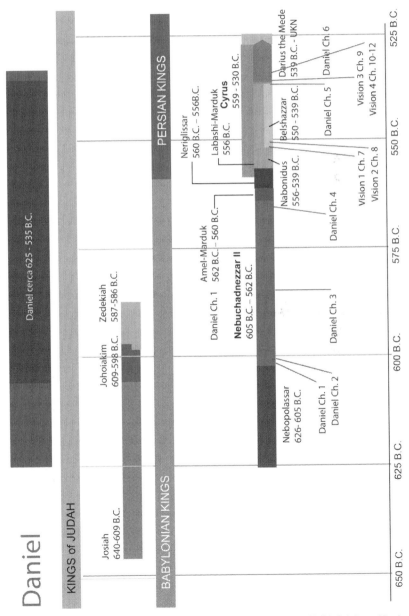

Timeline of the Life of Daniel overlaid with the kingdoms of Judah, Babylon and Persia

an unruly, even violent ruler and lost all favor with the Lord and the people. The records say that he was a godless tyrant who committed many atrocities and crimes. He reintroduced the sacrifices of children into the nation's idolatry. He lived in incestuous relations and was in the habit of murdering men (2 Kings 24:4) whose spouses he violated and whose property he seized. He tattooed his body in defiance of the law.[2] The exact nature of his death is unknown. One record says that "Nebuchadnezzar king of Babylon...bound him in fetters, to carry him to Babylon" (2 Chron. 36:6; Ezek. 19:5-9). When he died, his body was "buried with the burial of an ass, drawn and cast forth beyond the gates of Jerusalem" (Jer. 22:19). Daniel would have grown up under his contentious and unstable reign. The nation grappled with the evil king and corrupt officials and priesthood and the people themselves were largely wicked and unruly.

When Nebuchadnezzar conquered Jerusalem, he brought back "certain, [or specially selected] of the children of Israel, and of the king's seed, and of the princes" (Dan. 1:3) to be hostages in Babylon. His intent was also to reform them and make them part of the governing body and aristocracy. Daniel and his kin, Hananiah, Mishael and Azariah, were among those taken to be taught and molded in the Babylonian system and culture. We may surmise that Daniel's lineage was royal perhaps a cousin to the king and a prince in Israel. Whatever his lineage and most importantly, it meant that he was educated, skilled in government, learned, cultured, and well versed in the Law of Moses and the prophets.

Young Daniel and his companions were taken from Jerusalem after Nebuchadnezzar took control over the kingdom. He lived through the reign of four Babylonian kings and the Medo-Persian emperors Cyrus and Darius. This long time of service would place him in his late 80's or early 90's at the time of his death. He witnessed the first companies of Jews leave Babylon and return to the Promised Land.

The prophet was revered among his contemporaries and certainly a hero to the exiled of Judah in the Chaldean provinces. Ezekiel knew and spoke very highly of him, pointing to his life as a pattern of righteousness and one pleasing to God.[3] He held up Daniel as a man of great wisdom (Ezek. 28:3). Daniel's integrity was compared to that of father Noah and the great prince and priest Job (Ezek. 14:14, 20; 28:3). Wherever he went, he rose to prominence and prospered in every situation—from the courts of King Jehoiakim in Jerusalem, to the palaces of Nebuchadnezzar in Babylon, to high positions under Cyrus and Darius. His life's circumstance did not change his character. Whether he was promoted to great and powerful positions in government (Dan. 2:45-46) or passed through precarious and seditious plots against his life (Dan. 6), he remained faithful and steadfast.

His diligence and loyalty to God earned him great gifts of the spirit. Specifically mentioned were those of wisdom and understanding (Dan. 1:17, 20; 5:11-14), revealing and interpreting dreams (Dan. 1:17; 5:14), competence in administration and the diversity of operations (Dan. 2:48; 6:1-2), interpreting writings and languages (Dan. 5) and receiving visions. He possessed great humility, integrity, loyalty, charity and demonstrated unshakable faith in the Lord. He was beloved of the angels and of God (Daniel 9:23; 10:19).

By his late years, Daniel beheld many dreams and visions. Few individuals experienced and witnessed more sweeping and compressive visions than did he.

The Record of Daniel

Daniel's record is divided into both historical and prophetic sections. The historical accounts were written primarily in Aramaic and the visions in Hebrew.[4] His histories center in the experiences he and his companions had with the kings that ruled in Babylon. Chapters 1–6 present six poignant stories that prove pivotal in their lives, testing their faith and devotion to the God of Israel, demonstrating wisdom and fidelity. Their faithfulness brought benefits to the prophet and his fellow kindred as well as the kingdoms they served. At each point, Daniel and his companions passed the test and were prospered and elevated.

A brief synopsis of each chapter (1-6) is as follows:

Chapter 1   Daniel and his fellows are taken from Jerusalem to Babylon to be trained and educated in the courts of Nebuchadnezzar. They refuse to eat the king's meal and associate with the pagan rites connected with the meals. For their obedience, they are blessed with spiritual gifts in matters of wisdom and understanding. Daniel is given the gift of visions and interpretation of visions.

Chapter 2   Nebuchadnezzar dreams of a great statue and sees its destruction. He commands the wise men and astrologers to relate the dream and interpret its meaning. They cannot and the king orders their death. Daniel and his friends petition the Lord to see the vision and know its interpretation. He is granted his desire. He relays the dream and the meaning to the king and is promoted in the province along with his companions. Daniel's God is praised.

Chapter 3   Nebuchadnezzar creates a great statue of himself and commands that the rulers and people of the kingdom worship it. Shadrach, Meshach and Abed-nego refuse and are cast into a fiery furnace. The Lord preserves them from death by fire. The God of Israel is acknowledged and revered throughout the kingdom.

Chapter 4   Nebuchadnezzar dreams another dream of a large tree and its protective branches. The tree is cut down with only the stump and root remaining. Daniel interprets the dream as representing the king. The prophet warns that if he does not humble himself, care for the poor and acknowledge the God of Heaven as the source of his success, the kingdom will be taken from him.

Nebuchadnezzar disregards the warning and

is struck mad. After seven years, he is restored again to his throne. He testifies that God rules in the heavens and sets men up as earthly rulers.

Chapter 5   The historical background for this chapter is the time just prior to the Persians conquering of Babylon. The regent king Belshazzar, the son of King Nabonidus, revels in a lifestyle of wickedness and decadence. He calls upon the Babylonian idol god to save them from the invading Persians. Jehovah weighs his life in the balance and the end of his kingdom is decreed. The message of this judgement is written on the palace wall. Daniel is called to interpret the writing. That night Cyrus, king of Persia, overthrows the kingdom of Babylon.

Chapter 6   Leading governing princes in Babylon scheme against Daniel who is designated as the president of the Satraps. Darius, king of the province, is deceived into making a proclamation that all should pray to him for counsel. Daniel prays to the God of Israel and is arrested and cast into the lion's den. Angels attend him and close the mouths of the lions. His accusers are cast in for treachery and are devoured by the lions.

Chapters 7–12 present prophetic visions of Daniel relative to the children of the covenant and the history of future gentile kingdoms. These visions span from his day to the end of the world. A brief synopsis of each chapter is as follows:

Chapter 7   A panoramic vision of successive gentile kingdoms from Babylon, Persia, Greece, and Rome down to the latter-day gentile nations and the end of the world. The prophet sees the rise and fall of each gentile kingdom and the eventual establishment of the Kingdom of God and the coming of the Lord. He sees the millennial day when the saints are given the Kingdom and power to rule and reign on the earth.

instruction and insights. It serves as an epilogue to all the visions. In the last days, Michael will come in defense of the children of the covenant amidst great tribulation and provide special insight into the Abomination of Desolation of the last days. This period includes a time of persecution of the Saints. Such persecutions will involve the taking away the sacrifices or religious freedoms by the ruling anti-Christs. A vision and brief description of the resurrection and judgment is given. The record is sealed up along with the understanding of revelation. The meaning of the visions will unfold as history is fulfilled.

Chiasm, Style and Message

The entire book of Daniel follows a chiastic structure. A Chiasm is a literary style frequently used in scriptural text, which is arranged in a pattern of repetition to give emphasis or clarification of an overarching message. A sample pattern may order subjects in the form of ABBA or ABXBA, with "X" representing a central idea that is supplemented or supported by subjects A and B. These subjects may be arranged within verses or chapters. The ideas in the book of Daniel are presented in the chapters. The book of Daniel contains two interlocked chiasms arranged as follows: AB-CC-BA-DED (see: table below).

The Book of Daniel's Chiastic Structure			Style	Language
A	Introduction 1: Current Exile (Ch. 1) Nebuchadnezzar has a Dream of four gentile kingdoms and the Kingdom of God (Ch. 2)		Narrative (Story)	Hebrew
	B	Nebuchadnezzar sees God's servants rescued (Ch. 3)	Narrative	Aramaic
		C Nebuchadnezzar judged (Ch. 4)	Narrative	Aramaic

C Belshazzar judged (Ch. 5)	Narrative	Aramaic
B Daniel rescued from plot. Darius praises God of Daniel (Ch. 6)	Narrative	Aramaic
Introduction 2: Future Return from Exile A Daniel has Visions of 4 Kingdoms and the Kingdom of God (Ch. 7)	Vision	Aramaic
D Details on post-Babylonian gentile kingdoms: Persia, Greece (Ch. 8)	Vision	Hebrew
E *The children of Israel people restored (Ch. 9)*	Vision	Hebrew
D Additional insight into post-Babylonian kingdoms (Ch 10-12)	Vision	Hebrew

*Chiasm structure adapted from Andrew E. Steinmann in *Daniel Concordia Commentary*

The first central idea in Daniel is found in subjects **C-C** that focuses on God's dealings with Babylon and its rulers. In Chapter 4 (C^1), Nebuchadnezzar is chastened and shown his true fallen nature and station as a mortal in comparison to God and the heavens. In Chapter 5 (C^2), Belshazzar is removed from power because of decadence and disrespect for the sacred things of God and His commandment. Babylon falls. Supporting this idea of God's management of the kingdom of Babylon are the subjects found in patterns AB and BA (Ch. 2-3 and 6-7). These subjects center on Judah's positive influence in the Babylonian kingdom through faithful servants like Daniel. Insight into how chosen men like Daniel and the Chosen People assist God in managing the affairs the kingdoms is captured in the chiasm (**D-D Ch. 8-10-12**).[5]

This idea is evident again in the second chiasm that extends the theme of God's influence on the gentile nations to the end of the world. In **E (Ch. 9)**, God's people will be restored and play a critical role in God's hands to both bless and curse the nations.

We observe this pattern throughout the record. God oversees the rise and fall of kings and nations through the centuries. In the end, His purposes are fulfilled and the chosen people play an influential role of bearing the priesthood and the covenant blessing of the Gospel to the world (Abr. 2:9). In the latter-days, the kingdom is restored, the chosen of God are established as a mighty people and are preserved through the trials and machinations of the events leading to the coming of the Lord.

Daniel's record provides powerful insights into God's planning and watch care for His children as they pass through their mortal experience. The sequence of stories and visions demonstrates both the Lord's foresight and oversight. It emphasizes the prosperity of the obedient and the fall of the ruler, kings or kingdoms who ignored or rejected the influence of His spirit (Dan. 5). Babylon's rise and fall provides a vivid portrayal of the positive and negative consequences awaiting the nations of the earth based on the adherence to the counsel and direction of the God of heaven (Doctrine and Covenants 88:45-50). Elder Bruce R. McConkie taught: "When the real history of the world is written, it will show God's dealings with men, and the place the gospel has played in the rise and fall of nations."[6]

Just as in ancient days, in the latter-days, modern Babylon, or the modern nations of the earth, will be prospered or suffer according to their heed to the spirit of truth and inspiration as given through the Lord. If the nations reject Him and His spirit, they too will fall away into history. President Brigham Young counseled: "We expect that...[the] city, nation, government, or kingdom which serves not God, and gives no heed to the principles of truth and religion, will be utterly wasted away and destroyed."[7] The rise and fall of nations is a major theme encapsulated in the chiasm found in Daniel.

The impression of the record is that Daniel wrote the book himself towards the latter years of his life. The majority of the references and chapters are written in the first person. As far as we can tell this record is complete within itself. It is not a partial account or a fragmentation of a larger record. It clearly does not include all of his writings, experiences or prophecies, but seems to be complete with the essential stories and visions that the Lord would have Daniel present to the Jewish nation and the greater House of Israel and to the world.

Some scholars question the authenticity of the book, citing conflicts or lack of validating evidence from archeological sources. As with any scripture, the truthfulness of the book relies solely on the confirming witness of the Spirit. The Savior, Himself (Matt. 24:15. Mark 13;14) endorsed Daniels' prophecy, which is a powerful affirmation of its veracity. The accuracy of the prophecies themselves provide their own endorsing testimony, and further credence to the writings will be proven as each prophecy is fulfilled. While validation through other means such as archeological evidence can be helpful, they are not full proof evidence as there remain many limitations. We should anchor our belief on the "spirit of prophecy" (Doctrine and Covenants 11:25; 2 Pet. 1:20), which confirms the veracity of the record, including the visions and lessons taught.

The Record of Daniel is Sealed

Towards the end of his life and in the last chapter, Daniel was commanded to seal the book (Daniel 12:9). The final six chapters or the prophetic visions—principally the content in chapters 10 through 12—constitute the "sealed" portion of the record. They are not sealed, as we may traditionally understand. The gold plates given to Joseph Smith, for example, contained an abridged record of Mormon and were literally sealed with solid bindings or tree sap making a large portion of plates inaccessible.[8] The plates of Mormon were also sealed by virtue of their unique language, the reformed Egyptian characters, that no modern scholar could completely interpret. Only through the gift and power of God as manifest through the interpreters, or Urim and Thumim (Mos. 8:13), were the contents of this record brought forth. Other prophetic records were sealed and hidden in the earth or taken into heaven to come forth in a future day (JS-H 1:60; 2 Ne. 30:15). The Revelation of John was sealed in coded language and imagery and preserved through the centuries by this cryptic language.[9]

Daniel's revelations were deemed "sealed" primarily because, like many prophecies, they project into the future. Their meaning remains hidden from the understanding of men until the day that they are fulfilled. As we shall see, a large portion of Daniel's visions have already been fulfilled and looking back, we understand that he was given and wrote very detailed and precise prophecies. But for years they persisted, partially unknown and their meaning shrouded in code and images similar to those found in John's Revelation. Their interpretation became clear in the natural course of events. As the predicted kingdoms rose to power or fell in accordance with the vision, the students and scholars could readily see their fulfillment and observe that the visions unfolded with surprising accuracy. Today, only a few passages remain "sealed."

In the last vision recorded in the book, an angel explains to Daniel that as the end draws near, his visions will become clearer and the important messages and their fulfillment will be unfolded. And he said, "Go thy way, Daniel: for the words are closed up and sealed till the time of the end. Many shall be purified, and made white, and tried; but the wicked shall do wickedly: *and none of the wicked shall understand; but the wise shall understand"* (Dan. 12:9-10, *emphasis added).*

The diligent and wise student will comprehend Daniel's writings and use the principles preserved therein in their preparation to meet the Lord. As the coming of the Son of Man draws nigh, even at the doors, the final few sealed portions will be unlocked and opened. The key of knowledge will be turned to help the wise understand what is coming and what to do overcome the tempests, troubles and tribulations that will sweep across the earth. The purposes of Daniel's visions and commission will be completed and the will of the Lord fulfilled.

End Notes

1   McConkie, Millennial Messiah 579, 582-3

2   Hirsch, Pick, Schechter, Ginzberg. "JewishEncyclopedia.com." JEHOIAKIM - JewishEncyclopedia.com, Jewish Encyclopedia, www.jewishencyclopedia.com/articles/8562-jehoiakim.

3   Keil. *Biblical Commentary of the Old Testament, The Book of the Prophet Daniel.* Introduction

4   Hirsch, Emil G., Konig Edward. JewishEncyclopedia.com." BOOK OF DANIEL - JewishEncyclopedia.com, Jewish Encyclopedia, www://www.jewishencyclopedia.com/search?utf8=%E2%9C%93&keywords=book+of+Daniel&commit=search

5   Chiasm adapted from c. Steinmann, Andrew E., *Daniel Concordia.* 2008. See also: Walvoord. *Daniel, The Key to Prophet Revelation.* 119

6   McConkie, *Mormon Doctrine.* 327

7   Widstoe. *Discourses of Brigham Young.* 114

8   Henrichsen. "What Did the Golden Plates Look Like?" *New Era* July 31, 2007

9   McConkie. "Understanding the Book of Revelation." *Ensign.* Sept. 1975

1

Captives in Babylon

Nearly 800 years had passed since Moses led the Children of Israel from Egypt. Jehovah had nurtured and instructed them since the days of their deliverance. He had purposed in His heart to "set them above all the nations that are upon the earth" and make of them a peculiar people (Exod. 19:5; Deut. 14:2). At Sinai, He revealed again the Law to keep them in remembrances of Him, to straighten them, and to purify them in preparation to enter into His presence (Exod. 20; Gal. 3:24).[1] He strengthened them in battle to defeat the pagan nations when they crossed the Jordan to conquer Canaan (Josh. 5:13-15). He chastened in love and preserved them against their enemies for hundreds of years. When they followed His counsel, they were blessed above measure (Gen. 49:26).

A serious schism arose between Judah and ten of the tribes or the northern kingdom. Israel, as it was called, rebelled and separated themselves from the Rehoboam, the king of Judah (1 Kgs. 11:31-32). Almost immediately, Jeroboam ruler of Israel, fearing his people would turn their loyalty to Jerusalem and the temple, set up two golden calves in Bethel, wherein idolatry was introduced to the kingdom and the course set by Jehovah was abandoned (1 Kgs 12:28). They quickly adopted the culture and idolatrous practices of neighboring nations. By Isaiah's day,

Israel had long since fallen into apostasy (1 Kgs. 11:33). In 721 B.C., the superpower Assyria swept down and conquered Syria and Israel, killing many and carrying the surviving Israelites captive into Mesopotamia (2 Kgs. 15:29).

The kingdom of Judah remained faithful and retained its sovereignty for several more generations. But like their brethren, they too became prideful and adopted the pagan traditions with all their degenerate practices. By 610 B.C., they had become fully rebellious and the majority of the people no longer followed Jehovah. Ripening in iniquity, they were poised for destruction.[2] God's treasured people were left to protect themselves against the most powerful nations in the region. "Because of iniquity she lost her power and was not able to defend herself against her enemies. Strategically, she was in an awkward position. The powerful nations were Egypt on the south [and Babylon that threatened from the east]. Instead of doing battle on their own lands, these...nations took turns overrunning Israel and making her their battleground."[3] In the middle of the geopolitical struggles, Judah had to choose between supporting the longtime Egyptian-Syrian alliance or the new superpower from the east, Babylon. Not following the counsel of Jeremiah (Jer. 25), they chose wrong and sought an alliance with Egypt, wherein they paid dearly.

In 605 B.C. Nebuchadnezzar, prince of Babylon ascended to be the commander of the Babylonian armies and moved to expand his father's kingdom west to the Mediterranean. His father, Nebopolassar, had defeated the ancient superpower Assyria and taken much of Syria. He, being old, left the duty to defeat the Egyptians to his son.[4] In a decisive battle, Nebuchadnezzar crushed Pharaoh Necho at the fortress of Carchemish, in northern Syria (Jer. 46:2). The victory opened the door for the Babylonian forces to overrun Syria and push into the land of Judea and Gaza.[5] When the Egyptians lost, they retreated back to their own borders and Babylonian troops swarmed into the lands around Jerusalem. The historical backdrop for the Book of Daniel begins at this point.

Babylon Lays Siege to Jerusalem

———

1 In the third year of the reign of Jehoiakim king of
Judah came Nebuchadnezzar king of Babylon unto
Jerusalem, and besieged it.

2 And the Lord gave Jehoiakim king of Judah into his
hand, with part of the vessels of the house of God:
which he carried into the land of Shinar to the
house of his god; and he brought the vessels into the
treasure house of his god (Dan. 1:1-2).

———

Jerusalem was a major prize, positioned in the center of the
region, it was both strategically important and lush with treasure.
Nebuchadnezzar besieged the city to subjugate her. If they resisted,
he would destroy her and take her inhabitants as prisoners.
Jehoiakim, king of Judah, withstood him for three months, but
eventually relented and became subject to his power. According
to the writings of Jeremiah, Babylonian troops overran the capital
Jerusalem in the 4th year of the reign of King Jehoiakim (Jer. 25:1;
36:1). Any previous sovereignty that she might have enjoyed under
Egypt was lost, and they became subjects to Nebuchadnezzar as
a tributary state. They were forced to pay tribute from the temple
treasury in Jerusalem, which included a number of the temple vessels
and artifacts. The Babylonians had taken interest in the treasure at
Solomon's temple after Hezekiah showed them the treasury decades
earlier (2 Kgs. 20:13) and now the prizes were in their hands. It is
noteworthy that the Ark of the Covenant was not part of the bounty,
only sacred vessels from the temple. The king was forced by the
Babylonians to relinquish members of the royal family and nobility
to go back to Babylon as hostages.[6] It may have been that the king
was killed in the siege or died as a hostage. Jeremiah prophesied
that after his death his body would be "drawn and cast forth beyond
the gates of Jerusalem" like a dead donkey (Jer 22:18-19; 36:30).

Nebuchadnezzar commanded that the Jewish hostages be
removed to Babylon and settled in the land of Shinar, the ancient
location of the tower of Babel (Gen. 10:10; 14:1, 9). "Shinar was the
plain of the lower delta country between the Tigris and the Euphrates

Photo by Steerpike © Used with permission
Wall painting of the ancient city of Babylon in the Province of Shinar.

rivers where they approach the Persian Gulf. It was the ancient land of Chaldea, or Babylonia."[7] At the time, it was the largest province, and included the capital city Babylon, where Nebuchadnezzar's palace was established. It was the center of the Babylonian empire.

The youthful Daniel, along with a number of his kin, were taken captive into Babylon. There they would be integrated into the society, educated and trained to serve in the palace of the king. It seems that Nebuchadnezzar thought favorably of these captives and was satisfied to care for them as noble patrons in his land. Phillips comments that to be selected to go to Babylon "was very generous of the king. Most conquering kings would have beheaded or banished such captives sending them off, perhaps to concentration camps or to be exploited, tormented, and brutally slain. That Nebuchadnezzar was capable of great cruelty was well known."[8]

Nevertheless, Nebuchadnezzar resolved to select youth from among the nobility of Judah to serve in his court. They would help integrate the larger Jewish population while serving the interests of Babylon. Those selected demonstrated aptitude in intelligence, "showing understanding; possessing a faculty for knowledge, a strength of judgment. In whom was strength, [i.e. physical strength], who had the fitness in bodily and mental endowments appropriate to stand in the palace of the king, and as servants to attend to his commands."[9] Daniel, Hananiah, Mishael, and Azariah are specifically named as being among those deported. They were apparently cousins and related kin to the royal family of Judah. Nebuchadnezzar removed many noble youth to keep the Jewish king in line, but primarily that they might be taught in the language and culture of the Chaldeans, the elite ruling class of Babylon. He wished them to become nobles and administrators. Some scholars believe that Daniel's education and experience over time, combined with his spiritual endowments from the Lord, elevated him to be equal with Abraham, Moses or Solomon in learning, wisdom and understanding.[10] By any standard, Daniel grew in understanding and became skilled in government, political systems and science, and very powerful—a great asset to the Babylonian kingdom. Even as the Jews were being scattered and carried captive into Babylon, the Lord prepared to watch over and protect them in their new home. He placed Daniel and his companions in positions of great authority. They would oversee and preserve the Jews in the kingdom and help them to prosper and promote their interests.

All four of the nobles mentioned were in their youth and were probably between the ages of 15 and 20 years of age.[11] This fact becomes significant as we learn that Daniel's life will be preserved through the reign of the current king Nabopolasser, and of Nebuchadnezzar, Amel-Merodach his son, Neriglissar-Labashi-Marduk, Nabonidus and Belshazzar, all of Babylon. He also lived during the reign of Cyrus of Persia and Darius the Mede. In the end, Daniel's life would span 80 to 90 years, wherein he witnessed the fulfillment of the Lord's promises that the Jews return to their homeland after 70 years in captivity and rebuild the city and its walls (Jer. 25:9-12; Dan. 9 10).[12]

The Treasure and Vessels of the Temple

After the siege of Jerusalem, treasures from Solomon's Temple were placed in the caravan and transported to Babylon with the captives. Upon arrival the vessels were placed in the

Vincente Lopez y Portaña, Museo de Bellas Artes © Used with permission
King Hezekiah showing the treasures of Solomon's Temple to Babylonian ambassadors

"house" or temple of Nebuchadnezzar's pagan god, Marduk, often referred to as Bel-Marduk. "Bringing the vessels to the house of Nebuchadnezzar's god was a natural religious gesture, which would attribute the victory of the Babylonians over Israel to Babylonian deities. Later other vessels would be taken [from the temple] and added to the collection" (2 Chron. 36:18, Isa. 39:7).[13] They would be placed in the treasury of the palace near the giant Ziggurat Temple at the center of Babylon.

The vessels were not considered treasure in the sense of gold coins or jewelry, but were sacred artifacts and trophies of conquest. They remained in or near Marduk's temple for many years only to surface again on the fateful night when Belshazzar ordered them removed and added to the table settings of the festival (Dan. 5:2). His pride and irreverent actions sealed his fate and that of his kingdom. The Babylonian life of pride and wickedness came to epitomize the cultural symbol of spiritual Babylon as a fallen and disobedient people (Doctrine and Covenants 133:14).

Jews given to the care of Ashpenaz

---

3   And the king spake unto Ashpenaz the master of his eunuchs, that he should bring certain of the children

of Israel, and of the king's seed, and of the princes;

4   Children in whom was no blemish, but well favoured, and skillful in all wisdom, and cunning in knowledge, and understanding science, and such as had ability in them to stand in the king's palace, and whom they might teach the learning and the tongue of the Chaldeans (Dan. 1:3-4).

Upon arrival in Shinar, the Israelite captives were placed in the care of Ashpenaz, who was the chief officer of the court.[14] Among his many duties, he held the responsibility of preparing and training captives from conquered nations to serve in the king's government. Ashpenaz was considered the master or chief of the eunuchs. Scholars have debated the meaning of the word eunuch. It is the English form of the Greek word, which means *bed-keeper,*[15] but also has been translated *officer* or *chief.* The term often denotes emasculation. In reality, all of the "eunuchs" were officers in the kingdom, and while some duties required physical castration, the majority were captains or chiefs in the military or officers in the bureaucracy. Ashpenaz might be compared to Potiphar, a chief captain of Pharaoh's guard (Gen. 37:36), whom we know had a wife (Gen. 39:7).

"In selecting those youths for education in his court in Babylon, Nebuchadnezzar was accomplishing several objectives. As mentioned, those carried away captive could serve as hostages to help keep the royal family remaining in Judah in line. Their presence in the Kings court would help to be a pleasant reminder to the Babylonian king of his conquest and success in battle. Further, their careful training and preparation to be his servants might serve Nebuchadnezzar well in the later administration of Jewish affairs."[16] Most who enjoyed this privileged lifestyle were content to serve and to certainly not "rock the boat," but enjoy their new fortune.[17]

Those selected from among Israel's captives were enrolled in a royal program of education and culturalization. Their selection required that they be distinguished first and foremost on their physical excellence. There could be no blemish or malformation. Only handsome and beautiful able-bodied candidates were allowed entry into the system. "The master of the eunuchs was commanded

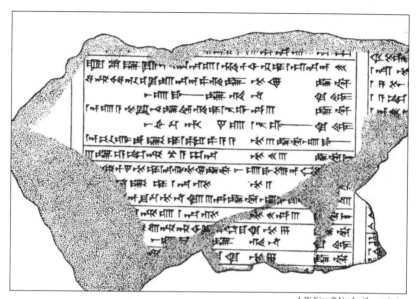

Ancient Cuneiform scripts outlining a Dynastic Chronicle. Similar documents were used in Babylonian education system

to have regard to bodily perfection and beauty as well as to mental endowments."[18] Royal blood alone was not enough, but those well favored physically, in character, intelligence and demeanor. "Corporeal soundness and a handsome form were considered indispensable among ancient Orientals for those who were destined for court service. Apparently this has been the case in Turkey and Persia, even in the nineteenth century."[19]

Nearly equal in importance to being physically handsome, the king required that the captives exhibit intellectual aptitude in all wisdom and disciplines.[20] They needed to demonstrate the ability to perceive or comprehend the complex knowledge found in the sciences and mathematics, astronomy, engineering, languages and diplomacy. Exactly how this was determined is unclear. Preliminary sorting processes were taken in Jerusalem and completed in Babylon. The initial selection was based purely in royal roots and physical appearance, and over time the aptitudes and talents of each person were manifest as they progressed in the program. Individuals were sorted and elevated based on understanding and performance. Among the candidates, Daniel always rose to the top.

Chaldean curriculum involved all the important subjects, including study of the Chaldean languages, which was evidently the beginning of their studies. Some have suggested that they were taught in the ancient cuneiform scripts. The old Babylonian scribal curriculum was presented in two clearly distinguished stages of education. In the earlier stage, students were introduced to the writing system as well as metrology. This included Sumerian vocabulary and grammar, as well as sentence structure. The second stage involved advanced literary texts that were copied with the help of masters. The study of these symbols were certainly part of the overall curriculum and necessary to unlock the knowledge of other ancient disciplines.

Not all the students continued in the specialized practice of the scribes. Whoever intended to branch into a particular administrative field, such as legal affairs, palace or temple administration, or military strategy generally did not need the knowledge of advanced literary writing, but only the ability to read the texts.[21] A sound linguistic foundation facilitated their studies and helped in the disciplines of the study of cultural letters, history, ancient languages, religion, philosophy, archeology, politics and government. Each step in their education expanded their knowledge and readied them to become functional and productive servants in the kingdom.

In reality, their proximity to the king afforded them opportunities and privileges that even the Babylonians and outside subjects of the kingdom would never enjoy. The tuition of such elegant education was very expensive, afforded only to the rich. While they lived far from their homes and family, they benefited from comfortable lives and the advantages of upper society, education, good living and access to government officials. Such benefits ultimately were used to influence many aspects of the treatment of the Jews.

Daniel and Friends given Babylonian Names

6   Now among these were of the children of Judah, Daniel, Hananiah, Mishael, and Azariah:

7   Unto whom the prince of the eunuchs gave names:

> for he gave unto Daniel the name of Belteshazzar;
> and to Hananiah, of Shadrach; and to Mishael, of
> Meshach; and to Azariah, of Abed-nego (Dan. 1:5-
> 7).

———

An important step in the transition occurred when Ashpenaz gave new Chaldean names to all the Hebrew youth. There were several reasons for this practice. "Name-giving in the Orient was primarily an exercise of sovereignty."[22] When Pharaoh Necho subjected Jerusalem, the king's name was changed from Eliakim to Jehoiakim (2 Kgs. 23:34), a sign of new leadership and reformations. Likewise, Nebuchadnezzar's goal was to thoroughly convert the young nobles to Chaldean thought and culture. The practice assisted the individual to become accepted by the locals who readily understood and could remember and pronounce their names.

There has been debate as to the meanings of the new names. Like their Hebrew names—whose meanings reflected their relationship or an attribute of God—the Chaldean titles were given to honor a person and the gods or to commemorate notable events.[23]

Hebrew Meanings	Babylonian Meanings
Daniel "God is my judge"	Belteshazzar is a variation of Babylonia Balatusu-usur or "Protect His Life"
Hananiah:"Jehovah is gracious"	Shadrach : "I am very fearful (of God)"
Mishael: "Who is what God is"	Meshach: "I am of little account or variation of Maraduk"
Azariah :"Jehovah has helped"	Abed-nego: "Servant of Nebo?" Second God of Babylon

Hebrew name meanings and Chaldean equivalent. [24]

What should be understood about their Hebrew names was the strong connection to Jehovah. Their deep devotion to the true God was not by chance. Devout parents gave them names to instill in them the conviction to serve Jehovah, observe His laws and walk in His ways in truth and soberness.[25] King Solomon wisely taught:

"Train up a child in the way he should go: and when he is old, he will not depart from it." (Prov. 2:6). Despite the serious deficiencies found generally in the Jewish culture, there still remained among the people and the royal princes those who would not bow their knees to Baal or any pagan god, but were firm and faithful (1 Kgs. 19:18). President Deiter F. Uchtdorf taught: "Daniel had been raised as a follower of Jehovah. He believed in and worshipped the God of Abraham, Isaac, and Jacob. He had studied the words of the prophets, and he knew of God's interaction with man."[26] Such devotion would bring valuable fruit in the Babylonian courts.

The Daily Provision of Meal

> 5   And the king appointed them a daily provision of
> the king's meat, and of the wine which he drank: so
> nourishing them three years, that at the end thereof
> they might stand before the king (Dan. 1:4).

Three years were provided to refine the comparatively rough and young Jewish nobility to serve in Nebuchadnezzar's courts. Among the amenities were privileged accommodations complete with royal rooms and meals. Daniel points out that the daily meals were "appointed" or mandated and that a prearranged diet of ample quantity and variety of food was part of the regiment. Everything had been preselected and deemed best for the health and enjoyment of the youths. If the menu paralleled that of the heathen king and his nobles, it would have been both rich, tasty and plentiful and considered the best that Babylon could offer.

The tables were set with all the amenities of the east. Undoubtedly they included exotic meats with combinations not in harmony with the Mosaic Law (Lev. 11, 18:20-24, Ezek. 20). Babylonians, like other heathens, ate all manner of beasts that had not been properly drained of blood (Lev. 3:17) and they indulged in many of the forbidden creatures of the earth and sea (Lev. 11, Deut. 14:7-10). Other delectable, but unacceptable dishes were likely offered to the devout followers of Jehovah. More importantly, the meals would be combined as part of the Babylonian pagan rites of worship;

something Daniel and his friends could not embrace. Daniel and his kin found themselves in a very serious dilemma.

Phillips comments on what surely would have been the general attitudes of all the new recruits: "They certainly would not want to press their 'good luck' by doing anything annoying to the Babylonian king. The food certainly smelled appetizing. It never occurred to the majority of ...[the trainees] to pause and think about whether the God of heaven might have something to say about it all. They certainly would not see any moral issues connected with the matter. After all, when you are in Babylon, you do as the Babylonians do."[27] The pressures on Daniel and his friends to abandon the old beliefs and embrace those of Babylon must have been immense. But they would not worship their gods by indulging in the feasts. They would not compromise. "He stayed true to his faith—in word and in deed."[28]

> Daniel resolved, or literally laid upon himself, the obligation not to defile himself, but to keep the covenant with Jehovah.

Daniel "resolved or literally, 'laid upon himself' the obligation not to defile himself." (cf: Isa. 42:25; 47: 7, 57:1,11; Mal 2:2)."[29] His commitment was to keep the Law of Moses, which explicitly commanded not to sacrifice unto strange or devilish gods (Deut. 32:16-17; see also 1 Cor. 10:20, 25-28). It was the covenant with God that he could not break, even if it brought disfavor or peril from the king, himself.

Daniel includes wine in the description of the offending banquet. While fermented wine was not expressly prohibited in the Law of Moses (except for Nazarites), those who understood the nature of the Lord and His spiritual influence refrained from strong drink, if not from alcohol altogether (Num. 6:3). Isaiah chastened the fallen tribes of Israel whose idolatry and disobedience had led them to heavy drinking and the foibles of excessive liquor. "But they also have erred through wine, and through strong drink are out of the way; the priest and the prophet have erred through strong drink, they are swallowed up of wine, they are out of the way through strong drink; *they err in vision, they stumble in judgment.* For all tables are full of vomit *and filthiness, so that there is no place clean* (Isa. 28:7-8, emphasis added; 24:9; Prov. 31:4). Isaiah taught the principle both figuratively and literally by condemning the fallen behavior of the apostate priesthood. These teachings and the light of his conscience certainly weighed heavily on the minds of the youth as they faced the problem of what to do about the king's meals.

Daniel's Courage, True to God and the Law

8 But Daniel purposed in his heart that he would not defile himself with the portion of the king's meat, nor with the wine which he drank: therefore he requested of the prince of the eunuchs that he might not defile himself.

9 Now God had brought Daniel into favour and tender love with the prince of the eunuchs.

10 And the prince of the eunuchs said unto Daniel, I fear my lord the king, who hath appointed your meat and your drink: for why should he see your faces worse liking than the children which are of your sort? then shall ye make me endanger my head to the king.

11 Then said Daniel to Melzar, whom the prince of the eunuchs had set over Daniel, Hananiah, Mishael, and Azariah,

12 Prove thy servants, I beseech thee, ten days; and let them give us pulse to eat, and water to drink.

13 Then let our countenances be looked upon before thee, and the countenance of the children that eat of the portion of the king's meat: and as thou seest, deal with thy servants.

14 So he consented to them in this matter, and proved them ten days.

15 And at the end of ten days their countenances appeared fairer and fatter in flesh than all the children which did eat the portion of the king's meat.

16 Thus Melzar took away the portion of their meat, and

the wine that they should drink; and gave them pulse
(Dan. 18-16).

————

When confronted with the reality of the king's regimen, Daniel resolved to be obedient and true to Jehovah. Given the environment and circumstances, such a resolution would not be a light decision.[30] The consequences were perilous and might at least disqualify him from the program, if not bring death. Furthermore, no Chaldean official would understand or accept the requirements of Jehovah's Mosaic Law as a valid excuse for non-conformance. In their eyes the God of Israel had been defeated and with Him all of the rites and requirements He exacted upon His people were disannulled. The youth's request would easily be interpreted as naive, if not an affront to Babylonian supremacy. Even so, Daniel resolved in his heart that despite the situation, defiling his body and the law was the greater issue and he vowed to be obedient.

Asking his benefactors for an exception represented an act of supreme faith and trust in God. But the Lord was with Daniel, for God had softened the heart of Ashpenaz, who "favored" and "loved" him. The young man approached the chief and asked to be exempted. Ashpenaz would have done many things to help the youth, but this request was met with fear, as disobedience to the king's command also placed the prince's life at risk. The practices and training were long established and produced good results. Allowing an untested regiment might yield unfavorable results. Despite his respect for the young servant, Ashpenaz did consider his request, but in the end the answer was "no."

Daniel remained undeterred. His response again demonstrated great faith and determination. He approached another of the eunuchs, one Melzar, and presented a very practical request. (Melzar was probably not the man's proper name, as it means "the steward, warden or guardian").[31] Daniel proposed that he and his companions be given *pulse* to eat and water to drink for ten days. His proposal carried relatively low risk, but would be sufficient to prove the point.

Daniel's Pulse - typical fruits and vegetables, grains and beans

"Pulse" is translated from the Aramaic word for seeds, with specific reference to grains and vegetables. When all the possibilities of foods that spring from seeds are considered, we readily observe that Daniel's diet could have included a broad and complete collection of fruits, herbs, nuts, vegetables and grains. A wide variety of food given by God was available, without the need for excessive or forbidden meats or the improper preparation that may have occurred under the king's menu. In practice, Daniel's meals were probably quite simple, but the selections where many.

Later in Chapter 10, Daniel records that during his fast, he "ate no pleasant bread, neither came flesh nor wine in my mouth" (Dan 10:3). He could eat meat and a variety of desirable foods, and nonalcoholic wine, but not the unclean meats, especially those slain to the idol gods or for the pagan festivals. The wine was probably juice from the vine, but pure and not fermented. Such a diet was set forth in the Garden of Eden and reaffirmed again in the latter days as described in the Word of Wisdom: "All grain is good for the food of man; as also the fruit of the vine; that which yieldeth fruit [or vegetables], whether in the ground or above the ground—" (Doctrine and Covenants 89:16, see also vs. 10). Staying away from inappropriate food was essential, but the key was also avoiding anything prepared for the pagan gods.

At the end of ten days the youths appearance confirmed the claim. They looked healthier than their peers. Scholars often assert that the result was just common sense and that any endowment or special blessing from the Lord was not necessary.[32] This may be true, but obedience to the Lord's commandments brings special heavenly blessings: "And all saints who remember to keep and do these sayings, walking in obedience to the commandments, shall receive health in their navel and marrow to their bones; And shall find wisdom and great treasures of knowledge, even hidden treasures; And shall run and not be weary, and shall walk and not faint" (Doctrine and Covenants 89:18-20). Acts in which faith and obedience are demonstrated bring the additional strength and wisdom that would be needed later on.

After the warden reviewed the young men, they were removed from any obligation to eat the prescribed diet. A regimen of "pulse" was regularly apportioned to them. We observe from this experience something about Daniel's demeanor and approach to applying the principles of the Gospel. He was a straightforward, even humble youth, but resolute to those principles very important to him. He recognized the value of the simple fare. However, he did not act irrationally by breaking off all contact with the heathen court [or the world], but was willing to learn what it could teach him. He acted as any believer in God should have acted under similar circumstances, with poise and calm.[33]

The record does not say how many youths and royalty were taken from Jerusalem, but when this first real test was presented, only these four are mentioned as desiring to remain clean and in harmony with the Lord. Daniel's reaction set the foundation and tone for his life's service in Babylon. It represented a simple yet powerful demonstration of faith and opened the way for the Lord to perform great works.

The Word and Blessings of Wisdom

_____

17 As for these four children, God gave them knowledge and skill in all learning and wisdom: and Daniel had understanding in all visions and dreams.

18 Now at the end of the days that the king had said he should bring them in, then the prince of the eunuchs brought them in before Nebuchadnezzar.

19 And the king communed with them; and among them all was found none like Daniel, Hananiah, Mishael, and Azariah: therefore stood they before the king.

20 And in all matters of wisdom and understanding, that the king inquired of them, he found them ten times better than all the magicians and astrologers that were in all his realm.

21 And Daniel continued even unto the first year of king Cyrus. (Dan. 1:18-21)

_____

The outcomes of their wise decision extended long term. The Lord blessed them in their studies and training. He bestowed upon them gifts and abilities to understand the material, to comprehend and discern the truths amidst all that was being conveyed by their Chaldean instructors. Wisdom was chief among these gifts, which enabled them to discern deeper truths and divine purposes behind the knowledge. As we shall see, because of his firmness and faithfulness, Daniel was also given the gift to interpret dreams and visions.

At the end of the three years of training and refinement, the youth were presented to Nebuchadnezzar in his court. The king sought to test the understanding of these new court members. Undoubtedly, he had done this many times with other youth, and compared their responses to the answers of previous "wise men." Among all the new candidates tested, none were found like Daniel and his companions. Even among all the astrologers and wise men in the kingdom, Nebuchadnezzar found their counsel and wisdom profoundly superior than the rest. No doubt their learning, coupled with the spiritual gifts of wisdom and understanding, set them apart more than any of the Chaldeans or the other wise men in the kingdom.

In modern revelation, the Lord gave the Word of Wisdom as a law that included the same promises extended to Daniel and his companions. Speaking of the spiritual benefits of the Word of Wisdom, President Boyd K. Packer admonished:

———

> The promise of health for living the standards of the revelation is not limited to members of the Church. Tell your nonmember friends about the Word of Wisdom and urge them to live it.
>
> And then there is a greater blessing promised in the Word of Wisdom. Those who obey it are promised that they "shall find wisdom and great treasures of knowledge, even hidden treasures" (Doctrine and Covenants 89:19). This is the personal revelation through which you can detect invisible crocodiles or hidden mines or other dangers.
>
> When you were confirmed a member of the Church, you had conferred upon you the gift of the Holy Ghost. "Know ye not," Paul wrote, "that your body is the temple of the Holy Ghost which is in you ... ?" (1 Cor. 6:19).
>
> And the Lord said, "The Comforter, which is the Holy Ghost, whom the Father will send in my name, he shall teach you all things, and bring all things to your remembrance, whatsoever I have said unto you" (John 14:26).
>
> There's a final promise in the revelation. Speaking again of those who keep and do and obey these commandments, the Lord said, "I ... give unto them a promise, that the destroying angel shall pass by them, as the children of Israel, and not slay them" (Doctrine and Covenants 89:21). That is a remarkable promise."[34]

All commandments are based on deeper principles of truth. The principles that surround the Word of Wisdom were established since the foundations of the earth when God placed Adam and Even in the Garden of Eden. These truths remain in force today and aid in the temporal well being of the obedient in the last days as it did for

Daniel and his fellows. It is "given for a principle with promise, adapted to the capacity of the weak and the weakest of all saints, who are or can be called saints." (Doctrine and Covenants 89:3).

Truth offers a secure, protected path against the evil designs of the wicked and conspiring men and women who seek to profit from the carnal weaknesses of fallen man. Elder D. Todd Christofferson explained that Latter-day Saint's should: "certainly not deface our body, as with tattoos; or debilitate it, as with drugs [or alcohol]; or defile it, as with fornication, adultery, or immodesty. As our body is the instrument of our spirit, it is vital that we care for it as best we can. We should consecrate its powers to serve and further the work of Christ. Said Paul, 'I beseech you therefore, brethren, by the mercies of God, that ye present your bodies a living sacrifice, holy, acceptable unto God" (Rom. 12:1).'"[35] They maintain their body as a pure temple, not to be defiled nor damaged, but a receptacle of the Holy Spirit.

> The destroying angel shall pass by them as the children of Israel, and not slay them.
>
> Doctrine and Covenants 89.91

Finally, one of the most important blessings mentioned, is protection from the works of the destroying angel. In one sense the devil embodies the role of a quintessential destroyer, for "...he goeth up and down, to and fro in the earth, seeking to destroy the souls of men" (Doctrine and Covenants 10:27; 105:15). In modern times, the world suffers from an epidemic crisis of drug and alcohol abuse.[36] Overdose deaths related to heroine alone reached more than 10,000 in 2016 in the United States.[37] Other deaths and sorrows associated to recreational drug and alcohol misuse are all too commonplace.[38] Certainly, adherence to the basic guidelines of the law combined with the companionship of the Holy Ghost will keep the devoted disciple on the straight and narrow path, safe from the deceptions and traps of the adversary.

The Lord also extends the "promise, that the destroying angel shall pass by them as the children of Israel, and not slay them"

(Doctrine and Covenants 89:91). The reference to the children of Israel is, of course, the circumstance when a destroying angel from heaven is sent to slay the firstborn of the Egyptians (Ex. 12:12, 29). When the judgments are poured out to cleanse the world at the last day, only those faithful to the commandments, including the Word of Wisdom, will be preserved. (Doctrine and Covenants 115:6).

The Challenge of Obedience

The Lord warned the Apostles: "If ye were of the world, the world would love his own: but because ye are not of the world, but I have chosen you out of the world, therefore the world hateth you" (John 15:19). Society can be very accommodating to those who subscribe to its own values. Among life's greatest challenges posed to the disciple of the Lord is the command to be obedient, even when His will sets you at odds with the cultural tide. In the latter-days, God has commanded his Church to "go ye out from among the nations, even from Babylon, from the midst of wickedness, which is spiritual Babylon." (Doctrine and Covenants 133:14). Nebuchadnezzar's world eventually comes to represent that which the Lord holds most detestable, a dangerous combination of affluence, hedonism and decadence. It was as spiritually dangerous for Daniel and his kin as the world is for the faithful today. Deciding not to define himself was a foundational step in securing his future.

It has been said that destiny swings on small hinges. Daniel could have easily gone along with the benevolence of Nebuchadnezzar's offer, settling in and counting his new station in life as good fortune. But the blessings that came from strict adherence to the Law, the enhanced spiritual gifts and the higher wisdom and understanding, the ability to interpret dreams and visions would have all been sacrificed in accommodating the requirements of this new station and opportunity to serve the king.

With the foundation of righteousness firmly established, Daniel and his friends were ready for far greater things.

Chapter Notes

1   Kimball, Spencer W. "Why Call Me Lord, Lord and Do Not the Thing Which I Say", General Conference April 1975, 9
"Moses came down from the quaking, smoking Mount Sinai and brought to the wandering children of Israel the Ten Commandments, fundamental rules for the conduct of life. These commandments were, however, not new. They had been known to Adam and his posterity, who had been commanded to live them from the beginning and were merely reiterated by the Lord to Moses. And the commandments even antedated earth life and were part of the test for mortals established in the council of heaven."

2   Brandt, "The Exile and First Return of Judah," *Ensign*, July 1974

3   Perry, "I Confer the Priesthood of Aaron," General Conference, October 1985

4   Uchtdorf, "Be Not Afraid, Only Believe", General Conference, October 2015

5   Walvoord, *Daniel, The Key to Prophet Revelation*, 39

6   Bullock C. Hassell, *An Introduction to the Old Testament Prophetic Books*, 340
In 601 BC, during the fourth year of King Jehoiakim's reign, Nebuchadnezzar attempted to overthrow Egypt, but was defeated, suffering heavy losses. Jehoiakim, along with several other cities in the region, rebelled and turned their loyalty back to Egypt. Three years later in 598 B.C. Nebuchadnezzar returned and retook Judea, including Jerusalem capturing another 10,000 Jews, many of which were sold and others deported to the Chebar River settlements in Tel Abib not far from Babylon. Ezekiel was among this group of exiles.

7   Smith, William (1813-1893), *A Dictionary of the Bible*, s.v. "Shinar."

8   Phillips, *Exploring the Book of Daniel, An Expository Commentary*, 32

9   Keil, *Biblical Commentary of the Old Testament, The Book of the Prophet Daniel*, 74

10   Walvoord, *Daniel, The Key to Prophet Revelation*, 52

11   Phillips, *Exploring the Book of Daniel, An Expository Commentary*, 28, Young, *The Prophecy Daniel: A Commentary*, 40, Keil, *Biblical Commentary of the Old Testament, The Book of the Prophet Daniel*, 73

12   Phillips, *Exploring the Book of Daniel: An Expository Commentary*, 28

13   Walvoord, *Daniel, The Key to Prophet Revelation*, 41

14   Keil, *Biblical Commentary of the Old Testament, The Book of the Prophet Daniel*, 73

15   Smith, *Bible Dictionary*, Ref: "Eunuch", The concept of a "eunuch" (a castrate) is described in the Bible primarily by two words, namely *saris* (Hebrew, Old Testament) and *eunouchos* (Greek, New Testament) (Hug 1918:449-455; Horstmanshoff 2000:101-114). In addition to "eunuch", however, both words can also mean "official" or "commander", while castration is sometimes indirectly referred to without using these terms. *Acta Theologica Supplementum* 7, 2005:1

16   Walvoord, *Daniel, The Key to Prophet Revelation*, 43

17   Uchtdorf, "Be Not Afraid, Only Believe", General Conference, October 2015, https://www.lds.org/general-conference/2015/10/be-not-afraid-only-believe?lang=eng

18   Keil, *Biblical Commentary of the Old Testament, The Book of the Prophet Daniel*, 73, See also: Perry, L. Tom, "The University of Mortality," BYU Speeches, February 07, 1988; "In The World," BYU Speeches, January 04, 1981

19   Young, *The Prophecy of Daniel, A Commentary*, 41, Quotes Zoeckler

20   Ibid 41

21   Tinney, Steve 1998; Texts, Tablets and Teaching: Scribal Education in Nippur and Ur, Expedition 40: 40-50 and 1999; On the Curricular Setting of Sumerian Literature, Iraq 61: 159-172. Vanstiphout, Herman L.J. 1978; Lipit-Eštar's Praise in the Edubba, Journal of Cuneiform Studies 30: 33-66 and 1979; How Did They Learn Sumerian?, Journal of Cuneiform Studies 31: 118-126.

22   Gerhard von Rad, Genesis rev ed. Philadelphia, Westminster, 1972, 83

23   Young, *The Prophecy of Daniel, A Commentary*, 43

24   Ibid 43, see also Walvoord, D*aniel, The Key to Prophet Revelation*, 42

25   Walvoord, *Daniel, The Key to Prophet Revelation*, 42

26   Uchtdorf, "Be Not Afraid, Only Believe," General Conference, October 2015, https://www.lds.org/general-conference/2015/10/be-not-afraid-only-believe?lang=eng

27   Phillips, E*xploring the Book of Daniel: An Expository Commentary*, 32

28   Ibid

29   Walvoord, *Daniel, The Key to Prophet Revelation*, 46; See also: Romney, "We Need Men of Courage," General Conference, April 1975; Stone, "Zion in the Midst of Babylon, "April 2006; Faust, "Where Is the Church?," BYU Speeches, Mar. 1 2005 and Ensign, Aug. 1990

30   Uchtdorf, "Be Not Afraid, Only Believe," General Conference, October 2015, https://www.lds.org/general-conference/2015/10/be-not-afraid-only-believe?lang=eng

31   Young, *The Prophecy of Daniel, A Commentary*, 45-46

32   Walvoord, D*aniel, The Key to Prophet Revelation*, 48-49

33   Young, *The Prophecy Daniel: A Commentary*, 48

34   Packer, "The Word of Wisdom: The Principle and the Promises,"April 1996, Ensign May 1996

35   Christofferson, "Reflections on a Consecrated Life," General Conference, October 2010, https://www.lds.org/general-conference/2010/10/reflections-on-a-consecrated-life?lang=eng

36   Staff Writer. "The Numbers Behind America's Heroin Epidemic." The New York Times. 30 Oct. 2015, www.nytimes.com/interactive/2015/10/30/us/31heroin-deaths.html.

37   Abuse, National Institute on Drug. "Overdose Death Rates." NIDA, U.S. Department of Health and Human Services, 15 Sept. 2017, www.drugabuse.gov/related-topics/trends-statistics/overdose-death-rates.

38   Katz. "Drug Deaths in America Are Rising Faster Than Ever." The New York Times, 5 June 2017, www.nytimes.com/interactive/2017/06/05/upshot/opioid-epidemic-drug-overdose-deaths-are-rising-faster-than-ever.html.
      Kindy and Keating. "For Women, Heavy Drinking Has Been Normalized. That's Dangerous." The Washington Post, WP Company, 23 Dec. 2016, www.washingtonpost.com/national/for-women-heavy-drinking-has-been-normalized-thats-dangerous/2016/12/23/0e701120-c381-11e6-9578-0054287507db_story.html?utm_term=.773e75077249.

Additional Notes: Babylonian Background:

Babylon was the world's great superpower… In its day, Babylon was the world's center of learning, law, and philosophy. Its military might was unparalleled. It shattered the power of Egypt. It invaded, torched, and looted the Assyrian capital, Nineveh. It easily conquered Jerusalem and carried away the best and brightest of the children of Israel back to Babylon to serve King Nebuchadnezzar. (Uchtdorf, "Be Not Afraid, Only Believe", General Conference, October 2015).

"Many scholars believe that Daniel was between 12 and 17 years old at the time. Think of it, my beloved young Aaronic Priesthood holders: Daniel was very likely your age when he was taken into the king's court to be educated in the language, laws, religion, and science of the worldly Babylon.

Can you imagine what it would have felt like to be forced from your home, marched 500 miles (800 km) to a foreign city, and indoctrinated in the religion of your enemies?" (Uchtdorf, "Be Not Afraid, Only Believe," General Conference, October 2015).

Vessels Taken to Temple of Babylonian God:

The carrying away of a part of the vessels of the temple and a number of the distiguished Jewish youth to Babylon, that they might be there trained for service at the royal court, was a sign and pledge of the subjugation of Judah and its God under the dominion of the kings and the gods of Babylon. (Keil, *Biblical Commentary of the Old Testament, The Book of the Prophet Daniel*, 73).

Defiling by Participation: The partaking of the food brought to them from the king's table was to them contaminating, because it was forbidden by law; not so much because the food was not prepared according to the Levitical ordinance, or perhaps consisted of the flesh of animals which to the Israelites were unclean, for in this case the youths were not under the necessity of refraining from the wine, but the reason of their rejection of it was that the heathen at their feasts offered up in sacrifice to their gods a part of the food and the drink, and thus consecrated their meals by a religious rite; whereby not only he who participated in such a meal participated in the worship of idols, but the meat and the wine as a whole were the meat and the wine of an idol sacrifice, partaking of which, according to the saying of the apostle (1 Cor. 10:20), is the same as sacrificing to devils. (Keil, *Biblical Commentary of the Old Testament, The Book of the Prophet Daniel*, 80.)

Daniel's Resolution: Daniel's resolution to refrain from such unclean food flowed therefore from fidelity to the law, and from steadfsastness to the faith that "man lives not by bread only, but by every word that proceedeth out of the mouth of the Lord" (Deut. 8:3), and from the assurance that God would bless the humbler provision which he asks for himself, and would by means of it make him and his friends as strong and vigorous as the other youths who did eat the costly provision from the king's table. (Keil, *Biblical Commentary of the Old Testament, The Book of the Prophet Daniel*, 80).

James Fergusson © Used with Permission

Artist conception of Ancient Nimrud (Nineveh) in her glory. Babylon was
patterned after the ancient Assyrian city

© Used with Permission

Reconstructed walls and gates of the ancient palace of Babylon

2

Nebuchadnezzar's Peculiar Dream

The King Dreams, A Dream

> 1 And in the second year of the reign of Nebuchadnezzar.
> Nebuchadnezzar dreamed dreams, wherewith his spirit
> was troubled, and his sleep brake from him.

Almost as soon as Daniel and his companions completed their training
and entered into the king's service, Nebuchadnezzar dreamed a series of
peculiar dreams. It seems that these dreams were given in answer to
"thoughts [that] came into [his] mind upon [his] bed, what should come
to pass hereafter" (Dan. 2:29). The destiny of the Babylonian kingdom
weighed heavily upon his mind. The Lord took the opportunity not only
to reveal something of the future of the king's empire, but also to unfold
the destiny of all the kingdoms that would follow to the end of the world.[1]

The number of dreams the king had is unclear, but one dream
in particular caught his attention and caused him to seek a true
interpretation. This dream so troubled him that he woke from his bed
extremely disquieted to the point that all sleep had left him. If our own
experiences are reliable, dreams where we are suddenly awakened
in the night are normally remembered, at least in part. Keil asserts

Britosh Museum © Used with permission
Babylonian boundary-stones and memorial tablets of Nebuchadnezzar I in the British
Museum. It is believed that Nebuchadnezzar II was named after this King.

that: "the reason of so great disquietude we may not seek in the
circumstance that on awaking he could not remember the dream.
This follows neither from Daniel 2:3, nor is it psychologically
probable that so impressive a dream, which on awaking he had
forgotten, should have yet sorely disquieted his spirit during his
waking hours. The disquiet was created in him, as in Pharaoh (Gen.
41), by the specially striking incidents of the dream, and the fearful,
alarming apprehensions with reference to his future fate connected
therewith."[2] Most individuals agree with this explanation of the
account.[3] The king suddenly awoke with a vivid recollection of the
dream. And if the dream came from God in answer to his pondering
and questions, then it surely would be remembered just as vividly
as Pharaoh recalled his dreams of the kine and corn (Gen. 41:1-7).

As we shall see, the king saw a great statue, strong and fearsome, that was destroyed by a rolling stone. The golden head was probably in the form of a familiar Babylonian character that he readily recognized, perhaps even something that resembled himself. The statue would have been both impressive and magnificent at the same time. Yet what happened to it was both violent and terrible; an event so startling that it startled him into consciousness.

In addition to providing the king answers, the vision's interpretation served as a framework for future revelations that Daniel would receive. It laid the foundation for him to understand future visions that came with greater detail about the succession of the Gentile nations. The prophet's reaction would be astonishment and dismay as he witnessed specific events that would not only involve future nations, but include many events of the House of Israel (Dan. 8, 11, 12).

The Timing of the Dream

Porphyry, a third century Christian antagonist, criticized a seeming inconsistency in Daniel's recorded timeframe. The alleged contradiction lies in the statement that Daniel's training lasted three-years and the time of Nebuchadnezzar's dream was in the second year of his reign. The two statements appear to be incongruent. If only two years had passed, Daniel would not have completed the courses and entered the king's service and therefore could not have provided the interpretation to the king.

A satisfactory explanation comes from the scholar Driver, who asserts that the three-year period merely extended over three years of his reign and was not a full three-year length of time.[4] The death and resurrection of the Lord, for example, spanned from 3 p.m. Friday evening, all day Saturday and into early Sunday morning, which was not a full 72 hours. But by Jewish tradition the duration satisfied three days.

Chaldean kings never considered the inauguration year as the first year of their reign. The inaugural year was filled with ceremony, bureaucratic re-organizations and festivals. Once solidly in office with his own staff, the king formally began his reign. Therefore, the second year of reign would be the third year that Nebuchadnezzar was in power, corresponding with Daniel's timeframe in Babylon (See the Table Below).

Nebuchadnezzar's "Second Year" Daniel 2:1	
May-June 605 B.C.	Babylonian victory over the Egyptians at Carchemish
June-Aug. 605 B.C.	Surrender of Jerusalem to Nebuchadnezzar. Daniel and his companions taken captive.
Sept. 7, 605 B.C.	Nebuchadnezzar, the general of the army, made king over Babylon after the death of Nabopolassar, his father.
September 7, 605 B.C. to April 1, 604 B.C.	Nebuchadnezzar's accession year as king and the first year of Daniel's training.
April 2, 604 B.C. to March 21, 603 B.C.	First year of the reign of Nebuchadnezzar and the second year of training for Daniel.
March 22, 603 B.C. to April 9, 602 B.C.	Second year of the reign of Nebuchadnezzar, third year of Daniel's training and the year of Nebuchadnezzar's dream.

Timeframes of Nebuchadnezzar's placement in office as outlined by Walvoord[5]

The Troubled King Demands an Interpretation

2   Then the king commanded to call the magicians, and the astrologers, and the sorcerers, and the Chaldeans, for to shew the king his dreams. So they came and stood before the king.

3   And the king said unto them, I have dreamed a dream, and my spirit was troubled to know the dream.

Extremely unsettled and sensing the vision to be from the gods in answer to his questions and concerns, the king sought an immediate answer—and it must be the true answer! While he felt that it came from the gods, he did not yet realize that it came from the true and living God. Nebuchadnezzar quickly sent for the wise men to be gathered. He hoped that they could provide a clear understanding of this important message. Four classes of advisors are mentioned as being summoned. They include: the magicians, the astrologers, the sorcerers and the Chaldeans. Each of these is listed in other portions of Daniel's record (Dan. 1:20; 2:10, 27; 4:7, 5:7, 11, 15). The combination constitutes the general quorum of "wise men" in the kingdom, which the king regularly consulted in all of the political affairs, battle campaign and religious matters.

"[The] magician is the translation of the Hebrew word with the root meaning of a 'stylus' or a 'pen,' and hence can be referred to as a scholar more than a magician in the ordinary sense."[6] Later in history, among the Persians, they are referred to as the Magi or the wise scholars. The equivalent in Jewish culture would have been the scribes. The wise men that generations later came to see the young boy Jesus were likely Jewish Magi from Babylon or Persia (Matt. 2:1-2). The astrologers were considered diviners or prophets; those who could discern future events by observing and interpreting signs in the skies. A few served as conjurers who spoke with the dead; sorcerers that practiced sorcery and incantations. Both astrologers and sorcerers would have been forbidden in Israel and punished by death for consulting with evil or peeping spirits (Deut. 18:10; see also 1 Sam. 28:5-20).

The fourth class was the Chaldeans or the upper class of nobles. Chaldeans in this context should not be interpreted in the broader ethnic sense (meaning people from the land of Chaldea), but only that group from southern Babylonia who took control when Nebopolassar conquered the Assyrians and rose as king. We might refer to these as the extended family aristocracy, royal nobles or tribes directly related to Nebuchadnezzar who benefitted from the rise of Nebopolassar's family to power.[7]

Inquiries on previous subjects from the king may have deserved the attention of only one or two groups of wise men, but this dream demanded all of the resources of the kingdom. The king assembled leaders from each of the four groups with the sole purpose of pooling the total intellectual and spiritual capacity of Babylon. The king was determined to gain an accurate interpretation of the dream.

After all, it came as an answer to his queries of the future of his own kingdom. In his mind the very destiny of the kingdom was at stake; there could be no misinterpretation.

Inquiries of the Wise Men

_____

4   Then spake the Chaldeans to the king in Syriack, O king, live forever: tell thy servants the dream, and we will shew the interpretation.

5   The king answered and said to the Chaldeans, The thing is gone from me: if ye will not make known unto me the dream, with the interpretation thereof, ye shall be cut in pieces, and your houses shall be made a dunghill.

6   But if ye shew the dream, and the interpretation thereof, ye shall receive of me gifts and rewards and great honour: therefore shew me the dream, and the interpretation thereof.

_____

It was not unusual for the king to call wise men into the court to give counsel and advice. It probably happened in the normal course of everyday business. Customarily, questions were asked, research and study were conducted in one form or another, thoughtful answers prepared and recommendations made. But this day would be different. When the Chaldean wise men heard that the king had a dream, the logical response was to ask for a summary of the dream. The king responded with a seemingly impossible request. He demanded that they provide both the dream and the interpretation of the dream. What made matters more interesting was this time there was the potential for reward and the penalties for nonperformance.

The king's command included the chance to receive great riches and position, which would be given to the one who could provide both the contents of the dream and an accurate interpretation. He would be elevated above the rest and be given generous gifts, status and honor. The punishment for nonperformance was death, a penalty that had never before been decreed. Both incentives, positive and negative, were in play, fueling the motivation to provide an accurate summary and a suitable explanation.

The proper interpretation was to Nebuchadnezzar essential as he was well aware of the patronizing disposition of the wise men. While they proved useful in many instances, they were also capable of conjuring the most nonsensical concoctions of poor advice imaginable. They would most often seek to provide answers pleasing to the king. In this matter, the king would take no chances. The fate of the kingdom was a subject not to be trifled with.

The wise men first replied by asking him to recite the contents of the dream. The king's response to the wise men's request was a reaffirmation of the decree: "The thing is gone from me" or in other words "is sure with me" (Dan. 2:5 footnote). This phrase has caused debate as to the meaning of "the thing" that had gone from the king. Did he mean that he could not remember the dream and that it was forgotten from his mind or was he saying something else? The linguistic constructs suggest that he did not say: "I forgot the dream," but rather "the thing" or the command had gone forth and it would not be rescinded. Other translations interpret the phrase to be "The command from me is firm" or "my decree is final."[8] In the Septuagint, the Greek translation of the Old Testament, the phrase, with slight alterations, is considered to mean: "is gone from me" or "it is a certainty from me"—in the sense of "I have decreed it."[9] The king was essentially saying, "my command on this matter has gone forth and is final."

> The king's response to the wise men's request was a reaffirmation of the decree: "The thing is gone from me" or I have decreed it.

Of course, the demand sparked terror in the hearts of the counselors. How could they know? How could they discover the dream with no information and then prepare an accurate interpretation? A request like this had never been made of the king or any previous king for that matter. The wise men were stunned and fear replaced anticipation for any reward.

The Wise Men's Second Appeal

----

7   They answered again and said, Let the king tell
    his servants the dream, and we will shew the
    interpretation of it.

8   The king answered and said, I know of certainty
    that ye would gain the time, because ye see the
    thing is gone from me.

9   But if ye will not make known unto me the
    dream, there is but one decree for you: for ye have
    prepared lying and corrupt words to speak before
    me, till the time be changed: therefore tell me the
    dream, and I shall know that ye can shew me the
    interpretation thereof.

The immediate reaction of the wise men was an attempt to persuade the king into giving details about the dream. The request was met with indignant wrath. Nebuchadnezzar accused them of stalling to buy time in an effort to create some elaborate falsehood or hoping that the circumstances would change (Dan. 2:9 footnote). There was but one mandate that applied and that was to make known the dream and its interpretation. By his edict "they see that the king is determined to punish them if they do not carry out his request, one law [or one decree], i.e. you can expect nothing else but the punishment,"[10] which will be sent forth, if you do not comply.

Again, the king's reluctance to grant more time and details was rooted in experience. He understood the shrewd nature of their craft. Given enough time, they could make up almost any interpretation. He was only interested in the true interpretation. They claimed the ability to speak to the divine or interpret the stars, therefore, let them apply their abilities and gifts. If they proved to be frauds the punishment of death would be justified.

The Final Petition of the Wise Men

----

10 The Chaldeans answered before the king, and said,
    There is not a man upon the earth that can shew
    the king's matter: therefore there is no king, lord,

nor ruler, that asked such things at any magician, or astrologer, or Chaldean.

11 And it is a rare thing that the king requireth, and there is none other that can shew it before the king, except the gods, whose dwelling is not with flesh.

12 For this cause the king was angry and very furious, and commanded to destroy all the wise men of Babylon.

———

In an act of desperation the Chaldeans made a final appeal. His request was not reasonable. No ruler or king had made such an impossible demand coupled with such severe penalties. They attempted to deflect responsibility by placing the interpretation in the hands of the gods. No one who dwells in the flesh would know, only the gods. If it came from the gods, let them provide an interpretation. "It was simply a confession of [the incompetence] on the part of the Chaldeans—no mortal man, only beings of a higher sphere can perform the king's request."[11]

Unwittingly, the council had set up the precise situation that the Lord intended. "God was shaping this matter to test the intrinsic futility of their (i.e. the Chaldeans) pretensions to superhuman knowledge, and to bring out in the most public manner his own infinite superiority over them all.[12] He alone gave the vision and He would unfold the secret through His servant Daniel.

The Death Sentence Sent Forth

———

13 And the decree went forth that the wise men should be slain; and they sought Daniel and his fellows to be slain.

14 Then Daniel answered with counsel and wisdom to Arioch the captain of the king's guard, which was gone forth to slay the wise men of Babylon:

15 He answered and said to Arioch the king's captain, Why is the decree so hasty from the king? Then Arioch made the thing known to Daniel.

16 Then Daniel went in, and desired of the king that he would give him time, and that he would shew the king the interpretation.

———

Unable to fulfill the requirements of their elevated positions, they were judged to be frauds and the death sentence was pronounced. The king ordered the chief of the guards to gather and slay the wise men and their families. All of the Chaldean priesthood, the magicians, the astrologers, the sorcerers and associated court members in the province of Babylon were to be immediately put to death. The execution order likely applied only to the local wise men in the province of Shinar and not to the whole kingdom.[13] Even so, these would have been the most noble and prestigious in the kingdom, even kindred to Nebuchadnezzar. There was great alarm.

"the Lord did bless Daniel. Though his faith was challenged and ridiculed, he stayed true to what he knew by his own experience to be right."

Daniel was not a part of the original assembly summoned to the court. The command for his death comes completely by surprise. It remains unclear exactly his relationship to the Chaldean elites other than he had begun to serve as an advisor in the court. He was not experienced enough, nor had he any preeminence to play a principle role. He had not joined any of the pagan priesthood orders that might have given him social advantage. Nevertheless, he was also a target scheduled for execution.

When the news of the king's command came to Daniel, he approached one Arioch, who was "the chief of the bodyguard, which was regarded as the highest office [over security] of the kingdom. It was his business to see to the fulfillment of the king's commands," including coordinating the execution.[14] The official knew and held great respect for the young prophet. Daniel's favorable relationship with those in high office is noteworthy. Despite the order, Arioch paused to consult with him and explain the situation.

Daniel's initial response was of concern over the "hastiness" of the king. He was not questioning the speed of execution alone, although that was a legitimate concern, but rather the harshness or rashness of the edict, given the circumstances.[15] It seemed very uncharacteristic of the king, even irrational. But exhibiting both poise and tremendous faith in the Lord, he requested to meet with the king, expressing confidence that he could fulfill the demand of interpreting the dream. Arioch seized upon the opportunity to avoid carrying out the king's order and agreed to arrange a meeting.

"Under ordinary conditions, Daniel might be filled with terror, but he is convinced that the Spirit of God is with him."[16] Men of deep faith are bold and confident. They possess a certainty rooted in their living in harmony with the commands of God (Doctrine and Covenants 121:45). President Deiter F. Uchtdorf asserted: "the Lord did bless Daniel. Though his faith was challenged and ridiculed, he stayed true to what he knew by his own experience to be right. Daniel believed. Daniel did not doubt."[17] Furthermore, Daniel exhibits humility. He makes no extravagant promises, but merely states that if the king will grant him time, he will declare the dream and its interpretation.[18] Something remarkable can be said about the spiritual maturity of the young man who stood calm amidst chaos and uncertainty.

If Daniel had only recently completed his education and entered service in the court, he would still be in his early twenties. The record affirms that his previous interaction with the king was positive (Dan. 1:20), but quite limited. Arioch introduced young Daniel to the king to make the plea (Dan. 2:24). He probably could not enter into his presence without an escort. Once in the court, the young Daniel confidently petitioned for additional time and promised that he would fulfill the tenants of the king's demand.

A pause in the execution order was granted. Daniel "went into his own house and showed the matter to his companions, that they might entreat God of His mercy for this secret, so that they might not perish along with the rest of the wise men of Babylon."[19]

Daniel Receives The Secret of the Vision

———

17 Then Daniel went to his house, and made the thing known to Hananiah, Mishael, and Azariah, his companions:

18 That they would desire mercies of the God of heaven concerning this secret; that Daniel and his fellows should not perish with the rest of the wise men of Babylon.

19 Then was the secret revealed unto Daniel in a night vision. Then Daniel blessed the God of heaven.

———

As soon as the young Daniel secured extra time, he returned to his house to elicit help from his friends: Shadrach, Meshach and Abed-nego. His focus was to combine their prayers and faith to petition the mercies of the Lord. The primary goal was that they not perish in the execution with all the wise men. Given Daniel's nature, he was doubtless concerned about the lives of all the wise men and their families as well as his kin and lastly, his own life.

The simple decision made years earlier, wherein they chose not to defile themselves with the king's meat, now loomed very large. President Deiter F. Uchtdorf reflected on the important choices the young lads had made:

———

> Just think about it. How much easier would it have been for Daniel to simply go along with the ways of Babylon? He could have set aside the restrictive code of conduct God had given the children of Israel. He could have feasted on the rich foods provided by the king and indulged in the worldly pleasures of the natural man. He would have avoided ridicule.
>
> He would have been popular.
>
> He would have fit in.
>
> His path might have been much less complicated. That is, of course, until the day when the king demanded an interpretation of his dream. Then Daniel would have found that he, like the rest of Babylon's 'wise men,' had lost his connection to the true source of light and wisdom.[20]

———

Living in harmony with God's will was essential to approaching God in faith. The Lord has taught: "Let thy bowels also be full of charity towards all men, and to the household of faith, and let virtue garnish thy thoughts unceasingly; then shall thy confidence wax strong in the presence of God" (Doctrine and Covenants 121:45). Not only had they not defiled themselves, but they had embraced their covenants in the Law of Moses with full commitment, both the tenants to be practiced as well as their spiritual meanings. Their strict obedience brought protection and instilled an assurance (Heb. 11:1) that they could come to the Lord in any situation. Like Ammon, the son of Mosiah, Daniel saw this crisis as an opportunity, and took advantage to act rather than succumb to fear (Alma 17:29). The situation was a matter of life and death, but he had been true and faithful. He could petition the Lord for mercy with trust and confidence that He would provide an answer for the king.

Daniel knelt and asked Jehovah to reveal the "great secret" of the king. He and his friends prayed earnestly explaining the gravity of the situation. And the Lord responded with a night vision. The specifics of the manifestation were not given, but it seems that he was given a vivid and detailed vision, more than Nebuchadnezzar's simple dream.

Other scriptural accounts provide insight into heavenly methods used to convey complex messages to prophets. These experiences involve seeing and understanding things and events accompanied by instruction from the Spirit (1 Ne. 11). Peter's vision of the sheet with the unclean animals, for example, is described thus: "I was in the city of Joppa praying: and in a trance I saw a vision, A certain vessel descend, as it had been a great sheet, let down from heaven by four corners; and it came even to me" (Acts 11:5, see also Acts 10:10). The vision was conveyed with impressions and instructions to take the Gospel to the Gentiles. Paul experienced a similar daytime manifestation (Acts 22:17), as did Balaam in his vision of the destiny of Israel (Num. 24:4,16). In the Book of Mormon King Lamoni was overcome by the Spirit and sees the Lord and angels and was taught by them (Alma 19:13-14, 34). Nephi, who was personally tutored by the Holy Ghost saw numerous panoramic visions about the Messiah, the Nephites and the Gentiles. In this experience the Spirit would command him to "look" to see each portion of the vision (1 Ne. 11:8, 12, 24, 25, 30, 32). Nephi's visions rank among the most impressive in scripture (1 Ne. 11-14).

Joseph Smith, the Seer, viewed the past, future and the eternities with unrivaled frequency. His First Vision (JS-H 1:17) experience coupled with later visitations of the Savior and other messengers set him apart from many of the prophets.

In like manner, Daniel's vision would have been detailed and complex, filled with a broad panorama of information. He not only saw Nebuchadnezzar's great statue, but was enlightened by the Spirit sufficient to provide the interpretation. Joseph Smith taught: "Could you gaze into heaven five minutes, you would know more than you would by reading all that ever was written on the subject."[21]

The young prophet was fully prepared to approach the throne of the king and reveal what no other "wise man' in the kingdom could. He became the true wise man and with the help of the Lord, the source of all wisdom. "The boy who believed and lived his faith had become a man of God. A prophet. A prince of righteousness."[22]

Thus instructed and prepared, Daniel blesses the Lord in a spirit of thanksgiving and gratitude for mercifully answering his prayers.

Daniel Praises the Lord in Thanksgiving

20 Daniel answered and said, Blessed be the name of God for ever and ever: for wisdom and might are his:

21 And he changeth the times and the seasons: he moveth kings, and setteth up kings: he giveth wisdom unto the wise, and knowledge to them that know understanding:

22 He revealeth the deep and secret things: he knoweth what is in the darkness, and the light dwelleth with him.

23 I thank thee, and praise thee, O thou God of my fathers, who hast given me wisdom and might, and hast made known unto me now what we desired of thee: for thou hast now made known unto us the king's matter.

Daniel's reaction to the vision is filled with awe and thankfulness. The Lord had heard their prayers and responded with a marvelous manifestation. He now knew the secret things that had been revealed to the king. Their lives were safe as well as the lives the wise men. In addition to the simple act of responding to the prayer, Daniel's mind had been enlarged as to the purposes and ways of the Lord. He began to grasp God's great power and wisdom over the earth and the kingdoms of the world. He marveled how the Lord governs over the "times" and "seasons" of the kingdoms of the earth. His power and benevolence were daily manifested.[23] He saw that God truly ordered and cared for all things. Nature was not a product of chance evolution, nor were the affairs of the earth guided by the wooden idols as the Chaldeans had asserted.[24]

> The vision enlightened Daniel's understanding of God's governing hand over all His creations. Kingdoms rise and fall according to their obedience to the laws of heaven.

The vision enlightened Daniel's understanding of God's governing hand over all His creations. Kingdoms rise and fall according to their obedience to the laws of heaven. As one kingdom is swept away, so the Lord raises up a new kingdom to spread peace and stability among His children. The cycle can be seen throughout history. Daniel seemed to have discerned the motives and intent of the Lord, acknowledging His genius, justice and wisdom in the use of His power.

The young prophet observed, through the aid of the Spirit, that God knows all. He sees every creation, every soul, even those things that occur in the darkest most secretive corners of society. In a similar manifestation, Moses saw the earth through the Lord's perspective. He "beheld the earth, yea, even all of it; and there was not a particle of it which he did not behold, discerning it by the Spirit of God. *And he beheld also the inhabitants thereof, and there was not a soul which he beheld not;* and he discerned them by the Spirit of God; and their numbers were great, even numberless as the sand upon the sea shore" (Moses 1:27-28, emphasis added).

President Harold B. Lee taught: "By faith in God you can be attuned to the Infinite and by power and wisdom obtained from your Heavenly Father harness the powers of the universe to serve you in your hour of need in the solution of problems too great for your human strength or intelligence."[25] The young prophet praises the "God of my fathers," recognizing his great heritage in the family of Israel. A part of that heritage included prophets who also received visions and revelation which gave them wisdom and knowledge.[26]

Daniel Approaches the King

———

24 Therefore Daniel went in unto Arioch, whom the king had ordained to destroy the wise men of Babylon: he went and said thus unto him; Destroy not the wise men of Babylon: bring me in before the king, and I will shew unto the king the interpretation.

25 Then Arioch brought in Daniel before the king in haste, and said thus unto him, I have found a man of the captives of Judah, that will make known unto the king the interpretation.

26 The king answered and said to Daniel, whose name was Belteshazzar, Art thou able to make known unto me the dream which I have seen, and the interpretation thereof?

27 Daniel answered in the presence of the king, and said, The secret which the king hath demanded cannot the wise men, the astrologers, the magicians, the soothsayers, shew unto the king;

28 But there is a God in heaven that revealeth secrets, and maketh known to the king Nebuchadnezzar what shall be in the latter days. Thy dream, and the visions of thy head upon thy bed, are these;

29 As for thee, O king, thy thoughts came into thy mind upon thy bed, what should come to pass hereafter: and he that revealeth secrets maketh known to thee what shall come to pass.

30 But as for me, this secret is not revealed to me for any wisdom that I have more than any living, but for their sakes that shall make known the interpretation to the king, and that thou mightest know the thoughts of thy heart.

———

Grant Romney Clawson © Used with permission
Young Daniel interprets Nebuchadnezzar's Dream

In the morning, Daniel enthusiastically approached Arioch with the good news that he had indeed received a manifestation. He reaffirmed the need to spare the wisemen and make arrangements to meet with Nebuchadnezzar. The Lord had set Daniel in full control of the situation.

Arioch hastens to the king and announces again that he had found someone who could interpret the dream. A significant amount of trust was expressed in Daniel, as he didn't preview or attempt to filter the response, but hastily approached the court. Some have expressed criticism at his taking honor unto himself by saying: "I have found a man of the captives of Judah, that will make known unto the king the interpretation" (Dan. 2:25) emphasizing his relationship with Daniel. His actions represented a classic human response, primarily of relief that a suitable resolution had been found. The situation was dire and he desired not to perform the executions. The chief also deserves credit for believing in Daniel and working to solve the crisis, without bloodshed. It is also interesting to note that Arioch's focus was on Daniel and not his God.

Notwithstanding his Jewish heritage, Daniel's proper introduction to the king was by his Chaldean name of Belshazzar, which was the only name the king recognized. Once in the court, the king immediately asked him about his ability to reveal the dream and give the interpretation. "The question, "*art thou able?*" i.e., has thou ability? does not express the king's ignorance of the person of Daniel, but only his amazement at his ability to make known the dream, in the sense, "art thou really able?"[27]

Daniel's initial response reinforces the unreasonableness of the king's demand as expressed by the wise men. What the king required "cannot the wise *men,* the astrologers, the magicians, the soothsayers, shew unto the king" (Dan. 2:27). He was in effect "defending [the position of the wise men] somewhat from the king's wrath while at the same time affirming their impotence."[28] He rebuked the king for demanding man to perform that which God had reserved for Himself alone.[29] At the same time he censured the system and art of the wise men who pretended to have great knowledge and skill in these matters. Daniel laid the groundwork to introduce his God as the true God and the only Being who could reveal the king's secret.[30]

The young prophet begins by testifying that there was indeed a God in Heaven who knows and reveals the secret thoughts of men, including the vision of the king. Again, the power and wisdom of the "God of Heaven" is emphasized. Jehovah's abilities compared to the pagan religions and idol gods is supreme. In reality, not only had the Chaldean priesthood and wise men put themselves to shame, but by association so were their gods. Neither they nor their idols of stone and wood were able to reveal the great secret.

Daniel tells the king that the dream came in consequence of his inner "thoughts." He had spent considerable time pondering the destiny of his kingdom. "Would it persist?" "What would become of it?" This statement certainly would have caught the king's attention, as no one else knew the thoughts or feelings that first spawned the vision. He reaffirmed that only God knew his thoughts and the feelings of his heart. Then in complete humility, he states: "… as for me, this secret is not revealed to me for *any* wisdom that I have more than any [other] living [being]." By himself, he had little ability or wisdom to fulfill the king's request. It was important for

Daniel to give all credit solely to that Being who had blessed and empowered him to fulfill the request. He proceeds to answer the questions in the king's heart.

He begins by revealing that what the king saw "…shall be in the latter days." The dream would come to its full fruition in the last or end days. Nebuchadnezzar's day (584 B.C.) was clearly not the last or latter-days or even the days when the gentiles had dominion in the world (Doctrine and Covenants 45:28). History had not progressed to the meridian of time. Babylon's moment was the beginning of the remarkable world events to come. Therefore, the vision showed the successive kingdoms from Nebuchadnezzar's reign to the end of days when all kingdoms of the world would come to an end. Each kingdom would be given dominion, but would fall into social decay and eventually be destroyed or break apart. In the end, the Lord will set up His kingdom which will be established forever. All this will come to fruition in the latter days.

The interpretation will not only answer Nebuchadnezzar's query, but provide to Daniel a view of the end from the beginning. He would later receive additional visions about these kingdoms and periods in greater detail. The combination of all that Daniel saw sets a framework and provides prophetic insight into the Lord's plan and intentions for His children in that part of the world. It reveals to the Chosen People what they can expect during this time and until the end of time.

President Joseph Fielding Smith explained: "This vision of the kingdom is a wonderful portrait of historical events down through the ages of time, from the day of Daniel to our present dispensation. Let us not forget that the promise of the Lord in this vision was that in the latter days of these kingdoms the Lord was to set up a kingdom that was not to be left to any other people, *'which shall never be destroyed,'* but which was to endure and consume all other kingdoms and stand forever."[31] Those who study with close attention will have understanding of what is to come.

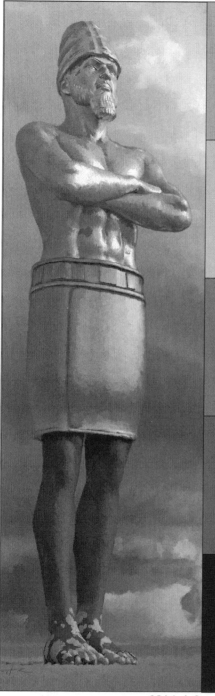

GOLDEN HEAD
The Babylonian Empire
beginning with
Nebuchadnezzar
612 B.C. - 539 B.C.
(The Lion Daniel 7:4)

SILVER TORSO
The Medo-Persian Empire
550 B.C. - 330 B.C.
(The Bear Daniel 7:5)

BRASS THIGH
The Macedonian-Grecian
Empire
331 B.C. - 168 B.C.
(The Leopard, Daniel 7:6)

LEGS OF IRON
The Roman Empire
753 B.C. - 479 A.D.
(The Beast, Daniel 7:7)
The Byzantium Empire
330 A.D. 1453 A.D.

TOES OF IRON AND CLAY
Divided Kingdoms
1400 A.D. - Present
(Ten Horns, Daniel 7:8)

© Painting by Steve Creitz and adapted by Erik Brandt, Used with Permission

The Statue in Nebuchadnezzar's Dream

The Dream Is Revealed

31   Thou, O king, sawest, and behold a great image. This great image, whose brightness was excellent, stood before thee; and the form thereof was terrible.

32   This image's head was of fine gold, his breast and his arms of silver, his belly and his thighs of brass,

33   His legs of iron, his feet part of iron and part of clay.

34   Thou sawest till that a stone was cut out without hands, which smote the image upon his feet that were of iron and clay, and brake them to pieces.

35   Then was the iron, the clay, the brass, the silver, and the gold, broken to pieces together, and became like the chaff of the summer threshing floors; and the wind carried them away, that no place was found for them: and the stone that smote the image became a great mountain, and filled the whole earth.

Daniel's explanation begins with the Hebrew translation of the Aramaic term for image. The language is not typically used to mean an idol, but rather a statue.[32] The statue was tall, beautiful and impressive and the size and form were terrible and frightening. "Even Nebuchadnezzar, the absolute ruler, recognized this as something greater than himself."[33] Its head was of gold, the chest and arms of silver, the belly and thighs of brass, the legs of iron and feet and toes of clay and iron mixed together. "The world-power is in all its phases in one, therefore all these phases are united in the vision in *one* image."[34]

The quality and weight of the metals decreases from the superior magnificent gold to the progressively inferior elements of silver, brass, iron and clay. "While the materials decrease in weight, they increase in hardness with the notable exception of clay in the feet. The image was obviously top heavy and weak in the feet."[35] The imagery, however, gives clues as to the nature of each kingdom to be given power on the earth.

By this time Nebuchadnezzar must have been sitting on the edge of his throne with his full attention focused on the young prophet and his heart pounding in his chest. The man that stood before him was relating exactly the contents of his dream. Daniel had his full consideration and admiration and he hung on every word.

The young prophet then spoke of an object of particular interest, a stone cut without hands. No human hands were used to cut this "stone," which implies that its origin was not of earthly powers, but from heaven.[36] "Without hands, without human help, is a litotes for: by a higher, a divine providence"[37] The stone comes from a mountain, a metaphor that Isaiah employed to mean temple: "The Mountain of the Lord's house shall be established in the top of the mountains" (Isa. 2:2). The figurative expression of mountain means habitation of the Lord. As Elder Bruce R. McConkie explains: the meaning of the phrase "top of the mountains" in reference to temples: "All of the holy temples of our God in the latter days shall be built in the mountains of the Lord, for his mountains—whether the land itself is a hill, a valley, or a plain—are the places where he comes, personally and by the power of his Spirit, to commune with his people."[38]

The metaphor "stone cut from the mountain without hands" symbolizes that messengers will be sent from God's heavenly temple (or mountain) to hew out or organize "the stone" or Kingdom of God on the earth. It is a reference to the restoration of the Gospel in the latter-days. President Spencer W. Kimball has taught: "The Church of Jesus Christ of Latter-day Saints was restored in 1830 after numerous revelations from the divine source; and this is the kingdom, set up by the God of heaven, that would never be destroyed nor superseded, and the stone cut out of the mountain without hands that would become a great mountain and would fill the whole earth."[39]

This impressive stone rolled forward smashing into the feet of clay causing the iron, brass, bronze and all the elements of the statue to shatter into fine pieces. The remaining elements were then blown as chaff from the thrashing floor, "that no place was found for them" (Dan 2:35). Any remaining vestiges of the old regimes were decimated and replaced by the Kingdom of Heaven. God's kingdom becomes the dominant power in the world. The stone cut from the heavenly mountain becomes a "great mountain" that fills the whole earth (Dan. 2:25).[40] This is a reference to the millennial day when righteousness reigns, when the whole earth is the Lord's mountain, a time when:

———

6   The wolf also shall dwell with the lamb, and the leopard shall lie down with the kid, and the calf and the young lion and fatling together; and a little child shall lead them.

7   And the cow and the bear shall feed; their young ones shall lie down together; and the lion shall eat straw like the ox.

8   And the sucking child shall play on the hole of the asp, and the weaned child shall put his hand on the cockatrice's den.

9   They shall not hurt nor destroy in all my holy mountain, for the earth shall be full of the knowledge of the Lord, as the waters cover the sea (2 Ne. 21:6-9; Isa. 11:6-9, emphasis added)

———

A number of scholars have described the stone as Christ, quoting the prophetic passage that portrays him as the "Stone of Israel" (Gen. 49:24) or a "rock [stone] of offense" (Isa. 28:16) or the "chief cornerstone" (Eph. 2:20; Matt. 21:42; Mark 12:10; Luke 20:17; Acts 4:11).[41] This interpretation is not incorrect as Christ is both the fashioner of the stone and the foundation stone of the kingdom (1 Cor. 3:11; Eph. 2:20). But in context, Daniel clearly states that it represents the heavenly kingdom set up by Christ, which shall one-day rule over all the earth (Dan. 2:44).

The stone smashing the statue was perhaps the portion of the dream that gave Nebuchadnezzar the most concern. If he had any inclination of the meaning of the statue, particularly the golden head, he certainly understood the implications of its destruction by the stone. Even if he did not know the particulars of the dream, it ends violently for the statue. That would be enough to motivate him to seek an explanation. Now a young man stood before him, who could not only tell him the contents of this dream, but it seems he was also prepared to reveal its meaning.

The Interpretation of the Dream

36　This is the dream; and we will tell the interpretation thereof before the king.

37　Thou, O king, art a king of kings: for the God of heaven hath given thee a kingdom, power, and strength, and glory.

38　And wheresoever the children of men dwell, the beasts of the field and the fowls of the heaven hath he given into thine hand, and hath made thee ruler over them all. Thou art this head of gold.

39　And after thee shall arise another kingdom inferior to thee, and another third kingdom of brass, which shall bear rule over all the earth.

Having presented the basic overview of the statue and its destruction from the powerful stone, the young prophet proceeded straight into the interpretation of the dream. He began with Nebuchadnezzar: "Thou, O king, *art* a king of kings" (Dan. 2:37). The language parallels very closely and a number of interpreters argue too closely, to praise or title of King of kings (Rev. 19:16). But Daniel simply intended to covey the fact that the king had a great dominion. He was, after all, the supreme king over many kings and kingdoms, the former of Judah, Jehoiakim, being one. His conquests covered lands and kingdoms from Egypt to the edge of the Median and Persian territories. He ruled as supreme sovereign over many nations. As a point of emphasis, Daniel relates the greatness of the king's territory: "wheresoever the children of men dwell, the beasts of the field and the fowls of the heaven hath he given into thine hand" (Dan. 2:38). Virtually, all that Nebuchadnezzar knew and understood made up his world and was under his control, but Daniel boldly pointed out that it was the God of heaven who had granted him the privilege to rule over such a vast kingdom (Dan. 2:37).

With the grandeur of the Babylonian Empire and the extent of the king's control thus described, Daniel confirms the kings suspicions by revealing that he, Nebuchadnezzar II, was embodied in the head. "Nebuchadnezzar was the head of gold. The head is the most important single member of the body, and gold is the most precious of all metals. This dual symbolism spoke of an absolute monarch. Other kings sat upon the throne of Babylon, but this vision ignores them…it ignores Nebuchadnezzar's successors… only Nebuchadnezzar was the head of gold."[42] Babylon was represented quintessentially as his monarchy; none previous and none thereafter wielded the unfettered power in like manner as that of Nebuchadnezzar.

Daniel moves on to speak of the kingdoms to come. "And after thee shall arise another kingdom inferior to thee, and another third kingdom of brass" (Daniel 2:39). The silver torso with two arms represented the Medo-Persians kingdom. The Macedonian empire, founded by Philip II and expanded by Alexander the Great, was embodied in the stomach-thighs of brass. Each kingdom would be given power to rule over "the world" for a season. Daniel does not say who these powers would be, only that there would be successors. The reader has the benefit of hindsight and the king may have had inkling, but the vision remained a mystery through all his days.

Daniel describes the second kingdom as inferior. But how so? Both the Persian and the Greek kingdoms were much larger geographically and controlled more nations and peoples, so by what standard could these be inferior? The Persians seemed less concerned with grandiose cities or wonderful exhibits of impressive architecture like those on display in Babylon, but only slightly. The real measure of inferiority was gauged by the king's standard of governance. He saw kingdoms in terms of raw power and unity invested in a single individual. By Nebuchadnezzar's standard their sovereignty and practices would have seemed much inferior.

The Persians, for example, did not rule by royal edicts spoken at the will or whim of the king. The monarch's edicts were written into law after consideration and deliberation among the aristocracy, councils and the review of the Magi. Royal pronouncements and proclamations were used as the primary instruments of governance. Greek rule introduced yet more deliberative and democratic principles as they sought to elevate the people through Hellenistic culture. Alexander's mighty kingdom collapsed after his death into four powerful but ever squabbling powers. His generals divided the empire and for years engaged in competitive conquests of intrigue designed to overthrow each other. Nebuchadnezzar would have viewed these kingdoms as greatly inferior.

Nebuchadnezzar would have concluded that the deterioration of the statue from pure gold to silver and then from silver to bronze and bronze to iron as an inferior digression from the unity and administrative efficiencies of his autocracy. The inefficiencies of petty wrangling and the jockeying for power comprised, in his mind, bureaucratic nonsense.

But from the Lord's point of view, the slow transformation was actually a deliberate progression towards broader and more reliable forms of government. Monarchies and dictatorships are rarely stable over the generations. They suffer from sibling strife, insurrection and slaughter at least as much, if not more than other more distributed forms of government. The principles of broader, more deliberative and structured kingdoms were represented in the metals. While they were lighter elements, they were also stronger and harder substances that could be fashioned into tools or instruments for the benefit of man.

Of course none of these kingdoms were by any means perfect or corruption free. History clearly demonstrates that they possessed a great capacity for brutality. Each kingdom engaged in cruel practices of conquest and plunder and the aristocracy was riddled with corruption, treachery and sycophants who fawned for position and favors. Despite the human frailties steady progress towards broader, more deliberative and representative forms of governance and greater prosperity was a constant thread. The Lord gave them sufficient enlightenment to establish order, progress and "bear rule over all the earth" (Dan. 2:39).

Each kingdom would be allowed dominion as it served the Lord's purposes. When the decay of tyranny and corruption spread in the kingdom and as unprincipled rulers became dominant, then the kingdom struggled, chastened with the consequences of their works. Eventually, the Lord forced a change. His over arching power prepared another kingdom suited to take their place.

Drawing of Rome by Architect Charles Cockerell

The Fourth Kingdom

40 And the fourth kingdom shall be strong as iron: forasmuch as iron breaketh in pieces and subdueth all things: and as iron that breaketh all these, shall it break in pieces and bruise.

41 And whereas thou sawest the feet and toes, part of potters' clay, and part of iron, the kingdom shall be divided; but there shall be in it of the strength of the iron, forasmuch as thou sawest the iron mixed with miry clay.

42 And as the toes of the feet were part of iron, and part of clay, so the kingdom shall be partly strong, and partly broken.

43 And whereas thou sawest iron mixed with miry clay, they shall mingle themselves with the seed of men: but they shall not cleave one to another, even as iron is not mixed with clay.

The fourth kingdom is described as strong like iron. It wields great power to bruise, break and subdue other kingdoms. The previous kingdoms portrayed in the statue also subdued peoples and nations, but this power extended its rule at unprecedented levels.

There can be no doubt that the iron legs and feet represented the Roman Republic and later the Roman Empire. For nearly a thousand years, Roman navies and legions crushed rival powers like the Etruscans, the Carthaginians, the Gauls, the Greeks, the Seleucids and Parthia. They pushed along the Mediterranean south into Africa and west into Hispania and Britannia.

Rome's initial goals were not necessarily conquest, but rather maintaining stability, prosperity and order. In their minds, however, this required crushing adversaries and subjugating rival kingdoms. Conquest for riches became increasingly more a part of Rome's policy over time. They always dealt ruthlessly with rebellion. The Judean uprising in 70 A.D. was quelled as Roman legions sacked the city and nearly annihilated the entire Jewish population. They burned and toppled the temple and slaughtered over a million Jews.[43] A second uprising, the Bar Kokhba Revolution of 132-135 A.D., brought the same brutal response. This time the inhabitants that survived were banned from the city and thousands were carried off to be sold as slaves. Rome abolished the sovereign nation of Judah all together. These punitive slaughters typified the retribution of Rome toward rebellious foes or subjects.

Rome's iron rule brought *pax romana* or the Roman peace, a stability that reached its pinnacle with Emperor Augustus and lasted for many generations. It was under this peace that the gospel was preached by the Apostles and Primitive Church. Eventually, Rome's serious internal strife and constant raids from outside tribes combined to diminish its power and break the great Roman Empire into separate, smaller nations and religious sovereigns.

Most scholars accept the two legs as symbolic of the major eastern and western partitions of the empire. "This was two-legged because it embraced two continents or two major geographical areas, the East and the West. The Roman Empire continued its sway over the entire Mediterranean area and the Byzantines to the east."[44] Ultimately, the newer eastern (Byzantine) empire separated from the western (Roman) kingdom. Rome remained the capital in the west and Constantinople the capital of the east. Through attrition, decay and constant conflict Rome's might crumbled and was eventually taken over by the barbarian Goths led by Odoacer in 476 A.D..[45]

Iron and Clay Mixed in Feet and Toes

The feet and toes of mixed clay and iron represent the kingdoms and nations that remained after the fall of Rome. In the east, the Byzantine Empire rose to control Eastern Europe and parts of the Middle East and Asia. Additionally, remnants of the Persian and Babylonian empires reestablished themselves, although into much lesser powers. Later they were transformed with the introduction of Islam into Muslim Caliphates and ultimately the Ottoman Empire. In the latter-days, the eastern kingdom has been separated into many countries scattered across the Middle East. In the west, the Roman Empire collapsed and the tribal nations throughout Europe reasserted themselves. These tribes developed into the modern European and Mediterranean countries of today. Ten toes, mixed with iron and clay, are appropriate symbols of the multinational condition of the world that evolved and transformed from the breakup of Rome's mighty empire.

Elder Orson Pratt, explaining why the toes were shown as being partly iron and partly clay, said: "the feet and toes were governments more modern to grow out of the iron kingdom (Roman Empire), after it should lose its strength. These are represented by the ten toes or ten kingdoms, which should be partly strong and partly broken. They should not have the strength of the legs of iron, but they should be mixed with miry clay, indicating both strength and weakness."[46] The strong unifying iron, the remnants of Rome and its powerful method of rule, manifested itself in part in the newly formed Catholic religion in the west and in Islam founded in the east. Harsh, heavy-handed methods of governance were the norm under the provincial kings, popes, imams and governors.

The clay brings an image of brittleness and symbolizes the various kingdoms broken into ethnic tribes or countries with all of the strengths and vulnerabilities that result. "The mixing of iron with clay represents that attempts to bind the two distinct and separate materials into one combined whole as fruitless, and altogether in vain. The mixing of themselves with the seed of men (Dan. 2:43), most interpreters refer to the marriage politics of the princes" a practice commonly employed among monarch powers.[47] Attempted alliances through marriage explains the meaning only in part as the symbolism "denotes all the means employed by the rulers to combine the different nationalities."[48]

In Daniel's day a strategic policy, employed first by the Assyrians and then the Babylonians, was to transplant peoples into different lands for the purpose of mingling them and creating one "homogenous race" under a single banner. In the end, the strategy proved to be a failure. The Romans employed this policy sparingly, but rather kept order through an effective bureaucracy and brute force when it was deemed necessary. Many nationalities became Roman citizens and integrated into the culture through immigration and naturalization.

Later the provincial kings used a variety of methods to build, mix or cleanse ethnic groups. In every case such efforts proved largely unsuccessful. The villages and townships were ethnically loyal and for the most part nationalistic with respect to their culture. The larger bonds between peoples—forces like religion, trade and political alliances—helped keep peace and stability, but the racial "clay" kept the peoples mostly separate and distinct. Even the Soviet Union's efforts in the twentieth century could not bring about a unified communist state through military oppression and secular indoctrination.

While not all nations and cultures survived the sweep of history, most did. The broad result is the modern world, a composite of many nations, a mixture of iron with clay. Latter-day stability among the nations is fragile, but peace has held together through a combination of influential superpower nations, religion, treaties, economic globalization and geography. The ethnic and national distinctiveness are still largely preserved, even within countries. God purposed to preserve the kindreds of the earth from the beginning. He understood that large central empires proved troublesome to His plan as we learn from the accounts of Babel (Gen. 11:1-9; 10:10).

The Kingdom of the God of Heaven

> 44 And in the days of these kings shall the God of heaven set up a kingdom, which shall never be destroyed: and the kingdom shall not be left to other people, but it shall break in pieces and consume all these kingdoms, and it shall stand for ever.
>
> 45 Forasmuch as thou sawest that the stone was cut out of the mountain without hands, and that it brake in pieces the iron, the brass, the clay, the silver, and the gold; the great God hath made known to the king what shall come to pass hereafter: and the dream is certain, and the interpretation thereof sure.

Daniel now addresses "the days of these kings" or the days when these kingdoms of iron mixed with clay have dominion in the world. These nations, primarily the Europeans, have come to power in what are called the "latter-days" or the "times of the Gentiles" (Dan. 2:28; Doctrine and Covenants 45:29-30). This period began about the 15th century with the exploration, expansion and colonization of the European Empires. The vision reveals that in the times of the Gentiles, the Kingdom of God would be established on the earth and that in the end, His kingdom would take dominion as the preeminent power over the world.

A number of commentators suggest that Christ's Church, established in the meridian of time, was this stone used to break the statue. But there is no evidence that the Primitive Church, as it was called, broke the gentile nations and ruled the world as described in the vision. In reality, the Apostles were delivered up and killed, and the faithful Church members were afflicted and hated of all nations (Matt. 24:9). Paul spoke of a great "falling away" from the Church (2 Thes. 2:3) and of the apostasy that followed wherein "false prophets" and "grievous wolves" entered in the flock, "not sparing it" (Acts 20:29).

The net effect of the apostasy was that the Church established by Christ was taken over and transformed. Its essence was destroyed and the remnant of the kingdom left to other peoples to pervert the doctrines and change the ordinances. Its history represents exactly the opposite of Daniel's prophecy. The Primitive Church could not be the great stone that would destroy the wicked kingdoms of the world. The Christian scholar Walvoord affirms: "There is certainly no evidence, two millennia after Christ, that the kingdom of God has conquered the entire world. In addition, there is no scriptural evidence whatsoever that Christ's first coming caused the downfall of gentile world power, which is still very much with us today.[49] God's kingdom would be cut from the mountain of heaven and established in some other way.

It is correct to look for a Church as the fulfillment of the predicted "stone" or God's Kingdom on the earth. It has always been established in this form. According to Daniel's interpretation, one should look for the stone or kingdom established in the latter days. It began small and as it rolled forth to become as a mountain and continued to grow until it filled the whole earth (Dan. 2:34-35). President Spencer W. Kimball further clarified the prophecy with the following explanation:

> Rome would be replaced by a group of nations of Europe represented by the toes of the image. With the history of the world delineated in brief, now came the real revelation. Daniel said: 'And in the days of these kings [that is, the European nations] shall the God of heaven set up a kingdom, which shall never be destroyed ...This is a revelation concerning the history of the world, when one world power would supersede another until there would be numerous smaller kingdoms to share the control of the earth. And it was in the days of these kings that power would not be given to men, but the God of heaven would set up a kingdom—the kingdom of God upon the earth, which should never be destroyed nor left to other people. The Church of Jesus Christ of Latter-day Saints was restored in 1830 after numerous revelations from the divine source; and this is the kingdom, set up by the God of heaven, that would never be destroyed nor superseded, and the stone cut out of the mountain without hands that would become a great mountain and would fill the whole earth."[50]

The cutting of the stone requires skill and must be performed with design and purpose. The establishment of the kingdom of God will be patterned from previous works. It must be fashioned in the likeness of the Kingdom of God established in preceding dispensations. Just as the Primitive Church had Apostles, Seventy, Pastors (bishops), evangelists (patriarchs), teachers and others (Eph. 2:20; 4:11), just as it enjoyed the gifts of the Spirit (Gal. 5:22) and engaged in missionary work and temple work (Mark 16:15; 1 Cor. 15:29), so too the latter-day kingdom will mirror the pattern set anciently and in the Primitive Church.[51]

The Lord declared to the prophet Joseph in Hiram, Ohio (1830): "The keys of the kingdom of God are committed unto man on the earth, and from thence shall the gospel roll forth unto the ends of the earth, as the stone which is cut out of the mountain without hands shall roll forth, until it has filled the whole earth. (Doctrine and Covenants 65:2).

Elder Neal A. Anderson has added further insight:

____

From the miraculous intervention of God to Daniel came the prophesied future of the gospel of Jesus Christ being restored to the earth, a kingdom that would fill the whole earth, 'never [to] be destroyed … [but to] stand for ever.' The number of members of the Church in the latter days would be relatively few, as Nephi prophesied, but they would be upon all the face of the earth, and the power and ordinances of the priesthood would be available to all who desired them, filling the earth as Daniel foretold (1 Ne. 14:12-14). In 1831 the Prophet Joseph Smith received this revelation: The keys of the kingdom of God [and the gathering of Israel from the four parts of the earth] are committed unto man on the earth, and from thence shall the gospel roll forth unto the ends of the earth, as the stone which is cut out of the mountain without hands shall roll forth, until it has filled the whole earth.[52]

____

God's kingdom will not destroy the gentile nations by military force or conquest. Rather these nations will eventually suffer under the judgments of the Almighty because of their own wickedness and evil deeds. They will largely reject the message of the gospel (3 Ne. 21:11-14; Doctrine and Covenants 45:28-29; 1 Ne. 14:15; JS-M 1:23). God's judgements will involve natural disasters, plagues and wars among themselves that will ultimately bring an end to all nations. "And thus, with the sword and by bloodshed the inhabitants of the earth shall mourn; and with famine, and plague, and earthquake, and the thunder of heaven, and the fierce and vivid lightning also, shall the inhabitants of the earth be made to feel the wrath, and indignation, and chastening hand of an Almighty God, until the consumption decreed hath made a full end of all nations" (Doctrine and Covenants 87:6).

In relation to the destiny of the latter-day kingdom, President Brigham Young noted: "The Lord God Almighty has set up a kingdom that will sway the sceptre of power and authority over all the kingdoms of the world, and will never be destroyed; it is the kingdom that Daniel saw and wrote of. It may be considered treason to say that the kingdom which that Prophet foretold is actually set up; *that* we cannot help, but we know it is so, and call upon the nations to believe our testimony. The kingdom will continue to increase, to grow, to spread and prosper more and more. Every time its enemies undertake to overthrow it, it will become more extensive and powerful; instead of its decreasing, it will continue to increase, it will spread the more, become more wonderful and conspicuous to the nations, until it fills the whole earth."[53]

Any remnants of all the previous kingdoms, the gold (Babylon), the silver (Persian), the brass (Greek), the iron (Roman Empire) and the brittle clay (gentile nations) that exist today will all be broken, their power annulled by the might and majesty of the King of kings and Lord of Lords. The millennial reign prophesied by the prophets will begin and the Lord Jesus Christ will be the sovereign over the earth (Isa. 2:2-7).

Daniel concludes his explanation by affirming that the dream and interpretation were correct and true. Keil asserts that: "the importance of the dream should put him [the king] in mind to lay the matter to hear, and give honour to God who imparted to him these revelations; but at the same time also the word assures the readers of the book of the certainty of the fulfillment."[54]

The Reward of King Nebuchadnezzar

---

46 Then the king Nebuchadnezzar fell upon his face, and worshipped Daniel, and commanded that they should offer an oblation and sweet odours unto him.

47 The king answered unto Daniel, and said, Of a truth it is, your God is a God of gods, and a Lord of kings, and a revealer of secrets, seeing thou couldest reveal this secret.

48 Then the king made Daniel a great man, and gave him many great gifts, and made him ruler over the whole province of Babylon, and chief of the governors over all the wise men of Babylon.

49 Then Daniel requested of the king, and he set Shadrach, Meshach, and Abed-nego, over the affairs of the province of Babylon: but Daniel sat in the gate of the king.

At the conclusion of Daniel's interpretation, Nebuchadnezzar falls upon his face in awe of the explanation. This was probably an unprecedented gesture of the king, not an act of worship, but to honor Daniel's God. In a similar incident, Josephus records that Alexander the Great bowed before the high priest of the Jews, and when asked by his general, Parmenion, as to the meaning of his action, replied "I do not worship the high-priest, but the God with whose high-Priesthood he has been honored."[55]

Nebuchadnezzar proclaimed Daniel's God, Jehovah, as "a God of gods" (Dan. 2:47). While he recognized the power and wisdom of his God, he was not converted to Jehovah, as he still expressed the polytheistic view that there were many gods. But as an expression of honor, he and others in the court offered sweet words of oblation that were a form of prayer directed to the God of Daniel for the blessing of wisdom and the revelation of his secret.

Nebuchadnezzar recognized Daniel's talent and the value of his abilities. He promoted the young prophet in the kingdom to be the governor (Satrap) over the province of Babylon. "Provinces such as Babel, etc., were ruled by an official known as *shakkanaku*."[56] Of all the provinces, however, Babylon (or Shinar) was the most prestigious and the most populous as it was the center of the kingdom, it epitomizes Babylonia. Daniel ruled over the province closest to Nebuchadnezzar and he was also made the chief president over all the wise men.

A few scholars have criticized Daniel for taking such a position over the astrologers and sorcerers, but the book affirms that he did not participate in their pagan and supernatural practices, only served as chief administrator and advisor.[57]

Just as any high official was privileged to do, Daniel selected those whom he trusted to serve closely and assist him. His kin from Jerusalem, Shadrach, Meshach, and Abed-nego, were set over the affairs of the province of Babylon, but he served in "the gate" or in the king's court at the pleasure of the king. He was informed of everything that was brought before the king, serving as a counselor, a trusted confidant to King Nebuchadnezzar.

Chapter Notes:

1   Kimball. "Church Growth and Lamanite Involvement," *BYU Speeches*. November 7, 1971

2   Keil. *Biblical Commentary of the Old Testament, The Book of the Prophet Daniel*. 87

3   Young, *The Prophecy of Daniel, A Commentary*, 60; *Biblical Commentary of the Old Testament*. 87

4   Quotes from Driver in Young. T*he Prophecy Daniel: A Commentary*. 55

5   Walvoord. *Daniel, The Key to Prophet Revelation*. 60

6   Leupold. *Exposition of Daniel*. 75

7   Walvoord. *Daniel, The Key to Prophet Revelation*. 61

8   See Daniel 2:5 in *New American Standard Bible* and *New International Versions (NIV)*

9   Walvoord. *Daniel, The Key to Prophet Revelation*. 63

10 Young. *The Prophecy Daniel: A Commentary*. 61

11 Bevan. S*hort Commentary on the Book of Daniel*. 1892

12 Butler. *The Bible-work, vol ix*

13 Walvoord. *Daniel, The Key to Prophet Revelation*. 66

14 Keil. *Biblical Commentary of the Old Testament, The Book of the Prophet Daniel*. 96

15 quote Kran, Keil. *Biblical Commentary of the Old Testament, The Book of the Prophet Daniel*. 96

16 Young. *The Prophecy Daniel: A Commentary*. 64-65

17 Uchtdorf, "Be Not Afraid, Only Believe." General Conference. October 2015

18 Young. *The Prophecy Daniel: A Commentary*. 64-65

19 Keil. *Biblical Commentary of the Old Testament, The Book of the Prophet Daniel*, 97

20 Uchtdorf, "Be Not Afraid, Only Believe, General Conference. October 2015

21 Smith. *Teachings of the Prophet Joseph Smith*, 324; cf. HC 6:50

22 Uchtdorf. "Be Not Afraid, Only Believe." General Conference. October 2015

23 Young. T*he Prophecy Daniel: A Commentary*. 67

24 Ibid, 67

25 Lee. *Church News*. 15 Aug. 1970, 2

26 The Hebrew term used for God was "Elohim," the father of Jehovah, signifying his praise and devotion to his Father in Heaven for the answer to his prayer. Walvoord. *The Key to Prophet Revelation*. 70

27 Keil. *Biblical Commentary of the Old Testament, The Book of the Prophet Daniel*, 100
    Anderson. "A Witness of God." General Conference, October 2016

28 Young. *The Prophecy Daniel: A Commentary*. 73

29 Ibid, 70

30 Leupold, *Exposition of Daniel*. 120

31 Smith. *Seek Ye Earnestly*. 310 Maynes. "The Truth Restored" https://www.lds.org/broadcasts/article/worldwide-devotionals/2016/01/the-truth-restored?lang=eng

32 Keil. *Biblical Commentary of the Old Testament, The Book of the Prophet Daniel*, 102

33 Walvoord. *Daniel, The Key to Prophet Revelation*. 77

34 Keil. *Biblical Commentary of the Old Testament, The Book of the Prophet Dan-*

iel. 102. Quotes: Klief

35   Charles. *A Critical and Exegetical Commentary on the Book of Daniel.* 24-25

36   Clark. *Bible Commentary*, Vol 4, 570-73

37   Keil. *Biblical Commentary of the Old Testament, The Book of the Prophet Daniel*, 108-09

38   McConkie. *The Millennial Messiah.* 275

39   Kimball. "The Stone Cut Without Hands." *Ensign.* May 1976

40   Joseph Smith taught: The Prophet called on all who held the Priesthood to gather into a little log school house, perhaps 14 feet square. But it held the whole Priesthood of the Church of Jesus Christ of Latter-day Saints who were then in the town of Kirtland...when we got together the prophet called upon the Elders of Israel to bear testimony of this work. ...When they got through the Prophet said, "Brethren, I have been very much edified and instructed in your testimonies here tonight, but I want to say to you before the Lord, that you know no more concerning the destinies of this Church and kingdom than a babe upon its mother's lap. You don't comprehend it" I was rather surprised. He said "It is only a little handful of Priesthood you see here tonight, but this Church will fill North and South America—it will fill the world" Woodruff. *Conference Report.* April 1898. 57

41   Clark. *Commentary of Daniel.* Vol 4. 573

42   Phillips *Exploring the Book of Daniel: An Expository Commentary.* 54-55

43   Oats. "The Great Jewish Revolt of 66 CE." *Ancient History Encyclopedia*, published on 28 August 2015 http://www.ancient.eu/article/823/

44   Walvoord. *Daniel, The Key to Prophet Revelation.* 87

45   Gibbons. *The Decline and Fall of the Roman Empire.* Vol. 4 Ch. XXXVI, 301-03

46   Pratt. *In Journal of Discourses.* 18:337; see also *Journal of Discourses.* 7:220-222

47   Keil. *Biblical Commentary of the Old Testament, The Book of the Prophet Daniel*, 108-09

48   Ibid

49   Walvoord. *Daniel, The Key to Prophet Revelation.* 88

50   Kimball. *Conference Report.* April 1976. 10

51   Callister. "What Is the Blueprint of Christ's Church?" CES Fireside January 12, 2014, https://www.lds.org/broadcasts/article/ces-devotionals/2014/01/what-is-the-blueprint-of-christs-church?lang=eng)

52   Anderson, "A Witness of God." General Conference, October 2016, see also *Teachings of Presidents of the Church: Joseph Smith* (2007), 444
See also: Christofferson. "Why the Church," General Conference, October 2015; Derrick. "Valiance in the Drama of Life." General Conference. April 1983; *Teachings of George Albert Smith* 2010, Chapter 17, Strengthening Power of Faith

53   In *Journal of Discourses* 1:202-3

54   Keil, *Biblical Commentary of the Old Testament, The Book of the Prophet Daniel.* 112

55   Josephus, *Antiquities*; Young. *The Prophecy Daniel: A Commentary.* 81

56   Meissner 1, 122

57   Young. *The Prophecy Daniel: A Commentary.* 82

Additional Notes: Dream of Nebuchadnezzar

Daniel said to the king that his dream was a portrayal of the history of the world. Then came the picture of the great image with head of fine gold, and breast and arms of silver, and belly and thighs of brass, and legs of iron, and feet of iron and clay. Then the revelation continued:

"Thou sawest till that a stone was cut out without hands, which smote the image upon his feet that were of iron and clay, and brake them to pieces." (Dan. 2:34.) (Kimball Spencer W. "The Stone Cut Without Hands." General Conference. April 1976)

Metals, Purity and Weight

"Gold has a specific gravity of 19.3, silver has a specific gravity of 10.51, brass has a specific gravity of 8.5, iron has a specific gravity of 7.6, and clay has a specific gravity of 1.9. So, right from the first, the image was doomed. So although God ordained as has allowed Gentle world empires to wax and wane and to rule and dominate the earth. He never intended this innovation, made necessary by Israel's sin to be permanent" (Phillips 53).

Daniel said to Nebuchadnezzar, "Thou art this head of gold" (v. 38). The dream revealed events that would take place over a long span of time. The culmination, however, was to take place in the last days. The Hebrew word that was used, *achariyth*, means "last or end" (James Strong. "A Concise Dictionary of the Words in the Hebrew Bible," in The Exhaustive Concordance of the Bible. 11). (LDS Old Testament Institute Manual Vol. 2).

3

The Great Statue

A Season of Babylonian Prosperity

An estimated 18 to 23 years passed after the time Daniel interpreted the dream (602 B.C.) to this chapter when Nebuchadnezzar built a great statue in the land of Dura (584–570 B.C.). During this time, Babylon enjoyed long seasons of success and prosperity. In the thirteenth-year, the siege of Tyre ended in a compromise with the Tyrian rulers accepting Babylonian authority.[1] In the nineteenth year (586 B.C.). Babylon sacked Jerusalem for the third time wherein it destroyed the temple (2 Kgs. 25:8), finally subduing the Jewish nation and leaving Jerusalem in rubble. A last group of Jewish captives were taken and united with their brethren in the Babylonian provinces. Nebuchadnezzar also went to Mitzraim in Egypt to wage war with Pharaoh Amasis. He conquered and brought the Egyptian empire under his subjection.

All of his victories brought a sustained peace and prosperity to the kingdom, especially the capital. Nebuchadnezzar turned from war to building. He invested significantly in construction and renovation projects. He expended resources to restore and expand many of the old temples including the Ziggurat of Marduk in the city itself. The palace, begun by his father Nabopolassar, was completed using only the finest materials of cedar wood, marble stones and precious ores.[2] The great protective walls and gates that surrounded the city were fortified and widened. In a number of places around the palace, he built a third layer of walls and ramparts that were considered impregnable. The iconic Hanging Gardens begun in 605 B.C. were finally completed, a magnificent accomplishment dedicated to the king's wife Amytis who missed the green hills of her homeland in Media. The gardens were connected to the royal palace that graced the city landscape.

It was during this great season of prosperity that Nebuchadnezzar decided that a statue should be erected as a monument to his greatness and a symbol of world dominance.[3] The statue would be fashioned in his image, a tribute and a memorial of the providence of the gods who had smiled so favorably on him and his kingdom. "Falling down before it [would be] a manifestation of reverence not only to the world-power, but also to its gods" and to him.[4]

The statue was layered with pure gold, likely a thick leaf overlaid onto wood, brick, and stone. It is argued that Nebuchadnezzar forged a statue of solid gold, but, in truth, this was neither practical nor probable. The shape and style would have conformed to traditional Babylonian design. "As to the upper part - the head, countenance, arms, breast —it may have been in the form of a man, and the lower part may have been formed like a pillar. This would be altogether in accordance with Babylonian art, which delighted in grotesque, gigantic forms."[5]

Building statue monuments and elevating kings to godhood was common in the eastern cultures, a form of self-deification. It probably began with Nimrod in Babel and served as a testimony of the favorable station they held among the gods, if not a witness that they were gods themselves. Nebuchadnezzar's statue "demanded the recognition of the national god, to whom the king supposed he owed the greatness of his kingdom, and was a command which the heathen subjects of Nebuchadnezzar could execute without any violence to their consciences."[6] But to the faithful Jews, it was an offense, an obstacle to their fidelity to Jehovah. The believing Jew would not violate the first law that there should be "no other Gods before me" (Ex. 20: 3).

The Affirmation of Loyalty

The record states that Nebuchadnezzar erected the statue on the plains of Dura where it would then be presented and dedicated.

---

1 Nebuchadnezzar the king made an image of gold, whose height was threescore cubits, and the breadth thereof six cubits: he set it up in the plain of Dura, in the province of Babylon.

Despite Babylon's great prosperity, not all was bliss. Records show that there were several coup attempts against the king's life, including one in the year 595 B.C.–594 B.C., which was recorded in the Babylonian chronicle as a major event in that year.[7] The statue therefore was not erected solely for the celebration of the king and his accomplishments, but would be used to test the loyalty of the officials, a ceremony to reaffirm their support of his position and power. "This ceremony is in keeping with the times. Such a display of officials was, on one hand, a gratifying demonstration of the power of Nebuchadnezzar's empire and on the other hand, was significant as recognizing the deities who in their thinking were responsible for their victories. The worship of the image was intended to be an expression of loyalty to Nebuchadnezzar…it was in effect saluting the flag, although because of the interrelationship with national loyalties, it may also have had religious connotations."[8] The important distinction here was that not "saluting the flag" could cost you your life, and it was a stated condition worth noting.

Dyre reaffirms that loyalty from the national officials was a primary focus of the event. He writes of a parallel account translated from a clay prism artifact found in modern Iraq. On the prism, Nebuchadnezzar wrote: "I ordered the [following] court official in exercise of the duties to take position in my [official] suite."[9] Then Dyre comments on the contents of the prism. "The prism then lists five ranks of individuals who were evidently summoned before Nebuchadnezzar at approximately the same time to appoint (or reappoint) official positions in the government of Babylon. The ranks include court officials, official of the land of Akkad, officials of towns, district officials and western vassal kings. This list [portrays] a high government gathering. If this assembly occurred after the unsuccessful revolt against Nebuchadnezzar in Babylon, it is likely that Nebuchadnezzar intended it as an awe-inspiring event to assure the future loyalty of those who held positions of authority under him."[10]

The statue was set-up in Dura although the exact location of the monument remains unknown, but archeologists suggest that it was about 12 miles south of Babylon in a place called Tolul Dura or the Mounds of Dura.[11]

Babylonian Dignitaries Gather at Dura

_____

2   Then Nebuchadnezzar the king sent to gather together the princes, the governors, and the captains, the judges, the treasurers, the counsellors, the sheriffs, and all the rulers of the provinces, to come to the dedication of the image which Nebuchadnezzar the king had set up.

3   Then the princes, the governors, and captains, the judges, the treasurers, the counsellors, the sheriffs, and all the rulers of the provinces, were gathered together unto the dedication of the image that Nebuchadnezzar the king had set up; and they stood before the image that Nebuchadnezzar had set up.

_____

The government officials invited to the dedication varied from princes to counselors and sheriffs. The breadth of dignitaries spanned all levels of the government. The princes were known as Satraps, a Persian title for the chief princes or provincial administrators. Satraps were the highest administrators, the watchers or overseers of the kingdom. These positions were just under the king and his council and appointed by the king himself. They were the principle representatives of the king in the provinces.[12] These offices were not given to just anyone, but solely to trusted and loyal confidants, mostly family.

The captains or prefects were military commanders, the chief generals over the army.[13] The governors and presidents constituted the local authorities that oversaw the civil administration of towns and villages. Counselors served as arbitrators: justices executed policy and administered the law. They often served as lawyers. Sheriffs or magistrates were lower judges involved in local law enforcement and disputes. And the treasurers administered the kingdom's assets by collecting taxes and accounting for the budget.[14]

No dignitary would have refused an invitation to come to the dedication, although it is interesting to note that nothing is said of the whereabouts of Daniel. Furthermore, there is no indication that the general populace was invited. The majority were dignitaries with important stewardships within the kingdom; perhaps others were allowed at the function, but focus was with the dignitaries.

For the majority of the attendees the dedication event would have been a time of excitement and anticipation; an occasion to reaffirm acquaintances, positions and status in the kingdom. Some might receive new assignments and responsibilities. It would have been a place of celebration and festivity, a kind of royal ball in which the reaffirmation of allegiance to the kings was in harmony with all the planned ceremonies.

Assembling to Worship the Great Image

When all were assembled at the appointed time, the royal caller cried for the attention of the assembled dignitaries.

4   Then an herald cried aloud, To you it is commanded,
     O people, nations, and languages,

5   That at what time ye hear the sound of the cornet,
     flute, harp, sackbut, psaltery, dulcimer, and all kinds
     of musick, ye fall down and worship the golden
     image that Nebuchadnezzar the king hath set up:

6   And whoso falleth not down and worshippeth shall
     the same hour be cast into the midst of a burning
     fiery furnace.

7   Therefore at that time, when all the people heard the
     sound of the cornet, flute, harp, sackbut, psaltery,
     and all kinds of musick, all the people, the nations,
     and the languages, fell down and worshipped the
     golden image that Nebuchadnezzar the king had set
     up.

A new command was pronounced to all the nations and subjects. At the sound of the anthem, representing Nebuchadnezzar and his great statue, every person was to bow and worship the image. Violators would suffer under pain of death. "The proclamation of the herald refers not only to the officers who were summoned to the festival, but to all who were present, since besides the officers there was certainly present a great crowd of people from all parts of the kingdom..., so that the assembly consisted of persons of various races and languages."[15]

The punishment for disloyalty was death in the fiery furnace. The brick kilns used in the many construction projects throughout Babylon were the most common furnaces. Doubtless a number of them stood nearby, used in the construction of the grand memorial and other projects in the area. These furnaces yielded heat in excess of 1500° Fahrenheit, more than sufficient to consume the bodies of any disobedient attendee.

An ensemble of royal musicians playing various musical instruments was positioned near the monument. The instruments consisted of a cornet, which is interpreted to be a horn. The horn was sometimes from an animal, but it probably was made of brass or wood. The flute was from the Hebrew, meaning to "hiss" or a "whistle." The harp, sackbut and psaltery were all string instruments ranging from a larger upright harp with traditional shape and as many as 10 to 14 strings, to the smaller organ-like sackbut held in the hand of a player, to the psaltery, which was fashioned after the Greek lyre. The dulcimer has been translated as panpipe or a bagpipe, which was imported by Greek merchants. Some scholars believe there is linguistic evidence that it was a drum, like small timpani.[15] The players with their instruments made up the small orchestra. The combination of instruments would have made an excellent assembly. It seems that they came prepared to perform all kinds of music, but the primary purpose was to introduce the new "Nebuchadnezzar national anthem."

Both the scene and circumstance instilled in Shadrach, Meshach, and Abed-nego something far more than an unsettled feeling, for they quickly understood the implications of the new command. It

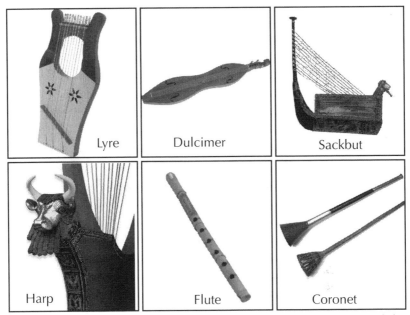

Ancient Instruments © Used with permission

ran contrary to every devotion they had for Jehovah and they well understood that their lives were in jeopardy.

When the music played, the masses bowed in unison according to the command. But there was more going on here than simply acknowledging Nebuchadnezzar as king or showing loyalty. This was a religious ceremony. "Since the dominion of Nebuchadnezzar was founded not by right, but by the might of conquest, and the homage which he commanded to be shown to the image was regarded not only as a proof of subjection under the power of the king, but comprehended in it also the recognition of his gods as the gods of the kingdom...In the demand of the king there was certainly a kind of religious oppression."[17]

As the great company fell to their knees and prostrated towards the statue, three individuals from the Babylonian contingent remained on their feet. If there were any feelings of peer pressure at the time they refused to eat from the king's table, this situation heightened similar concerns by several fold. The result of their actions was clearly a matter of life and death, and their decision to stand would likely mean death.

Chaldeans Accuse Shadrach, Meshach and Abed-nego

----

8   Wherefore at that time certain Chaldeans came near, and accused the Jews.

9   They spake and said to the king Nebuchadnezzar, O king, live forever.

10   Thou, O king, hast made a decree, that every man that shall hear the sound of the cornet, flute, harp, sackbut, psaltery, and dulcimer, and all kinds of musick, shall fall down and worship the golden image:

11   And whoso falleth not down and worshippeth, that he should be cast into the midst of a burning fiery furnace.

12   There are certain Jews whom thou hast set over the affairs of the province of Babylon, Shadrach, Meshach, and Abed-nego; these men, O king, have not regarded thee: they serve not thy gods, nor worship the golden image which thou hast set up.

The local Chaldean representatives knew that the three administrators had just violated the law. Among them were loyal, but ambitious dignitaries who sought for opportunity to rise in position. Since Shadrach, Meshach and Abed-nego were high appointees in the Babylonian province and were Jews, the situation presented a perfect chance. Jealousy among the aristocracy was always at play, and the envious officials seized upon the moment. No doubt the promotions of these foreign Jewish captives and the high nature of their positions weighed heavily for years upon a few of the Chaldean officers. This opened a perfect opportunity to get rid of them and take posts once and for all.[18]

Other objectors might simply have been loyal Babylonian nationalists offended at the disrespectful manner with which Shadrach, Meshach and Abed-nego remained on their feet. After all the worship command had been given, and any response other than bowing was viewed as a severe demonstration of disrespect.

The Chaldeans immediately approached the king and spitefully indicted the offenders. The accusers were quick to point out the nationality of the three and their important positions in the central province. Foreigners were obviously not as loyal as indigenous citizens and therefore must be more susceptible to treachery. After rehearsing to the king the command and the consequences for non-compliance, the officials then accused the three of disloyalty and disrespect. "O king, have not regarded thee: they serve not thy gods, nor worship the golden image" (Dan 3:12). The three charges leveled against the three were: first, a disregard and disrespect to the king,

Shadrach, Meshach and Abed-nego refuse to bow before the image of king
Nebuchadnezzar of Babylon

second, not worshiping the national gods and third, and not bowing down to the image according to the command. The combination of the three offenses was tantamount to insubordination and worthy of the pronounced punishment, death.

Nebuchadnezzar's Anger

13 Then Nebuchadnezzar in his rage and fury commanded to bring Shadrach, Meshach, and Abed-nego. Then they brought these men before the king.

14 Nebuchadnezzar spake and said unto them, Is it true, O Shadrach, Meshach, and Abed-nego, do not ye serve my gods, nor worship the golden image which I have set up?

15 Now if ye be ready that at what time ye hear the sound of the cornet, flute, harp, sackbut, psaltery, and dulcimer, and all kinds of musick, ye fall down and worship the image which I have made; well: but if ye worship not, ye shall be cast the same hour into the midst of a burning fiery furnace; and who is that God that shall deliver you out of my hands?

Philip Galle in Haarlem Holland, 1537-1612, © Used with permission

The Three Jews (Shadrach, Mechach, Abed-nego) brought before Nebuchadnezzar

Nebuchadnezzar's reaction to the accusation was predictable. Had he not clearly presented the command and the consequences for disobedience? News of the obstinate non-conformists from among the delegation had not only spoiled the spirit of the occasion, but confirmed suspicions of possible traitors in his midst. If true, he would deal swiftly with the dissenters. In a fit of anger, but not yet uncontrolled rage, he commanded that they be brought before him.

We must remember that they had served in high offices of the Babylonian province for over a decade. They were probably known to the king and performed their tasks with fidelity. These new accusations would have come as a surprise to the king, who upon seeing them offered a chance to refute the charges. The statements :"Is it true?" and "If ye be ready...fall down and worship" suggest a merciful second chance. He would allow acquittal to all charges if they simply denied the claim and lay prostrate to the idol image when the music played. If they complied, no further questions would be asked, but if they refused to worship the idol and his gods, the result was clear.

Nebuchadnezzar then adds a tone of defiance. If they stand firm in their decision "who is that God that shall deliver you out of my hands?" Again, no nation or opposing gods had overthrown him in the long history of battles and conquests. No kingdom had challenged his dominion and survived. In his mind, he reigned supreme, and his statement was not arrogant. He did not expect the gods from other nations to be able to exercise power or interfere.[19] The whole purpose of this event was to herald his supreme standing. Anyone who defied this station would be challenged directly. Again, unwittingly, Nebuchadnezzar had set the table for the God of Heaven to show forth his power before all of Babylon.

Shadrach, Meshach, and Abed-nego Stand Firm

16 Shadrach, Meshach, and Abed-nego, answered and said to the king, O Nebuchadnezzar, we are not careful to answer thee in this matter.

17 If it be so, our God whom we serve is able to deliver us from the burning fiery furnace, and he will deliver

us out of thine hand, O king.

18   But if not, be it known unto thee, O king, that we will not serve thy gods, nor worship the golden image which thou hast set up.

19   Then was Nebuchadnezzar full of fury, and the form of his visage was changed against Shadrach, Meshach, and Abed-nego: therefore he spake, and commanded that they should heat the furnace seven times more than it was wont to be heated.

20   And he commanded the most mighty men that were in his army to bind Shadrach, Meshach, and Abed-nego, and to cast them into the burning fiery furnace.

21   Then these men were bound in their coats, their hosen, and their hats, and their other garments, and were cast into the midst of the burning fiery furnace.

22   Therefore because the king's commandment was urgent, and the furnace exceeding hot, the flame of the fire slew those men that took up Shadrach, Meshach, and Abed-nego.

23   And these three men, Shadrach, Meshach, and Abed-nego, fell down bound into the midst of the burning fiery furnace.

———

The three Jewish princes answered with clarity and boldness, holding back no words in their response to the king. They declared that "our God is able to deliver us from the burning fiery furnace, and he will deliver us out of thine hand, O king" (Dan. 3;17). Then came an expression of unshakable commitment and trust: "but if not...we will not serve thy gods." Elder Vaughn Featherstone suggests: "they stood in royal priesthood dignity before the king and defied him with power and assurance. Not even his kingly authority could force them to compromise the least or greatest commandments of God."[20]

In the contest between the king's gods and their God, they chose Jehovah. He "quenched the violence of fire" (JST. Gen. 14:26; Heb. 11:34) and they knew that the God of Israel was able to save them. He had promised the faithful of Jacob: "When thou passest through the waters, I will be with thee; and through the rivers, they shall not overflow thee: when thou walkest through the fire, thou shalt not be burned; neither shall the flame kindle upon thee" (Isa. 43:2).

The expression "but if not," was not rooted in doubt of His ability to protect or redeem them, but demonstrated their pure trust, submissiveness and willingness to give their lives as a testimony of their faith and confidence in the Savior. If it was His desire that they suffer death in defense of Him and His name, they were willing to do so. Of this level of deep personal commitment, President Howard W. Hunter has taught: "The ability to stand by one's principles, to live with integrity and faith according to one's belief—that is what matters, that is the difference between a contribution and a commitment. That devotion to true principle—in our individual lives, in our homes and families, and in all places where we meet and influence other people—that devotion is what God is ultimately requesting of us."[21]

> Our God is able to deliver us from the burning fiery furnace, and he will deliver us out of thine hand, O king... but if not... we will not serve thy gods.

For king Nebuchadnezzar, the response represented an unmitigated expression of treason and an affront to him in the presence of the royal crowd. The statement of Shadrach, Meshach and Abed-nego was a provocation of the king's command in defiance of the occasion, Babylon's gods and of him. And as a result the text says that: "the form of his visage was changed" (Dan. 3:19). Any feelings of mercy or appreciation that he might have had for them and their service in the kingdom was gone, replaced by pure, white-hot fury. An urgent command to heat the fiery furnace was given. The kiln was to be heated seven times the normal temperature. This of course was an expression of hyperbole to indicate that the furnace fires were to be stoked as hot as possible. The chances of heating the kiln to 10,000 degrees was unlikely, but it would, nevertheless, be very, very hot.

The "most mighty men" were ordered to immediately bind the three and take them to the furnace. No time was wasted to remove uniforms, emblems or superfluous clothing. They were to be cast in hats and all. Archeologists have suggested that the point of entrance might have been from above.[22] The soldiers would lower or cast the captives down from a door above the fire. Hence, the soldiers were also at great risk from exposure to heat or falling into the fire themselves. No matter where or how the fugitives were cast in, they too were exposed to the tremendous heat and died. As it was, all three fell into the flames of the very hot furnace.

Shadrach, Meshach and Abed-nego Saved in the Furnace

24 Then Nebuchadnezzar the king was astonied, and rose up in haste, and spake, and said unto his counsellors, Did not we cast three men bound into the midst of the fire? They answered and said unto the king, True, O king.

25 He answered and said, Lo, I see four men loose, walking in the midst of the fire, and they have no hurt; and the form of the fourth is like the Son of God.

26 Then Nebuchadnezzar came near to the mouth of the burning fiery furnace, and spake, and said, Shadrach, Meshach, and Abed-nego, ye servants of the most high God, come forth, and come hither. Then Shadrach, Meshach, and Abed-nego, came forth of the midst of the fire.

27 And the princes, governors, and captains, and the king's counsellors, being gathered together, saw these men, upon whose bodies the fire had no power, nor was an hair of their head singed, neither were their coats changed, nor the smell of fire had passed on them.

The king and his officers expected that as soon as the young protestors fell into the kiln, they would be consumed almost at the moment they were thrown in. As the crowd stood and attempted to see the fate of the condemned, the king pointed to something in the midst of the flames that astonished him. They were not consumed at all. Furthermore, he thought he saw a fourth Person with them, whose stature and appearance was most impressive, even glorious.

18th Century Biblical Art © Used with permission
Artist's depiction of Shadrach, Meshach and Abed nego with an angel in the fiery furnace

A heavenly being had been sent to protect and sustain them from the intense fire.

The king's initial reaction was to question whether there were actually three thrown into the fire or were there more? Those in the assembly affirmed the number was indeed three. In disbelief, Nebuchadnezzar then proclaimed that he could see four in the finance, mingling without harm and the fourth was "like the Son of God" (Dan. 3:25). Without doubt their God, Jehovah, had indeed supported them in the trial. Whether the Lord, Himself, preserved the three by His personal presence or by the assistance of an angel, we do not know. Verse 28 suggests that it was an angel, but it certainly could have been the Lord, Himself.

As Christians and students of the Gospel, the statement "like the Son of God" makes perfect sense, but it is unlikely that Nebuchadnezzar understood the relationship of Jehovah, the God of the Jews, as being the Son of the Father. The king's orientation was still steeped in paganism and his statement would have been according to his own world view. Young states that: "the translation of the [KJV], the Son of God is not grammatically defensible. The meaning is son of deity, i.e. a divine person, one of the race of the gods, or a super natural being...No doubt the king spoke in the spirit and meaning of the Babylonian doctrine of the gods."[23] Even so, Nebuchadnezzar had challenged the God of the Jews, as to whether or not He could deliver them. And He did deliver them.

Certainly impressed and perhaps even a little anxious, the king commands them to come out of the furnace. The fire had not consumed them, nor did it have any power over them, neither to burn, nor to singe; nor had the smell of fire and smoke passed upon them. They were preserved and unaffected by the incident. The impact of the event sunk deep into the king's soul. Nebuchadnezzar's rage turned to honor for them as the servants of the "most High God." Again, unaware that their God was the only true and living God, Nebuchadnezzar nevertheless proclaims Jehovah as the Most High above all the gods, still believing in many gods.

Nebuchadnezzar Honors Shadrach. Meshach and Abed-nego

———

28 Then Nebuchadnezzar spake, and said, Blessed be the God of Shadrach, Meshach, and Abed-nego, who hath sent his angel, and delivered his servants that trusted in him, and have changed the king's word, and yielded their bodies, that they might not serve nor worship any god, except their own God.

29 Therefore I make a decree, That every people, nation, and language, which speak any thing amiss against the God of Shadrach, Meshach, and Abed-nego, shall be cut in pieces, and their houses shall be made a dunghill: because there is no other God that can deliver after this sort.

30 Then the king promoted Shadrach, Meshach, and Abed-nego, in the province of Babylon.

———

It is difficult to fully appreciate the king's reaction. At one moment he was consumed by unmitigated anger, willing to demand forced worship by authoritarian decree. But in the face of the marvelous manifestation, his pride was tempered, and his attitude mellowed. He announced that their appearance "had changed his word." The decree that all should bow to the statue was rescinded, that "[these three] might not serve nor worship any god, except their own God" (Dan. 3:28). Their trust had not been in vain, but rather their faithfulness was rewarded and their God glorified.

The God of Israel delivered them from the fire, and "at the same time [the king] not only openly announced that [their God] had saved (Dan. 3:28) His servants, but also by an edict, issued to all the peoples of his kingdom, he forbade on pain of death the doing of any dishonour to the God of the Jews (Dan. 3:29)."[24] This edict redounded to the benefit of the Jews scattered throughout the empire. Any persecution against their God was condemned under penalty of death. The actions of these faithful men extended to the entire Jewish population in the Babylonian diaspora. The Lord had opened the way for Israel to freely worship without fear of reprisal.

Of their miraculous faith, Elder Dennis E. Simmons said: "They knew that they could trust God—even if things didn't turn out the way they hoped. (Mos. 7:33) They knew that faith is more than mental assent, more than an acknowledgment that God lives. Faith is total trust in Him.

Faith is believing that although we do not understand all things, He does. Faith is knowing that although our power is limited, His is not. Faith in Jesus Christ consists of complete reliance on Him.

Shadrach, Meshach, and Abed-nego knew they could always rely on Him because they knew His plan, and they knew that He does not change (Alma 7:20; 3 Ne. 24:6; Mor. 9:19; Moro. 8:18). They knew, as we know, that mortality is not an accident of nature. It is a brief segment of the great plan (2 Ne. 11:5; Alma 12:25; D&C 84:35–38) of our loving Father in Heaven to make it possible for us, His sons and daughters, to achieve the same blessings He enjoys, if we are willing."[25]

In true Nebuchadnezzar form, he again promotes Shadrach, Meshach and Abed-nego in the government. Their positions in the Babylonian province were reaffirmed, and even augmented with greater responsibilities. "Whatever former rank and authority, they were promoted. Although they probably remained in the same office, they were relieved of any opposition and had special favor of the king in what they did."[26] Any disposition or conspiracy held by their Chaldean peers to remove them from office was squelched and they were forced to acknowledge their authority and their God. Notwithstanding the separation from parents and the corrupting influences of Babylon, and despite the deep political pressures or the threat of mortal danger, they did not waver in their hour of testing.[27]

Chapter Notes

1   Youngblood, Bruce and Harrison, ed. *Unlock the Bible: Keys to Exploring the Culture and Times.* 347

2   Smith, William and Fuller. *A Dictionary of the Bible: Comprising Its Antiquities, Biography, Geography, and Natural History.* Vol. I, 314

3   Klief quoted by Keil. *Biblical Commentary of the Old Testament, The Book of the Prophet Daniel.* 120

4   Keil. *Biblical Commentary of the Old Testament, The Book of the Prophet Daniel.* 120

5   Ibid, 118

6   Ibid, 118

7   Shea. *Daniel's Extra-Biblical Text and the Convocation on the Plains of Dura.* 29-52

8   Walvourd.. *Daniel, The Key to Prophet Revelation.* 101

9   Dyre. *Musical Instruments.* 427; See also Walvoord. *Daniel, The Key to Prophet Revelation.* 103

10 Ibid. 427; See also Walvoord. *Daniel, The Key to Prophet Revelation.* 103

11 Oppert. *Expedition Scientifique on Mesopotamie* 1:238 ff

12 Walvoord. *Daniel, The Key to Prophet Revelation.* 103

13 Ibid

14 Ibid

15 Keil. *Biblical Commentary of the Old Testament, The Book of the Prophet Daniel.* 122

16 Dyre. *Musical Instruments.* 436

17 Keil. *Biblical Commentary of the Old Testament, The Book of the Prophet Daniel.* 124

18 Wood. *Daniel.* 87, Walvoord. *Daniel, The Key to Prophet Revelation.* 107 "The word 'accused' translates from the Aramaic expression common to sematic languages that literally means 'they ate their pieces,' that is, to devour piecemeal.' This is why their accusation is identified as malicious."

19 Walvoord. *Daniel, The Key to Prophet Revelation.* 109

20 Featherstone. "Incomparable Christ: Our Master and Model." Ensign, September, 1995

21 Hunter. "Standing As Witnesses of God" *Ensign*, May 1990 , See also: Brown, Victor L. "Where Are You Going," BYU Speeches. June 04, 1978

22 Young. *The Prophecy of Daniel, A Commentary.* 93- 94

23 Keil. *Biblical Commentary of the Old Testament, The Book of the Prophet Daniel.* 131

24 Keil. *Biblical Commentary of the Old Testament, The Book of the Prophet Daniel.* 132

25 Simmons. "But If Not…" General Conference. April 2004

26 Walvoord. *Daniel, The Key to Prophet Revelation.*115

27 Ibid. 115-116

Additional Notes: The Mounds of Dura:

"We must, without doubt, much rather seek for this plain in the neighborhood of Babylon, where, according to the statement of Jul. Oppert (Expéd. Scientif. en Mésopotamie, i. p. 238ff.), there are at present to be found in the S.S.E. of the ruins representing the former capital a row of mounds which bear the name of Dura, at the end of which, along with two larger mounds, there is a smaller one which is named el Mokattat (la colline alignée), which forms a square six metres high, with a basis of fourteen metres, wholly built en briques crues (Arab. lbn), which shows so surprising a resemblance to a colossal statue with its pedestal, that Oppert believes that this little mound is the remains of the golden statue erected by Nebuchadnezzar." Keil, *Biblical Commentary of the Old Testament, The Book of the Prophet Daniel*, 119

Brick kilns common to Mesopotamia   © Used with Permission

© Used with Permission
Relief of Shadrach, Mechach and Abed-nego on a sarcophagus at the Vatican

4

The Heart of Nebuchadnezzar

The voice and tone in Chapter 4 appears to be unique and different from Daniel's other historical accounts (Chapters 1-6). The record was written in the first person voice of King Nebuchadnezzar himself, through one of his scribes. It is a general proclamation sent throughout the Babylonian kingdom. Daniel may have helped compose it, but the narrative clearly originates from the king, himself.

Nebuchadnezzar's Journey

From the beginning of his reign as king, Nebuchadnezzar was a destined to undergo a long sequence of experiences and trials designed to elevate and expand his understanding of Jehovah, the Most High and True God. His training began years earlier with the dream of the statue of gold, other metals and feet of iron and clay (Dan. 2). In this experience, Nebuchadnezzar at least knew that Daniel's God was a "revealer of secrets" and held exceptional insight and wisdom (Dan. 2:47). His perception increased in the confrontation with Shadrach, Meshach and Abed-nego. They defied his command to bow to the great image and to worship his gods. In anger, he pronounced their deaths and challenged their God, in whom they trusted, whether He was able to deliver them. Jehovah did intervene to protect them from the heat and flames of the furnace. The king realized through their miraculous preservation that their God was able to preserve them. Nebuchadnezzar blessed the God of Shadrach, Meshach, and Abed-nego, exclaiming that "no other God that can deliver after this sort" or in this way (Dan. 3:29). There was something to be revered and respected in the God of Jews, Jehovah.

Now, at this later stage of the king's life, Jehovah intended to provide a much more personal tutoring experience that would instruct and humble the king. The trial would persist: "till thou know that the most High ruleth in the kingdom of men, and giveth it to whomsoever he will" (Dan. 4:35). "So profound [would be] the impression graven into the conscience of this pagan king by his seven-year discipline…that he at once acknowledged the supremacy of the living God. All his life had been pagan. True, he had briefly acknowledged the God of Daniel (Dan. 2:46-48), the God of Shadrach, Meshach, and Abed-nego (Dan. 3:28-39), but he had soon lapsed back into his native paganism. But this time a genuine work of grace seems to have been done to his soul."[1]

His struggle would touch him profoundly and as a result, he would prepare and send this "proclamation … to all the peoples of his kingdom, informing them of [the wondrous] event in which the living God of heaven [had wrought, making] Himself known as the ruler over the kingdoms of men."[2]

The King's Proclamation

———

1   Nebuchadnezzar the king, unto all people, nations, and languages, that dwell in all the earth; Peace be multiplied unto you.

2   I thought it good to shew the signs and wonders that the high God hath wrought toward me.

3   How great are his signs! and how mighty are his wonders! His kingdom is an everlasting kingdom, and his dominion is from generation to generation.

———

These first three verses form the preamble to the official proclamation sent throughout the Babylonian kingdom. The declaration was given with salutations of peace and good wishes. The king glories in the signs and wonders shown to him by "the high God" (Dan. 4:2). He expresses praise and wonder at the kingdom and dominion of God that has persisted through the generations of families on the earth. Words such as these had never come from Nebuchadnezzar in previous years. "Remember that he was a Babylonian King who was steeped and raised in idolatry, [a product from]...the very country where idolatry was born back in the distant days of Nimrod" (Gen. 10:8-20; 21:1-9).[3] Nebuchadnezzar was perhaps the most successful king of his age. He had led victorious armies to conquer many nations, including Judah. He had destroyed and sacked the city of Jerusalem and the sanctuary of Jehovah. He had triumphantly carried off trophies from Solomon's temple and installed them in Esagila, the temple of the patron deity, Bel–Marduk, the head of the Babylonian pantheon of gods. Therefore, in his mind, the evidence of victory confirmed the superiority of his gods over the God of the Jews.[4] But now, everything was different. There was a new tone in his voice, a proclamation that led the people to believe that something in him had changed. His praise to "the high God" carried with it a profound respect and understanding not previously grasped, let alone expressed.

The years prior to this declaration had been among the most grueling and humbling ordeal of his life. Nebuchadnezzar had undergone a momentous transformation. His language reflects a man whose heart had changed (Dan. 7:4). Portions of the letter actually echo sentiments we would find familiar to the followers of Jehovah. They are reflective of someone who knows and understands something of the God of Israel. His tenor speaks of one converted and enlightened through the experience and the Spirit of the Lord.

The words of Lamoni, who was a wicked and hard-hearted Lamanite king, reflect a man who had also undergone a similar miraculous conversion: He exclaimed: "Blessed be the name of God, and blessed art thou. For as sure as thou livest, behold, I have seen my Redeemer; and he shall come forth, and be born of a

woman, and he shall redeem all mankind who believe on his name…
and he sunk again with joy… being overpowered by the Spirit
(Alma 19:12-13). Ammon explained that Lamoni was changed
from a hardened Lamanite to a converted brother, enlightened by
the spirit of truth: "for he knew that king Lamoni was under the
power of God; he knew that the dark veil of unbelief was being
cast away from his mind, and the light which did light up his mind,
which was the light of the glory of God, which was a marvelous
light of his goodness—yea, this light had infused such joy into his
soul, the cloud of darkness having been dispelled" (Alma 19:6).

The depth of Nebuchadnezzar's "conversion" or "enlightenment"
remains unclear. It's probable that he was not converted like king
Lamoni. He still referred to "my gods," meaning the pagan gods
of Babylon in his proclamation (Dan. 4:8). Nevertheless, his
understanding demonstrated a much deeper, clearer and illuminated
view of God and His power and works. When he built the great
statue and boasted of himself, his accomplishments and his self-
made kingdom, it was all about him (Dan. 3:1, 5-7). He, with the
help of his gods, was both the maker and the master of his destiny.
But now, his attitude was about the true God of Heaven. Interestingly
enough the transformation corresponds to the introduction of
another terrifying dream.

Nebuchadnezzar's Troubled Dream

4   I Nebuchadnezzar was at rest in mine house, and
    flourishing in my palace:

5   I saw a dream which made me afraid, and the
    thoughts upon my bed and the visions of my head
    troubled me.

6   Therefore made I a decree to bring in all
    the wise *men* of Babylon before me, that they might
    make known unto me the interpretation of the
    dream.

7   Then came in the magicians, the astrologers, the
    Chaldeans, and the soothsayers: and I told the dream
    before them; but they did not make known unto me
    the interpretation thereof.

Marten van Heemskerck © Used with Permission

Babylon's Famous Hanging Gardens and the Ziggurat Temple known as Esagila

Years earlier, Nebuchadnezzar reflected with great contentment on his life situation, "after having subdued all the neighboring countries, and greatly enriched and adorned his own, [he] became so intoxicated with his prosperity."[5] In his mind, there were no threatening nations to be conquered, no major projects to build, no further lessons to be learned and no greater people than the Babylonians. He could finally rest. His surroundings were filled with peace and contentment. There was nothing left to do but "flourish" in the palace. The goal was to sit back and enjoy the kingdom. But the God of Heaven had other ideas. From the king's description, it appears that another dream occurred just at the moment when as he was enjoying the opulence of the palace and reflecting on the accomplishments of the kingdom. Unlike the previous dreams, which were spawned by questions and concerns in his heart, this dream came, not by request, but by the will of the Lord.

The dream troubled the king deeply. While the exact interpretation remained a mystery, unlike the first dream, he must have known deep down that the subject of the vision was either himself or his kingdom. And the content of the dream was not favorable. Immediately, he called for the wise men of the kingdom to assist in the discovery of its interpretation.

This time, the king was willing to reveal details about the dream to the wise men. And having learned their lesson, the college of Chaldeans, scholars, magicians and soothsayers were wise enough to hold their peace unless they could provide a truly reliable interpretation, but no such explanation was forthcoming. The prophet Daniel still oversaw the wise men (Dan. 4:9), but for unknown reasons he was not at the first session with the king. The mystery of the dream remained cloaked until the true prophet arrived to provide a clear interpretation.

The Dream Explained to Daniel

————

8   But at the last Daniel came in before me, whose name was Belteshazzar, according to the name of my god, and in whom is the spirit of the holy gods: and before him I told the dream, saying,

9   O Belteshazzar, master of the magicians, because I know that the spirit of the holy gods is in thee, and no secret troubleth thee, tell me the visions of my dream that I have seen, and the interpretation thereof.

10 Thus were the visions of mine head in my bed; I saw, and behold a tree in the midst of the earth, and the height thereof was great.

11 The tree grew, and was strong, and the height thereof reached unto heaven, and the sight thereof to the end of all the earth:

12 The leaves thereof were fair, and the fruit thereof much, and in it was meat for all: the beasts of the field had shadow under it, and the fowls of the heaven dwelt in the boughs thereof, and all flesh was fed of it.

13 I saw in the visions of my head upon my bed, and, behold, a watcher and an holy one came down from heaven;

14 He cried aloud, and said thus, Hew down the tree, and cut off his branches, shake off his leaves, and scatter his fruit: let the beasts get away from under it,

and the fowls from his branches:

15 Nevertheless leave the stump of his roots in the earth, even with a band of iron and brass, in the tender grass of the field; and let it be wet with the dew of heaven, and let his portion be with the beasts in the grass of the earth:

16 Let his heart be changed from man's, and let a beast's heart be given unto him; and let seven times pass over him.

17 This matter is by the decree of the watchers, and the demand by the word of the holy ones: to the intent that the living may know that the most High ruleth in the kingdom of men, and giveth it to whomsoever he will, and setteth up over it the basest of men.

18 This dream I king Nebuchadnezzar have seen. Now thou, O Belteshazzar, declare the interpretation thereof, forasmuch as all the wisemen of my kingdom are not able to make known unto me the interpretation: but thou art able; for the spirit of the holy gods is in thee.

———

This portion of the proclamation carried with it a feeling of anticipation. And while the king called for all the wise men, his true faith lay in Daniel and his abilities. In essence, he says, "finally, or at long last, Daniel has arrived to provide true counsel." The tension and expectation surrounding the meaning of the dream was palpable as the king awaited an explanation.

The record shows that the king refers to Daniel by both his Hebrew name, as well as his Chaldean name, Belteshazzar. A few scholars have questioned the significance of using both names in the letter. The Babylonian people would have known Daniel only by his Chaldean title. However, "In recognition of the fact that Daniel's God is the interpreter of the dream. Nebuchadnezzar called Daniel by his Hebrew name, the last syllable of which refers to Elohim, [the name of the Father]. The king explained that the name Belteshazzar was given 'after the name of my god,' that is, the god Bel. The double name [was] not unnatural in view of the context and the dream explanation."[6] By this point in their relationship, the king had developed great admiration for the prophet and chose to

A large shade tree common to Mesopotamia and Africa

address him by his Jewish name out of respect for him, his gifts, and talents, and the wisdom gained from his God (Dan. 4:8).

The mind of the king reflected a key attitudinal shift. Nebuchadnezzar knew that "the spirit of the holy gods" resided in Daniel and that any true interpretation of the dream required this special Spirit. "The word *holy* refers to the gods which are divine with special powers and ability, rather than purity alone."[7] It seems that Nebuchadnezzar also had great regard for the God of Israel and may have had more faith in the True God of Daniel than in the pagan gods, which he knew were made of wood and gold.[8]

With Daniel present and prepared to hear the king, Nebuchadnezzar then revealed the contents of the dream. He described a great tree in the middle of the earth. "The use of trees in the Bible for symbolic purposes as well as in extrascriptural narratives is found frequently. (cf. 2 Kgs. 14:9; Ps. 1:3; 37:35; 52:8; 92:12; Ezek. 17)."[9] Nebuchadnezzar probably sensed that the tree represented him or his great kingdom. He associated the tree as the center of the world, the protector of the people. "The position of the tree would then indicate its importance to the entire earth."[10] He had been the heart of Babylon, their hero if you will and Babylon was at the heart of the world.[11] He states that the tree grew until it reached heaven. Using a western form of language, we might say that "the tree was very high, and could be seen from a great distance."[12]

The tree provided food, rest and an umbrella of protection for the fowls and animals. All peoples fed from and were nourished by this benevolent tree. The imagery gives the impression of a great and prosperous haven. It presents a scene of stability and tranquility. The overarching protection of the empire and a prosperous economy all rested under the benevolent hand of Nebuchadnezzar, the Babylonian protectorate.

It is true that in the years of conquest and the expansion of the kingdom, bloody battles were fought; terrible sieges mounted and national disruptions were common. But once the supremacy of the kingdom was established, a period of peace and prosperity prevailed. The Babylonians, and later the Persians, Greeks, Romans and subsequent kingdoms, all managed to create periods of stability for long stretches in their administrations. The Lord blessed and prospered each kingdom and the people as they adhered to moral laws and order. But when wicked monarchs or tyrants reigned or when secret combinations prevailed, then contention, strife and instability were the norm.

It should be noted that while the Lord was the true provider of food, water, prosperity and rest, He respected the role given the king and gave him honor as the ruler of the kingdom.

The king speaks of a messenger, "a watcher, an holy one came down from heaven" (Dan. 4:23). "In Babylonian religion, it was customary to recognize 'council deities' who were charged with the special task of watching over the world."[13] This tradition extended into the Babylonian government with its own "watchers," or the princes (Satraps) that oversaw or watched over large regions of the empire. The Hebrew or Jewish belief would be to refer to the heavenly watchers simply as angels or messengers charged with the commission to watch over and protect the people, in some cases specifically the House of Israel.

The stewardship of this heavenly "watcher" was to look after the Babylonian kingdom. Similar references are found in Zechariah who spoke of "the servants of the Lord, which run to and fro through the whole earth" (JST Zech. 4:10). In a later vision, an angelic watcher visits Daniel near the Tigris River. He relates that his responsibility was to battle the forces of evil and darkness to protect the Persian leadership and the people of Israel to insure the will of the Lord is fulfilled (Dan. 10:13, 20-21).

The watcher that visited the king in the dream is a messenger and teacher sent by the decree of the "holy ones: to the intent that the living may know that the Most High ruleth in the kingdom of men, and giveth it to whomsoever he will, and setteth up over it the basest of men" (Dan. 4:17). Nebuchadnezzar sensed that reference "basest of men" applied to him. The watcher directly challenged his belief of independent sovereignty and his nobility as the most powerful man in the world. The angel chastened him for his coarse and brutal mannerisms, which represented the Lord's view. Later, the king would admit that he was not noble by God's standard, but indeed, among the basest of men.

Jehovah had sent a messenger to reveal to him "things as they really are" (Jacob 4:13) and challenge the king to change his attitude and heart. A warning was given that he must open his mind to a higher understanding and perspective, and if he would not the branches of the great tree would be cut, the leaves scattered and the animals and birds that benefited from the tree would seek another refuge. Only a stump and green grass would remain. The imagery was clear, if he did not change, the king would lose his ability to rule and be forced to forage like the beasts of the field.

God had granted the blissful situation that graced his kingdom, and he could easily be removed. He could be smitten and become equal to the basest and lowest of beasts. The watcher announced that the root of the tree would remain as a "band of iron or brass." Nebuchadnezzar would not lose the kingdom. His position would be held in reserve until the appointed lessons were learned. But the decree was firm. The trial would not be removed until its ends were met. "The messenger then concluded his decree and states its

Old Bible Art © Used with Permission
Daniel interprets Nebuchadnezzar's dream of the tree

purpose: that all people would recognize the true God, 'the Most High,' and acknowledge Him as the true ruler of mankind who had power to place 'the lowliest of men' over earthly kingdoms."[14]

With the essence of the dream revealed, Daniel immediately discerned its meaning. In an expression of confidence, the king anxiously appealed for an interpretation, stating: "thou *art* able; for the spirit of the holy gods *is* in thee" (Dan. 4:18).

Daniel's Reaction to the Dream

19 Then Daniel, whose name was Belteshazzar, was astonied for one hour, and his thoughts troubled him. The king spake, and said, Belteshazzar, let not the dream, or the interpretation thereof, trouble thee. Belteshazzar answered and said, My lord, the dream be to them that hate thee, and the interpretation thereof to thine enemies.

20 The tree that thou sawest, which grew, and was strong, whose height reached unto the heaven, and the sight thereof to all the earth;

21 Whose leaves were fair, and the fruit thereof much,

and in it was meat for all; under which the beasts of
the field dwelt, and upon whose branches the fowls
of the heaven had their habitation:

22 It is thou, O king, that art grown and become strong:
for thy greatness is grown, and reacheth unto heaven,
and thy dominion to the end of the earth.

23 And whereas the king saw a watcher and an holy
one coming down from heaven, and saying, Hew
the tree down, and destroy it; yet leave the stump
of the roots thereof in the earth, even with a band
of iron and brass, in the tender grass of the field;
and let it be wet with the dew of heaven, and let his
portion be with the beasts of the field, till seven times
pass over him (Dan. 4:19-23).

――――

When the king completed his summary of the dream, Daniel
stood astonished, because he readily knew the interpretation. He
was a friend to the king and became concerned about revealing
its meaning. He stood silent before his throne for an hour. It was
Nebuchadnezzar who finally encouraged him by reassuring him that
neither the dream's contents nor its interpretation should trouble
him, but that he should be forthcoming without fear, there would
be no reprisal.

Before proceeding, Daniel begins with a traditional eastern
expression. He wishes the interpretation of the dream be applied to
the king's enemies, and not to the king. What he was about to say
would be considered bad news and tradition held that Daniel wished
the curse be removed and placed upon someone else. The prophet
was genuinely concerned about things that might befall the king and
the kingdom.

He begins by explaining the meaning of the tree. "It [the tree]
is thou, O king, that art grown and become strong: for thy greatness
is grown, and reacheth unto heaven, and thy dominion to the end
of the earth" (Dan. 4:22). The dream reflected Nebuchadnezzar's
very thoughts as he sat in his palace pondering the greatness of
his kingdom (Dan. 4:1). Daniel restated his thoughts as part of
the explanation to help him understand that self-absorption and
ungratefulness were sizable portions of the problem. The king never

considered the possibility that his successes were not of his own making nor blessings from a God different from his pagan gods. He was also blind of his neglect of the poor and the disadvantaged, many of which had worked as slaves to build the impressive city. He did not understand that the God of Heaven, the True God, held the successes and destiny of his kingdom in His hand.

The watcher warned of unfavorable judgments that would befall the king if these perceptions did not change. Just as a tree can be cut down to the earth, so he would be hewn down and driven from the throne to mingle with the beasts and to frolic in the dew of the fields (Dan 4:23). The judgment would last "till seven times pass over him" (Dan. 4:23). This is generally interpreted to mean seven years. Given the symbolic nature of the number seven, we might conclude that the duration of the judgment would remain until the purposes of the Lord were fulfilled or completed. Calvin thinks that it merely meant "a long time."[15]

The Lord is no respecter of persons (Acts 10:34; Doctrine and Covenants 38:16) and He chastens those whom He loves (Hel. 15:3). Despite the greatness of the king and his abilities, the Lord saw in Nebuchadnezzar a person who could benefit from soul shaping tutoring. He was ready to be instructed and enlightened about the true nature of God, the ruler of the earth and the universe. While it seems a big deal to require that Nebuchadnezzar pass through such a humiliating trial, it was important that he glean from it this meaningful lesson: "till thou know that the most High ruleth in the kingdom of men, and giveth it to whomsoever he will" (Dan. 4:25).

Elder Neal A. Maxwell taught of the necessity of trials and tutoring opportunities and the blessing to those who endure well.

———

Thus, enduring is one of the cardinal attributes; it simply cannot be developed without the laboratory time in this second estate. Even the best lectures about the theory of enduring are not enough. All the other cardinal virtues—love, patience, humility, mercy, purity, submissiveness, justice—they all require endurance for their full development. Puzzlement, for instance, is often the knob on the door of insight. The knob must be firmly grasped and deliberately turned with faith. The harrowing of the soul can be like the harrowing of the soil to increase the yield with things being turned upside down. Moses experienced such topsy-turvy change. A lesser individual couldn't have forsaken Egypt's treasures and privileged status only to be hunted and later resented as a prophetic presence in the royal courts, which he had doubtless known earlier, but as an insider. Yet we are told Moses endured by faith (Heb. 11:24–29)...God is easily pleased, but hard to satisfy. As a Father, God is delighted with our first and further steps, but He knows how straight, how narrow, and how long the ensuing path is. Again, how vital endurance! Happily, while the Lord has promised us a tutoring mortality, He has also promised us glorious things as well!"[16]

As the Father of all the inhabitants on the earth, God's tutoring hand is ever extended, actively teaching to bless the lives of every child who will submit to His gentle hand. It was evident that Nebuchadnezzar had arrived at a point in his life where the Lord could teach valuable character building lessons. But because of the seriousness of his transgression and the difficult nature of the trial, the king was forewarned to make the necessary corrections of his own volition, rather than to be placed into more dire circumstances.

Daniel Provides Additional Interpretation of the Dream

24 This is the interpretation, O king, and this is the decree of the most High, which is come upon my lord the king:

25 That they shall drive thee from men, and thy dwelling shall be with the beasts of the field, and they shall make thee to eat grass as oxen, and they shall wet thee with the dew of heaven, and seven times shall pass over thee, till thou know that the most High ruleth in the kingdom of men, and giveth it to whomsoever he will.

26 And whereas they commanded to leave the stump of the tree roots; thy kingdom shall be sure unto thee, after that thou shalt have known that the heavens do rule.

27 Wherefore, O king, let my counsel be acceptable unto thee, and break off thy sins by righteousness, and thine iniquities by shewing mercy to the poor; if it may be a lengthening of thy tranquility.

———

Daniel emphasized again that the dream was a warning from the "most High." He in essence begged him to hearken to his counsel. If he does not repent, "They [the watchers] shall drive thee from men" (Dan. 4:25). His mental faculties would be stricken and he would be removed from the throne and suffer from madness to mingle and graze as an ox or a horse in the field.

He admonished the king with all the feelings of a friend to take seriously the charge and harken to the message. If he truly believed the interpretation, he would repent of his pride and would begin to show kindness to others and generosity to the needy. "With utmost courtesy, he urges Nebuchadnezzar to turn from his sins and show mercy to the poor. Nebuchadnezzar undoubtedly had been morally wicked and cruel to those over whom he ruled. His concern had been to build a magnificent city as a monument to his name rather than to alleviate the suffering of the poor."[17] Here, the Lord provides the stark contrast between a king that mortal men might consider to be accomplished versus what is important to Him. History records very few men in power attain to the greatness emphasized by God. Nevertheless, the king of Babylon had arrived at the point that he must learn this valuable lesson. If he was compliant, his peace and prosperity would be extended all the remainder of his days.

The Curse Comes Upon the King

———

28 All this came upon the king Nebuchadnezzar.

29 At the end of twelve months he walked in the palace of the kingdom of Babylon.

30 The king spake, and said, Is not this great Babylon, that I have built for the house of the kingdom by the might of my power, and for the honour of my majesty?

31 While the word was in the king's mouth, there fell a voice from heaven, saying, O king Nebuchadnezzar,

to thee it is spoken; The kingdom is departed from thee.

32 And they shall drive thee from men, and thy dwelling shall be with the beasts of the field: they shall make thee to eat grass as oxen, and seven times shall pass over thee, until thou know that the most High ruleth in the kingdom of men, and giveth it to whomsoever he will.

33 The same hour was the thing fulfilled upon Nebuchadnezzar: and he was driven from men, and did eat grass as oxen, and his body was wet with the dew of heaven, till his hairs were grown like eagles' feathers, and his nails like birds' claws.

———

For twelve months Nebuchadnezzar seemed to remember the admonitions of Daniel, but there was little change of heart, no real understanding, no consideration to apply the counsel from the "Most High." The implementation of the prophetic warning, while not immediately fulfilled, was inevitable.[18] In a moment of characteristic pride and forgetfulness, the king exclaims: "Is not this great Babylon, that I have built for the house of the kingdom by the might of my power, and for the honour of my majesty?" (Dan. 4:30).

He could not help himself. "When he surveyed the great and magnificent city from the top of his palace, 'pride overcame him,' so that he dedicated the building of this great city as the house of his kingdom to the might of his power and the honour of his majesty."[19] And indeed, he *was* a great conqueror, administrator and builder! Babylon boasted the largest and most grand city in the world. "The discovery of the cuneiform inscription has remarkably confirmed the accuracy of this. From these we learn that Nebuchadnezzar was primarily, not a warrior, but a builder... He renovated the temple of Marduk in Babylon, and of Nebo in Borsippa. He then declared how he restored fifteen other temples in Babylon and completed the two great walls of the city, adding a large rampart."[20]

Babylon's imposing city features were impressive by any standard. The historian Herodotus and archeological studies reveal that the circumference of the city extended about 56 miles.[21] Nebuchadnezzar augmented the walls and ramparts surrounding the

© Used with Permission

Ishtar Gate with Nebuchadnezzar's Palace in the background

city to a reported height of 335 feet and 87 feet in width.[22] Herodotus also reports that chariots could race side by side along the top of the walls. One hundred bronze gates 87 feet high provided access to the inner city, while protecting its citizens from their enemies. Some of these historical descriptions are thought to be hyperbole, but the overall impression of the city's grandeur is accurate. One of the most impressive accomplishments was the hanging gardens. Seen from the palace and towards the center of the city. It was considered one of the seven structural wonders of the world, comparable to the pyramids in Egypt. Truly Babylon was a marvelous place and a wonder to the eyes of all, but his consideration of the poor and disadvantaged left much to be desired.

Nevertheless, as the words left his mouth, a voice from heaven responded to Nebuchadnezzar's boastful utterance. The voice declared that the kingdom had departed from him, and the judgment pronounced would be executed. The voice repeats the punishments and immediately he becomes mad. The king collapses onto his hands and knees and is lead from the palace into a field or garden to eat grass with the beasts. He would remain in this condition until he was convinced that the God of heaven, who granted him the kingdom and his victories, was the source of his success and could give or take away such blessings.

The proclamation remains silent about the details of the trial during this period. "It is probable that he was kept in the palace gardens, away from abuse bfoy common people. Although he was allowed to live in nature, he was protected, and in his absence his counselor, possibly Daniel himself, continued to operate the kingdom efficiently.... It is reasonable to assume that Daniel had much to do with the kind treatment and protection of Nebuchadnezzar. He undoubtedly informed the counselors of what the outcome of the dream would be and that Nebuchadnezzar would return to sanity. God must have inclined the hearts of Nebuchadnezzar's counselors to cooperate, while in contrast to what was often the case in ancient government when at the slightest sign of weakness, rulers were cruelly murdered. Nebuchadnezzar seems to have been highly respected as a brilliant king by those who worked with him, and this helped set the stage for his recovery."[23]

As for the king's actual experience, the record provides no details concerning his mental capacity or the struggles of his soul. Was the king completely mad? Had he lost all his cognitive abilities? Or was there sufficient awareness to allow him to process the situation, even though he had lost mental control? For tutoring to take place and lessons to be learned, there must remain some mental ability, he must have comprehended somewhat what was happening, otherwise he could not consciously have arrived at the level of contrition and submission we find in the letter. He would not have attained the needed understanding to meet the conditions required to remove the curse.

The Days of Trial End for the King

34 And at the end of the days I Nebuchadnezzar lifted
up mine eyes unto heaven, and mine understanding
returned unto me, and I blessed the most High, and
I praised and honoured him that liveth for ever,

whose dominion is an everlasting dominion, and his kingdom is from generation to generation:

35 And all the inhabitants of the earth are reputed as nothing: and he doeth according to his will in the army of heaven, and among the inhabitants of the earth: and none can stay his hand, or say unto him, What doest thou?

36 At the same time my reason returned unto me; and for the glory of my kingdom, mine honour and brightness returned unto me; and my counsellors and my lords sought unto me; and I was established in my kingdom, and excellent majesty was added unto me.

37 Now I Nebuchadnezzar praise and extol and honour the King of heaven, all whose works are truth, and his ways judgment: and those that walk in pride he is able to abase.

———

When the requirements of the trial were fulfilled, after his heart changed and his understanding matured, Nebuchadnezzar's reason returned. "Looking to the heavens was possibly the first step in his recognition of the God of Heaven and his regaining of his sanity."[24] It is clear that he was a new man, his heart had changed, and his understanding of his role and place in the world had expanded. With this new enlightenment the king could lift his eyes and bless the "True and Most High God."

The suffering and struggles over the prescribed period had produced in him a slow transformation from the self-centered ruler to one who acknowledged the hand of the Lord. His strength and intellect had been enabled through the power of the King of Heaven. King Benjamin taught this very principle to the Nephites when he reminded them that the very Being that has "created you from the beginning, and is preserving you from day to day, [is] lending you breath, that ye may live and move and do according to your own will, and even supporting you from one moment to another—" (Mosiah 2:21). The Lord instructed Enoch: "Behold these thy brethren; they are the workmanship of mine own hands, and I gave unto them their knowledge, in the day I created them; and in the Garden of Eden, gave I unto man his agency" (Moses 7:32).

For many this doctrine would be hard to accept. "What? I am my own person!" Many would exclaim, "I have my own intellect, I move and act of my own accord!" Few mortals realize that it is only by the power and grace of God that they live, move, think and progress. But eventually, everyone will come to the same realization as Nebuchadnezzar, they will know that it is only through the enabling grace of God that they have power to do these things. The Lord has said: "the day shall come when you shall comprehend even God, being quickened in him and by him. Then shall ye know that ye have seen me, that I am, and that I am the true light that is in you, and that you are in me; otherwise ye could not abound." (Doctrine and Covenants 88:49:50).

The king's confession revealed a newfound understanding that, compared to God, the inhabitants of the earth are "nothing," a thought that he had never previously supposed (Moses 1:10). It is doubtful that prior to this experience Nebuchadnezzar thought of himself as nothing, but now he understood that even his great accomplishments and the greatness of Babylon were insignificant compared to God's dominion. He recognized that his knowledge, abilities and the resources used to build the great empire were gifts from heaven. The king acknowledged God's great gifts and abilities by declaring that "none can stay the hand" (Dan. 4:25). He challenged the fool or ignorant who might question God's wisdom and purposes by asking, "What have you done?" (Dan. 4:35).

With great benevolence and mercy, the Lord restored Nebuchadnezzar to his position as head of the kingdom. With Daniel's help, he was reinstated. His advisors and counselors returned to seek council and fulfill his commands. The Lord even bestowed additional "excellency and majesty" upon him. The king was transformed. He saw "things as they really are" (Jacob 4:13). "His issuing of a decree while somewhat humiliating to his pride and containing an abject recognition of the power of God gives some basis for believing that Nebuchadnezzar had a true conversion."[25] While the experience was doubtless painful, in the end it brought joy and appreciation, a grateful realization of the marvelous transformation that had taken place in his heart.

A feeling of profound gratitude for the experience is evident in the letter (Dan. 4:37). He expresses an indebtedness to God for this newfound wisdom and extols honor to the King of heaven, who had chastened him in truth and love. He was humble. His expressions of gratitude tell just how far Nebuchadnezzar had come. Of God's foresight and tutoring ability. Elder Maxwell taught: "It is extremely important for you to believe in yourselves not only for what you are now but for what you have the power to become. Trust in the Lord as He leads you along. He has things for you to do that you won't know about now but that will unfold later. If you stay close to Him, you will have some great adventures…the Lord will unfold your future bit by bit."[26]

From the world's perspective, Nebuchadnezzar had it all. He was king. He ruled over the largest and most powerful kingdom of his age. He had gold, comfort, power, adoration and respect. What more could he want? And yet God saw fit to teach him that there are lessons and qualities more precious than anything the world could offer. The Lord was interested in Nebuchadnezzar's character and progression, not in his comfort or maintaining his earthly station.

Nebuchadnezzar's experience provides obvious spiritual lessons for each of us. Elder Maxwell continues: "God knows even now what the future holds for each of us. In one of his revelations these startling words appear, as with so many revelations that are too big, I suppose, for us to manage fully: 'In the presence of God,…all things . . . are manifest, past, present, and future, and are continually before the Lord' (Doctrine and Covenants 130:7). The future 'you' is before him now. He knows what it is he wishes to bring to pass in your life. He knows the kind of remodeling in your life and in mine that he wishes to achieve. Now, this will require us to believe in that divine design."[27] This was true of Nebuchadnezzar and it is true of each individual. Even the great earthly sovereigns are completely subject to God's absolute power and correction.[28] The Lord chastens and straightens, He humbles and teaches, He molds and shapes all of His children who will submit to His masterful hand.

Future monarchs, dictators and presidents should take note of the king's experience as being applicable to them. Those that harken to the Lord or His servants will also be guided and prospered. Cyrus of Persia was an example of a future king who followed the light of the Lord within him. His efforts were blessed and he prospered. Belshazzar, on the other hand, ignored these valuable lessons and paid with his life (Dan. 5:17-23, 30).

The Lord has declared: "I am able to do mine own work" (2 Ne. 27:21). His foreknowledge and plans for the kingdoms and peoples of the earth will come to pass. Throughout the mortal estate, His purposes will be accomplished either with the assistance of earthly leaders and mankind, to their benefit and glory, or in spite of their rebelliousness and pride. "God, the Father of us all, uses the men of the earth, especially good men, to accomplish his purposes. It has been true in the past, it is true today, it will be true in the future."[29] In every case, He brings to pass His special work for the blessing, progress and benefit of His children on the earth.

Chapter Notes

1   Phillips. *Exploring the Book of Daniel: An Expository Commentary*. 70-71
2   Keil, *Biblical Commentary of the Old Testament, The Book of the Prophet Daniel*. Introduction, 133
3   Josephus, *Antiquities*, 30
4   Phillips. *Exploring the Book of Daniel: An Expository Commentary*. 71
5   Clarke. B*ible Commentary Vol. IV Isaiah - Malachi*, Introduction. 580
6   Walvoord. *Daniel, The Key to Prophet Revelation*. 125
7   Young. *The Prophecy Daniel: A Commentary*. 99, cf Driver. *Daniel*. 48
8   Walvoord. *Daniel, The Key to Prophet Revelation*. 126
9   Ibid. 126
10 Young. *The Prophecy Daniel: A Commentary*. 101
11 Ibid. 101, (Barnes), 101
12 Stuart. *A Commentary of the Book of Daniel*. 1850
13 Walvoord. *Daniel, The Key to Prophet Revelation*. 127
14 Ibid. 129
15 Young. *The Prophecy Daniel: A Commentary*. 105
16 Maxwell. "Endure It Well." General Conference. April 1990
17 Walvoord. *Daniel, The Key to Prophet Revelation*. 132
18 Ibid. 133
19 Keil. *Biblical Commentary of the Old Testament, The Book of the Prophet Daniel*. 158
20 Young. *The Prophecy Daniel: A Commentary*. 119
21 Herodotus. *Histories* I. 179, See also: Tanner. *Ancient Babylon: From Gradual Demise To Archaeological Rediscovery*. APP. P.1
22 Herodotus. *Histories* I. 179
23 Walvoord. *Daniel, The Key to Prophet Revelation*. 135
24 Ibid. 137
25 Ibid. 138
26 Maxwell. Interview with Janet Peterson, Friend to Friend https://www.lds.org/liahona/1984/06/friend-to-friend?lang=eng
27 Maxwell. "But for a Small Moment" BYU Devotionals. September 1, 1974
28 Walvoord. *Daniel, The Key to Prophet Revelation*. 138
29 Benson. "Civic Standard for Faithful Saints." Conference Report. April 1972. 48-49

Additional Notes:

Regarding the statement, "his hair grew as the feathers of an eagle," etc., Friedr. remarks that besides the neglect of the external appearance, there is also to be observed the circumstance that sometimes in physical maladies the nails assume a peculiarly monstrous luxuriance with deformity. Besides, his remaining for a long time in the open air is to be considered, "for it is an actual experience that the hair, the more it is exposed to the influences of the rough weather and to the sun's rays, the more does it grow in hardness, and thus becomes like unto the feathers of an eagle." (Keil. *Biblical Commentary of the Old Testament, The Book of the Prophet Daniel*. 160).

Technical Name for Illness: God may have struck Nebuchadnezzar with clinical lycanthropy, a mental illness that causes a person to believe they are an animal and to act like one. A person with this form of insanity remains somewhat unchanged in his inner consciousness, but his outer behavior is irrational. Walvoord. *Daniel, The Key to Prophet Revelation.* 136

5

The Fall of Babylon

Nebuchadnezzar's reign ended with his death in 562 B.C., roughly one year after his sanity returned and he regained the throne. From that point on the seat of the kingdom became very unstable. His son and heir Evil-Merodach (Amel-Marduk), ascended to the throne and ruled for two years. Keil says that "[he] reigned badly" and therefore was assassinated by his brother-in-law Neriglissar, in 560 B.C..[1] Neriglissar reigned four years and then died,seemingly of natural causes. His young son, Labashi-Marduk, was placed on the throne and ruled for a mere two months before being murdered by a band of conspirators "because he gave many proofs of a bad character."[2] Included in the conspiring band was Nabonidus, a son-in law of Nebuchadnezzar. He was also believed to be partly of Assyrian descent through his mother. "The marriage was probably political, designed to strengthen his claim to the throne, which he claimed in 556 B.C."[3]

After obtaining the crown, Nabonidus did not like the duties of monarch, nor was he a very good king. Historians described him as "a person who was altogether unfit to occupy [the throne]."[4] As a partial Assyrian, he was resented by the Chaldean aristocracy and not favored by some of the military. He became very unpopular with the powerful Marduk priesthood by favoring Sin, the moon god rather than Bel-Marduk. His attempt to consolidate the differing religions in the temple

Jona Lendering © Used with Permission
Relief of Nabonidus worshiping the moon god Sin

of Marduk, which proved to be a serious misstep with the Marduk priesthood. Their disfavor forced him to leave the throne in Babylon and the religious festivals. Nabonidus moved to Tema (Tayma) in Northern Arabia (553 B.C.) to build a new commercial empire and engage in archaeology.[5] In truth, he was an archaeologist at heart and spent much time excavating a number of Assyrian sites near Harran.[6] His removal from Babylon forced him to place his son, Belshazzar—a capable soldier—as the vice regent over the empire. "This continued for at least five years—from the seventh through eleventh year of Nabonidus's reign—and probably longer."[7]

Belshazzar governed over all of the Babylonian provinces. "Although, technically, Belshazzar occupied a position of authority subordinate to that of Nabonidus, actually, he seems to have had nearly all the prerogatives of monarch."[8] He would have been the official through which Daniel and the Jews petitioned all of their government business. Therefore, referring to Belshazzar as the king in a Jewish document (the Book of Daniel) was an appropriate application of the title.[9]

Babylonian society was much like Rome during its pinnacle of power and prosperity. It was a metropolitan city lush with money, commerce, paganism, tradition and ceremony and of course pride for the gods and their country. Self-absorption, pleasure–seeking and entertainment were dominant characteristics of the opulent culture, especially with the elite class. Among Belshazzar's chief responsibilities was keeping the people contented, especially the religious priesthood and the aristocracy. As the regent-king, he underwrote the most important royal celebrations and was happy to host them as the presiding authority. The Babylonian Chronicles provide the precise date for the grand festival spoken of in Daniel 5:1. "The Chronicle states that on the sixteenth day of the month Tashritu [Hebrew month of Tishri] in Nabonidus's seventeenth year (Saturday, October 12, 539 B.C.) year of rule, the army of Cyrus entered Babylon without a battle."[10]

The Royal Festival

———

1   Belshazzar the king made a great feast to a thousand of his lords, and drank wine before the thousand.

2   Belshazzar, whiles he tasted the wine, commanded to bring the golden and silver vessels which his father Nebuchadnezzar had taken out of the temple which was in Jerusalem; that the king, and his princes, his wives, and his concubines, might drink therein.

3   Then they brought the golden vessels that were taken out of the temple of the house of God which was at Jerusalem; and the king, and his princes, his wives, and his concubines, drank in them.

4   They drank wine, and praised the gods of gold, and of silver, of brass, of iron, of wood, and of stone.

———

Royal feasts were common in the Orient. Ashunsnasirpal II (Neo-Assyrian king of 883 B.C.-859 B.C.) hosted a great feast for

69,574 guests when he dedicated the capital city of Calah (Nimrud) in 879 B.C..[11] The Persian kings were known to dine daily with about 15,000 royal guests.[12] Belshazzar's royal feast was not so large, but by all accounts it was both impressive and exclusive. The celebration boasted a great fare. "The [courtyard] dining room was enormous, reportedly 1,650 feet wide and [it is said a mile in length.] Some 4,500 pillars in the form of giant elephants were part of the walls. They were carved out of stone and stood roughly twenty feet high. The tables were fashioned in the form of horseshoes."[13] It literally was a great and spacious building (1 Ne. 8:26). The elite dressed in their finest outfits of gold or silk laced in ornate jewels and fashionable colors to enjoy the evening.

This festival might have been like another typical Babylonian celebration except that all was not well in the kingdom. Babylon had suffered a series of crushing defeats to Cyrus and the Persian army was marching on the last strongholds of the empire. Only a few days earlier he had attacked the Babylonian army of Akkad in Opis on the Tigris. Seeking to side with Cyrus, the inhabitants of Akkad revolted, but Nabonidus, who had returned from Arabia, massacred the city. On the 14th day, Sippar was seized with very little opposition and Nabonidus fled into Babylon with the remaining troops to support and rally the citizens within the city walls.[14]

The Persians camped outside the outer gates near the Euphrates and Cyrus planned to mobilized warriors to divert the river long enough to allow troops to cross and penetrate the outer ramparts. Within Babylon there were pockets of discontentedness and insurrection. King Nabonidus with his troops worked to quell the internal rebellion as well as defend against the Persian threat.

The night of the great festival, Cyrus's army crossed the river and entered the city, but they had to travel a fair distance and it took time to traverse other walls and secure the boroughs before arriving at the palace. They would not reach the great temple and the feasting guests for several hours. It was in this setting that the peculiar happenings of the festival began.

It is believed that the festival was organized in an attempt to petition their gods to assist in defending the city.[15] "Nabonidus was a

John Martin 1789-1854, © Public Domain
Belshazzar's Feast 1820, oil painting on canvas

committed idolater. He had recently made a clean sweep of the idols in all of the surrounding towns around Babylon and brought them to the capital. He foolishly imagined that these confiscated images would help him ward off the Medo-Persian threat. Belshazzar likely set them up in his vast banquet hall. It was expressly to honor them that he planned this feast."[16] As the celebration began, none of the dignitaries was aware that Cyrus had circumvented the walls and was closing on the center of the capital and the palace. "It was hard for the Babylonians to believe that even the Medes and the Persians who had surrounded their beloved city could possibly breech the fortifications or exhaust their supplies that were intended to be ample for a siege of many years. Their confidence in their gods was bolstered by their confidence in the city."[17]

As the evening progressed, Belshazzar led a series of toasts and tributes to the empire and the gods. The excessive consumption of wine brought on heavy intoxication. Perhaps in a moment of weakness and certainly in disregard of judgment, the king ordered that the "golden and silver vessels" taken from the holy sanctuary in Jerusalem, be removed from the temple treasury of Bel and brought to the feast.

The holy vessels were distributed among the guests: his wives, friends and officials, who filled the sacred vessels with wine and drank freely. "It was the reckless madness of the drunken king and of his drunken guests during the festival which led them to think of the God of the Jews, whom they supposed they had subdued along with His people, although He had by repeated miracles forced the heathen world-rulers to recognize his omnipotence."[18] In a careless and undisciplined state, they began to speak against the God of heaven, as "Belshazzar hoped it would boost morale....This was blasphemy in a high degree, and therefore presently punished by God."[19] Nebuchadnezzar had decreed by law that the citizens of Babylon not blaspheme against the God of Daniel (Dan. 3:29). But the wickedness of the king brought on the adverse conditions, which set in motion the end of the reign of Belshazzar and completed the downfall of the kingdom.

The Finger Writes on the Wall of the Palace

5   In the same hour came forth fingers of a man's hand, and wrote over against the candlestick upon the plaster of the wall of the king's palace: and the king saw the part of the hand that wrote.

6   Then the king's countenance was changed, and his thoughts troubled him, so that the joints of his loins were loosed, and his knees smote one against another.

7   The king cried aloud to bring in the astrologers, the Chaldeans, and the soothsayers. And the king spake, and said to the wise men of Babylon, Whosoever shall read this writing, and shew me the interpretation thereof, shall be clothed with scarlet, and have a chain of gold about his neck, and shall be the third ruler in the kingdom.

8   Then came in all the king's wise men: but they could not read the writing, nor make known to the king the interpretation thereof.

9   Then was king Belshazzar greatly troubled, and his countenance was changed in him, and his lords were astonied.

Rembrandt in National Art Gallery, London © Public Domain
Belshazzar's sees the writing on the wall

The large dining court was apparently positioned near the palace. In the late hour of revelry, a human-like hand appeared and began etching character symbols upon the wall. King Belshazzar was seemingly the first to see the actual hand, which caused "his countenance to change" as the high spirit of the festival was quickly replaced with fear. The sudden transformation in his features meant that 'the king changed color as to his countenance, became pale from terror, and was so unmanned by fear and alarm, that his body lost its firmness and vigor."[20] The specter of the hand triggered such fright in him that his knees knocked together. "The apparition had appeared too closely after the kings blasphemous boast and condemning behavior. Belshazzar at least suspected that Jehovah, the God of the Jews, whose golden vessels he had desecrated, had spoken."[21] Apparently, the intoxicating effects of the evening were swept aside by the unnerving events playing out on the wall.

The characters appeared to be unreadable to both the king and the assembly. The writing was encoded Aramaic and not entirely known to the Babylonians. "It is not specified what made the words unreadable as well as unintelligible....But most straightforwardly the story envisage them written in unpointed consonants; being able to read out unpointed text is partly dependent on actually understanding it, and Daniel later reads the words out one way and then interprets them another."[22]

With the peculiar characters etched on the wall and the king unable to read them himself, he called for the astrologers, Chaldeans and soothsayers. Only three classes from the royal councils were mentioned, supposedly because they were the most likely to interpret the writing. It is possible that all classes of wise men were summoned, especially since the magicians, with their scholarly learning, possessed the best expertise for interpreting the writings.[23] There is no reason to believe that all the resources available to the king were not summoned to interpret the important code.

Each class of wise men studied the inscription to no avail. Deep with concern and greatly troubled, the king's countenance again changed; this time he was engulfed with despair and confusion as he assessed the situation. He worried that somehow the urgent message might not be deciphered. "The alarm was heightened by a bad conscience, which roused itself and filled him with dark forebodings."[24] A troubled atmosphere permeated the entire assembly as the lords and dignitaries feared that no satisfactory solution could be found.

Daniel Summoned to the Festival

10 Now the queen, by reason of the words of the king and his lords, came into the banquet house: and the queen spake and said, O king, live for ever: let not thy thoughts trouble thee, nor let thy countenance be changed:

11 There is a man in thy kingdom, in whom is the

spirit of the holy gods; and in the days of thy father light and understanding and wisdom, like the wisdom of the gods, was found in him; whom the king Nebuchadnezzar thy father, the king, I say, thy father, made master of the magicians, astrologers, Chaldeans, and soothsayers;

12 Forasmuch as an excellent spirit, and knowledge, and understanding, interpreting of dreams, and shewing of hard sentences, and dissolving of doubts, were found in the same Daniel, whom the king named Belteshazzar: now let Daniel be called, and he will shew the interpretation.

13 Then was Daniel brought in before the king. And the king spake and said unto Daniel, Art thou that Daniel, which art of the children of the captivity of Judah, whom the king my father brought out of Jewry?

14 I have even heard of thee, that the spirit of the gods is in thee, and that light and understanding and excellent wisdom is found in thee.

15 And now the wise men, the astrologers, have been brought in before me, that they should read this writing, and make known unto me the interpretation thereof: but they could not shew the interpretation of the thing:

16 And I have heard of thee, that thou canst make interpretations, and dissolve doubts: now if thou canst read the writing, and make known to me the interpretation thereof, thou shalt be clothed with scarlet, and have a chain of gold about thy neck, and shalt be the third ruler in the kingdom.

———

In this moment of deep distress and confusion, the queen appears at the banquet. Apparently, the words of the king and the stirring in the courtyard had caught her attention. Up until that point she had not previously been at the event. Most interpreters rightly assert that she was either the mother of the reigning king, or the widow of the late Nebuchadnezzar, since according to the record the wives of Belshazzar were already present at the festival (Dan. 5:2). "The stately manner in which she makes her appearance seems to imply that she is not his wife…[but] the high station of the queen is further shown by the fact that she entered the banquet hall of her own accord."[25] Young believes that she was indeed the Queen Mother, and the widow of the deceased Nebuchadnezzar. As the queen mother, she was able to approach the king where others could not.[26] She was highly regarded and handled with great respect. When she spoke, all others remained silent.[27] And from her testimony it is clear that she lived when Daniel served in Nebuchadnezzar's court.

At the time of the festival, it is unclear the nature of Daniel's station in the kingdom. Nabonidus had displaced the old Chaldean leadership in the coup and if Daniel was still serving, he was probably removed to a secondary role or retired. Whether he had been replaced by one of the subsequent kings, or Belshazzar himself, or had taken leave (because he was over seventy years of age), remains unknown.

The queen spoke of a man in the kingdom "in whom is the spirit of the holy gods" (Dan. 5:11). She explained that Nebuchadnezzar held great confidence in him and placed him in authority as the "chief" of the wise men. When Daniel was present the light of wisdom and understanding permeated the administration. She further explained that Daniel had an excellent spirit and gifts that he used for "interpreting of dreams and shewing of hard sentences, and dissolving of doubts" (Dan. 5:12). As the wife of the former king, she would have witnessed his impressive deeds first hand and heard of his interpretation of the king's first dream. Since that moment she observed countless other expressions of his wisdom and sensible handling of the king's business. She knew of his character and admired how Daniel cared for her husband during his final and very difficult trial. It is interesting that she called him Daniel and not Belteshazzar. When he was summoned it was by his Hebrew name, which meant that she honored and trusted his God.

"The words of the queen do not prove that Belshazzar was not acquainted with Daniel, but only show that he had forgotten the service rendered by him to Nebuchadnezzar; for according to Daniel 5:13 he was well acquainted with the personal circumstances of Daniel."[28] Her counsel was considered good fortune and immediately the prophet was called to the festival.

Daniel presented himself before the king. Notwithstanding the circumstances and fear in the assembly, the tone of Belshazzar was somewhat contemptuous towards the prophet. He did not recall his great deeds or service in working with Nebuchadnezzar, but rather his heritage as a Jew and a captive. Perhaps he was flustered by the moment. Nevertheless, for Daniel, associating him with his Jewish heritage was perfectly fine.

Belshazzar reiterates the words of the Queen Mother and then highlights the failure of the wise men to interpret this great mystery. In typical Babylonian monarch fashion, he promised that if Daniel could solve this great mystery and reveal the meaning of the "hard sentences" on the wall, taking away his fears and doubts, he would be rewarded with treasures and exalted again by being granted the third position in the kingdom.

Daniel, who had already held high positions and had more treasure than he needed, was not at all interested in the reward or position. Nevertheless, in a spirit of service, he prepared to interpret the sentences and bring clarity to the situation. As in previous instances the wise men demonstrated their total inability to solve the problem. "Too often the world, like Belshazzar, is not willing to seek the wisdom of God until its own bankruptcy becomes evident. Then help is sought too late, as in the case of Belshazzar, and the cumulative sin and unbelief that precipitates the crisis in the first place becomes the occasion of downfall."[29]

Daniels Explains the Message in Context

17 Then Daniel answered and said before the king, Let thy gifts be to thyself, and give thy rewards to another; yet I will read the writing unto the king, and make known to him the interpretation.

18 O thou king, the most high God gave Nebuchadnezzar thy father a kingdom, and majesty, and glory, and honour:

19 And for the majesty that he gave him, all people, nations, and languages, trembled and feared before him: whom he would he slew; and whom he would

he kept alive; and whom he would he set up; and whom he would he put down.

20 But when his heart was lifted up, and his mind hardened in pride, he was deposed from his kingly throne, and they took his glory from him:

21 And he was driven from the sons of men; and his heart was made like the beasts, and his dwelling was with the wild asses: they fed him with grass like oxen, and his body was wet with the dew of heaven; till he knew that the most high God ruled in the kingdom of men, and that he appointeth over it whomsoever he will.

22 And thou his son, O Belshazzar, hast not humbled thine heart, though thou knewest all this;

23 But hast lifted up thyself against the Lord of heaven; and they have brought the vessels of his house before thee, and thou, and thy lords, thy wives, and thy concubines, have drunk wine in them; and thou hast praised the gods of silver, and gold, of brass, iron, wood, and stone, which see not, nor hear, nor know: and the God in whose hand thy breath is, and whose are all thy ways, hast thou not glorified:

———

Daniel expresses that he has no interest in the reward, in part because he was not the least bit interested in more gold or power, but also because he wished the king to know that his interpretations would be presented without bias. He could have full confidence in the explanation given. "Daniel rejected the gift and the distinction promised to avoid, as a divinely enlightened seer, every appearance of self-interest in the presence of such a king, and to show the king and his high officers of state that he was not determined by a regard to earthly advantage, and would unhesitatingly declare the truth, whether it might be pleasing or displeasing to the king."[30] He probably knew that the kingdom was at its end (Isa. 44:28; 45:1) and that any position given in the Babylonian monarch was short-lived.

The prophet begins by recounting previous lessons about the kingdom and the experiences of his father Nebuchadnezzar. He reminds Belshazzar how the God of heaven had set up Babylon and gave power to his father to subdue the nations and become a dominant power on the earth. Nebuchadnezzar had recorded his experience and sent a proclamation throughout the kingdom (Dan 4). The lessons were still in force. He rehearsed the punishment his father brought upon himself because of pride and self-aggrandizement (Dan. 5:18-21). Nebuchadnezzar spent several years deprived of his faculties milling about as a beast in the palace gardens, eating grass with feather-like hair and claw like nails (Dan. 4:33).

Daniel's brief review of this history impressed upon Belshazzar's mind that even though his father was a greater man in power and majesty, he abased himself before the God of heaven. He learned to be accountable before the true Sovereign of the kingdom.[31] In the end, Nebuchadnezzar confessed that the real Source of his success and prosperity was the God of Heaven. Perhaps the most valuable lesson learned was that "it is the Most High God who sets up and takes down mortal rulers, and those human rulers need to acknowledge that the Most High God 'rules the kingdom of mankind.'"[32] Belshazzar should have remembered and harkened to the teachings provided by his former king and exemplar.

> But has lifted up thyself against the Lord of Heaven;...and has praised the gods of silver and gold of brass, iron and wood, and stone...and the God in whose hand thy breath is...hast thou not glorified.

Ignoring the lessons of the past, Belshazzar reigned wickedly before God. He had not simply disregarded the lessons of his father, but now had come out in open disrespect against the God of Heaven. He had blasphemed Jehovah by removing the sacred temple vessels and defiled them in the feast (Dan. 5:23). It was a direct affront, an act of contempt against the God of Israel in favor of his pagan gods. "[Daniel] points to the great contrast that there is between the gods formed of dead material and the living God, on whom depend the life and fortune of men. The former Belshazzar praised, the latter he had not honoured."[33]

Daniel's chastisement highlights a truth about most idolatrous people. Deep in their soul, they are aware that their idol gods have no life, nor do they breath, nor wield power, but are dumb fashioned creations "of silver, and gold, of brass, iron, wood, and stone, which see not, nor hear, nor know." (Dan. 5:23; see also Hab. 2:18, 1 Cor. 12:2, Abr. 1:7). "One can well imagine the tense moments as these ringing words reached every ear in the vast hall in the deathly silence that greeted Daniel's prophetic utterance."[34] Their consciences were cut to the quick and the shame of their actions were overwhelming.

Daniel rebuked the attitudes, riotous practices and blasphemy of the king and the assembly of lords and priests. They had come to epitomize the type of society that God detests. The Lord held this lifestyle as the example of rebellion, idolatry and pride and declared all such behavior as "spiritual Babylon" (Doctrine and Covenants 133:14). They were worthy of destruction and for these reasons the sign was given.

The Message Interpreted

_____

24 Then was the part of the hand sent from him; and this writing was written.

25 And this is the writing that was written, MENE, MENE, TEKEL, UPHARSIN.

26 This is the interpretation of the thing: MENE; God hath numbered thy kingdom, and finished it.

27 TEKEL; Thou art weighed in the balances, and art found wanting.

28 PERES; Thy kingdom is divided, and given to the Medes and Persians.

_____

Daniel proceeded to decipher the writings on the wall and provide an explanation for the message given. As mentioned, most scholars believe that the message was written in the Hebrew form of Aramaic, which would be familiar to Daniel, but less familiar to the Chaldeans. The original message properly interpreted translates to: MENE, MENE, TEKEL, UPERES, the U being the conjunction

Gustave Doré 1832-1883, © Public Domain
Daniel interprets the writing on the wall

"and."[35] The writing in true Aramaic would also contract or omit all vowels from each word. The end result would be something like this: MN, MN TKL PRS or more appropriately:

P T M M

R K N N

S L

Another possibility is that the prophet saw the message as follows, noting that the characters are written from right to left:

S R P L K T N M N M

To interpret the code, Daniel simply applied the vowel *E* and the required spacing to divide the letters into words, so that the inscription read (reading now from left to right) as follows:

MENE MENE, TEKEL, PERES[36]

In English, the interpretation of the message would read:

NUMBERED!, NUMBERED!, WEIGHED!, DIVIDED!

Having thus properly separated the code, its interpretation still required spiritual insight in order to understand and the meaning of the message. The background had been given by Daniel, now the message would come.

The repeated use of the word *mene* was given for emphasis. "*Mene* is related to the Hebrew word *Mina*. A *Mina* was equal to fifty shekels. The word can also be translated "to count" or "to number."[37] Daniel explained that: "God hath numbered thy kingdom, and finished it" (Dan. 5:26). Implicit in the meaning was that an evaluation of the kingdom had been performed after which its end was determined. The double use of the word meant that the kingdom was "counted" twice, each time resulting in the same judgment. A similar process occurred when the Lord reviewed Sodom and Gomorrah's condition in which Abraham bargained that the city might be spared if ten righteous souls could be found (Gen. 18: 23-33). When ten good souls were not found, the city's fate was sealed and it was destroyed. Since the penalty is so severe, the counting must occur twice.

Tekel is similar to the Hebrew word Shekel. A shekel was a unit of weight, but can also be translated "to weigh" or in this case weighed and "found light or wanting."[38] The counting process involved weighing the works, deeds and character of the kingdom against their understanding of God's will and truth. Could the king be held accountable for his actions? Did he understand that his deeds were offensive? Had he ignored harkening to the lessons of his kingly fathers? Apparently, the answer was yes! His character and actions were weighed against his understanding and he was found unworthy to continue his reign. His kingdom would come to an end. Daniel portrays this message by saying: "Thou art weighed in the balances, and art found wanting" (Dan. 5:27).

The word *pheres* is related to the Hebrew *peres*, which was a unit of weight equal to a half of a shekel. "The word can also be translated 'divided,' and as a play on words it could also refer to the Persians."[39] Daniel interpreted the symbols to mean: "Thy kingdom is divided, and given to the Medes and Persians" (Dan. 5:28).[40] After Babylon is overthrown, the spoils will be divided among the princes of the Medes and the Persians. "[Daniel explained] it accordingly, so that he brings out, along with the meaning lying in the word, the allusion to Persians: thy kingdom is divided, or broken into pieces, and given to the Medes and Persians. The meaning is not that the kingdom was to be divided into two equal parts, and the one part given to the Medes and the other to the Persians; but [*peres*] is to divide into pieces, to destroy, to dissolve the kingdom."[41]

> Thy kingdom is divided and given to the Medes and Persians...one part to the Medes and the other to the Persians.

The interpretation sank deep into the conscience of the king. His heart despairs as he realizes his doom is near. God is patient. However, men must not mistake His long-suffering for weakness or disinterest. Over time justice must be satisfied and if there is no repentance, the consequences of their actions will overtake the wicked. The writer of Ecclesiastes despaired over his misspent life: "Because sentence against an evil work is not executed speedily, therefore the heart of the sons of men is fully set in them to do evil." (Eccl. 8:11).[42] Belshazzar felt his error and had been given time to repent, but took no advantage of the opportunity.

Stone relief in Perceoplis depicting the victorious Persian kings   © Public Domain

The Kingdom Falls to the Medes and Persians

---

29 Then commanded Belshazzar, and they clothed Daniel with scarlet, and put a chain of gold about his neck, and made a proclamation concerning him, that he should be the third ruler in the kingdom.

30 In that night was Belshazzar the king of the Chaldeans slain.

31 And Darius the Median took the kingdom, being about threescore and two years old.

Daniel's interpretation provided a solid and complete explanation of the writings on the palace wall. Belshazzar fulfilled his promise. The prophet was arrayed in a royal robe and a proclamation was sent to the officers, lords and priests naming him as the third regent in the kingdom. This would place Belshazzar's father as the king and first ruler, Belshazzar as the second ruler and now Daniel the third. But Daniel believed it to be a short-lived privilege, as he well knew the fate of the kingdom. He did not feel that the Persians would honor his position in the new kingdom.

In its rise to power, the Babylonian empire had conquered Jerusalem, taken its inhabitants into captivity, looted its beautiful temple, and destroyed the city. Yet Babylon was to have as its last official act the honoring of one of the Hebrew captives who by divine revelation not only predicted its downfall, but also outlived the empire and its glory. Man may have the first word, but God will have the last word.

The fall of the King and Babylon came within hours. Herodotus, the Greek Historian, recorded the acts of Cyrus when he diverted the Euphrates river, allowing his troops entrance into the city from under the wall.

———

> ...Cyrus, with the first approach of the ensuing spring, marched forward against Babylon. The Babylonians, encamped without their walls, awaited his coming. A battle was fought at a short distance from the city, in which the Babylonians were defeated by the Persian king, whereupon they withdrew within their defenses. Here they shut themselves up, and made light of his siege, having laid in a store of provisions for many years in preparation against this attack; for when they saw Cyrus conquering nation after nation, they were convinced that he would never stop, and that their turn would come at last.

> Cyrus was now reduced to great perplexity, as time went on and he made no progress against the place. In this distress either someone made the suggestion to him, or he bethought himself of a plan, which he proceeded to put in execution. He placed a portion of his army at the point where the river enters the city, and another body at the back of the place where it issues forth, with orders to march into the town by the bed of the stream, as soon as the water became shallow enough: he then himself drew off with the unwarlike portion of his host, and made for the place where [legendary former queen] Nitocris dug the basin for the river, where he did exactly what she had

done formerly: he turned the Euphrates by a canal into the basin, which was then a marsh, on which the river sank to such an extent that the natural bed of the stream became fordable. Hereupon the Persians who had been left for the purpose at Babylon by the river-side, entered the stream, which had now sunk so as to reach about midway up a man's thigh, and thus got into the town.

Had the Babylonians been apprised of what Cyrus was about, or had they noticed their danger, they would never have allowed the Persians to enter the city, but would have destroyed them utterly; for they would have made fast all the street gates which gave access to the river, and mounting upon the walls along both sides of the stream, would so have caught the enemy, as it were, in a trap. But, as it was, the Persians came upon them by surprise and so took the city. Owing to the vast size of the place, the inhabitants of the central parts (as the residents at Babylon declare) long after the outer portions of the town were taken, knew nothing of what had chanced, but as they were engaged in a festival, continued dancing and reveling until they learnt about the capture. Such, then, were the circumstances of the first taking of Babylon."[43]

––––

Persian troops stormed into the city, overwhelming the light resistance of Babylonian troops on the walls and at the gates. They then moved to take the palace. The fall of the capital was swift and short, with little bloodshed. In fact, some of the population was unaware that the city had been taken and the king executed.[44] Isaiah and Jeremiah both give accounts of Babylon's ruin and particularly Belshazzar's downfall. Jeremiah wrote: "recompense her according to her work; according to all that she hath done, do unto her: for [the king] hath been proud against the Lord, against the Holy One of Israel. Therefore shall her young men fall in the streets, and all her men of war shall be cut off in that day, saith the Lord" (Jer. 50:29-

30). Isaiah spoke specifically of the dinner feast and the siege of the Persians: "Go up, O Elam: besiege, O Media; all the sighing thereof have I made to cease. Therefore are my loins filled with pain...I was dismayed at the seeing of it. My heart panted, fearfulness affrighted me: the night of my pleasure hath he turned into fear unto me. Prepare the table, watch in the watchtower, eat, drink: arise, ye princes, and anoint the shield." (Isa. 21:2-5). An evening, which started with festive eating and drinking to petition the gods for protection, ends in fear, and for many who attended the festival, death. A few days afterwards Belshazzar the son of Nabonidus died in battle. Cyrus' son Cambyses held a public mourning lasting six days and accompanied the corpse to the tomb.[45]

© Public Domain
Portrait of King Cyrus

As Babylonian forces fell, king Nabonidus fled the city and sought refuge in Borsippa. With the city in control, Cyrus raised the Persian flag on the massive walls and lined the ramparts with Persian warriors. In time, he pursued and captured king Nabonidus, who was exiled to Carmania where he died.[46] About seventeen months after the capture of Babylon, Cyrus ordered major sections of the walls torn down and destroyed, fearing that if kept intact, the population could easily retake the city and fortify it against his army.

A study of the full account of the prophecies of Isaiah (Isa. 13:17-21) and Jeremiah (Jer. 50-51) foretell of the bloody collapse of Babylon. This seems to contradict the historical accounts of the actual taking of the city, with the exception of pockets of resistance and the purging of the palace leadership. But these prophecies have duel meaning. While they speak of the fateful end of Babylon, their complete fulfillment will come when modern Babylon meets its doom and collapses in horrific bloodshed prior to the Second Coming. "For after today cometh the burning—this is speaking after the manner of the Lord—for verily I say, tomorrow all the proud and they that do wickedly shall be as stubble; and I will burn them up, for I am the Lord of Hosts; and I will not spare any that remain in Babylon" (Doctrine and Covenants 64:24).

Babylon's Ignominious End

It took several generations after the Persian and Greek empires, but the great city Babylon, the source of King Nebuchadnezzar's pride and effort, lost its appeal and fell into disrepair and ruin. Isaiah's prophetic word predicted the end of the mighty city:

---

20 It shall never be inhabited, neither shall it be dwelt in from generation to generation: neither shall the Arabian pitch tent there; neither shall the shepherds make their fold there.

21 But wild beasts of the desert shall lie there; and their houses shall be full of doleful creatures; and owls shall dwell there, and satyrs shall dance there.

22 And the wild beasts of the islands shall cry in their desolate houses, and dragons in their pleasant palaces: and her time is near to come, and her days shall not be prolonged. (Isa. 13:20-21)

From Babel to the prosperous and mighty days of Babylonia under Nebuchadnezzar, this empire has symbolized opulence and idolatry at its worst. It is often portrayed as the prototype for wickedness and rebellion against the God of Heaven. The Lord refers to the latter-day gentile nations collectively as "the world" or "spiritual Babylon" (Doctrine and Covenants 133:14). The ancient civilization introduced idolatry to the world, and modern Babylon will follow a sordid path perverting itself in pagan and hedonistic living. Like its predecessor modern Babylon embraces its own idols, covets power and embellishes itself with riches and riotous living. Like the ancients, modern idolaters are consumed with themselves and the works of their own hands. They pride themselves in their sophisticated philosophies and crafty lifestyles all of which cause them to forget the God who created them and lends them their very breath. "For they have strayed from mine ordinances, and have broken mine everlasting covenant; They seek not the Lord to establish his righteousness, but every man walketh in his own way, and after the image of his own god, whose image is in the likeness of the world, and whose substance is that of an idol, which waxeth old and shall perish in Babylon, even Babylon the great, which shall fall." (Doctrine and Covenants 1:15:16)

Just as Belshazzar turned from the Lord and trusted in his own gods, so too will many in modern Babylon forget Him to their fateful destruction. The Lord has promised: "[I will]...suddenly come to [my] temple; the Lord who shall come down upon the world with a curse to judgment; yea, upon all the nations that forget God, and upon all the ungodly among you." (Doctrine and Covenants 133:2).

Chapter Notes

1   Keil. *Biblical Commentary of the Old Testament, The Book of the Prophet Daniel*, 164; Phillips. *Exploring the Book of Daniel: An Expository Commentary.* 85

2   Ibid. 164

3   Phillips. *Exploring the Book of Daniel: An Expository Commentary.* 85

4   Keil. *Biblical Commentary of the Old Testament, The Book of the Prophet Daniel.* 165

5   Olmstead. *History of the Persian Empire.* 38, Phillips. *Exploring the Book of Daniel: An Expository Commentary.* 85, 249

6   Watrall. "ANP203 History of Archaeology Lecture 2". Anthropology.msu.edu. Retrieved 7 April 2014.

7   Grayson. *Assyrian and Babylonian Chronicles, repr.* 109-10

8   Young. *The Prophecy Daniel: A Commentary.* 117

9   ?Ibid, 117

10   Grayson. *Assyrian and Babylonian Chronicles, repr.* 109-10

11   Mallowan. "Nimrud", in *Archeology and Old Testament Study.* 62

12   Walvoord. *Daniel: The Key to Prophetic Revelation.* 143

13   Phillips. *Exploring the Book of Daniel: An Expository Commentary.* 85

14   Prichard. *Ancient Near Eastern Texts Relating to the Old Testament.* 1969

15   Walvoord. Daniel: *The Key to Prophetic Revelation,* 144

16   Phillips. *Exploring the Book of Daniel: An Expository Commentary.,* 86

17   Walvoord. *Daniel: The Key to Prophetic Revelation.* 147

18   Keil. *Biblical Commentary of the Old Testament, The Book of the Prophet Daniel.* 180-81

19   Trapp. *A Commentary on the Old and New Testaments Vol X*

20   Keil. *Biblical Commentary of the Old Testament, The Book of the Prophet Daniel.* 182, See also Walvoord. *Daniel: The Key to Prophetic Revelation.* 148

21   Phillips. *Exploring the Book of Daniel: An Expository Commentary.* 88

22   Goldinggay. *Daniel, Word Biblical Commentary.* 148

23   Keil. *Biblical Commentary of the Old Testament, The Book of the Prophet Daniel.* 182

24   Ibid. 182

25   Young. *The Prophecy Daniel: A Commentary.* 122

26   Ibid. 122

27   Walvoord. *Daniel: The Key to Prophetic Revelation.* 150

28   Keil. *Biblical Commentary of the Old Testament, The Book of the Prophet Daniel.* 186, Walvoord. *Daniel: The Key to Prophetic Revelation.* 150

29   Walvoord. *Daniel: The Key to Prophetic Revelation.* 152

30   Keil. *Biblical Commentary of the Old Testament, The Book of the Prophet Daniel.* 187

31   Young. *The Prophecy Daniel: A Commentary.* 124

32   Walvoord. *Daniel: The Key to Prophetic Revelation.* 154

33   Keil. *Biblical Commentary of the Old Testament, The Book of the Prophet Daniel.* 189

34   Walvoord. *Daniel: The Key to Prophetic Revelation.* 155

35   Young. *The Prophecy Daniel: A Commentary.* 125-26

36   Phillips. *Exploring the Book of Daniel: An Expository Commentary.* 93

37   Walvoord. *Daniel: The Key to Prophetic Revelation.* 156

38   Ibid. 157

39   Ibid. 157
40   Young. *The Prophecy Daniel: A Commentary.* 127
41   Keil. *Biblical Commentary of the Old Testament, The Book of the Prophet Daniel.* 190
42   Phillips. *Exploring the Book of Daniel: An Expository Commentary.* 91
43   Herodotus, *Histories* 1.189-191
44   Phillips. *Exploring the Book of Daniel: An Expository Commentary.* 95
45   Chisholm, Hugh, *Encyclopedia Britannica 11ᵗʰ Ed.* 105-6
46   Young. *The Prophecy Daniel: A Commentary.* 138

Additional Notes

Identity of Belshazzar: Herodotus, relates that Cyrus entered the city by damming off the Euphrates during a festival of its inhabitants, and that the king was put to death, whose name he does not mention, but whom he describes as a youth, and as a riotous, voluptuous, cruel, godless man. (Keil. Biblical Commentary of the Old Testament, The Book of the Prophet Daniel. 166, who quotes: Xenophon (Cyrop. vii. 5, 15ff.).

Fate of Nabondus: But in their statements concerning the last king of Babylon they both stand in opposition to the accounts of Berosus and Abydenus. Herodotus and Xenophon describe him as the king's son, while Nabonidus, according to both of these Chaldean historians, was not of royal descent. Besides this, Xenophon states that the king lost his life at the taking of Babylon, while according to Berosus, on the contrary, he was not in Babylon at all, but was besieged in Borsippa, surrendered to Cyrus, and was banished to Carmania, or according to Abydenus, was made deputy of that province. (Keil. 167)

6

Daniel and
the Lion's Den

The Persians Set up the Kingdom

Daniel and the lion's den is one of the most widely known stories in scripture. This important event occurs late in his life, several years after Nebuchadnezzar's death, after the Medo-Persian Empire had overthrown the kingdom. He was in his seventies, possibly close to eighty years of age. It comes shortly after the new Persian government established order in Babylon, "when Darius the Median took the kingdom, *being* about threescore and two years old" (Dan. 5:31). It is generally accepted that this Darius (the Mede) did not reign over Cyrus's vast Medo-Persian Empire. Rather, as a powerful Mede, he was "set" or placed as ruler over Babylon and some of its territories. In verse 28, Daniel mentions the reign of both Darius and Cyrus. But Darius would have been the official through which He and the Jews conducted most of their business.[1]

After the fall of Babylon, Cyrus and the army quickly went to work to rebuild the city and gain the favor of the surviving lords and the people. "The conquerors did what they could to set up friendly relationships

© 2009 Monica Boorboor, Used with Permission
Stone relief depicting the standard of Cyrus and the Achaemenid Empire (Persia)

with the people in their power, and although Belshazzar was slain, his father Nabonidus lived for some years afterward. Even some of the gods of Babylon were honored by the conquerors."[2] Cyrus claimed to be chosen by the god Marduk to conquer Babylon and rescue the gods of Sumer and Akkad, whose temples had fallen into disrepair under Nabonidus.[3]

Darius Establishes the Government

1   It pleased Darius to set over the kingdom an hundred and twenty princes, which should be over the whole kingdom;

2   And over these three presidents; of whom Daniel was first: that the princes might give accounts unto them, and the king should have no damage.

3   Then this Daniel was preferred above the presidents and princes, because an excellent spirit was in him; and the king thought to set him over the whole realm. (Dan 6:1-3).

Much of the Babylonian leadership was swept aside in the battles. The Persians and Medes quickly set out to establish order over the city and the provinces. Darius the Mede, having been set in place by Cyrus, began appointing satraps, or princes, in the several provinces that comprised the Babylonian portion of the Empire. These princes were chief officials designated "for the government of the affairs of the kingdom [which Darius] had received, and especially for regulating the gathering in of the tribute."[5] Historians have found variations in the actual number of satraps proposed, ranging from 20, 21, 23 to 120. Whatever the number, they represented the senior administrators required to fulfill the work of the kingdom.

As Darius reorganized the government, he found in Daniel "an excellent spirit" (Dan. 6:3). He placed him in the high position of senior president over two other presidents. Keil provides an excellent explanation as to how else Daniel might have received favor: "The successor [to Belshazzar] would be inclined toward the recognition [of Daniel's promotion] by the reflection that by Daniel's interpretation of the mysterious writing from God, the putting of Belshazzar to death appeared to have a higher sanction, presenting itself as if it were something determined in the councils of the gods, whereby the successor might claim before the people that his usurpation of the throne was rendered legitimate. Such a reflection might move him to confirm Daniel's elevation to the office to which Belshazzar had raised him."[4] With Nabonidus captured and Belshazzar dead, Daniel, as the third in the kingdom, was a logical candidate to set ahead of the others. By placing Daniel as first president, Darius also confirmed upon him the position given by Belshazzar's promotion, that of third ruler in the kingdom.[5] Furthermore, Darius was thinking who might succeed him if he were to die or be assassinated. Despite Daniel's advanced age, he was chosen as vice-regent over the new province.

While Keil's explanation is plausible, in the end Darius needed someone that he could trust and who was respected by the Babylonians. He saw and sensed in the prophet that man. Daniel's unwavering integrity and abilities helped pave the way for him. The responsibility of the chief presidents would be to oversee the satraps who gave an account of their provinces. They ensured efficient government, the even application of the laws and faithful

Stone relief depicting the king Cyrus of Persia   © Used with Permission

dispersion of revenue according to the king's will. They were accountable for the tribute and expenses, doing no "damage" to the treasury or assets. "Eastern courts were always hotbeds of bribery and corruption. Rarely was a person in any place of power not given to feather his own nest. The various satraps under Daniel came to hate him. He stood in the way of lining their pockets…Darius soon discovered that his revenues would be in safe and capable hands."[7] Daniel, as the chief or "first" among the presidents, answered only to Darius. The Lord opened the door of opportunity and placed him in a position of responsibility among the new conquerors.

Flag of Achaemenid Empire

The record is silent on who served as the other presidents or prominent satraps in the kingdom. Doubtless many were Chaldeans, newly appointed or re-appointed by the king. These men were familiar with Daniel as he served under Nebuchadnezzar for forty-seven years. The combination of his position, his heritage and his integrity caused jealousy among them, especially among the more senior members of the assembly. His removal would be beneficial to the princes and certainly to the members in the presidential quorum.

The Grand Scheme to Trap and Remove Daniel

_____

4 Then the presidents and princes sought to find occasion against Daniel concerning the kingdom; but they could find none occasion nor fault; forasmuch as he was faithful, neither was there any error or fault found in him.

5 Then said these men, We shall not find any occasion against this Daniel, except we find it against him concerning the law of his God.

6 Then these presidents and princes assembled together to the king, and said thus unto him, King Darius, live for ever.

7 All the presidents of the kingdom, the governors, and the princes, the counsellors, and the captains, have consulted together to establish a royal statute, and to make a firm decree, that whosoever shall ask a petition of any God or man for thirty days, save of thee, O king, he shall be cast into the den of lions.

8 Now, O king, establish the decree, and sign the writing, that it be not changed, according to the law of the Medes and Persians, which altereth not.

9 Wherefore king Darius signed the writing and the decree.

_____

A conspiracy was hatched among the senior presidents and a few of the princes to snare Daniel in a trap and remove him from office. "We can expect that these men, most of them probably were much younger than Daniel and anxious to get ahead."[8] Their initial strategy was to "find occasion against [him]" (Dan. 6:4). They likely searched for discrepancies among the official records with the intent to scrutinize his conduct or expose any evidence to accuse him of fraud, embezzlement or abuse of power. The presidents would have access to key records and any incriminating evidence; but their efforts revealed nothing. It is important to contrast the character of the conspirators with that of the prophet. While Daniel's integrity protected him from such conspiratorial schemes, their works were laced with calculated dishonesty and conniving for power. Those seeking a cause for accusation revealed their own manipulative character. "Daniel's colleagues appear as simply (in both senses of the word) plotters. Most of the speech in the story is theirs, and they condemn themselves out of their own mouths; every word they speak, as well as every move they make, concerning intrigue, manipulation, treachery, duplicity and scheming."[9] The tactics and spirit of Daniel's enemies mirror that of the devil, who, in the war in heaven, waged a continual campaign both day and night of faultfinding and slander against his brethren in an effort to unseat or destroy them. (Rev. 12:10).

Unable to find culpability in his administrative practices and knowing of Daniel's devotion towards his God, they sought occasion to find some peculiarity in his religious observance to use against him. If they could leverage his devotion to Jehovah, then the trap would yield the desired fruit. Their focus changed. After reviewing several possibilities, they sought to test his adherence to the basic principles of prayer and adoration. They would strike at the core of Daniel's dedication to his God by ironically proving his resolve in petitioning Jehovah in prayer. In reality, they knew that Daniel's disposition was to be faithful. He would ignore any edict commanding him to cease worshipping his God.

The cabal carefully planned a scheme that for 30 days no man could petition another god or seek high advice from any man other than from Darius. Inherent in the edict would be the flattering supposition that Darius was either the son of the gods or a god himself. "The object of the law was only to bring about the general recognition of the principle that the king was the living manifestation of all the gods, not only of the Median and Persian, but also of the Babylonian and Lydian, and all the gods of the conquered nations."[10] Pagan tradition allowed for the deification of kings and leaders. "According to the general principle of heathenism, the ruler is the son, the representative, the living manifestation of the people's gods, and the world-ruler, thus the manifestation of all the gods of the nations that were subject to him. Therefore, all heathen world-rulers demanded from the heathen nations subdued by them, that religious homage should be rendered to them in the manner peculiar to each nation. Now that is what was here sought."[11]

The institution of the Persian government played perfectly into the implementation of the scheme and the proposed law. The presidents would inaugurate and formally recognize Darius as the living manifestation of the gods, not only of the Medes and Persians, but also of the Babylonians and Lydians, and all the gods of the conquered nations. "All the nations…were required not to abandon their own special worship, but in fact to acknowledge that the Medo-Persian world ruler Darius was also the son and representative of their national gods. For this purpose, they must for the space of thirty days present their petitions to their national gods only to him as their manifestation."[12]

Such edicts were fairly common practice of newly installed monarchs who wished to claim the blessing of the people, by either declaring divine approval, as did Cyrus, or by maintaining that they were a descendant of deity. As Young and others have pointed out, "there is nothing unusual in ascribing to Persian kings worship such as would be afforded the pagan gods."[13] Such assertions would legitimize their high station and engender loyalty. "And the heathen nations could all do this without violating their consciences; for since in their own manner they served the Median king as the son of their gods, they served their gods in him."[14] Of course the Jews were not afforded the latitude of regarding the king as the manifestation of Jehovah; therefore, the law became a mechanism for accusation and persecution targeted precisely at Daniel.

The assembly flattered the king by suggesting that: "All the presidents of the kingdom, the governors, and the princes, the counsellors, and the captains, have consulted together to establish a royal statute" (Dan. 6:7). The pledge of loyalty was brought to Darius with the pretended universal consent of the whole leadership of the kingdom. It was claimed that every relevant officer, military commander and local governor was supportive of the proclamation. The whole kingdom was bestowing honor on their new king by elevating him with this special edict.

Exactly what matters and policies qualified as worthy to be petitioned to the king is not clear, but the logical conclusion was that the business of the kingdom was the focus of the requests. Chiefs, officers, military captains and governors all sent business and requests for permission or counsel only to the king. It is unknown how many traditionally petitioned their pagan gods for wisdom in matters of state, but for the time being this would be expressly forbidden.

Much of the business of the kingdom might have been presented to the king anyway, but the formality of demanding that only he be petitioned re-affirmed his supreme station and served as a high gesture of loyalty. The request from the embassy, presented with such flattery, was accepted. As a point of emphasis, the law was to be enacted with the king's seal. Such a formality meant that once the king signed it into law, it could not be changed or revoked. The Medes and Persians adopted this policy as a method of presenting fairness in governance and certitude in the law.

Of course, the intent of the seal was to bind the king and ensure the arrest and death of violators, namely Daniel. Otherwise, as he was trusted and a friend, the king might reverse the order or draw exception. Darius signed the wicked decree and the deed was done.

Daniel Offers Prayers towards Jerusalem and is arrested.

———

10 Now when Daniel knew that the writing was signed, he went into his house; and his windows being open in his chamber toward Jerusalem, he kneeled upon his knees three times a day, and prayed, and gave thanks before his God, as he did aforetime.

11 Then these men assembled, and found Daniel praying and making supplication before his God.

12 Then they came near, and spake before the king concerning the king's decree; Hast thou not signed a decree, that every man that shall ask a petition of any God or man within thirty days, save of thee, O king, shall be cast into the den of lions? The king answered and said, The thing is true, according to the law of the Medes and Persians, which altereth not.

13 Then answered they and said before the king, That Daniel, which is of the children of the captivity of Judah, regardeth not thee, O king, nor the decree that thou hast signed, but maketh his petition three times a day.

14 Then the king, when he heard these words, was sore displeased with himself, and set his heart on Daniel to deliver him: and he laboured till the going down of the sun to deliver him.

15 Then these men assembled unto the king, and said unto the king, Know, O king, that the law of the Medes and Persians is, That no decree nor statute which the king establisheth may be changed.

16 Then the king commanded, and they brought Daniel, and cast him into the den of lions. Now the king spake and said unto Daniel, Thy God whom thou servest continually, he will deliver thee.

17 And a stone was brought, and laid upon the mouth of the den; and the king sealed it with his own signet, and with the signet of his lords; that the purpose might not be changed concerning Daniel.

———

The record is clear that Daniel knew of and understood the edict signed by Darius. Nevertheless, as he had done for decades, he went to his chamber and opened the windows toward Jerusalem to begin to offer his soul to the Lord. "A discontinuance of it on account of that law would have been, [to Daniel] a denying of the faith and a sinning against God."[15] The presidents and princes united in the cabal assembled themselves outside his window. Daniel probably prayed aloud, not so others could hear, but out of devotion and tradition. Such a practice made it easier for his accusers to provide witnesses and present charges to the king. With the prayers uttered, the contemptible group hasted away to the king. In the same way the Chaldeans accused Shadrach, Meshach and Abed-nego of being disloyal to Nebuchadnezzar, so too the "loyal patriots" approached Darius and accused Daniel of disrespect and disloyalty against the king and in violation of the newly signed law.

Daniel was presented to the king together with witnesses who shared their evidences and testimony. At this moment, he

Briton Riviere © 1872 Public Domain
Daniel in the Lion's Den by Briton Riviere

immediately understood his folly and that he had been taken by the scheming plots of the presidents and princes. The record says that he was displeased with himself, not having connected the dots or discerned the deception from its proposal. In an attempt to release his trusted servant, the king consulted the judges of the law to determine whether he could circumvent the binding seal of the edict. During the process, the princes and presidents reminded him of the unchangeable nature of the decree and that it could not be altered, but must be fulfilled. It should be understood that "the rigidity of the Medo-Persian law was not a bad thing. Later, in the days of Ezra, the adversaries of Judah wrote letters to Ahasuerus, the Persian king, slandering the Jews and endeavoring to have a decree signed to prevent the Jews from continuing with the work of reconstruction. They succeeded (Ezra 4:1-24). Later, the decree of Cyrus was found, the original document that led to the release of the Jews in the Promised Land. That changed the whole picture."[16] In that case, the law favored the Jews.

The king labored, perhaps even stalled the execution of the judgment to the last moment, waiting until sunset. Disgusted with himself and horrified by the situation, he finally ordered Daniel to be cast into the lion's den. In an expression of confidence and of hope, Darius admonished Daniel by stating that his God could deliver him from the lions and professed that was the desire and anticipation of his heart. The prophet was lowered into the den and a stone was placed over the entrance and sealed with the signet of the king. There Daniel remained undisturbed until morning light.

Most scholars believe that the den was a cistern-like hole, with access from above with a ladder, through which the lion's caretakers lowered down food as well as condemned prisoners. A small hole above the cavern also made it easy to close and seal. Maintenance of the cistern-like den and the lions would be difficult without a side access, but Daniel 6:24 makes it clear that the primary access came from above and that there were multiple ledges or layers around the sides of the cave where prey could temporarily escape from the lions who wait for prisoners to lose their grip and fall. They would then attack them at the bottom of the cave.

Daniel Emerges from the Lion's Den

18 Then the king went to his palace, and passed the night fasting: neither were instruments of musick brought before him: and his sleep went from him.

19 Then the king arose very early in the morning, and went in haste unto the den of lions.

20 And when he came to the den, he cried with a lamentable voice unto Daniel: and the king spake and said to Daniel, O Daniel, servant of the living God, is thy God, whom thou servest continually, able to deliver thee from the lions?

21 Then said Daniel unto the king, O king, live forever.

22 My God hath sent his angel, and hath shut the lions' mouths, that they have not hurt me: forasmuch as before him innocency was found in me; and also before thee, O king, have I done no hurt.

23 Then was the king exceeding glad for him, and commanded that they should take Daniel up out of the den. So Daniel was taken up out of the den, and no manner of hurt was found upon him, because he believed in his God.

24 And the king commanded, and they brought

> those men which had accused Daniel, and they
> cast them into the den of lions, them, their children,
> and their wives; and the lions had the mastery of
> them, and brake all their bones in pieces or ever they
> came at the bottom of the den.

Darius spent the night in his bedchamber fasting. It was a very sleepless night as he worried about the fate of his faithful servant Daniel and his unwise role in the prophet's condemnation. It appears that even the musicians tasked with playing relaxing and beautiful music to help him sleep were dismissed. His night was probably filled with tossing and turning, even pacing back and forth awaiting the first light of dawn. At the break of day, the king speedily made haste to the lion's den to discover whether Daniel had survived. The seal on the door was broken and the stone removed. Darius peered into the darkened den. With a lamentable voice, but in an expression of faith, he shouts down to Daniel asking whether his God, who is the living God, was able to protect him from the lions.

To his great joy, Daniel responds "O king, live forever," confirming that he was indeed alive and spared from the hungry lions. Just as Shadrach, Meshach and Abed-nego were preserved from the furnace fire, so too the Lord sent an angel to temper the hunger and shut the lion's mouths. Daniel relates that the reason the Lord had spared him was because he was innocent before God and the king. He was not disloyal to the king as his accusers had testified and his survival in the cave was evidence of this fact. He maintained his integrity despite the trap set by his colleagues in the presidency and among the princes.

With indescribable joy the king commands that Daniel be lifted from the den. We can only imagine the shock and horror of the accusers when Daniel and the king return to the palace that morning for breakfast.

In an act of justified anger, the king then turns on Daniel's accusers. The fact that the prophet had come out of the den unscathed was interpreted as proof of his innocence, just as he had testified. The conclusion therefore was that Daniel had been falsely accused. His adversaries were summarily rounded up with their families and cast into the same den. "The punishment of the wives and children was in accordance with Persian custom cf Her. 11:119; Amm. Mar. xxiii; 6, 81 (some laws are abominable, through which, because of the crime of one person, all his relatives are put to death)."[17] The Persian tradition was intended to preemptively quench any future uprising from family members who may hold deep resentment to punishments inflicted by the empire.

We should not conclude that all 120 satraps and the presidents were part of the conspiracy, nor were there hundreds cast into the den. Only a relative few who combined together to trap and remove Daniel. These were arrested and thrown in the den of hungry lions. Of course, if they were also preserved, as was the prophet, they would have been acquitted as well. The resulting night brought a much different result. As each person hung onto the edges around the den, eventually they lost their strength or grip and fell or "came to the bottom" (Dan. 6:24) where the lions had "mastery" and they were consumed.

The Proclamation to the Kingdom

---

25 Then king Darius wrote unto all people, nations, and languages, that dwell in all the earth; Peace be multiplied unto you.

26 I make a decree, That in every dominion of my kingdom men tremble and fear before the God of Daniel: for he is the living God, and steadfast for ever, and his kingdom that which shall not be destroyed, and his dominion shall be even unto the end.

27 He delivereth and rescueth, and he worketh signs and wonders in heaven and in earth, who hath delivered Daniel from the power of the lions.

28 So this Daniel prospered in the reign of Darius, and in the reign of Cyrus the Persian.

In a fashion similar to Nebuchadnezzar's proclamation (Dan. 3:29) praising the God of Shadrach, Meshach and Abed-nego, Darius announces to the kingdom Daniel's faithfulness and his preservation at the hand of the "living God" (Dan. 6:26). "Darius acknowledged the God of Daniel, indeed, as the living God, whose kingdom and dominion were everlasting, but not as the only true God, and he commanded Him to be reverenced only as a God who does wonders in heaven and on earth, without prejudice to the honour of his own gods and of the gods of his subjects."[18] The king commands, that Daniel's God should be feared and respected by all throughout the kingdom.

Even so, from the jaws of conflict and conspiracy, the God of Israel, through the faithfulness and instrumentality of His servant Daniel, was reaffirmed as the "living God" to be honored and revered. No doubt such a proclamation engendered respect for Jehovah and respect for the Jews throughout the Medo-Persian Empire. This event reaffirmed Daniel's position as chief President in the government and set the stage for his influence and service in the Persian kingdom. Later when the Jews approached Cyrus to reveal the writings of Isaiah (Isa. 45:1), which prophesied of their return to Jerusalem. He surely was impressed with the prophetic reference that added to his respect for the Jews gained through Daniel's influence. All these factors affected his decision to issue the command for their release and return.

The commentator Young drew this lesson from the faithfulness of Daniel: "Our lot on this earth is to walk more by faith than by sight. This is the chief exercise of the soul, which is essential to our vitality and growth. We must have, at times, our mountains of vision as well as our valleys of the shadow of death. Never let us doubt the essential preeminence of justice, and righteousness and truthfulness. By this we shall be borne up through the regions of cloud into realm of light."[19]

Chapter Endnotes

1   Keil and Delitzsch,*Biblical Commentary of the Old Testament, The Book of the Prophet Daniel*, Vol. 6. 1872, 548, See also: Karst, Josef ed., *Die Chronik aus dem Armenischen übersetzt mit textkritischem Commentar.* Vol 5 of *Eusebius Werke* . Die griechischen christlichen Schriftseller der ersten drei Jahrhunderte, vol. 20 (Leipzig: J. C. Hinrichs, 1911), 246

Darius the Mede proves to be a controversial figure in historical circles. Unlike Cyrus the Great, a royal Darius that reigned contemporary to the fall of Babylon cannot be identified through historical and archeological records. A statement written by the Babylonian historian Berossus, cited in the *Chronicon* of Eusebius, mentions a king named Darius, and Berossus associates this Darius with Cyrus's victory over Nabonidus and the fall of Babylon in 539 B.C.. The translated passage reads as follows: "To this one [Nabonidus] Cyrus gave, when he had taken Babylon, the governorship of the land of the Carmanians; [but] Darius the king took away some of the province for himself."

Berossus's account suggests that the Persians and Medes, while kindred allies, had still not solidified their kingdom under a single monarch. This union would not be complete until Cyrus the Great married the daughter of the King of the Medes, Cyaxares II. Cyrus already had assumed the throne of his father Cambyses 1 when he died in 559 B.C., but waited to gain the dowry of the Median kingdom through marriage. The record of Xenophon states that: "After the conquest of Babylon the [Median] army regarded Cyrus as king, and he began to conduct his affairs as if he were king (vii. 5. 37); but he went to Media, to present himself before Cyaxares [II]. He brought presents to him, and showed him that there was a house and palace ready for him in Babylon, where he might reside when he went thither (viii. 5. 17f.). Cyaxares [II] gave him his daughter to wife, and along with her, as her dowry, the whole of Media, for he had no son (viii. 5. 19)." Keil. *Biblical Commentary of the Old Testament, The Book of the Prophet Daniel.* 195; Xenophon. *Cyropaedia. 194-95*

Trusting in the account of Berossus as true, we conclude that it was unlikely that Darius took the Babylonian Kingdom from Cyrus by his own power, but Cyaxares II influenced the bestowal of Babylon upon him by soliciting Cyrus. Not yet king of the Medes, Cyrus would be willing to appease the Median king and grant this favor upon Darius. Eventually Cyrus married Cyaxares's daughter, thus solidifying the kingship over both Persia and Media. Darius would have reigned for about two years, then Cyrus would take back the Babylonian Kingdom for himself just as Daniel's record suggests. This explanation seems to satisfy all historical records.

Another prominent explanation purports that Cyrus placed the conquering general, a Mede named Gubaru as governor over the province. "On the 16th day, Gubaru (Darius the Mede) the leader of Gutium along with the army of Cyrus entered Babylon without any opposition. Later they arrested Nabonidus when he returned to Babylon. On the third day of the month of Arahshamnu, Cyrus marched into Babylon, and they laid down green branches in front of him. The city was no longer at war, peace being restored. Cyrus then sent his best wishes to the residents living there. His governor, Gubaru, then installed leaders to govern over all Babylon." Gubaru would have changed his name when he ascended to the throne and Cyrus would, however, take back the kingdom when Darius died or retired. Keil, *Biblical Commentary of the Old Testament, The Book of the Prophet*

Daniel, 195; Xenophon. *Cyropaedia. 194-95*

2   Ibid. 316

3   Ibid. 166-67, also cites Prichard, *Near Eastern Studies*

4   Keil. *Biblical Commentary of the Old Testament, The Book of the Prophet Daniel.*
     190-191

5   Ibid. 207

6   Ibid. 201

7   Phillips. *Exploring the Book of Daniel: An Expository Commentary.* 98

8   Walvoord. *Daniel: The Key to Prophetic Revelation.* 168

9   Goldingay. *Daniel.* 125

10   Keil. *Biblical Commentary of the Old Testament, The Book of the Prophet Daniel.*
     211

11   Ibid. 211

12   Young. *The Prophecy Daniel: A Commentary.* 134

13   Walvoord. Daniel: *The Key to Prophetic Revelation.* 169

14   Keil. *Biblical Commentary of the Old Testament, The Book of the Prophet Daniel.*
     211

15   Keil. *Biblical Commentary of the Old Testament, The Book of the Prophet Daniel.*
     213; See also: *Teachings of George Albert Smith*, 2010, Ch. 17,. "Strengthening
     Power of Faith."

16   Phillips. *Exploring the Book of Daniel: An Expository Commentary.* 103

17   Young. *The Prophecy Daniel: A Commentary.* 139

18   Keil. *Biblical Commentary of the Old Testament, The Book of the Prophet Daniel.*
     218

19   Young. *The Prophecy Daniel: A Commentary.* 139

7

The Vision of the Kingdoms of the World

SECTION I

Chapter 7 transitions the record of Daniel into the second of the two major collections. Chapters 1- 6 portrayed key events of personal and historical significance, some of which tested and then confirmed the righteousness of the prophet and his companions. Their faithfulness elevated them into powerful positions in the Babylonian and Persian kingdoms, which opened many doors and opportunities both for themselves and the Jews. The experiences served to make known the name of Jehovah and His exalted station in the eyes of the kings and the empires (Dan. 2:47; 3:28-29; 4:34-35). The Babylonian queen testified that Daniel had the "spirit of the holy gods" and brought "light and understanding and wisdom" to the kingdom (Dan 5:10:11).

In their elevated positions, they provided protection and oversight for the Jewish people, who were strangers in a strange and occasionally very hostile land. Jehovah used Daniel to guide the circumstances by which He watched over and safeguarded His people from the initial days of exile until they returned to their homeland.

The second section marks the beginning of a series of visions recorded in chapters 7-12. The summaries of visions revealed important events about the gentile nations and the Jew to the prophet. Chapter 7 opens with an exhibition of several images, each representing a mighty kingdom that will rule in power on the earth. It serves as a transitional chapter between the previous personal section to the series of visions featuring future nations and kingdoms. Structurally, chapter 7 completes the chiastic arrangement of chapters 2-7 (See the Preface for an explanation) and parallels Nebuchadnezzar's dream in Daniel 2.

This expansive vision shows the succession of Gentile kingdoms beginning with his day and ultimately concludes in the last days with the establishment of God's kingdom and His millennial reign.[1] This panoramic vision serves as an overview and portrays images and messages that the Lord feels are necessary for Daniel, and the reader to understand of the future. It lays the framework upon which subsequent visions will then be given showing the same kingdoms in greater detail [8-12].

> This commentary addresses Daniel's visions and writings precisely within the context that they are presented, as though angelic messengers delivered them by the spirit of prophecy and revelation.

For a few individuals dubious of the spirit of prophecy, the visions contained in chapters 7-12 are a source of controversy. Early scholars like Porphyry, a third century Christian antagonist, argued that the writings were actually 2nd century B.C. records written after the historical fact.[2] Some of Daniel's accounts are so rich in detail that if one does not subscribe to Divine foreknowledge, they must argue that it could only be a historical account, not a prophecy. This commentary addresses Daniel's visions precisely as they are presented, as though angelic messengers visited the prophet and delivered them by the spirit of prophecy and revelation.

We should remember that the Lord himself quoted from Daniel as He spoke of the "Abomination of Desolation" (Dan. 9:27; 11:31; 12:11) to His disciples on the Mount of Olives (Matt. 24:15). Additionally, Joseph F. Smith saw Daniel in the vision of the Redemption of the Dead, describing him as the seer who "foresaw and foretold the establishment of the kingdom of God in the latter-days, never again to be destroyed nor given to other people" (Doctrine and Covenants 138:44). This prophetic reference is recorded in Daniel 2:44, with other references found in Daniel 2:14, 18, 22-23; 7:18.

As we read and study the visions, we marvel at their accuracy, and the Spirit confirms its prophetic origins. We know that God is able to foresee all things past, present and future (Doctrine and Covenants 130:7). Through this omniscience, He reveals the future in great detail to His servants the prophets (Amos 3:7) and the world.

History will pass from Daniel's day (circa 620-537 B.C.) to the Meridian of Time and the Savior's mortal ministry (0-33 A.D.), and then will proceed to the latter-days. As it passes, the student of Daniel's record will, in each age, witness remarkable fulfillments of each vision. They will see God's foreknowledge of events and His hand in the direction and destiny of the kingdoms. Each account provides understanding of things yet to come. Daniel's writings will prove useful to the Jews who returned to Jerusalem (539 B.C.) during the periods when they navigate alliances and in times when they suffer persecutions. They will be a source of insight for the Apostles who live during the Lord's mortal ministry and they will be valuable again to the latter-day faithful, who desire understanding into events leading to the Second Coming.

Daniel's Dream of the Kingdoms of the Gentiles

This first vision recorded in chapter 7 came several years after Nebuchadnezzar's death. Belshazzar reigned in Babylon under his father, Nabonidus. The year was 553 B.C., about fourteen years before the fall of Babylon.[3] Nabonidus had entrusted the kingdom to his son Belshazzar as co-regent while he resided in Tayma, Arabia. He had left the city because of serious contentions with the priests of Marduk and he sought the opportunity to study archeology and conduct military expansions in the region.[4] Previous chapters (Daniel 5) reveal that unlike `Nebuchadnezzar's regime, Daniel was not a principle officer in Belshazzar's government. He likely had been replaced and remained in retirement until the night of the fateful feast when Cyrus took the city.

The Vision of the Beasts

1   In the first year of Belshazzar king of Babylon Daniel had a dream and visions of his head upon his bed: then he wrote the dream, and told the sum of the matters.

2   Daniel spake and said, I saw in my vision by night, and, behold, the four winds of the heaven strove upon the great sea.

3   And four great beasts came up from the sea, diverse one from another.

In the first year of Belshazzar's reign, the Lord showed Daniel in vision the Babylonian kingdom and the three great kingdoms that would follow. The vision came in the night while in his bedchambers. It is not stated whether his experience was presented in the form of a dream or an actual vision. But given the detailed nature of the account, it is likely that the experience was more of a vision with vivid presentations and interplay.

Daniel recorded the "sum of the matter" meaning a summary or "the chief contents of the dream, omitting secondary things, e.g., the minute description of the beasts."[5] Most of the details, including the panoramic scope and the complexities of each kingdom were omitted. He was not capable of recording everything revealed by the Spirit. But for the purposes of the prophecy, the key elements or "the sum of the matter" was sufficient.

Daniel begins by speaking of "the four winds of the heaven, which strove upon the great sea," a vast sea symbolic of the masses of humanity (Dan. 7:2). It represents the millions of inhabitants on the earth, the kindreds, tribes and nations that interact and live out their lives (Rev 13:1).[6] The tossing of the seas can be compared to the "tumults of the peoples, and the commotions among the nations of the world."[7] The heavenly winds that "strove upon the sea" provide a divine and subtle influence directing and orchestrating lives and events. Daniel's account provides no specifies about the nature of the "winds of heaven" that "blow." These powerful heavenly forces as essential in the organizing of nations and the guiding and blessing of individuals that therefore prosper the kingdoms in which they reside.

The Lord's omnipresence and penetrating spirit broods over humanity, and together with ministering angels work to persuade the peoples of the earth to do good, to achieve greatness, to accomplish much, thus fulfilling His purposes. He blesses the obedient and hedges up the way or curses the rebellious. The scriptures teach about the watchers, "angels sent forth from God, to whom is given power over the four parts of the earth, to save life and to destroy... having power to shut up the heavens, to seal up unto life, or to cast down to the regions of darkness" (Doctrine and Covenants 77:8). A multitude of divine factors are ever at play represented as winds that blow upon the sea.

The devil provides an opposing wind that churns chaos and brings strife, contention and machinations. His influence is seen in the brutality, unrest and disorder so common within the kingdoms of the earth. He destroys lives, families and peoples as they yield themselves to his spirit and influence. He enjoys great success among the peoples of the earth, many of whom suffer in sorrow, war and privation.

"As a consequence of stirring up the sea, four beasts arise, but as the subsequent context reveals, not simultaneously. Three beasts although differing one from another, have this in common, that each rises from the sea, i.e., represents a kingdom of human origin and nature."[8] Each kingdom in turn strengthens in power, prospers and exercises dominion for a season and then, as it decays in wickedness, is over thrown or breaks apart according to their works and the will of the God of Heaven.

The events of Daniel's vision follow the same pattern given to king Nebuchadnezzar in his dream (Chapter 2). He saw successive kingdoms represented by symbols incorporated in a great statue. The statue was imposing and impressive, made of gold, silver, brass, iron and clay. The figure's metallic components each signified a future kingdom. The glorious statue represented something with which the king could identify. Man considers empires to be magnificent and glorious powerful entities.[9] The statue served as an icon of future political powers in their strength and importance.

Like Nebuchadnezzar's dream, Daniel is also shown images, but not in the form of glorious statues of gold and silver, but as ferocious beasts: a lion, bear, leopard and an eclectic combination of beastly features. Joseph Smith clarified the purpose of the vision's symbols: "The prophets [Daniel and John] do not declare that they saw a beast or beasts, but that they saw the *image* or *figure* of a beast. Daniel did not see an actual bear or a lion, but the images or figures of those beasts. The translation should have been rendered 'image' instead of 'beast,' in every instance where beasts are mentioned by the prophets....When the prophets speak of seeing beasts in their visions, they mean that they saw the images, they being types to represent certain things. At the same time they received the interpretation as to what those images or types were designed to represent."[10] The prophet Joseph's explanation clarifies the abnormal characteristics of the beasts: lions and leopards with wings, the leopard with multiple heads. The bear held three ribs in its mouth and the multiformed fourth creature was made up of all the afore mentioned animals with added horns.

Daniel's vision presented the same earthly kingdoms seen by Nebuchadnezzar, but they were not noble or imposing statues, but rather fearsome, savage and abusive creatures. They are not always be admired as might man might do. Rather, they were presented from God's point of view. He drew out the metaphor of vicious animals, crafty and wild, that attack and devour prey.

While each earthly kingdom was indeed great, those who governed were fallen men, often brutal and murderous, susceptible to the faults and foibles of the natural man. The prophet Joseph elaborates further: "You see that the beasts are spoken of to represent the kingdoms of the world, the inhabitants whereof were beastly and abominable characters; they were murderers, corrupt, carnivorous, and brutal in their dispositions."[11] The lion, the bear, and the leopard were well-known ferocious creatures that hunted and exhibited dominance in their realms of influence. The ten-horned beast represented something powerful and to be dreaded if it were confronted as a foe. The prophet adds: "When God made use of the figure of a beast in visions to the prophets He did it to represent those kingdoms which had degenerated and become corrupt, savage and beast-like in their dispositions, even the degenerate kingdoms of the wicked world; but He never made use of the figure of a beast nor any of the brute kind to represent His kingdom."[12]

Keil observes: "There yet remains for our consideration the question, what are the historical world-kingdoms which are represented by Nebuchadnezzar's image (Dan. 2), and in Daniel's vision of four beasts rising up out of the sea? Almost all interpreters understand that these two great revelations are to be interpreted in the same way. 'The four kingdoms or dynasties, which were symbolized (Dan. 2) by the different parts of the human image, from the head to the feet, are the same as those which were symbolized by the four great beasts rising up out of the sea.' …. These four kingdoms, according to the interpretation commonly received…are the Babylonian, the Medo-Persian, the Macedo-Grecian, and the Roman empires."[13]

Historical accounts are replete with acts of brutality employed by the Babylonians, the Persians, Alexander and his Greek successors, and the Romans. They led powerful armies that crushed adversaries and obliterated cities and peoples as they conquered or when it was deemed necessary to maintain order. Oft times their governance practices employed cruel methods to enslave whole populations or subdue rebellions. In a few cases, exceptions like Cyrus were comparatively just and honorable, men of "boldness, courage, temperance, perseverance and generosity."[14] Nevertheless, the majority of rulers were disposed to deceitful crafts of inequity and intrigue; some were murderers, succumbing to the temptations common to those who covet great power, or they indulged in sexual gratification; all seemed to revel in opulence and fame. Too much success and prosperity emboldened the empires and the aristocracy with pride and avarice, which frequently wrought competition among fractious power mongers whose machinations resulted in assassinations and revolution.

Like their rulers, the nobility and the people often turned indulgent and became culturally coarse, even brutal. As society increased in wickedness, it would begin to reject and "revile against that which [was] good." (2 Ne. 28:16). They would, over time, "ripen in iniquity" until the cup of wickedness was full (Doctrine and Covenants 101:11; 18:; 29:9,103:3). The natural consequences of their actions would turn against them (Rev. 14:13; 3 Ne. 27:32). The despotic rulers would be deposed and the rebellious like Belshazzar would be removed. In many cases the kingdoms fall into internal unrest or civil war bringing famine and destruction. Outside forces generally combined to help bring about their destruction. In time the kingdom would be overthrown, broken or destroyed. The justice of God brings the natural consequences of actions, which when played out over time overtake the wicked to their downfall. The prophet Nephi spoke of this pattern in the 17th Chapter of 1 Nephi. (1 Ne. 17:35-37).

The kingdoms shown do not include all the dominions on the earth. By this time, several empires had already been established in the Far East. Notable and powerful tribes were spread across Africa and the mighty Nephite and Lamanite nations populated the Promised Land (1 Ne. 12:1-3). As far as we know none of these kingdoms were included in the vision. Daniel's dream focuses on the Gentile nations that would govern in the Middle Eastern lands, Europe, western Asia and northern Africa. It is worth noting that the Holy Land is situated centrally in the midst of all these kingdoms. The vision provides an important long-term perspective on kingdoms wherein the covenant people are placed squarely in the middle. By providing this visionary perspective, the covenant people can see the Lord's hand in their lives and the destiny of their nation. Let us review each of these four kingdoms in turn.

Artists rendition of the Lion with wings representing the Babylonian Empire

The First Beast – The Babylonian Empire

———

4   The first was like a lion, and had eagle's wings: I
beheld till the wings thereof were plucked, and it
was lifted up from the earth, and made stand upon
the feet as a man, and a man's heart was given to it.

———

The first image presented to Daniel is in the form of a lion
fitted with eagle's wings. "[It] corresponds to the head of gold in
Chapter 2 and stands for Babylon and represented the reign of
Nebuchadnezzar...The lion is the king of the beasts and the eagle
as the king of the birds, [which] well corresponds with gold (Dan.
2) the most precious of metals, Thus, Babylon is represented by the
lordliness of the animals."[15]

Scripturally and in Babylonian architecture, Babylon is
represented as both a lion and an eagle. Jeremiah spoke of
Nebuchadnezzar as a "lion...the destroyer of the Gentiles" (Jer.
4:7; see also 49:19); and as "a lion that had broken the bones of
the Assyrians and her neighbors" (Jer. 50:17, 44). Jeremiah applies
the symbol of a strong predator that overwhelms his prey just as
Babylon overthrew their Assyrian rivals. The lion characterizes
Nebuchadnezzar's great conquests throughout the region. It

possesses an unconquerable spirit, symbolic of a young energetic king that overran the Mideast from Tyre and Egypt to the borders of the Medes and the Arabians. His methods for maintaining order was more often strong and ruthless as a lion hunting prey.

When Zedekiah and the Jews rebelled against the Babylonian king, Nebuchadnezzar laid siege to the city. Eventually, his armies broke down the walls, and burned the central buildings, including the temple and captured thousands to be carried away and sold as slaves. The Jewish king Zedekiah saw his sons slain before his eyes. The guards were then ordered to "put out the eyes of Zedekiah, and bind him with fetters of brass, and carry him to Babylon." (2 Kgs. 25:7; See also Jer. 39:6-7; 52:10-11). These ruthless measures were exercised to establish supremacy over their foes and to bring order in the kingdom.

Like Jeremiah, Ezekiel also compared Babylon to "a great eagle with great wings, longwinged, full of feathers" (Ezek. 17:3, 12). The spread of the eagle's wings points to Babylon's range of influence that encompassed much of that region of the world. Nebuchadnezzar's father had already subdued Assyria, but "[his] swift conquests [were] depicted under the symbol of the lion and eagle's wings. The battle at Carchemish in 605 B.C., which humbled Egypt to Nebuchadnezzar, opened the way to the west."[16] Babylon's reach extended thousands of miles, even down into Ethiopia.

Nevertheless, Babylon's, or rather, Nebuchadnezzar's, wings were "plucked." The Lord subdued the king's passion for expansion and changed his attention towards building great cities and monuments in the Empire. His own statue served as one of many impressive projects (Dan. 3). Nebuchadnezzar looked inward to finish the great Babylonian temples and other structural icons, such as the hanging gardens or the great multi-faceted wall around the capital. Additionally, God purposed to temper the harsh and dynamic nature of the king. He would undergo his own personal trial, which wrought in him a mighty change of heart (Dan. 4:16). The king's chastening experience tutored him and he gained a greater understanding of the True God. The experience changed his nature and outlook from a self-willed and tyrannical monarch to one who ruled with greater charity and compassion, knowing of the greatness and strength of God. His heart mellowed with time and he gave consideration and care to his fellow man. Chapter 4 reveals the details of this tutoring experience.

While Daniel lived in the center of the Babylonian Empire and witnessed firsthand the governance and supremacy of the empire, he no doubt saw, through the Spirit, the whole scope of influence of this vast kingdom.

The Bear - The Medo-Persian Empire

> 5   And behold another beast, a second, like to a bear, and it raised up itself on one side, and it had three ribs in the mouth of it between the teeth of it: and they said thus unto it, Arise, devour much flesh.

A second beast comes into view, a fearsome and aggressive bear represented as the silver torso in Nebuchadnezzar's dream (Dan. 2:32, 35). While "the bear is inferior to the lion in strength and appearance, and is heavy and ungainly in its movements,"[17] it nonetheless represents a formidable predator and adversary. It was

Steve Creitz © Used with Permission

Artists rendition of the bear with three ribs representing the Medo-Persian Empire often considered second to lions in its ability to track and kill prey.

Daniel sees the bear rise up on one side. The description is difficult to envision; a bear rising up on a side or perhaps on its hind legs. The imagery provides an accurate portrayal of the simultaneous rise of the Median and Persian Empires and the eventual dominance of the Persians. The bear itself, or the ethnic peoples are the same—the early Iranian tribes—with one tribe that would come to dominate all others. "The animal itself, the bear, represents the Medo-Persian Empire, and the dual nature of this empire is symbolized by the beast lifting itself on one side."[18] Countless scholars have devoted considerable effort studying to provide a variety of alternative explanations for this image, but the historical realities match the symbol, the Medo-Persian empire is correct.

The Medes and the Persians are generally viewed as kindred nations. They have common roots that go back to the Iranic Aryan tribes that emerged in the regions of northern and western Iran about 1000 B.C.. For centuries they were nomadic and remained subservient tributaries to the Middle Assyrian and neo-Assyrian Empires.[19] But as they learned to master irrigation and agriculture and with the fall of the Assyrian Empire, the opportunity for the two most dominant Iranian tribes, the Medes and Persians, to exert their power in a mighty alliance became reality. The Medes had assisted Babylon in the capture of Nineveh in 612 B.C., which resulted in its overthrow in 605 B.C., and brought the rise and preeminence of the Babylonians. During the reign of Babylon both the Medes and the Persians unified other tribes to the two powerful nations. They grew in population, sophistication and influence with the Medes gaining a slight advantage.

Cyrus the Great unified both nations when "he rebelled against his grandfather, the Mede King, Astyages. He won a decisive victory in 550 B.C. resulting in Astyages' capture by his own dissatisfied nobles, who promptly turned him over to the triumphant king."[20] The familial, tribal and cultural connections that existed between the two kingdoms allowed for a relatively smooth transition under Cyrus, who united the peoples with him as king. President Wilford Woodruff had high regard and praise for Cyrus: "Now I have thought many times that some of those ancient kings that were raised up, had in some respects more regard for the carrying out of some of these principles and laws, than even the Latter-day Saints have in our day. I will take as an ensample Cyrus. ... To trace the life of Cyrus from his birth to his death, whether he knew it or not, it looked as though he lived by inspiration in all his movements. He began with that temperance and virtue which would sustain any Christian country or any Christian king. ... Many of these principles followed him, and I have thought many of them were worthy, in many respects, the attention of men who have the Gospel of Jesus Christ."[21]

Daniel sees that "*[the bear] had* three ribs in the mouth of it between the teeth of it" (Dan. 7:5). The ribs represent the remains of the prey or kingdoms subdued in the expansion of the Persian Empire. "Those who regard the second empire as Medo-Persian, have generally taken the ribs to Babylon, Lydia and Egypt."[22] Geographically, these kingdoms were the most proximate and therefore, were subjugated in the early years of Persia's expansion. In time, Persia's borders would far exceed those of Babylon, extending past ancient Lydia into Greece, up into the Black Sea region of Armenia and Azerbaijan in Central Asia. They also pushed east as far as India. While the three kingdoms or "ribs" were subsumed in Persia's initial campaigns, the kingdom grew to eventually include an estimated 50 million people,[23] which at the time was believed to be about 45% of the world population.[24] No subsequent empire fully reached the geographic size of ancient Persia, which came to be called by the founder Cyrus as the Achaemenid Empire. Even the vast Macedonian empire under Alexander was not so expansive.

Rise and Devour Much Flesh

Persian conquests were substantial military efforts, both logistically and in battle. The command to "arise, devour much flesh" (Dan. 7:5) was fulfilled with massive armies that marched to conquer in overpowering force. "A characteristic of the Medo-Persian [empire was its] method of waging war. It never moved unless it had an overwhelming force with which to crush all resistance. It was wasteful of human life...When Darius marched through Scythia for instance, he mobilized nearly three-quarters of a million men, not counting his fleet of six hundred ships. In Xerxes's [campaign against Greece, it is believed that] he took two and a half million troops with him; the movement of this mass of men looked more like a migration than an army. Even Persia's last and most pacific king brought more than a half million men to the Battle of Issus and two years after their defeat was able to find another million for his final battle [at Gaugamela]." Historians question the numbers given by ancient writers, but the principle of the Persians assembling incredible numbers in their armies and large impressive fleets is factual.[25]

The Persians gathered troops from all quarters of the kingdom and from neighboring allies. Herodotus mentions infantry from at least 47 nations[26] and warships came from as many as twelve maritime powers to help their campaign against the Greeks.[27] Phillips writes: "The policy of the Persian emperors was to fill the ranks of their armies with hordes of people from conquered lands, territories stretching all the way from India to the Mediterranean. Herodotus counted and described no less than fifty-six nationalities conscripted by Xerxes for his march against Greece. The feats of organization, the logistics and the provisioning of such enormous hordes staggers the imagination. And these troops were swelled by camp followers of all kinds. We can see the disregard for human life that was involved in these wars."[28]

Persian governance and administration was, for the most part organized, sensible and impressive. Cyrus set the tone in the kingdom by approaching rule with equity and benevolence. The Achaemenid Empire was organized into an estimated 23 major Satrapies or provinces, each led by trusted governors called satraps. The organization proved so successful that when Alexander conquered Persia, he kept much of the leadership and customs in place. He did so in part because they were effective, but also to conciliate the Persian elite.[29]

The Persians fostered great road works, city construction and expansion. They taught the arts, sciences and mathematics, and maintained a postal system. They even emancipated many slaves. The emperors loved gardening and created many beautiful and impressive garden grounds throughout the empire. Once in power

Artists rendition of the Leopard with four heads and four wings, the Grecian Empire

and their realms secure, they served as stabilizing overseers, bringing peace and prosperity. In this regard, they fulfilled the purposes of the Lord.

The Third Beast – The Macedonian-Greek Empire

6   After this I beheld, and lo another, like a leopard, which had upon the back of it four wings of a fowl; the beast had also four heads; and dominion was given to it.

Next, Daniel sees a third image of a beast, a powerful leopard fitted with four wings and four heads that rises and is given dominion over the inhabitants of the earth. In Nebuchadnezzar's dream this kingdom was presented as thighs of brass and represented the Grecian Empire (Dan. 2:32, 35). The leopard or panther, while still powerful and agile, "is neither so kingly as the lion nor so strong as the bear, but is like to both in rapacity, and superior to them in the springing agility with which it catches its prey."[30] Visually, a leopard with four wings and four heads is a curious image. But again, focus must be on the symbolism of the image rather than to attempt to conceive a literal picture of the figure.

Carlsberg Glyptotek © Used with Permission

Bust of Alexander the Great

Keil succinctly reveals that: "wings are everywhere an emblem of rapid motion; heads, on the contrary, where the beast signifies a kingdom, or are the heads of the kingdom."[31] If wings symbolized the empire's power to "move and act" (Doctrine and Covenants 77:4), then applied to the Macedonian armies and their ability to make rapid advancements and conquer in battle is both accurate and appropriate. Alexander the Great led swift campaigns from Greece to Hellespont on the tip of Lydia all the way to Babylon and on to India. Another less cited interpretation of the leopard was symbolized by the use of leopard or panther pelts on the backs of the Macedonian cavalry, known as the *Hetairoi*, or the Companion Cavalry. These riders represented the elite regiment of which Alexander was the commander[32] and was composed primarily of the Macedonian royalty and aristocracy.[33] Alexander's cavalry proved a key advantage in battle and helped the Greeks strike decisive wins against their foes.

Alexander's Youth and Rise in Power

From the day Alexander took a command in the Macedonian army at age 16, he never lost a battle.[34] He proved a brilliant tactician and exceeded all others in warfare strategy, a quality which he proved over and over again throughout his campaigns. The Greek armies were not nearly as numerous as were the Persians. Generally, they attacked with between 35,000 and 50,000 hoplites or *pezhetairoi*, also known as the "foot companions."[35] The Macedonians foot soldiers and calvary were professionally trained and led by excellent generals accomplished in battle tactics. Alexander's father, Philip was a "ferocious disciplinarian…he trained and drilled his troops repeatedly,"[36] which created a familiarity in the army and bred

Johnny Shumate © Used with Permission
The Greek hoplites ready for battle in Phalanx formation

cohesion in the stress of battle.[37] One of the most effective and enduring military formations in Greek warfare was the Phalanx, which is interpreted in Greek as the finger. The Phalanx formation moved in close-rank, dense grouping of warriors armed with long spears with sarissas (long sharp tips) and interlocking shields. It was like an ancient form of tank, difficult to penetrate and a lethal advancing force.

The Macedonians mastered warfare using the Phalanx combined with the adept and swift support of cavalry. Unlike the Persians who massed hundreds of thousands of mostly enlisted troops, Greek armies were well-trained, conditioned and battle hardened professionals familiar with field tactics and strategy, which Phillip had drummed into their every fiber.[38]

The Macedonians began the conquest of fellow Greeks by first subduing rival states such as Athens, Sparta, Thebes and Thrace. After his father died, Alexander continued to secure Greek loyalty until he controlled the entire peninsula. His passion, however, quickly turned to the conquest of Asia and within a few years, he began expansion of the empire by crossing into Lydia at Hellespont (Istanbul, Turkey). Having perfected his style of warfare in campaigns against his fellow Greeks, he sought to prove his troops against the Persians.

The leopard's four wings would come to represent the speed of expansion and geographical reach of Alexander and his Macedonian armies. They swept across the Persian Empire of Darius II from Lydia to Egypt, to Babylon, Bactria (Afghanistan) and the Indus Valley in India (Modern Pakistan). "The lightning character of his conquest is without precedent in the ancient world. And this is full in keeping with the speed embodied in the leopard and the four wings in his back."[39] His juggernaut forces captured the Persian empire in just twelve years, a feat that might have taken three lifetimes under most kings. He secured major victories over regions and strongholds almost every year until he penetrated India. He had already drawn up plans to take his Hoplites west to the Empire of Carthage (Tunisia), Hispania and Britannia and move south into Arabia, which he would have done had he lived longer.[40] His spirit seemed to thrill at the thought of battle, conquest and expansion of the empire.

Alexander's conquests opened the door for the dissemination of classic Hellenism eastward into Asia. Its philosophical ideals and cultural influences poured into the art, architecture, science, language and government. While Alexander was Greek, a student of Aristotle, the advancement of Hellenism was not his highest priority. In reality when he married Roxana, the Persian princess of Bactria, his Greek companions were dismayed.[41] He encouraged even mandated that the Macedonian elite follow his example to marry other royal Persian women, a practice that caused serious discord among the Greek generals and troops.[42] Nevertheless, Hellenism's influence poured into the region and was upheld by the subsequent kings and administrations. Koine Greek became the predominant language used in trade, education and government. Hellenistic thought and culture dominated both traditional Greek cities and non-Greek communities alike, influences which remained into the Roman Empire and the ministry of the Savior. In reality, the widespread influence of Greek culture helped pave the way for the promulgation of the Gospel. While there was much in Greek Hellenism to be admired, the pagan application of many elements ran counter to the Gospel and proved problematic culturally to both the Jews and later to the Christians.

Alexander's life and reign was a brief 32 years. He died abruptly from illness and over drinking. Foul play and complications from a serious injury received in India have not been ruled out. In June of 323 B.C., He died in the palace of Nebuchadnezzar, in Babylon, at the age of 32. His death came at the peak of his power and upon his death, the kingdom was divided among his generals. Antigonus, followed by Cassander, retained Macedonia (Greece); Lysimachus took Asia Minor and Thrace; Perdiccas and later Seleucus I, retained Syria, Babylonia and the majority of Asia to India; and Ptolemy ruled in Egypt and Arabia Petrea, which included Palestine.[43]

The leopard's four heads represented the four kings and the major kingdoms carved out of Alexander's vast empire. "The heads indicate that in contrast with earlier beasts that had only one head, the third empire would have four governmental divisions with corresponding heads."[44] Biblical accounts have portrayed kings using the symbols of both horns and heads (Zech. 1:18-19, Dan. 7 and 8; Rev 13:1, 11; 17:3,7,12,16). The symbol used on the leopard is fitted with heads.[45] In subsequent verses of this chapter, the term "horn" is used to describe future kings and kingdoms (Dan. 7:7-8,1, 21-21, 24-25).

This Greek empire described in the vision is the "third kingdom under the providence of God. It can conquer and rule only because God gives it power to do so."[46] Alexander brought a dynamic personality, passion and military skill to command the Macedonian armies and to organize an empire, but he would not be allowed to retain the kingdom. Once the Lord's purposes were fulfilled, Alexander was removed and the empire was divided into smaller kingdoms. In this way, a balance of power was established across the region. Greek influence expanded according to the limits set by the Lord.

The Forth Beast - Roman Empire and European Kingdoms

7   After this I saw in the night visions, and behold a fourth beast, dreadful and terrible, and strong exceedingly; and it had great iron teeth: it devoured and brake in pieces, and stamped the residue with

the feet of it: and it was diverse from all the beasts that were before it; and it had ten horns.

8   I considered the horns, and, behold, there came up among them another little horn, before whom there were three of the first horns plucked up by the roots: and, behold, in this horn were eyes like the eyes of man, and a mouth speaking great things.

———

The vision continues with a fourth beast described as "dreadful and terrible and strong exceedingly" (Dan. 7:7). The Roman Empire and the Gentile kingdoms that followed are represented in the fourth beast. It was portrayed in Nebuchadnezzar's dream as the legs of Iron and the feet (or toes) of clay (Dan. 2:33, 40). "The empire had [previously] been symbolized by legs of iron that took up half the total height of the image. The iron depicted the great strength of the Roman Empire. The long legs revealed that the Roman Empire, and later the divided Byzantine Empire, would far out last the others."[47] Rome's reign lasted nearly 1000 years. Even after it was broken, its influence continued to be felt into the latter-days.

Brief overview of the Rise of Rome

Rome's history and rise to power is complex, perhaps more complicated than the previous kingdoms combined. A complete review of Roman history is neither possible nor practical for this book. A brief overview is, however, helpful to understanding the overall meaning of the vision.

Rome initially obtained power by gaining independence from the Etruscans in 509 B.C. It coalesced from smaller groups as a city-state in Latium and grew as it allied or subdued a confederation of the Latin tribes along the western coast of central Italy. Almost from its inception it had democratic roots; a king worked with a representative Senate (*senatus*), or council. While the Senate had existed since 753 B.C. after the defeat of the Etruscans, Rome formed a republic under a Senate and replaced the king with two consuls.[48] The Latin letters *SPQR* symbolized *Senātus Populusque Rōmānus*, meaning "The Roman Senate and People," or "The Senate and People of Rome."[49] This symbolized the ideology that inspired

© Used with Permission

Ruins of the forum and Colosseum in the ancient city of Rome

Roman culture for centuries. Even after the Emperors took power, pride in the representative Senate remained a powerful influence. The historian Le Glay argues that Rome's spirit of a representative republic still thrives in nations today.[50]

Rome conquered or incorporated rival tribes (Samnites, Lucani and Sabini) of Italy over a period of 230 years. By 266-265 B.C. the Roman Republic had consolidated its power over much of the southern Italian peninsula. The Mediterranean rival Carthage threatened its expansion and security, which triggered the first Punic War and resulted in Rome's occupation of Sicily in 241 B.C..[51] As a result of their victory, Rome rapidly moved to dominate the Mediterranean Sea, and began campaigns into Illyria (Croatia, Bosnia and Albania), which was governed by the *Greeks.*

In 202 B.C. a second Punic War ensued with Carthage and Hannibal. In a campaign of revenge, he marched troops to the walls of Rome, threatening the republic itself. But in the end, Hannibal was defeated in the Battle of Zama near Carthage, in North Africa.[52] Rome's victory continued the policy of the empire expansion with the acquisition of the former Carthaginian territories as they expanded into Hispania (Spain), establishing the provinces of Hispania Ulterior and Hispania Citerior on the Iberian Peninsula (197 B.C.).

Rome pushed more forcefully eastward into Greece and Macedonia, eventually crushing both Greek and Seleucid (Syrian) forces in separate campaigns spanning a decade (196-188 B.C.). They ultimately subdued Greece in a series of victories spanning over 30 years, defeating Perseus, son of Phillip V in 168 B.C. and finally quelling a last uprising in the fourth Macedonian War (150-146 B.C.). Roman troops moved across the Hellespont and by ship across the Mediterranean into the ancient kingdoms of Lydia and Phrygia (133 B.C.), who bequeathed their kingdoms without a major conflict.

In 109 B.C. the Romans suffered from serious incursions by tribes on their northern borders. Feeling threatened, they moved to subjugate the Celts in northern Italy and the Gauls in France. The general Gaius Marius won two victories over the numerous Cimbri and Teutones tribes by slaughtering hundreds of thousands of nomadic Gauls and German tribesmen (104-103 B.C.).

In 64-63 B.C., general Pompey swept south from Lydia into the Middle East overrunning the remnants of the Seleucid Empire (Syria) to take Judea (64-63 B.C.). Julius Caesar completed the subjugation of the Gauls, through what many considered a genocidal campaign, as he moved Roman influence into northern France and across the channel into southern Britannia (55 B.C.).

The transition from Republic to Empire came about with the rise of Julius Caesar and through a series of internal civil strifes. Augustus secured control as Emperor in the famous battle of Actium against Mark Antony in 31 B.C. Augustus's reign initiated a long period of relative peace. It was in this season of *Pax Romana* that the Savior was born (Luke 2) and the promulgation of the Gospel began. Later in 43 A.D., Emperor Claudius continued in Britannia where Julius Caesar had started and failed. He also pushed northward into France, Switzerland and as far as the Rhine river of Germany (84 A.D.).[53] Tajan added Davia beyond the Danube among the German tribes and subdued the Parthians in Mesopotamia (Northern Iraq).[54] But by 300 A.D. the empire separated into two major kingdoms, the eastern Byzantine Empire in Constantinople and the traditional western Roman Empire.

Eventually, by 476 A.D., Rome was overrun by the "barbarians" and the western Empire separated into autonomous nations with the central authority regaining strength under the Holy Roman Church and Charlemagne. Most of the European nations became their own sovereign powers and ruled under the dominion of local kings.

Daniel Unsettled by the Fourth Beast

Unlike the previous beasts, Daniel's impression of this fourth was filled with horror. It is unclear exactly why he reacts this way, as all of the kingdoms demonstrated a propensity to be ruthless and brutal to any who opposed them. However, there are clear and abundant examples of the Romans exercising special vindictiveness to defeat foes or to subdue or punish rebellious tribes, communities and nations. Rome obliterated their rival Carthage in the third Punic War (149–146 B.C.), wherein they burned the city, enslaved the population and systematically sowed salt into the fields to prevent the planting of crops. They overran barbarian tribes and clansmen who resisted them, killing tens of thousands, if not hundreds of thousands. Roman soldiers trampled tribes and communities in Britannia in an effort to subdue the Druid resistance. The Jews in Galilee and Jerusalem were massacred by centurion soldiers to quell the rebellion in 67-70 A.D. Roman legions slaughtered over a million Jews throughout Judea. Titus,

James Tissot © Used with Permission
The Centurion (Le Centurion) Brooklyn Museum

embarrassed at the brutality of his troops, chastened them for overreaching,[55] but the death and carnage was done.

All are examples of Rome's harsh and methodical conquering methods and governance practices. The record says that they first "devoured and brake in pieces" (Dan. 7:7) by overwhelming and humiliating peoples with their armies. The beast was fitted with great iron teeth that broke and tore its prey and stamped down any resistance (Dan. 7:7). The stamping of the "residue with the feet of it" represented its iron rule. There was no tolerance for rebellion against Rome and they trampled all opposition and rebellions with impunity.

No doubt Daniel witnessed Roman soldiers clad in iron and crimson as they marched into Hispania, Gaul and Britannia, or across the Mediterranean and North Africa. The Romans took slavery and capital punishment to a new level, capturing and selling millions and imposing harsh punishments such as crucifixion. They sacrificed men at the hands of other men or to beasts in the gladiator games of the grandiose circus in the Colosseum. Uprisings from slaves within the Republic brought on the Servile Wars (135-132 B.C., 104-100 B.C.), which featured serious unrest in Sicily and later in central Italy where the gladiator Spartacus lead a three-year revolt against the empire (73-71 B.C.). All three major uprisings were crushed and thousands of defectors were crucified along the roads. Perhaps Daniel witnessed the crucifixion of the Savior, Himself, at the hands of Roman soldiers. Whatever was shown in the vision sickened his spirit and filled him with dread and disgust.

But not all was death and carnage, nor were all of Rome's enemies victims. Ancient altars near Carthage show grizzly evidence of human sacrifice, primarily infant sacrifice. Similar rites were had among the various tribes in Europe, especially among the Druids of Britain. In some respects, the peoples conquered were indeed barbarians, as the Romans called them, and Rome brought order and civilization, even if at a terrible price. Those who submitted to Roman rule were protected and prospered under a well-organized, evenly administered communities. The Greek born Polybius "justified Rome's domination by the excellence of its institutions (which he judged well balanced) and by the superiority of its army, though adding an important factor in a world permeated by the divine. 'It is in the domain of religious concepts that the superiority of the Roman state is at its greatest' (VIII.56)"[56]

Citizens and nations of the Empire enjoyed the benefits of *Pax Romana*, an environment of stability and peace that enabled commerce, education, the arts and literature. A suitable living was available for many, including many of the servant slaves, who often worked to purchase their freedom. It was the setting in which the Savior undertook to conduct His ministry and the environment wherein the Gospel prospered across the Empire for a season. But the Roman system, under the Emperors, also proved to be the same force by which the Primitive Church was brutalized and scattered, leaving the remnants in a state of Apostasy.

"The Roman Empire gradually grew for four centuries (reaching its pinnacle at 60 million inhabitants in A.D. 117. This was in contrast to the sudden rise and fall of the preceding empires. It likewise declined slowly, beginning in the third century. The decline became obvious in the fifth century A.D. with [Roman legions] leaving Britain and Rome being sacked in A.D. 410 by the Visigoths. It was not until A.D. 1453 that the last Byzantine ruler was killed in battle when Mehmed II conquered Constantinople."[57] The remnants of the Empire separated into many smaller kingdoms described in the vision as ten horns. These were primarily composed of European and Middle Eastern nations from Portugal to Russia and from Tunisia to Pakistan. These kingdoms ebb and surged in power and dominance for centuries and most remain as countries in the latter-days or times of the Gentiles. The era of the ten horns is characterized either by major conflicts between the Christians and Muslims or wars among kingdoms themselves.

Rome's dominance lasted for more than 500 years, longer than the Babylonian (70), Persian (200) and Macedonian (180) kingdoms combined. Its influence, its civil governance and justice system, its medical and scientific advances, its adaptation of Greek architecture, literature and philosophy endured for more than a millennium and still permeate governments, justice systems and society today.

The Little Horn

Daniel sees an ominous figure emerge from among the ten horns in the latter-days. It is presented as a "little horn [that] arises" to power and "three of the first horns plucked up by the roots" (Dan. 7:8). The three horns make up a portion of the original ten. The roots of the kingdoms are symbols of traditions, culture and ancestry. The "uprooting" comes in combination with the rise of the "little horn." It first involves conquest and then the subversion of cultural traditions and ethnic roots. It also means the systematic incorporation of political and philosophical ideologies, and it includes the dissolution of existing regimes, the overthrow of political systems and the realigning of national borders.

The number three (3 of 10) has proportional meaning and should be interpreted like the number 1/3, which John frequently used in the Revelation (Rev. 8:7-12).[59] Three signifies that a limited portion of the ten kingdoms came under control of the little horn.

In the twentieth century, Marxist communists swept into power in Eastern Europe and uprooted many traditional, cultural and political systems, beginning with the October Revolution of 1917. Joseph Stalin solidified their grip on power through the horrors of collectivization and his terrible purges. During and after World War II, Stalin and the Soviets extended the Marxist system into the whole of Eastern Europe including Central Asian countries like Yugoslavia, Georgia and Uzbekistan. They began a systematic indoctrination of communism and atheistic philosophies among all the countries conquered. Mao Zedong led a similar revolution in China, where the communist party obtained control in 1947. Both regimes spread Communist ideology and control through force and intimidation for most of the twentieth century. Other successes were had in places like Vietnam and Pol Pot's Cambodia. President Ezra Taft Benson said of this latter-day geopolitical threat: "Never before on the face of this earth have the forces of evil and the forces of good been as well organized. Now is the great day of the devil's power, with the greatest mass murderers of all time living among us [meaning on the earth]."[60] President Benson spoke of the Communists centered in Russia and China.

For the majority of the twentieth century, the Communists worked to expand Marxist doctrines and grow influence throughout the world. Ultimately, the Soviet Union collapsed in the late 1980s under the weight of their rigid totalitarian control and a failed economy. China was forced to enacted economic and political reforms to maintain control. Despite the failures, the doctrines of state centered government remains alive and well in the world, especially in the university and among government elites.

The Stalinist, Pol Pot   Adolf Hitler

Mao Zedong   Joseph Stalin

After the fall of the Soviet Union, elements of the corrupt political apparatus and entrenched bureaucratic cabals within Russia persisted. While many hoped the Communist fall would bring the dawn of a new liberal democratic Russia, the situation deteriorated into an autocratic regime under a rejuvenated corrupt pay-to-play kleptocracy.[61] These strong political figures combined to create another totalitarian regime wherein an elite few control major sectors of the economy, trade and the military; and therefore, the country.

Daniel sees that the "little horn" or anti-Christ is a person with "eyes like the eyes of man," and "a mouth speaking great things" (Dan 7:8). And in fact, he is a man. Keil compares the latter-day tyrant to Antiochus Epiphanies and his rise to power as described in Chapter 8. The language suggests that "it [the little horn] arose out of littleness' there lies the idea that [he] grew to great power from a small beginning; for [he] became very great, i.e., powerful." [62]

The origins of the latter-day little horn stems from small beginnings or ordinary social conditions. But employing the force of personality, a drive for status, combined with craftiness of deceit and corruption, he rises through the ranks to a position of great power. Similar historical examples include: Adolf Hitler, Joseph Stalin, Mao and Napoleon, who all began in relatively "little" circumstances. This latter-day anti-Christ emerges from a similar background, but will persist in his craft until he rises to the top.

The little horn demonstrates a proficiency to speak great words and to persuade the peoples and kingdoms. In addition to the talent of persuasion, and perhaps more importantly, he leverages economic and military resources to rejuvenate the "empire." The combination of his personal qualities and his many resources opens up opportunities to influence international policy, create alliances and solidify his preeminence in the community of countries. Both John's and Daniel's visions show that he will be successful. John records that in the latter days the "ten horns which thou sawest are ten kings, which have received no kingdom as yet; but receive power as kings one hour with the beast. *These have one mind, and shall give their power and strength unto the beast.*" (Rev. 17:12-13, emphasis added).

> the little horn, "shall make war with the Lamb" or as the record says, he "shall wear out the saints of the most High, and think to change times and laws"

The little horn or beast, as John calls him, will successfully create alliances that unite the leaders of the ten horns. The combination of powerful resources, military armies and bribes enable this cabal of autocrats (kings) to influence control over the nations. Once the alliance is in place, Ezekiel says they will combine forces to march against the nation of Israel (Ezek. 38-39).

John also speaks of a False Prophet who becomes a key player in the alliance with the beast and the nations (Rev. 13:11-15; 16:13). The joining of the beast and the false prophet foretells of a sordid combination between political governments and corrupt religious groups. The false prophet figure could be interpreted in several ways, but certainly radical Jihadists in the Middle East, North

Africa and Europe will be part of the fulfillment of the prophecy. Fundamentalists continue to gain influence among the Muslim peoples forming their own political and religious centers of power. The struggle—or great Jihad—focuses on establishing again the promised worldwide Islamic Caliphate. Under a self-proclaimed successor to the prophet Muhammad (the 12th Imam), Jihadists will rally to forcibly establish Sharia law as the preeminent system and do so by waging war against "the infidel."

A diabolical, but primary goal of the Jihadists, will be to coerce the conversion, eviction or destruction non-Muslims living in their own lands and to make war with the Christian and Jewish nations. In addition, they will sound the call to fulfill a long held manifesto to annihilate Israel, pushing the Jewish people out of their land into the sea.[63] Statements outlining this goal are already in the charters of nations like Iran and of radical groups such as Hezbollah, Hamas, and ISIS. The prophecy foresees that radical Islamic states and their satellite surrogates will ally with the little horn (eighth beast) and combine their resources to war against Israel. Given current latter-day conditions, it is reasonable to assume the Jihadists will continue to export terror and violence to disrupt nations and government in most every other area of the world.

With the general rise of wickedness, the false prophet will not be limited to Islamic radicals, but will include other major religious groups and organizations as well. Nephi describes the mixture of latter-day anti-Christs as follows: "…But it is the kingdom of the devil, which shall be built up among the children of men, *which kingdom is established among them which are in the flesh.* For the time speedily shall come that all churches which are built up to get gain, and all those who are built up to get power over the flesh, and those who are built up to become popular in the eyes of the world, and those who seek the lusts of the flesh and the things of the world, and to do all manner of iniquity; yea, in fine, all those who belong to the kingdom of the devil are they who need fear, and tremble, and quake; they are those who must be brought low in the dust; they are those who must be consumed as stubble; and this is according to the words of the prophet" (1 Ne. 22:22-23). Elder Neal

A. Maxwell taught that this "church", [meaning the church of the devil] comprised an eclectic consolidation of many kingdoms, both political, religious and in other forms.[64]

The alliance between the little horn and the false prophet will emerge as a powerful and potent force in the world. The beast's thirst for conquest and the false prophets quest for religious dominance will threaten the stability of humankind and bring the foretold calamites of Armageddon and terror to billions (Doctrine and Covenants 87:6). Daniel's vision also reveals that the little horn, "shall make war with the Lamb" (Rev. 17:14) or as the record says, he "shall wear out the saints of the most High, and think to change times and laws" (Dan. 7:25). The term little horn can also be extended generally to those who oppose the Saints the doctrines of their Redeemer. More will be discussed on this later.

The Thrones Cast Down

The natural course of their dark alliance and murderous works plays out in the vision. Conflict and war, cultural and political strife, wickedness and unrest all permeate the world. So much unrest and conflict is sown that eventually the kingdoms of the earth are thrown down and left in ruin.

> 9   I beheld till the thrones were cast down, and the Ancient of days did sit, whose garment *was* white as snow, and the hair of his head like the pure wool: his throne *was like* the fiery flame, and his wheels as burning fire.
>
> 10 A fiery stream issued and came forth from before him: thousand thousands ministered unto him, and ten thousand times ten thousand stood before him: the judgment was set, and the books were opened.

At some point, the focus of the vision shifts. The subject moves from the beastly kingdoms and anti-Christs to a council of heavenly beings. Despite the change in venue, Daniel's vision is continuous and remains in the context of the events in motion. The council convenes to rule on the state of affairs among the nations. They will judge the beast's alliance, its objectives and works and what is to become of it. At the head of this council is the Ancient of Days. The title means "one of advanced days or the oldest man."[65] By revelation, we understand that Adam is the oldest or most ancient man. The scriptures also refer to him as Michael, or the archangel, the head of the heavenly hosts (Doctrine and Covenants 27:11; 107:54; 116:1; 138:38; 128:21, Dan. 10:13, 21).

Daniel provides a brief description of Adam as a glorious being of majesty and beauty to whom thousands and tens of thousands attend. He is depicted as a personage in the likeness of God. His hair is white as snow, and his countenance shines with glory and his presence projects the heat of fire. "The white garment of the judge indicates both majestic dignity and purity."[66] Even his "wheels," or chariot is covered with fire. With such an impressive description, one might easily misinterpret him to be Christ or even the Father. But the ancient figure at the head of the council is Michael, the Prince of the holy people, the archangel.

The Gospel promises a glorious resurrection to all who remain faithful and inherit the celestial kingdom. They become just men made perfect, beings of impressive and noble character, they are like unto God (1 Cor. 15:40; 1 Jn. 3:2, Doctrine and Covenants 76:50-70, 92-96). John, the Apostle, taught: "Beloved, now are we the sons of God, and it doth not yet appear what we shall be: but we know that, when he shall appear, we shall be like him; for we shall see him as he is" (1 John 3:2). Daniel's descriptive account of Adam is a testament of the fulfillment of this glorious doctrine.

The purpose of the council declared is "the judgment;" not the final judgment (Rev 20), but a hearing to judge the little horn and the nations of the world. The Lord taught that the Father had given Him responsibility to preside at the great and final judgment (John 5:22). Three verses later Daniel records that Christ, the Son of Man, comes to the Ancient of Days at the council (Dan. 7:13). Adam "sits" or presides at the council that judges world conditions brought about by the little horn and his alliance. The judgment seems to be in the form of a trial. The proceedings involve heavenly records that contain the acts of men, with the principle subject being the works of the little horn and the corrupt alliance of nations.

The prophet Lehi was given a record similar to the one reviewed in Michael's court (Dan. 7:10). Lehi's account proclaimed the abominations of Jerusalem and then decreed destructions against the city and her inhabitants based on their works (1 Ne 1:11-13). In consequence of the immoral condition of Jerusalem, the record pronounces that "it should be destroyed, and the inhabitants thereof; many should perish by the sword, and many should be carried away captive into Babylon" (1 Ne. 1:13). Ezekiel had a similar experience regarding the same situation in Jerusalem (Ezek. 2:9-10).

Adam's council reviews the actions of the beast and adjudicates his works. In the end, he is found worthy of removal. The beast's kingdom, his alliance and for that matter the whole kingdom of the devil is decreed to end (Dan. 5:27; 7:11). The outcome of the council is "set" (Dan. 7:10) and the verdict is pronounced. The beast's earthly throne is to be cast down and the kingdom destroyed.

Earlier in Daniel's record, Nebuchadnezzar spoke of "watchers" (Dan. 4:13, 17, 23) or angels of authority who oversee the kingdoms of the earth. These angels record the acts of men (3 Ne. 27:26) and execute the decrees of God. Later, we learn that these "watchers" play a prominent role in the successes or failures of the nations. One "watcher" was engaged in defending the king of Persia for a time (Dan. 10:13, 21). The record does not relay any specifics, nor the extent of their involvement, but shows that heavenly representatives are indeed engaged in the destiny and affairs of men on the earth. Chief among the watchers is Michael (Dan. 12:1) who executes and coordinates all heavenly designs and purposes for the inhabitants of the earth according to the will of God.

While a verdict is declared, it seems that the purpose of Adam's council goes beyond the scope of determining the fate of the beast alone. Phillips writes that: "The rendering 'I beheld till the thrones were cast down' can [also] be translated 'I beheld till thrones were set.'"[67] A dual meaning is assigned to the statement. The kingdoms of the world are to be cast away and at the same time the Kingdom of God set up. This record reveals that not only does the Ancient of Days judge the fate of nations, but also prepares the way for

Christ, the Son of God, to take the kingdom and with Him the Saints receive inheritance in that kingdom (Dan. 7:14).

The Great Council at Adam-ondi-Ahman

Daniel's record is the only Biblical account that speaks of this great council. However, latter-day revelations add light to Michael's visitation and the purpose of the grand meeting. Modern scripture and prophets tell us that it is a General Conference and those in attendance include representatives of the great dispensational leaders, "watchers," other important figures and members. The location is a place called Adam-ondi-Ahman.

Additional background in Doctrine and Covenants 107, which says: "Three years previous to the death of Adam, he called Seth, Enos, Cainan, Mahalaleel, Jared, Enoch and Methuselah, who were High Priests, with the residue of his posterity, who were righteous, into the valley of Adam-ondi-Ahman, and there bestowed upon them his last blessing. And the Lord appeared unto them, and they rose up and blessed Adam, and called him Michael, the Prince, the archangel. And the Lord administered comfort unto Adam, and said unto him, I have set thee to be at the head: a multitude of nations shall come of thee, and thou art a Prince over them forever" (Doctrine and Covenants 107:53-55). The ancient Patriarchs gathered to receive instructions and give honor to Adam just prior to his death. At that first great priesthood meeting, Adam was set as prince over the nations. As the prince of humankind, he holds keys over the human family, including the priesthood organization under Christ. In this station, he has the right to sit in judgment over the works of mortal men and to execute heavenly decrees according to the will of Christ and the Father.

In the latter-day council, they will gather again at Adam-ondi-Ahman. During the march of Zion's Camp (May-June 1837), Heber C. Kimball, Brigham Young and a few of the early brethren went with Joseph Smith to see the place where Adam offered sacrifice and met with the ancient priesthood brethren. Heber's account reads as follows: "The Prophet Joseph called upon Brother Brigham, myself and others, saying, 'Brethren, come, go along with me, and I will show you something,' He led us a short distance to a place where were the ruins of three altars built of stone, one above the other, and one standing a little back of the other, like unto the pulpits in the Kirtland Temple, representing the order of three grades of Priesthood; 'There,' said Joseph, 'is the place where Adam offered up sacrifice after he was cast out of the garden.' The altar stood at the highest point of the bluff. I went and examined the place several times while I remained there."[68]

In addition to the meeting of judgement, we learn that attendees in this meeting will give an account of their stewardship in the kingdom of God over all the ages of the earth.[69] This meeting is set in preparation for the Millennial reign of the Savior. Elder Bruce R. McConkie wrote: "Adam... will call his children together and hold a council with them to prepare them for the coming of the Son of Man. By his children it is meant the residue of his posterity that are righteous; all of his posterity are not to be involved, only those— as it was in the days of the original Adam-ondi–Ahman—who are worthy...all who have held keys shall stand before him who holds all the keys. They will be called upon to give an account of their stewardships and to report how and in what manner they have used their priesthood and their keys for the salvation of men within the sphere of their appointments."[70]

Each leader in attendance—from Adam to Enoch and Noah, to Abraham and Moses, to Peter and the Twelve Apostles, and finally to Joseph Smith—will each give an account of their stewardship and performance in their dispensation. It seems logical that each prophet provides records as evidence of his works and stewardship. The records in heaven will be opened and read, witnessing of their obedience and accounting for their stewardship.

Just as Daniel's vision presents in that hour the Son of Man will appear to receive their reports and then declare His eminent return (Dan. 7:13-14). President Joseph Fielding Smith also commented of His appearance at the meeting: "Adam will direct this judgment, and then he will make his report, as the one holding the keys for this earth, to his Superior Officer, Jesus Christ. Our Lord will then assume the reins of government; directions will be given to the Priesthood; and He, whose right it is to rule, will be installed officially by the voice of the Priesthood there assembled."[71] Adam will [surrender] to Christ all authority. "Then Adam will be confirmed in his calling as the prince over his posterity and will be officially installed and crowned eternally in this presiding calling."[72] This gathering of the children at Adam-ondi-Ahman will involve thousands of participants, even tens of thousands, and will be one of the greatest conferences ever convened on the earth.

By the end of the conference, Christ will take His rightful place on the throne as King of kings and Ruler over the earth. His Millennial reign is imminent. The council will adjourn to execute the verdict on the fate of the beast and the earthly kingdoms.

Beast Thrown into the Flame of Fire

11 I beheld then because of the voice of the great words which the horn spake: I beheld even till the beast was slain, and his body destroyed, and given to the burning flame.

12 As concerning the rest of the beasts, they had their dominion taken away: yet their lives were prolonged for a season and time.

The vision returns back to the beast and his doomed dominion. The council's judgment is executed and the beast is slain and his body given to burning flames. Both physical and spiritual interpretations apply to this imagery. The actual man, who is the anti-Christ, dies by the decrees of God and his soul is cast into hell. There he suffers intense misery as the eternal flames of torment sear his conscience for the vile atrocities he has committed (Rev. 21:8; cf. Rev. 20:14). The beast's kingdom and the kingdoms over which he presides are also destroyed. Those nations and leaders who supported the "little horn" are overthrown in a combination of natural disasters and war. Their punishment is similar to the fate of the beastly leader. Modern Babylon is destroyed and their wicked inhabitants cast into the flames of hell.

John's Revelation says that the "ten horns which thou sawest upon the beast, these shall hate the whore, and shall make her desolate and naked, and shall eat her flesh, and burn her with fire." (Rev. 17:16). The consequences of the wicked, those who have yielded to the spirit of the destroyer (Doctrine and Covenants 105:15), bring consuming judgements that strip modern Babylon naked. She is burned in the carnage of war and anarchy. The Lord executes vengeance on the kingdom of the beast. He has stated: "I will send a fire on Magog, and among them that dwell carelessly in the isles: and they shall know that I *am* the Lord" (Ezek. 39:6). Nephi reports that "every nation which shall war against thee, O house of Israel, shall be turned one against another, and they shall fall into the pit which they digged to ensnare the people of the Lord. And all that fight against Zion shall be destroyed, and that great whore, who hath perverted the right ways of the Lord, yea, that great and abominable church, shall tumble to the dust and great shall be the fall of it." (1 Ne. 22:14)

Additional details surrounding the downfall of the anti-Christ and his kingdom will be reviewed later in Chapters 11-12. Daniel is content to relate that the kingdoms of the world are thrown down and the Kingdom of Christ is given to the saints (Dan. 7:14). "The passage is another illustration of how quickly God can dispose of the mightiest of earthly rulers, and how evil men are ultimately brought to divine judgment."[73]

Finally, Daniel comments on the remnants of the previous beastly kingdoms. The "lives" of the nations that came from ancient Babylon, Persia, the Macedonian-Greek empire and ancient Rome were "prolonged" (Dan. 7:12). The Lord will surely make a full end of all sovereign governments (Doctrine and Covenants 87:6; see also: Jer. 46:28), but the kindred families of the earth, the ethnic peoples, their cultures and righteous traditions will persist in their many curious and divers forms. The numerous peoples and nations of the earth will retain their rich traditions and cultures, which will persist into the millennium. When the Lord returns, He brings with Him the Kingdom of Heaven, which becomes the ruling government over the remnants who endured the events of His Coming.

Christ Takes the Kingdom

---

13 I saw in the night visions, and, behold, one like the Son of man came with the clouds of heaven, and came to the Ancient of days, and they brought him near before him.

14 And there was given him dominion, and glory, and a kingdom, that all people, nations, and languages, should serve him: his dominion is an everlasting dominion, which shall not pass away, and his kingdom that which shall not be destroyed.

Daniel sees that One like the "Son of man came in the clouds of heaven" (Dan. 7:13) to the Ancient of days. President Joseph Fielding Smith spoke further of this grand series of meetings to be held at Adam-ondi-Ahman:

"Then Christ will be received as King of kings, and Lord of lords. We do not know how long a time this gathering will be in session, or how many sessions may be held at this grand council. It is sufficient to know that it is a gathering of the Priesthood of God from the beginning of this earth down to the present, in which reports will be made and all who have been given dispensations will declare their keys and ministry and make report of their stewardship according to the parable [of the talents]. Judgment will be rendered unto them for this is a gathering of the righteous, those who have held and who hold keys of authority in the Kingdom of God upon this earth. It is not to be the judgment of the wicked. When all things are prepared and every key and power set in order with a full and perfect report of each man's stewardship, then Christ will receive these reports and be installed as rightful Ruler of this earth. At this grand council he will take his place by the united voice of the thousands who by right of Priesthood are there assembled. This will precede the great day of destruction of the wicked and will be the preparation for the Millennial Reign."[74]

The kingdom of heaven is "set" or established on earth and all the final preparations for His glorious return can also be set in motion. The glory and honor that the Savior rarely received while in mortality is rightfully bestowed upon Him. The Kingdom will never to be taken from the earth, nor removed in the eternities. His rightful place as the Head is confirmed and the beginning of an everlasting dominion formalized.

SECTION II

Daniel Reacts to the Vision

15 I was grieved in my spirit in the midst of my body, and the visions of my head troubled me.

16 I came near unto one of them that stood by, and asked him the truth of all this. So he told me, and made me know the interpretation of the things.

17 These great beasts, which are four, are four kings, which shall arise out of the earth.

18 But the saints of the most High shall take the kingdom, and possess the kingdom forever, even for ever and ever.

Portions of the vision clearly left Daniel disturbed, especially the events involving the final beast, the little horn and his war against the Saints. His reaction demonstrates the gentle and pure nature of his character. Clearly the night vision distressed him greatly and continued to be a source of apprehension for some time thereafter. He was so concerned about the vision's contents that he approached a messenger that stood nearby and asked "the truth of all this" (Dan. 7:16). He was not asking "Is this really true?" Rather, the root of his concern was over the details of what he just witnessed: "What does it mean?" "Do I really understand?" "Will history play out as it has been presented?" His shock over the latter day events is so profound that he sought for greater understanding, "a more sure explanation."[75]

The messenger responds by reassuring the prophet that he indeed understood the vision clearly and accurately, but then provides additional explanation.

The messenger reaffirmed the reality and destiny of the four kingdoms, beginning with Babylon and the successive powers that followed. Each kingdom would rise and fall according to their obedience to the Lord's law and designs. Mighty men would be allowed to assemble armies and subdue nations and then build powerful kingdoms. The Lord would bless or curse their efforts and assist them or place stumbling blocks according to what He deemed to be best for His children. Nevertheless, the agency of mankind was always respected. A good example is found in the prophecies written by Isaiah about Cyrus. The king of Persia would be granted the privilege to raise up a mighty nation. God would take him by "the right hand" and lead him to subdue other nations in order to build the great Persian (Achaemenid) Empire. Jehovah would open the doors to his success (Isa. 45:1).

The same would be true of Alexander the Great who was permitted to conquer the Persians and as a result Greek Hellenism spread across the region. Likewise, the Roman Republic and Empire served the Lord's purposes for centuries until it also decayed and broke apart. It should be remembered that none of these kingdoms were righteous like Enoch's Zion or the Nephites to whom Christ visited. They were beastly kingdoms composed of fallen leaders with weaknesses and frailties common to mankind. Nevertheless, the Lord's purposes were accomplished despite the failings and wickedness of the people.

The angel explains that in the end, Christ and His Saints will rule over the earth. All other "beastly" nations will fail and be swept aside. The Kingdom of God will prevail as the preeminent power on the earth (Matt. 6:10). The Lord and the saints will take the kingdom after the reign of the little horn and when the kingdom of ten kings is destroyed. The little horn takes power, just as the previous beastly kingdoms had done. His control is both ruthless and expansive. Together with the false prophet, he will be allowed to war against the holy people. When his works reach the limits that

God has set, then Michael, the archangel, and his hosts will sweep away their kingdom through plagues and judgments. The Lord will then give the keys of His Kingdom to the Saints and it shall never be taken from the earth.

The Fourth Kingdom Revealed to Daniel

——

19 Then I would know the truth of the fourth beast, which was diverse from all the others, exceeding dreadful, whose teeth *were of* iron, and his nails *of* brass; *which* devoured, brake in pieces, and stamped the residue with his feet;

20 And of the ten horns that *were* in his head, and *of* the other which came up, and before whom three fell; even *of* that horn that had eyes, and a mouth that spake very great things, whose look was more stout than his fellows.

21 I beheld, and the same horn made war with the saints, and prevailed against them;

22 Until the Ancient of days came, and judgment was given to the saints of the most High; and the time came that the saints possessed the kingdom.

——

Daniel seems almost obsessed with the fourth kingdom, specifically the little horn. He asks for additional clarity, the truth or the exact meaning of the creature and the ten horns. This beast was unlike any of the previous kingdoms, which in many respects mirrored the image of Babylon both in character and dominion. But questions about the fourth fixated in his mind and consumed his attention and concern.

He rehearses back the descriptive language the fourth beast, especially a depiction of the "little horn." His description provides greater insight into what he saw. For example, the anti-Christ was "more stout" than his companions (Dan 7:20). Most leaders of nations are great in their own right, but this man carried an imposing presence. The combination of his talent to speak and motivate the masses, together with perhaps his physical presence, not stature alone, but other prominent features and personality traits that make him a striking figure. Adolf Hitler, for example, was not physically impressive at 5'8" tall, but he was "stout" in that he held a presence more impressive than many other leaders on the world stage at the time. His demeanor seemed confident and he could move the masses by speech, but his eyes and expressions were cold and sinister. Anyone with discernment could tell that he was not a nice man. The anti-Christ in the last days will be neither congenial, nor will he be compassionate or warm, but he will, however, carry a presence that strike respect, if not fear in the world.

Daniel asks again about the little horn who "warred" against the chosen people (Dan. 7:21). His campaign to persecute or wear down the saints seems, at least initially, to be successful and imposes on them great discomfort. The horn succeeds until the judgment of the Ancient of Days. Daniel is intent on gaining as much understanding as he can relative to the fate of the people of God.

A Final Explanation of the Fourth Beast

23 Thus he said, The fourth beast shall be the fourth kingdom upon earth, which shall be diverse from all kingdoms, and shall devour the whole earth, and shall tread it down, and break it in pieces.

24 And the ten horns out of this kingdom are ten kings that shall arise: and another [little horn] shall rise after them; and he shall be diverse from the first, and he shall subdue three kings.

25 And he shall speak great words against the most High, and shall wear out the saints of the most High, and think to change times and laws: and they shall be given into his hand until a time and times and the dividing of time.

26 But the judgment shall sit, and they shall take away his dominion, to consume and to destroy it unto the end.

The messenger rehearses yet a third explanation of the fourth beast. This time he explains it in a way that we understand that the beast will pass through three phases.

Phase I (v23): The first phase describes a beast as having power to "devour the whole earth, and shall tread it down, and break it in pieces" (Dan. 7:23). Previously, Daniel saw that with "iron teeth" and "nails of brass" it devoured and brake in pieces, and stamped kingdoms and peoples (Dan. 7:19). The reference is, of course, to the Roman Empire, which trampled and consumed what seemed to be "the whole world," crushing most every foe and subduing many peoples. The Empire remained intact and held power until the fourth century. As mentioned, Walvoord argues that remnants of this creature could be traced until the death of the Byzantine king at Constantinople in 1453 A.D. when Mehmed II, an Ottoman sultan, took the city and kingdom.[76]

Phase II (v24): The second phase of the beast rises out of "this kingdom" meaning that it draws its origins from the residue of the broken Roman and Byzantine Empires. From Rome's ashes come smaller kingdoms represented by ten horns. They make up the European and Middle Eastern nations ruled by kings until the 19th and 20th centuries. The symbolism of horns represents kings or monarchies who together with their co-partners, the state churches, ruled over all the nations, many of which were formerly of the empire. When the times of the Gentiles comes in (Luke 21:24), these kingdoms will reach their zenith of power. They will be the beneficiaries of God's inspiration during the Renaissance, Reformation and colonial expansion. European nations, especially the British, Spanish, Portuguese, Dutch and Germans spread their influence across the world into the Americas, Africa, Asia and the Pacific. It could be argued that these kingdoms continue to have influence today. The remnants of classic Hellenism and the Roman Empire were carried with the gentiles into the world in the form of architecture, the sciences, engineering, medicine, rational philosophy and many elements of democratic government.

Phase 3 (v.24-25): The third and final phase of the beast is symbolized by the rise of the "little horn," or as John calls him, the eighth beast (Rev. 17:11). The angel explains that this horn shall "arise after them," meaning after phase two, or the period where the gentile nations (ten horns) have power. He will rise as their power begins to dwindle. "He shall be diverse from the first," meaning his kingdom shall not follow the pattern of the previous kingdoms. Unlike the ten horns who had monarchs and adopted traditions and practices from the Roman Empire, the nature and world-view of this beast shall be different (diverse) from those of the ten horns. The angel notes that the ascension of this power is accomplished through the subjugation of three kings, which were once part of the original ten horns.

As previously noted, the logical explanation involves the rise of the modern Communists and their revolutions and wars to take power primarily in Eastern Europe. Under Lenin, the communists seized control in Russia and then under Stalin, they enveloped Eastern Europe from the Ukraine to Berlin. The land and population was roughly one-third of the total area controlled by the kings. The same was true of the Middle East and northern Africa, with the communists heavily influencing countries like Libya, Egypt, Syria and Lebanon. Even if you look at Communist influence worldwide, it expanded to reach roughly one-third of the earth's countries and populations. The little horn will emerge from the kingdom built by the Communists.

John's account provides additional insight. The beast is wounded and then comes to life again (Rev. 13:3). A generally accepted meaning of this scripture refers to the death of Nero and the resurgence of the Emperors via Vespasian and others that follow. This, of course, provides an adequate explanation for John's day. The latter-day interpretation involves the ultimate fall or death of Soviet Communism in 1989, but in accordance with the pattern revealed by John, the head is healed and the whole world wonders at the rise of the beast (Rev. 13:3).

Just as new emperors rose to replace Nero, so too in Russia totalitarian minded leaders took power to reassert the old ways. Many of the old guard communists remade themselves in the new republic, maneuvering into new positions and taking control of what would become a new oligarchy. Russia's fragile democracy after Yeltsin faded away and the new government emerged resembling more the old style totalitarian regime of Soviet Communists, than a liberal democracy. The new actors represent a potent strain of Stalin-like despots and nationalists, who through pay to play and Secret Combinations maintain control over Russia. Such an environment is fertile soil in which an anti-Christ, the wounded head, the "little horn" could rise to power.

With power in hand, they seek to disrupt the West and gain greater influence in the Middle East. They sow seeds of corruption and discord, buy influence and work to destabilize adversaries. In the long run they will gain traction and build alliances to exert much greater influence in the world.

An alternative interpadmilretation offered by the scholar Phillips argues that the three kings are the three principle powers on the earth in the latter days, namely the United States, Russia and China. Given the context of the vision and other scriptural accounts in Ezekiel, Joel, Zechariah and Revelation, this interpretation seems unlikely.

A more universal interpretation of the "little horn" is applied to any individual who seeks power and comes out in opposition against the principles of righteousness. The situation in democratic countries like the United States will also be precarious. Anti-Christs in this country will seek to change the laws and culture in an active campaign against the righteous (Dan. 7:25). Given the wicked conditions in the world, anti-Christs will be plentiful and wield great influence in the governments and societies across the globe.

The Anti-Christ Speaks Great Words

The anti-Christ speaks great words against the most High. History shows that anti-Christs hold little to no regard for the true and living God. Most are completely oblivious to Him, or they sneer at the concept of god or religion or righteousness. They are however, prolific in self-aggrandizement, setting themselves up as objects of worship and establishing their own will. "The sin of the king is placing himself with God, therefore, … he does not regard the fundamental conditions given by God, but so changes the laws of human life that he puts his own pleasure in the place of the divine arrangements."[77]

The angel says that he "think[s] to change times and laws" (Dan. 7:25). The great words of "the horn" are accompanied by changes in culture and traditional values in favor of new laws and government policy. The Book of Mormon provides an account where corruption of the laws spread among the Nephites: "And that they had altered and trampled under their feet the laws of Mosiah, or that which the Lord commanded him to give unto the people; and they saw that their laws had become corrupted, and that they had become a wicked people...And because of their iniquity, the church had begun to dwindle; and they began to disbelieve in the spirit of prophecy and in the spirit of revelation; and the judgments of God did stare them in the face" (Hel. 4:22-23). The changing of the times and laws is a natural result of wickedness in the world. It occurs among every people and in every nation. It opens the door for dramatic changes in moral standards, political policies and social attitudes.

Speaking of the United States Constitution, the Savior said: "Therefore, I, the Lord, justify you, and your brethren of my church, in befriending that law which is the constitutional law of the land; And as pertaining to law of man, whatsoever is more or less than this, cometh of evil." (Doctrine and Covenants 98:6-7). The Lord established the laws and patterns of governance that brought about the most freedom and agency to mankind. He cultivated prosperity and happiness. He commanded that these principles be upheld and maintained. Conversely, the adversary desires to pervert God's work by injecting changes or new laws to allow his servants to exert greater control or to justify his program of wickedness.

His servants, anti-Christs, ever promote major cultural transformations that move society away from the laws and teachings that God has established. They propose reforms that by their very nature run contrary to the will of the Lord. Such changes unsettle, even upset the righteous, and if passed, make them weary and dispirited. The angel explains that the goal of the anti-Christ is, in part, to "wear out the saints of the most High" (Dan. 7:25). As wickedness increases in society, it vexes the peace of the upright (2 Pet. 2:7). The result is more brazen enmity and social strife, which is injected into the political climate in the form of contention. As the disparity widens, the pressures against righteousness heightens. In time the wicked will rage against the righteous and their anger will reach a tipping point where it breaks into persecution (2 Ne. 28:2). These are the conditions that greatly concerned the prophet Daniel.

The angel explains that they, the saints, shall "be given into his hand until a time and times and the dividing of time" (Dan. 7:25). The term "time (1) and times (2) and the dividing of times (1/2) and equals 3 1/2, which corresponds to the duration that the anti-Christs hold power in the world. It is a symbolic number representing a period when evil rules on the earth. John's language says that they have power for forty and two months or 3 and ½ years (Rev 11:3).

A Perspective from the Revelation of John

During this time of crisis, John's Revelation states that the ten kings "receive power as kings one hour with the beast. These have one mind, and shall give their power and strength unto the beast. These shall make war with the Lamb, and the Lamb shall overcome them" (Rev. 17:12-14). Leaders from many nations (ten kings) will join together with the little horn to make war with the Lamb. Obviously, they don't make war directly with the Lord, but rather with His servants and Saints scattered in the earth. The Lord, of course, sees the conflict as His battle. It's probable that the alliance between the kings, the false prophet and the little horn will be an uneasy alliance; nevertheless, millions will be assembled in armies for battle.

Ezekiel speaks of the alliance of Gog, from Magog, who marches against Israel in holy war of total annihilation (Ezek. Ch. 38-39). Gog was the ancient king of the kingdom Magog, which today lies in modern day Russia. The army consists of "two hundred thousand thousand (200,000,000)" or myriads upon myriads of troops equipped with modern weapons massed against the nation of Israel. The desire is to wipe them from the earth. The Lord, through two of His prophets (Apostles), defends the Jewish people for the 3 1/2 years. In the end, a tremendous earthquake and other calamities destroy the great army. (Rev. 11:13). The little horn (beast) dies in the judgment (Ezek. 39:11) and by both accounts—Daniel and the Revelation of John—he is speedily cast down to hell (Dan. 7:11; Rev. 19:20).

The earthquake and calamites send the alliance, even the world, into a state of chaos and anarchy. Nation turns against nation and kingdom against kingdom. New alliances rise up to fight others, and the only peace that to be found will be in Zion (Doctrine and Covenants 45:68-69). Only after these judgments are sent to chasten the earth will the Lord come in glory. His brightness and glory will destroy all remnants of the wicked and usher in His Millennial reign.

Christ's Comes and Dominion Given to the Saints

⎯⎯⎯

27 And the kingdom and dominion, and the greatness of the kingdom under the whole heaven, shall be given to the people of the saints of the most High, whose kingdom is an everlasting kingdom, and all dominions shall serve and obey him

28 Hitherto is the end of the matter. As for me Daniel, my cogitations much troubled me, and my countenance changed in me: but I kept the matter in my heart.

⎯⎯⎯

The angel reinforces the prophecy that the Lord will subdue all worldly kingdoms, and in the end His kingdom will rule. The righteous are given power and authority in the kingdom to preside over the nations. Those who desire a part in these glorious events must endure the terrible trials brought by the anti-Christ. Their challenge will be to remain faithful throughout the turbulent events when the "beastly kingdoms" reign. Righteous men and women will be found in all nations. Despite attempts from the beast to change the times and laws, to dishearten the saints and destroy the Jews, they will fail.

The vision's impact on the prophet Daniel was so profound that he was left greatly troubled and pondered it for many days. Certainly part of the horror was watching the war and destruction perpetrated against his fellow Jews in Jerusalem. But also, he empathized with the Saints in the latter times who would suffer under persecution in the world. The imagery and vision experience seemed almost too much for his sensitive spirit to bear. He writes that his countenance changed or "my face grew pale" (Dan. 7:28), sickened by what he had seen. For months, he replayed the events over and over in his mind and his soul was heavy. No one exposed to such evil presented at such a scale could not be moved. Daniel's tender heart was changed, and he kept all these visions unto himself.

Chapter Endnotes

1   Gleason L. Archer, Jr. "*The Expositor's Bible Commentary, vol. 7*, Frank E Gaebelein, ed. 85; See also Walvoord. *Daniel: The Key to Prophetic Revelation.* 181

2   Walvoord. *Daniel: The Key to Prophetic Revelation*, 182

3   Wood, *Commentary on Daniel.* 179

4   Wiseman. "Belshazzar, in the New Bible Dictionary, J.D., Douglas, ed. 139

5   Keil. *Biblical Commentary of the Old Testament, The Book of the Prophet Daniel.* 222

6   Walvoord. *Daniel: The Key to Prophetic Revelation.* 188

7   Keil. *Biblical Commentary of the Old Testament, The Book of the Prophet Daniel.* 222

8   Young. *The Prophecy Daniel: A Commentary.* 143

9   Walvoord. *Daniel: The Key to Prophetic Revelation.* 187

10   Smith. *Teachings of the Prophet Joseph Smith.* 289, 291

11   Ibid. 289, 291

12   Smith, *Scriptural Teachings of the Prophet Joseph Smith*, 289

13   Keil. *Biblical Commentary of the Old Testament, The Book of the Prophet Daniel.* 245

14   Pratt. *Autobiography of Parley Parker Pratt.* 46

15   Young. *The Prophecy Daniel: A Commentary.* 143-144

16   Phillips. *Exploring the Book of Daniel: An Expository Commentary.* 112

17   Driver, Young. *The Prophecy Daniel: A Commentary.* 144

18   Ibid. 145

19   Young. "The early history of the Medes and the Persians and the Achaemenid empire to the death of Cambyses", in Boardman, John; Hammond, N. G. L.; Lewis, D. M.; Ostwald, M., *The Cambridge Ancient History* 4. 1–52

20   Briant. *From Cyrus to Alexander: A History of the Persian Empire.* Eisenbrauns. 3

21   *Journal of Discourses,* vol. 22, 207

22   Young. *The Prophecy Daniel: A Commentary.* 145

23   Yarshater. *Iranian Encyclopedia.* 47

24   Guinness Entry: "Largest empire by percentage of world population." *Guinness World Records.* Retrieved 11 March 2015

25   Phillips. *Exploring the Book of Daniel: An Expository Commentary.* 114-15

26   Herodotus. *The Histories* VII. 69-80, 84-87

27   Ibid. 89-90

28   Phillips. *Exploring the Book of Daniel: An Expository Commentary.*115

29   Briant. *Alexander the Great and his Empire.* 111-118; Cartledge. *Alexander, the Great.* 102-103

30   Keil. *Biblical Commentary of the Old Testament, The Book of the Prophet Daniel.* 227

31   Keil. *Biblical Commentary of the Old Testament, The Book of the Prophet Daniel.* 227

32   Briant, *Alexander the Great and His Empire*, 129; Fuller. *The Generalship of Alexander the Great.* 49-51

33   Lonsdale. *Alexander the Great: Lessons in strategy.* 47-49, 51

34   Cartledge. *Alexander, the Great.* 165

35   Lendering. *Phalanx and Hoplites*, Livius.org July 27, 2013. http://www.livius.

org/pha-phd/phalanx/phalanx.html

36 Phillips. *Exploring the Book of Daniel: An Expository Commentary.* 115; Cartledge. *Alexander, the Great.* 165-167

37 Cartledge. *Alexander, the Great.* 166

38 Mark."The Greek Phalanx" *History Encyclopedia*, 181, January, 2012, http://www.ancient.eu/article/110/

39 Walvoord. *Daniel: The Key to Prophetic Revelation*, 194

40 Cartledge. *Alexander, the Great.* 219-221

41 Ramirez-Faria. *Concise Encyclopedia of World History.* 450

42 Cartledge, *Alexander the Great.* 121, 199-201; Briant, *Alexander the Great and His Empire.* 129-132

43 Keil, *Biblical Commentary of the Old Testament, The Book of the Prophet Daniel.* 293, See also Hochner. *"Between the Testaments* in The *Expositor's Bible Commentary, Vol. 1.* 75

44 Walvoord. *Daniel: The Key to Prophetic Revelation.* 194

45 Young. *The Prophecy Daniel: A Commentary.* 146

46 Ibid. 146

47 Phillips. *Exploring the Book of Daniel: An Expository Commentary.* 116

48 Abbott. *A History and Description of Roman Political Institutions.* 3

49 Article by Tim. J. Cornell, in *A Comparative Study of Thirty City-state Cultures: An Investigation, Volume 21*, edited by Mogens Herman Hansen, Study conducted by the Copenhagen Polis Centre (Historisk-filosofiske Skrifter 21, 2000, 209 (Cornell says the form was used by the *fetiales* for declaring war and cites *Livy 1.32.11-13)*

50 Le Glay. *A History of Rome.* 548

51 Fields. *The Roman Army of the Punic Wars 264–146 B.C. (Battle Orders).* 15

52 Carey. *Hannibal's Last Battle: Zama and the Fall of Carthage.*

53 Ibid. 196, Phillips. *Exploring the Book of Daniel: An Expository Commentary.* 116

54 Phillips. *Exploring the Book of Daniel: An Expository Commentary.* 116

55 Josephus, *War of the Jews.* VI.3, 584

56 Le Glay. *A History of Rome.* 1996, 92

57 Walvoord. Daniel: *The Key to Prophetic Revelation,* 197

58 Gaskill. *The Lost Language of Symbolism. 132*

59 Ibid. *118*

60 Benson. "In His Steps," *BYU Speeches.* March 04, 1979
Ezra Taft Benson: "Today, the international, criminal, communist conspiracy fits this Book of Mormon description perfectly, for there is a combination of gangsters who lust for power, who have liquidated some 70 million people, brought one-third of the world's population under bondage, and who seek to overthrow the freedom of all nations. I have talked face to face to some of these godless leaders, on both sides of the Iron Curtain." Benson "The Book of Mormon Warns America" *BYU Speeches*, May 21, 1968
President David O. McKay has said: "The position of this Church on the subject of communism has never changed. We consider it the greatest satanical threat to peace, prosperity, and the spread of God's work among men that exists on the face of the earth. (*General Conference Address*, Priesthood Session, April 9, 1966.)

61 Dawisha. *Putin's Kleptocracy: Who Owns Russia?.* 267-315

62 Keil, *Biblical Commentary of the Old Testament, The Book of the Prophet*

Daniel, VIII 9, 294-95

63 In a 416-page manifesto called Palestine, Iran's Ayatollah Ali Khamenei details his view on the destruction of Israel and the deception of the US. The book, which credits Khamenei as "The flag bearer of Jihad to liberate Jerusalem," is only available in Iran, the NY Post revealed. http://www.*ibtimes.co.uk*/irans-ayatollah-ali-khamenei-publishes-book-destroy-israel-deceive-us-1513761

64 Kingdom of the Devil: "kingdom of the devil, brothers and sisters, must be regarded as a collective, generic designation. We must not confuse it with any of its subsets, as ominous and bad as they may be for their season in human history. We must not confuse the subsets with the whole of it. Maxwell. "Insights from My Life," *Ensign*. August 2000

65 McConkie. *The Millennial Messiah: The Second Coming of the Son of Man.* 582

66 Young. *The Prophecy Daniel: A Commentary.* 151

67 Phillips. *Exploring the Book of Daniel: An Expository Commentary.* 118

68 Whitney. *Life of Heber C. Kimball.* 209-210

69 McConkie. *The Millennial Messiah: The Second Coming of the Son of Man.* 584-85

70 Ibid. 582

71 Smith. *Way to Perfection.* 291

72 Smith. *The Progress of Man*, 3rd ed. 481–82; also McConkie. *The Millennial Messiah: The Second Coming of the Son of Man.* 578–88

73 Walvoord. Daniel: The Key to Prophetic Revelation. 204

74 Smith. *The Progress of Man*, 3rd ed. 481–82; also McConkie, *The Millennial Messiah: The Second Coming of the Son of Man.* 578–88

75 Young. The Prophecy Daniel: A Commentary. 157

76 Walvoord. *Daniel: The Key to Prophetic Revelation.* 197

77 Keil. *Biblical Commentary of the Old Testament, The Book of the Prophet Daniel.* 242

The Beast in Daniels and John's Revelation

Daniel points out peculiar characteristics of the fourth beast that made it "diverse" or different from the previous three. While there is not an exact correlation of characteristics between the beast in John's Revelation and the beast in Daniel's account, they are, nevertheless, one and the same. A comparison of the two accounts is in order.

1 And I stood upon the sand of the sea, and saw a beast rise up out of the sea, having seven heads and ten horns, and upon his horns ten crowns, and upon his heads the name of blasphemy.

2 And the beast which I saw was like unto a leopard, and his feet were as the feet of a bear, and his mouth as the mouth of a lion: and the dragon gave him his power, and his seat, and great authority (Rev. 13:1-2).

John's Revelation shows features from all the previous creatures embodied in this fourth beast. "And the beast which I saw was like unto a leopard, and his feet were as the feet of a bear and his mouth as mouth of a lion." (Rev 13:2). Daniel's vision portrays them as independent beasts. Rome's rule extended from Hespania to Greece and beyond to Parthia. It controlled virtually the same lands as the ancient kingdoms of Babylon, Persian and Greece. While Rome had its own dominant culture and values, its governance policies where tolerant of the cultural and traditional peculiarities in each nation. Rome provided space for most ethnic beliefs to thrive including the ancient cultures in Mesopotamia, Persia and Greece. The Jews were afforded the privilege of worshiping Jehovah, until their national rebellions brought punishment and eviction. The Christians were not initially persecuted on religious grounds by Rome, but out of political misunderstandings. The creature did possess fierce iron teeth, symbolizing Rome's aggressive methods in conquering and punishment, against those who resisted them.

John's account adds features like: "seven heads and ten horns, and upon his horns ten crowns, and upon his heads the name of blasphemy" (Rev. 13:1). Daniel only mentions the ten horns. Other than the horns, Daniel does not speak of heads or crowns or of blasphemy. These features

Artist Unknown © Public Domain

Caesar Augusta with a Wreath (Civic) Crown, Glyptothek Museum, Munich

were shown to John to emphasize the emperors of his day that took power from the republic Senate and ruled in Rome from 44 B.C. until its fall to the Visigoths. A number of emperors brought serious trouble to the Primitive Church and subsequent Christians as they made "war with the saints" (Rev. 13:7). Nero, Domitian, Diocletian, Decius, among others mounted serious campaigns of persecution over several centuries.

When John's beast was first presented, seven heads are depicted, but later an eighth is prophesied to come symbolizing the rise of an anti-Christ in the latter days, who would be in the likeness of the emperors (Rev 17:11). John's "eighth beast" can be compared to the "little horn" seen by Daniel (Dan. 7:8), who "shall speak great words against the most High, and shall wear out the saints of the most High, and think to change times and laws (Dan. 7:25). And as mentioned, heads and horns denoted power figures, i.e. kings or rulers (1 Sam. 2:10, Jer. 48:25, Zech. 1.19, 21).

The horns of John's beast are fitted with crowns that have the title blasphemy. They symbolize royalty; first the laurel wreaths of the emperors, and later the golden crowns for the kings of the nations or the religious leaders (Rev. 13:1). The practice of self-deification was evidence of the blasphemous attitudes of the emperors against the God of heaven.

The ten horns correspond to the ten toes of iron mixed with clay on the statue spoken of in Daniel 2 (Dan. 2:41-42). As horns, these diverse kings ruled over kingdoms (toes) that came into power after Rome's rule had diminished. The European nations from Britain to Russia make up the majority of the "horns" symbolized in the beast. For centuries monarchs ruled these kingdoms and it is still true for some countries, even today. It could also be argued that the nations of northern Africa to western Asia (Afghanistan) are to be included as part of the ten horns, as they were formerly parts of the several empires seen by Daniel.

There is no reason to believe that there were literally ten kings or ten kingdoms, but rather, the number ten was given symbolically to mean the whole of that part of the world. These horns remain as sovereign powers in one form or another until, as Daniel states, "the thrones were cast down, and the Ancient of days did sit" (Dan. 7:9). As the events of the latter-days and the Second Coming are fulfilled, the remnants of this final beast and its horns will be swept away in war and with divine judgments. Plagues and calamities will be poured out to cleanse the earth in preparation for the Lord's return and millennial reign (Doctrine and Covenants 77:12).

8

The Kingdoms of Persia and Greece

The vision of Chapter 7 provided a panoramic view of the great kingdoms that would rule from Daniel's day to the end of the world. In subsequent chapters, the Lord offers additional details and insights through additional visions and visitations given to the prophet. This vision (Chapter 8) addresses the two powers that will succeed the Babylonian Empire: the Medo-Persian (or Archaemenid) empire and the Macedonian (or Greek) Empire, which rose to greatness from among the rival Greek states. Chapter 9 gives insight into the Jew's return to their homeland and prophesies of the coming of the Messiah into mortality. It presents clues to Israel's history from the time of "Ezra and Nehemiah to the inauguration of the kingdom of heaven."[1] The reign of the Greek Seleucid and Ptolemaic dynasties are addressed in Chapters 10 and 11 (11:1-35). They expound with exquisite details and unusual interest on what are now called the Syrian Wars (1-IV) and provide special insight into Antiochus Epiphanies, an archetypical anti-Christ.

The final verses of Chapter 11 (vs. 36-45) and Chapter 12 preview latter-day anti-Christs and the troubles they bring to the world along with the persecutions they enact against the Saints. Daniel receives counsel relative to the end of the world and the Second Coming.

The record shows that these final visions were originally written in Hebrew. This language signals a change in the intended audience. These messages are specifically for his people, the chosen people of Israel. The prophetic details of future kingdoms will prove a helpful guide to the Jews as they pass through the coming centuries. God foresees their destiny from the beginning to the end. They must negotiate the rise and reign of the Persian, the Greek and the Roman Empires and the perplexities that will accompany each kingdom.[2] The visions also provide insight and counsel for the holy people, or the Saints, during very perilous times in the last days. They too must glean valuable lessons from the visions to help them endure well.

The Vision in Susa of Elam

————

1   In the third year of the reign of king Belshazzar a vision appeared unto me, *even unto* me Daniel, after that which appeared unto me at the first.

2   And I saw in a vision; and it came to pass, when I saw, that I *was* at Shushan *in* the palace, which *is* in the province of Elam; and I saw in a vision, and I was by the river of Ulai.

————

Daniel's vision begins as he "saw [himself] in vision" near the banks of the river Ulai near the city of Shushan or Susa in the Persian province of Elam. Ulai was "apparently ...a large artificial canal (c. 900 feet in breadth) which connected two other rivers,... and passed by the capital city on the north east."[3] Susa was located about 225 miles east of Babylon roughly equal distance between Babylon and the Persian Empire.[4] It was an ancient and holy city to the Medes, a principle capital. Its relationship to the Babylonian Empire is unclear, although Daniel does call it a province (Dan. 8:2); presumably a Babylonian province. Babylon and the Medes enjoyed previous alliances against the Assyrians, and it is very likely that Babylon and Elam were at least allies.[5] Given Daniel's description it is probable that Elam was part of the greater Babylonian protectorate, even though very little is known of Susa from that era. Cyrus conquered the land of Elam and Susa about 540 B.C. and the city became a principle capital of the Persian Empire thereafter.[6]

Marcel-Auguste Dieulafoy © Public Domain
Reconstruction by French archaeologist of the palace of Artaxerxes II Mnemon in
Susa or Shushan (KJV Bible)

A sizable population of Jews lived in the capital and greater region. Later, Esther lived in Susa, or Shushan (Esther 1:5) as the Persians called it, and in her day it, was the capital city to King Ahasuerus (or Xerxes I, See Esther 1:1). It was there that Esther married the king and later with the help of Mordecai saved the Jews from Haman's genocidal plans (Esther 7-8). It is reasonable to assume that a large Jewish community lived in and around Susa in Daniel's day. By this period of history (551 B.C.), Susa was both impressive and beautiful. He seemed to be familiar with its environs, the palace and the surrounding communities.

The Shushan palace lay near the center of the city and was one of the settings where he saw himself. The other was near the river Ulai. The prophet wrote that the vision "appeared unto me" (Dan. 8:1) as the first, meaning that the format of this vision was similar to the first one recorded in Daniel 7. It has been debated whether Daniel was actually at the city in person or only saw himself in vision. Josephus asserts that he was indeed in Elam,[7] and while he may have visited the city many times in his life, the language suggests that he saw himself in vision, carried away in a dream or by the Spirit.

The vision came in the third year of Belshazzar, which sets it chronologically between chapters 4 and 5. "On the basis of the Babylonian Chronicle, it is now known that Nabonidus began his reign in 556 B.C., and apparently Belshazzar became co-regent in 553 B.C. when his father took residence at Telma [Temã in Arabia]....The vision of chapter 8 occurred in 551 B.C., or twelve years before Belshazzar's [infamous] feast."[8]

The setting for the dream in Elam was deliberate, as it served to impress upon the prophet's mind from whence the next great empire would arise. The capital city lay before him and eventually became one of three Persian centers (Persepolis and Ecbatana being the other two). It was impressive, flowing with prosperous markets and beautiful Persian styled gardens. Tradition holds that Daniel might have been buried at Susa in a sepulture memorialized today as the Tomb of Daniel. Josephus writes: "Now when Daniel was become so illustrious and famous, on account of the opinion men had that he was beloved of God, he built a tower at [Susa], in Media: it was a most elegant building, and wonderfully made, and it is still remaining, and preserved to this day.... Now they bury the kings of Media, of Persia, and Parthia in this tower to this day, and he who was entrusted with the care of it was a Jewish priest."[9]

Since Daniel died during the reign of the Persian kings and was regarded prominently by them, a dignitary with such a high station could easily have been designated as royalty and buried in or near a capital. Other than tradition, no evidence supports that he was actually buried there. If the prophet had his way, he might have requested to be taken back to the Promised Land for burial. Nevertheless, Susa was a special city to the prophet and a place of much tutoring from the Lord.

Kingdoms represented by the Ram and the Goat

3   Then I lifted up mine eyes, and saw, and, behold, there stood before the river a ram which had *two* horns: and the two horns were high; but one *was* higher than the other, and the higher came up last.

4   I saw the ram pushing westward, and northward, and

southward; so that no beasts might stand before him, neither was there any that could deliver out of his hand; but he did according to his will, and became great.

The vision presents a ram with two horns. The Biblical symbol of horns represents power, primarily invested in the kings (Zech. 1:21; Ps. 112:9; Rev 13:1). In Daniel's day, the Persian kings displayed crowns featuring a ram's head and horns. "The king of Persia wore a jeweled ram's head of gold instead of a diadem, such as are seen on the pillars at Persepolis. Also the Hebrew for 'ram' springs from the same root as 'Elam,' or Persia. The 'one horn higher than the other' corresponds to the bear 'raising itself on one side'"[10] Daniel recognized the symbol of the ram both in terms of its linguistic roots and as a symbol of the Persian crown and the kingdom.

The dual ram horns represented the kingdoms of the Medes and the Persians. Among the Iranian tribes, the Medes rose in power and might first, but eventually they were surpassed under the dynamic character of Cyrus the Great. Cyrus took control of the Median Empire by overthrowing his grandfather. Through diplomacy and marriage, Cyrus pacified several nearby provinces including the Bactrians, Parthians and Saka.[11] Once the two kingdoms were unified, Cyrus and the Medo-Persians expanded their influence

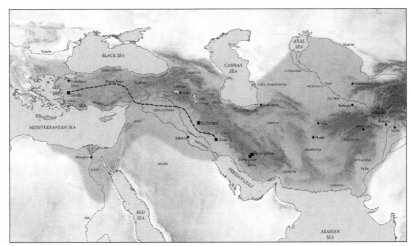

Map by Gabriel Moss © Used with Permission
The Persian or Achaemenid Empire at its greatest extent

throughout the region. "The directions [mentioned in scripture] ...indicate the directions in which the Persian Empire made her greatest conquests [west, north and south]."[12] The Persians first pushed westward into Babylon, Syria and as far as Egypt. They also conquered west into Phrygia and Lydia in Asia Minor (Turkey). In Africa, Persian troops marched southward to the kingdom of Ethiopia. Later Cyrus moved northward into the Black Sea. They conquered Armenia, and moved up around the Caspian Sea.

In addition to Cyrus, the most notable of the Persian kings were Darius and Xerxes who expanded the kingdom as far as Greece. In 492 B.C. the first Persian invasion was their first invasion into Macedon and Greece by king Darius I. The conflict was sparked by Greek lead rebellions in Persian ruled Lydia. In the campaign, he successfully subjugated Thrace and Macedon, which became a sore point for Philip and a rallying cry for Alexander, the Great years later. Their conquest of Greece ended with their defeat at Marathon (490 B.C.). In a second war with the Greeks, the Persians returned under Xerxes I. At Thermopylae they broke through in the north and marched south to Athens where he ordered the city burned. The next day, under duress for what he had done, he ordered the city rebuilt. He was eventually defeated by general Themistocles in a naval battle at Salamis in 479 B.C..[13] The Greeks repulsed the Persians from the peninsula. The Lord had set the bounds of Persian domination and influence so that they could not overcome the Greeks.

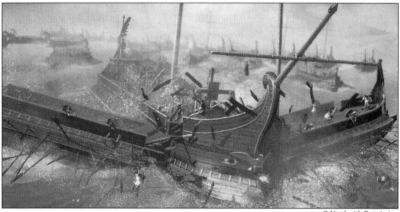

© Used with Permission

Ancient trireme ships in battle similar to the fleet Themistocles
used to defeat the Persian invasion of Greece

Persian soldiers depicted on a relief at Percepolis in Iran

Under Darius II, Persian troops pushed eastward into Bactria (Afghanistan) and the Indian Hindus, now Pakistan. The Farce language, architecture and other cultural influences remain in Pakistan and India even today. In its supremacy, the Persian empire and rule was as large as any major kingdom before or since. It indeed became "great," just as the vision represents.

The founder of the Medo-Persian Empire, Cyrus, was considered by most historians to be benevolent and humble and treated his subjects with tolerance and fairness. He is noted for freeing slaves, including the Jews, a few of which returned to Jerusalem in the time of Ezra. Persian governance practices were very impressive. The kingdom was divided into 23 major Satrapies or provinces and about 120 minor provinces. Each was presided over by a very influential Satrap who collected taxes, maintained the armies and oversaw the day-to-day operations of the kingdom. Shadrach, Meshach and Abed-nego served as the Satraps over the Babylonian province and Daniel as a president of all of the Satrapies under the local ruler, Darius (Dan. 6). For nearly 200 years the Persians—or Achaemenid Empire as Cyrus designated it—ruled with might and brought great order. Nevertheless, Daniel sees a he goat rise from the west. The Macedonian-Greeks were destined to come to power, conquer the Persians and sweep across their empire.

The He Goat and Notable Horn

5   And as I was considering, behold, an he goat came from the west on the face of the whole earth, and touched not the ground: and the goat *had* a notable horn between his eyes.

6   And he came to the ram that had *two* horns, which I had seen standing before the river, and ran unto him in the fury of his power.

7   And I saw him come close unto the ram, and he was moved with choler against him, and smote the ram, and brake his two horns: and there was no power in the ram to stand before him, but he cast him down to the ground, and stamped upon him: and there was none that could deliver the ram out of his hand.

Greece is represented in Daniel's vision as a he goat, a familiar animal often characterized in Greek mythology. They fashioned the mystic figure as a man combined with a goat feature, or a satyr. The figure given in the vision was probably just a goat. Historically, the Grecian states had influenced the Middle East and Asia through trade and immigration, but its rise as a potent military power and its thirst to conqueror did not come until the reign of Philip II of Macedonia (359–336 B.C.). Their newfound power ultimately facilitated the spread of Hellenistic (or Greek) culture far and wide across the continent. During the reign of the Persians, the Greek city-states were fiercely independent and frequently quarrelled among themselves. Philip led an effort to unify the states through a combination of conquests and diplomacy.[14] His emphasis on advanced military discipline and strategic weaponry gave him an advantage among his rivals. Macedonians were traditionally herdsmen, which may also account for the symbolism of the goat. Despite being looked upon as backward, the superior Macedonian military enabled them to gain great advantage in battle. Eventually, they subjugated most of the Grecian peninsula. Alexander the Great inherited his father's kingdom and maintained rule in Greece, but afterwards expanded the kingdom into Asia and Africa. He is represented in the vision by the "notable horn" between the eyes of the goat. "The unusual horn—one large horn instead of the normal two—symbolically represents the single leadership he provided."[15]

Philip saw that even at a young age, Alexander was ambitious and courageous. After bridling a seemingly untamable horse, Bucephalus, the king told his son: "My boy, you must find a kingdom big enough for your ambitions. Macedon is too small for you."[16] By the age of sixteen, Alexander was installed as regent king over Macedonia while his father waged war against Byzantium.[17] During these early years, Alexander successfully subdued rebellions from Thrace and other uprisings from competitive city-states. "Very early, he displayed an uncanny trait of always being able to discern the enemy's tactics in advance."[18] He reacted quickly to situations on the battlefield to gain the victory. He conquered with exceptional tactical insight and unparalleled speed and efficiency.

In 336 B.C. one of Philip's bodyguards, Pausanias, murdered the king at a wedding. A few historians believe that his wife Olympias and Alexander were at the center of the plot. Philip had married Cleopatra of Macedon whose son was the rightful heir to the throne leaving Alexander on the outside. No evidence can be found to substantiate the claim that Alexander was ever involved, but after his father's death the stepbrother was quickly dispatched

The statue Taming of Bucephalus by Alexander the Great

and the flamboyant son assumed the throne. Alexander obtained the kingdom at the age of 20 and swiftly moved to consolidate support among the Greek cities. His brutal subjection of Thebes warned fellow cities of the necessity of making peace with the new king.[19]

Once firmly in control, he expanded his sights to move south and east into Asia. The love of conquest seemed to coarse through his veins. Some describe his passion as *pathos,* or an insatiable drive for battle. What motivated him was probably more than just the need to conquer, but he indeed excelled in the art of war. His principle goal was to liberate the Greeks in Asia and deprive the

Persians of their kingdom, a passion energized in part by revenge for previous Persian incursions into Macedon and Greece.

Josephus writes of a dream wherein Alexander saw the Jewish high priest and felt the command of God to march from Greece to take the Persian kingdom. Speaking to the Syrian king in Palestine, he recounted the words of Alexander:

> I did not adore him [meaning the Jewish high priest], but that God who hath honored him with his high priesthood; for I saw this very person [the priest] in a dream, in this very habit, when I was at Dios in Macedonia, who, when I was considering with myself how I might obtain the dominion of Asia, exhorted me to make no delay, but boldly to pass over the sea thither, for that he would conduct my army, and would give me the dominion over the Persians; whence it is that, having seen no other in that habit, and now seeing this person in it, and remembering that vision, and the exhortation which I had in my dream, I believe that I bring this army under the Divine conduct, and shall therewith conquer Darius, and destroy the power of the Persians, and that all things will succeed according to what is in my own mind. [20]

This sign and other experiences gave Alexander the confidence to act decisively on what he felt. He left Pella with fifty thousand troops and crossed the Hellespont (Dardanelles in Istanbul) into Asia Minor. "Halfway across [the strait], he sacrificed a bull to Poseidon and made libation with a golden vessel, just as Xerxes had done long ago."[21] Upon arrival he thrust a spear in the ground designating his intention to conquer the whole of Asia.[22]

Alexander's first confrontation with Darius and the Persian army was at the Granicus River in ancient Lydia. The battle by no means favored Alexander, nevertheless, he managed to cross the 60 foot river with his companion cavalry and disrupt the left flank of the Persians, which opened a door in the center for hoplite soldiers to cross and crush their foes.[23]

Johnny Shumatte © Used with Permission
King Philip and the Companion Cavalry (Hetairoi) arrayed with leopard pelts

He extended his campaign into Lydia and greater Asia Minor beginning with Sardis.[24] Macedonian troops swept south through the cities wherein they handed Darius a second decisive defeat at Issus. In that battle, he took the Persian king's mother and sisters captive, whom he retained to symbolize his right as heir to the kingdom.[25] He pushed further south along the Ionian coasts to Tyre where he laid siege to the city by blockading the island for seven months, both by land and sea. His army built a causeway allowing troops access to breach the fortifications. Isaiah prophesied the destruction of the city (Isa. 23:1-9) and thereafter, it was never a significant power. The fall of Tyre brought real fear throughout the region.

Hearing of the downfall of Tyre, Darius sent a peace envoy. He offered terms wherein Alexander would take his daughter Stateira to wife, which would make him co-regent of Persia. Believing that he could have the kingdom anyway, the offer was summarily rejected. Alexander responded that he was sure that he could have these gifts and the kingdom as well.[26] From Tyre, he moved along the coast seizing control of all the ports and taking the Phoenician stronghold of Gaza. He then marched towards the capital of Jerusalem.

Josephus's account of Alexander's entrance into Jerusalem provides insight into the Lord's preparation for the preservation of His people and demonstrated His will that they accept the rule of the Greeks. "God warned [Jaddua, the High Priest] in a dream, which came upon him after he had offered sacrifice, that he should take courage, and adorn the city, and open the gates; that the rest should appear in white garments, but that he and the priests should meet the king in the habits proper to their order, without the dread of any ill consequences, which the providence of God would prevent."[27] The combination of Alexander's dream and the revelation to Jaddua prevented any slaughter or pillaging of Jerusalem by the Macedonian army.

The Egyptians capitulated and hailed Alexander both as a liberator and a new Pharaoh, a son of the gods.[28] One of his first acts was to commission the construction of a new city, Alexandria, which would later become a center of Hellenization and one of the most important cities in the region.

Daniel's vision states that the "he goat came from the west on the face of the whole earth, and touched not the ground" (Dan. 8:5). His expansive conquests were swift by any standard. Alexander's expeditions extended from Greece into India, but the campaign lasted only twelve years. In reality, he hardly touched the earth. He swept into one region and then moved quickly to take the next. Not only was his advance rapid, but Daniel wrote that "he was moved with choler (anger) against him, and smote the ram, and brake his two horns" (Dan 8:7). "An unusual feature of the goat's attack was its fury, borne out of history. The Persians had attacked Greece earlier. Now it was time for retaliation."[29] The Macedonian army marched across the old empire of Darius III. On his way to Babylon, he crossed the Tigris, where Darius had assembled another impressive army of several hundred thousand to met him again. The Greek general routed the king in a pitch battle at Gaugamela, fulfilling Daniel's vision that "there was no power in the ram to stand before him, but he cast him down to the ground, and stamped upon him: and there was none that could deliver the ram out of his hand" (Dan 8:7).

Charles Le Brun, 1619-1690, © Public Domain

Triumph of Alexander the Great in Babylon

The logistics involved in conquering lands and securing peoples would have been difficult if not impossible for Greece. As a means of maintaining order, Alexander recruited and trained troops from among the Persian ranks. In the beginning, these were meant to support the Macedonian elite and keep the peace, but over time they proved valuable in battle.[30] The Macedonian army and nobles protested the integration of the Persians. Nevertheless, it signaled Alexander's larger strategy to incorporate the Persian aristocracy and Satrap governance to keep the control over the heart of the empire.[31]

Alexander's victory at Gaugamela left the 300 mile march to Babylon virtually unprotected. The ancient city became a prestigious prize. He sent ambassadors ahead to the city proclaiming that he desired no part in its destruction or defacement. "Alexander wanted a bloodless victory and promised to honor the gods of Babylon. The glittering city of the plain opened its gates in mid-October 331 B.C., and Alexander entered triumphantly."[32]

His stay in Babylon was short lived. Alexander had set his eye on Susa in the heart of Persia where he would set himself on Darius' throne beneath the famous golden canopy.[33] Afterwards, he would quickly march again in the winter to Persepolis, the most prominent of the Persian capitals and a holy city. "The gates were forced and Alexander entered the famous city on January 31, 330 B.C.."[34] Unlike previous cities, Persepolis was sacked and looted by Greek troops and Alexander, as king, took the treasury. Eventually, he burned the Hadish Palace (Xerxes I residence), which spread to the other buildings and eventually consumed the great Palace of 100 columns. Several reasons have been given for the destruction of the capital. Some say he did it in revenge for the burning of Athens, but in reality Alexander wished to send the message that the Achaemenid Empire had come to an end.[35]

Darius had fled from Gaugamela to Ecbatana and then to the Caspian Sea in Bactria (Afghanistan), where he was deposed in a coup and murdered by Bessus,[36] a relative and one of his own generals. Before he died, Alexander found him lying on the ground. After his death, he "covered [the body] with his own cloak and sent it back in state to Persepolis to be given a royal burial."[37]

The Persian Empire had fallen. The Lord had given Alexander power to defeat the largest empire in the world. But the king's thirst

The gates of the ancient capital of Persepolis in Iran

for conquest remained unsatisfied. In the summer of 327 B.C., he marched into India with weary troops. Holding to a desire to return to Greece they rebelled. "Coenus, one of his faithful officers, now old and ill, tried to reason with the infatuated Alexander, saying to him, 'Sir, if there is one thing a successful man should know, is when to stop.'"[38] Alexander was furious and persisted. It took another year for him to listen. In the mean time, he conquered the Hindus valley and defeated the great kingdom of king Porus (Purushottama).[39] Eventually he and the army made their way back to Susa and finally to Babylon where Alexander died in 323 B.C..

His conquest and reign brought Greek culture to Asia, which influenced the language, philosophy, science and classic art for centuries. It also introduced a basic form of democratic ideals, which settled into the region and planted the seeds for the foundation of western civilization. One historian said: "He was one of the supreme fertilizing forces in history. He lifted the civilized world out of one groove and set it in another, he started a new epoch; nothing could again be as it had been....Greek culture, heretofore practically confined to Greeks, spread throughout the world; as for the use of its inhabitants, in place of the many dialects of Greece, there came up the form of Greek known as the *koine*, 'the common speech.'"[40] This was the language spoken throughout the region in the day of the Lord's ministry.

The end of the Macedonian Empire, Antiochus IV Epiphanies, The Anti-Christ

_____

8   Therefore the he goat waxed very great: and when he was strong, the great horn was broken; and for it came up four notable ones toward the four winds of heaven.

9   And out of one of them came forth a little horn, which waxed exceeding great, toward the south, and toward the east, and toward the pleasant *land*.

_____

At the height of his power, Alexander died; the great horn was broken (Dan. 8:8). He passed away in Nebuchadnezzar's palace

Karl von Piloty © Public Domain
The death of Alexander the Great in Babylon by Polity

having suffered from complications of malaria or flu symptoms. Some argue that he died from the poison or the poisonous effects of over intoxication.[41] Signs of sickness were manifest shortly after a celebration in Babylon, and worsened over a period of 10 days. Historical accounts mention chills, sweats, exhaustion and high fever, typical symptoms of infectious diseases, including typhoid fever.[42] He succumbed to the illness in early June 323 B.C..

Alexander's Kingdom Broken Apart

In consequence of Alexander's death, the Empire fell into chaos and conflict. For several years, rival generals, known as the *Diadochi* or *the dynasties*, divided up and then fought for control over the kingdom. Battles, combinations for power and intrigue raged for more than a decade as they jostled for supremacy. Eventually, "four notable ones" or horns came up "toward the four winds of heaven" (Dan. 8:8). The Greek successors (or notable ones) were primarily generals who served and conquered under Alexander. Cassander remained in Macedonia and Greece; Lysimachus ruled over Thrace, Bithynia, and Phrygia of Asia Minor; Seleucus eventually secured Syria, Babylon, Persia and the regions eastward and Ptolemy assumed power in Egypt, Palestine and Arabia Petrea.[43]

These four Greek kingdoms represented the major powers established after Alexander's death. The wars and competition would continue to plague them for years to come.

The vision progresses from one kingdom to the next and doubtless included details about the kings and their kingdoms. But the vision's focus becomes a "little horn," which rose up from one of the kingdoms, the Syrian realm. As always, the horn symbolizes a king (Dan. 8:9). The Hebrew word used for *little* reflects "a horn less than little" or "a horn from littleness" meaning it "arose out of littleness, there lies the idea that it grew to great power from a small beginning; for it became very great and powerful toward the south, toward the east, and toward the [pleasant land] (*the splendour, glory*), i.e., toward the glorious land."[44] The prophecy emphasizes that this little horn, while rising from small beginnings, "waxed exceedingly great" (Dan. 8:9).

The "little horn" spoken of in this prophecy is Antiochus IV Epiphanies, the 8th Greek king of the Seleucid Empire who reigned from 175 B.C. to 164 B.C. Antiochus was the third son of Antiochus III, the Great. His father had expanded the Seleucid Kingdom from Phrygia (Turkey) to Parthia (Afghanistan), envisioning himself as a second Alexander. While attempting to expand into Greece, the Romans defeated him at the Battle of Magnesia (190 B.C.). Scipio subdued Antiochus III who was obliged to pay an indemnity of 15,000 talents of silver over a period of 12 years. He surrendered his elephants and his fleet, and gave up hostages, including his son Antiochus IV. The boy was carried captive into Rome to keep his father in good behavior.[45] Antiochus IV lived comfortably in Rome for 14 years. Antiochus the Great was killed near Susa while attempting to loot money from the temple treasury.[46]

The eldest son, Seleucus (Philopator), assumed the throne. In accordance with the Roman treaty, he sent his young son Demetrius to replace Antiochus IV as a hostage in Rome. While on the way back to Antioch, he heard news that his brother Seleucus had been murdered by a usurper Heliodorus, the treasurer. Antiochus immediately elicited help from the king of Pergamum to overthrow the usurper and retake the kingdom.[47] After a short battle, Antiochus took possession of the Syrian throne, which rightly belonged to his nephew Demetrius.[48] Eventually, he eliminated all other possible heirs to the kingdom, including his nephew and became the king of the Seleucid Empire.

Berlin Museum © Public Domain

Bust of Antiochus Epiphanies in Berlin Museum

Historians record that Antiochus was considered by many to be emotionally unstable and violent by nature. Later in his rule, he added Epiphanies to his name, which meant "manifestation" or the "Illustrious One." His contemporaries nicknamed him Epimanes, meaning "madman."[49] His demeanor revealed a penchant for passionate excesses, competition and ambition. And when it came to conquests, his desires were tempered only by the Roman Empire. He did "prosper" by securing and expanding the kingdom into the east and the south. He reinforced his hold on Babylon, Persia and Armenia. His father had taken Coele-Syria (Palestine) or as Daniel called it, "the pleasant land," or the Holy Land. It was ever a disputed possession of the Ptolemaic and Seleucid kingdoms.

In 170 B.C., a contest arose between the young Egyptian Pharaoh Ptolemy VI (Philometor) and Antiochus over Coele-Syria. The Pharaoh demanded the return of the territory from Egypt to Damascus traditionally held by the Ptolemies. Antiochus responded by preemptively invading Egypt and conquering the entire region except for the city of Alexandria. In the invasion, he managed to capture the king. Since Ptolemy's wife Cleopatra was his niece, Antiochus claimed that he was merely the protector of the land, not an invader, hoping that would suffice Roman concerns. When Egypt appealed to Rome in 168 B.C., Antiochus led a second attack and also sent a fleet to capture Cyprus. His assault was halted with the arrival of the Roman ambassador (*Gaius Popillius Laenas*), who delivered a message warning him that if he continued, the Senate would consider the Syrians to be in a state of war with Rome. He capitulated and withdrew.

Antiochus's Campaign Against the Jews

———

10 And it waxed great, even to the host of heaven; and it cast down some of the host and of the stars to the ground, and stamped upon them.

11 Yea, he magnified himself even to the prince of the host, and by him the daily sacrifice was taken away, and the place of his sanctuary was cast down.

12 And an host was given him against the daily sacrifice by reason of transgression, and it cast down the truth to the ground; and it practised, and prospered.

———

The detail of Daniel's prophecy of the 'little horn' becomes relevant at this point in history after Antiochus was ordered to withdraw from Egypt. During the campaign, a rumor spread throughout the Jewish kingdom that he was killed in battle. At the time the rightful heir to the High Priest position, Jason, had been replaced by Menelaus an appointee of Antiochus. At first news of his death, Jason gathered a thousand men and drove Menelaus out and retook his station at Jerusalem. Forced to flee, the deposed high priest retreated south and met with Antiochus and his armies bearing news of the Jewish insurrection.

Enraged with Judah's rebellion and smarting from his failure in Egypt, the Syrian King marched to Jerusalem to restore Menelaus. The Maccabean account describes the assault as follows: "When these happenings were reported to the king, he thought that Judea was in revolt. Raging like a wild animal, he set out from Egypt and took Jerusalem by storm. He ordered his soldiers to cut down without mercy those whom they met and to slay those who took refuge in their houses. There was a massacre of young and old, a killing of women and children, a slaughter of virgins and infants. In the space of three days, eighty thousand were lost, forty thousand meeting a violent death, and the same number being sold into slavery" (2 Macc. 5:11–14).

Antiochus himself entered the temple, sacrificed a pig on the altar and ordered the worship of the Olympian Zeus as the supreme god. Two years later, a statue of the pagan god—cast in the image of the king himself—was placed in the temple. Antiochus claimed that Zeus had manifested himself to the king. He therefore became Antiochus Epiphanies, or god has "manifest" himself. (2 Macc 4:7)[50] He appointed "an elderly Athenian (Philip) to conduct a campaign to force the Jews to abandon their religion and the customs of their ancestors" (2 Macc. 6:1). By the edicts of Antiochus, Philip moved with an army of soldiers disrupting Jewish worship by subverting the Mosaic temple rites. The temple was desecrated again on December 25, 167 B.C. when the sacrifices were forcibly ordered to cease (Dan. 8:12). A Greek altar was erected in place of the Mosaic altar.[51] Antiochus's soldiers ransacked the local houses and destroyed all copies of scripture (scrolls) that could be found, "casting truth to the ground" (Dan 8:12). A few Jews discovered in possession of the Holy Writ were put to death. Antiochus resorted to every conceivable method to force them to renounce their religion.

The phrase "and an host was given *him* against the daily *sacrifice*" (Dan 8:12) meant that because of pride and rebellion, the daily sacrifices were given to the transgressors. The High Priest's office had become corrupt and the secular (Hellenized) Jews allowed the temple mount to be modified to reflect the pagan gardens and courtyards of Greek temples. Frequently, Greeks and sympathetic Jews (or the transgressors) in control of the temple participated in celebrations with drinking and the sacrificing of forbidden animals. Those Jews, faithful to their religion, were prohibited attendance at the temple and could not worship according to the Mosaic Law. "The neighboring Greek cities were also instructed to require Jews to eat the [unclean] sacrifices; they were told to put to death every Jew who refused to adopt the Greek way of life" (Macc. 6:8-9). All efforts to pervert or destroy the Jewish culture and religion prospered (Dan. 8:12).

The vision states the king cast down the "hosts of heaven" (Dan. 8:10) and "magnified *himself* even to the prince of the host" (Dan. 8:11). The term "host of heaven" serves as a poetical description of God's chosen people. Job, for example, referred to the host of heaven—primarily the chosen people—as the stars of heaven, who shouted and sang for joy in the pre-mortal realm before the foundations of the earth. (Job 38:7). In this vision these "stars" were cast down "to the ground, and stamped upon" (Dan. 8:11).

In addition, "he magnified himself even to the prince of the hosts" (Dan 8:11). Most of the eastern kings by tradition magnified themselves proclaiming to be favored by the gods or the incarnation of their god on the earth. The "magnification" described in this vision, however, directly pits Antiochus against the Prince of the hosts, or Jehovah. The act of placing the idol statue of Zeus created in his own image within the Holy of Holies amounted to a clear act of blasphemy. "Antiochus gave orders that they should 'forbid burnt-offerings, and sacrifice, and drink-offerings in the temple; and that they should profane the Sabbath and festival days.'"[52] The added use of military force and political edicts prohibiting the worship of Jehovah became a serious imposition upon the hosts of the faithful and a total affront to the God of Heaven.

It was during this period of persecution that "Antiochus issued coins with the title '"Epiphanies' which claimed that he had been blessed by the gods, which manifested divine honors and showed him as beardless and wearing a diadem."[53] Certainly, his successes resulted in a high level of self-preoccupation sufficient for him to believe that he was "enlightened" by the gods. Having adopted the idea of a favored ruler served to embolden his resolve to replace the religion of the God of Israel with that of the Greek god Zeus.

Antiochus's motivations against the Jews were very political. His distaste for the Jewish religion was palpable. In his mind, unifying the kingdom meant Hellenizing the kingdom. He felt that their religion engendered disloyalty to the state, which was evidenced by their rebellion. If he could convert (or subvert) the more pious Jews from their traditions, then the cultural differences would fade and loyalty would be the natural outcome. Antiochus elicited help from the secular Jews who already supported Hellenized culture and, he felt, would help bring about the ultimate political goals. These "transgressors" (Dan. 8:23) did align with the Greek authorities.

James Tissot © 1902 Public Domain

Depiction of the Second Temple by James Tissot Brooklyn Museum

The Jews claimed to have rejected idolatry in its traditional forms of graven statues and grove festivals. But those enamoured with the classical, philosophical, scientific and artistic ideals of Greek Hellenism also adopted the pagan, mystical and carnal aspects of the culture. These secularists had become just as idolatrous as their ancestors. They formed the upper class or the more "sophisticated" and "refined" secular Jews in Jerusalem's society. They looked down upon their pious brethren. Many jockeyed for acceptance in the "high society" and for positions and favors granted by their rulers, as was the case of Jason and Menelaus. Such efforts meant drinking in with Greek traditions, approving of the pagan beliefs and in most cases falling into moral transgression. These compromises proved just as destructive as the ancient worshiping of Baal or Moloch. Hence the Lord referred to them as "transgressors" (Dan. 8:23). The Jewish apostates or "transgressors" clearly enabled, even supported, the campaign "against the daily *sacrifice* by reason of transgression" (Dan. 8:12). They, together with the Greek rulers and the army, cast the "truth" and the hosts of chosen to the ground. In the short term, they prospered under the grateful hand of their political rulers.

The Duration of the Persecutions

13 Then I heard one saint speaking, and another saint said unto that certain saint which spake, How long shall be the vision concerning the daily sacrifice,

and the transgression of desolation, to give both the
sanctuary and the host to be trodden under foot?

14   And he said unto me, Unto two thousand and three
hundred days; then shall the sanctuary be cleansed.

———

Daniel writes that in the vision he hears one messenger speak
to another asking: "How long *shall be* the vision *concerning* the
daily sacrifice, and the transgression of desolation, to give both
the sanctuary and the host to be trodden under foot?" (Dan. 8:13).
Apparently, an angel prompts another to explain to the prophet how
long these events will be allowed to continue. Daniel, obviously
very concerned at the tribulations inflicted on the Jews, "sought for
meaning" (Dan 8:15) as to the length and purpose of these very
difficult trials.

The angel in the vision reveals that the stopping of "the daily
sacrifice" continued for "two thousand and three hundred days" (Dan.
8:14), the period in which the sanctuary was "cast down" or under
control of the Greeks (Dan. 8:11). Young adds that "Antiochus did
not actually tear down the temple although he evidently desecrated
it to such a point that it was hardly fit for use."[54]

The messenger responds with 2300 days; "then shall the sanctuary
be cleansed" (Dan. 8:14). While Antiochus's violent assault began
two years prior to the desecration of the temple and the erection of
the Greek altar, the focus is the stoppage of religious worship in the
temple. By applying a traditional Hebrew interpretation, we arrive
at a meaningful conclusion. Kiel explains: "This separation of the
expression "days" into evenings and mornings, so that to number
them separately would make 2300 evening-mornings or 1150 actual
days *is appropriate*. ...When the Hebrews wish to express separately
day and night, the component parts of a day, then the number of
both is expressed. They say, forty days and forty nights (Gen.
7:4, 7:12; Ex. 24:18; 1 Kgs. 19:8), and three days and three nights
(Jonah 2:1; Matt. 12:40). ...In the designation of time, 'till 2300
evening-mornings,' could be understood the evening and morning
sacrifices, and the words be regarded as meaning, that till 1150
evening sacrifices and 1150 morning sacrifices are discontinued."[55]

The scholar appropriately focuses on the morning and evening worship exemplified by the daily sacrifices at the temple, which had been suppressed. By replacing 2300 days to mean 1150 morning sacrifices and 1150 evening sacrifices we arrive at about 3 and ½ years. The number 3 ½ is consistent with other passages frequently used to symbolize a period of crisis or oppression when the anti-Christs persecute the people of God (Dan. 12:11, Rev 11:2). It doesn't necessarily have to be 3 ½ years, but serves symbolically to highlight a critical time in which the covenant people find themselves persecuted and unable to openly worship their God. In most cases, it also provides a rough estimation of the actual timeframe.

Both the vision and the interpretation of the vision caused a tender-hearted Daniel serious concern.

The Interpretation of the Dream

———

15 And it came to pass, when I, *even* I Daniel, had seen the vision, and sought for the meaning, then, behold, there stood before me as the appearance of a man.

16 And I heard a man's voice between *the banks of* Ulai, which called, and said, Gabriel, make this *man* to understand the vision.

17 So he came near where I stood: and when he came, I was afraid, and fell upon my face: but he said unto me, Understand, O son of man: for at the time of the end *shall be* the vision.

18 Now as he was speaking with me, I was in a deep sleep on my face toward the ground: but he touched me, and set me upright.

19 And he said, Behold, I will make thee know what shall be in the last end of the indignation: for at the time appointed the end *shall be.*

———

Another heavenly messenger comes into view and instructs Gabriel to help the prophet understand the meaning of the vision.[56] The messenger was probably Michael, who stands above Gabriel in authority (Doctrine and Covenant 107:54; 130:5).[57] This vision marks the first time that Gabriel is mentioned in the Bible. He is referred to again in Daniel 9:21 and in Luke 1:19, 26, where he announces the births of John the Baptist and of Jesus to Mary.

Daniel's reaction to the exchange between the messengers was that of fear. He writes that he fell facedown as asleep. He was probably overwhelmed with the entire experience. Gabriel reaches down to provide strength so he could lift himself up. His touch gave him sufficient power to stand and receive the remaining portion of the interpretation. A similar event occurs in the Revelation of John, when the Apostle fell and worshipped a messenger from heaven (Rev. 19:10) and was commanded to rise. Both Daniel and John were blessed or empowered sufficiently to continue with the vision experience.

The Last End of the Vision

Gabriel's explanation focuses on "the last end," speaking of the end of the persecutions or when the trials shall end. "That which is to take place in the close of the indignation-period is the most prominent thing in the vision and that which Daniel and the Jewish people were most interested to know."[58]

The messenger also refers to the end of God's indignation (Dan. 8:19).[59] The reference here does not reflect Jehovah's anger against Antiochus, although His judgments eventually befell the persecutor, but rather God's divine wrath against the Jews themselves.[60] The question may be asked, why allow Antiochus's terrible brutality? But as was discussed, it was paganism and apostasy that had crept deeply into many corners of Jewish culture that brought the wrath of the Lord. We know of the intrigue that plagued those who sought the High Priest's office. Even though Jason was the rightful heir prior to being ousted, he built a Greek Gymnasium in Jerusalem for the training of boys for the games and the education of Hellenism. The ills of Greek paganism cankered many of the aristocracy and learned who had drifted from or completely abandoned the Mosaic Law. The Lord saw fit to chasten Israel for "[He] doth chasten his people with many afflictions, yea, except he doth visit them with death and with terror, and with famine and with all manner of pestilence, they will not remember him" (Hel. 12:3).

Similar events are recorded in early Church History. The Latter-day Saints underwent terrible persecutions in Missouri. The Lord explains that He "suffered the affliction to come upon them, wherewith they have been afflicted, in consequence of their transgression…there were jarrings, and contentions, and envyings, and strifes, and lustful and covetous desires among them; therefore by these things they polluted their inheritances…They were slow to hearken unto the voice of the Lord their God" (Doctrine and Covenants 101:2, 6-7). But in mercy, He promised: "Yet I will own them, and they shall be mine in that day when I shall come to make up my jewels. Therefore, they must needs be chastened and tried, even as Abraham, who was commanded to offer up his only son. For all those who will not endure chastening, but deny me, cannot be sanctified." (Doctrine and Covenants 101:3-5).

Jehovah allowed trials to fall upon the Jews with the intent to purge wickedness, purify the righteous and seal up the transgressors. Those who were martyred for faithfulness entered into His rest to receive their rewards. Others, who remained true despite the persecutions, came through purer and more suitable for the kingdom of God. Yet there were many who participated in the persecutions because they were lured away into worldly paths to be sifted and rejected in the final Day of Judgment (Doctrine and Covenants 63:63). The trial was doubtless severe, even a painful process, but necessary for the testing and purification of the Jewish nation to fulfill the covenant and the Plan of Redemption. The Lord was able to both chasten and purify those who would endure and remain faithful while at the same time seal up the wicked unto darkness (Doctrine and Covenants 133:72). Antiochus was held accountable for his brutality. He died of an illness while fighting in a campaign in Tabae.[61]

Gabriel's explanation of "the last end of the indignation" (Dan. 8:19), came with the assurance that when the full measure of the transgressor's cup was filled and the chastisement of the Jews complete, "the time appointed the end *shall be*" fulfilled (Dan. 8:19, see also Doctrine and Covenants 103:3). The objectives and duration of the trial were fixed according to the foreknowledge of

God.[62] The angel assures Daniel that Judah's pain would eventually end. "This sense of 'end' is probably based upon the use of the word in Amos 8:2, Ezek. 7:2, 'An End!…'For still the vision awaits its appointed time; it hastens to the end—it will not lie. If it seems slow, wait for it. It will surely come; it will not delay.'"[63] The time of indignation is set and will not be allowed go an additional day, but must persist until the Lord's purposes are fulfilled.

A note in the Septuagint states that "The End" means the end of the Gentiles or the end of the world. "But this is to read into the [meaning] what is not found there. Gabriel explicitly states that the vision has reference to the latter part of the Wrath [or indignation] (not the end of the times of the Gentiles)."[64] The vision's focus clearly means the end of the persecutions in Judah.

While "the end" refers to the days of Antiochus's rage, the lessons taught in these passages are instructive for the latter-days. The Jews experience provides a pattern for events that will be repeated again at the end of the world (Dan 12;10:11). We consider that in the latter-days, there will come again a "little horn" (Dan. 7:8), whose attitude and disposition bring again persecutions and trials like those imposed by Antiochus Epiphanies. The record states that he will also exalt himself, "speak great words against the most high" and seek to "wear out the saints and change times and laws" (Dan. 7:25).

The end of Chapter 11 and Chapter 12 provide insight into the persecutions sent upon the righteous in the latter days. They speak of a similar "time that the daily sacrifice shall be taken away, and the abomination that maketh desolate set up. (Dan 12:11). Just like the ancient trials of Antiochus, it will involve much sifting and chastening to prepare of the Saints in preparation for the Coming of the Lord. The Lord will use these events to separate the people, both saints and gentiles alike into their own place to prepare the world for burning (Doctrine and Covenants 86:7; 3 Ne. 18:18).

Additional interpretations of the Vision

20 The ram which thou sawest having *two* horns *are* the kings of Media and Persia.

21 And the rough goat *is* the king of Grecia: and the great horn that *is* between his eyes *is* the first king.

22 Now that being broken, whereas four stood up for it, four kingdoms shall stand up out of the nation, but not in his power.

Again, Gabriel confirms that the ram with the two horns represented the nearby powers of Media and Persia—a supposition that Daniel had likely suspected. He may also have determined the explanation of the "rough goat" to be Greece, an influential power from the west whose citizens had already impacted Asia and the Middle East through immigration and trade. As mentioned, a popular figure worshiped in Greece was the rustic Pan, the half man-half goat god of the wild and shepherds. Gabriel explained that the "great horn" was the first king, referring, of course, to Alexander the Great. While his father Philip II, was the king that made Macedonia the dominant power among the Greek states, Alexander used this power to expand the Grecian Empire from Athens to India and Northern Africa to the Caspian Sea. Alexander died and his kingdom fractured into multiple smaller kingdoms. Eventually, four Greek generals took reign over four major kingdoms that would rule for the next 200 years.

The Latter-time of their kingdom and the transgressors

23 And in the latter time of their kingdom, when the transgressors are come to the full, a king of fierce countenance, and understanding dark sentences, shall stand up.

24 And his power shall be mighty, but not by his own power: and he shall destroy wonderfully, and shall prosper, and practise, and shall destroy the mighty and the holy people.

25 And through his policy also he shall cause craft to prosper in his hand; and he shall magnify *himself* in

> his heart, and by peace shall destroy many: he shall
> also stand up against the Prince of princes; but he
> shall be broken without hand.

———

Gabriel provides greater explanation on the latter era of the Seleucid Kingdom. He mentions specifically the time when the transgressors had come into the full. He speaks of Apostasy in Judah, when the hearts of many Jews had abandoned the Mosaic religion in favor of the Greek culture. "Hellenism spread in Judaea as it did everywhere else. The richer and more aristocratic Jews— those closest in contact with the...authorities—tended to embrace Hellenistic culture...Hellenism intrigued many wealthy and educated Jerusalemites because of its emphasis on human reason, science, art and architecture, physical beauty, aesthetics, nature, the glorification of the human body and the observable world."[65] While the Greeks promote much pagan evil, Young explains that "the transgressor[s] are not the heathen, but the apostate Jews who introduced heathen rites among the Jews, and built in Jerusalem a heathen Gymnasium for their games."[66] Gabriel reaffirms that at this time when the transgressors have so much influence in Judah that "a king of fierce countenance...shall stand up" (Dan. 8:23).

Antiochus is described as having a "fierce countenance" (Dan. 8:23) or translated, a violent disposition. His ferocious, even vindictive nature would rise in full display in his campaign against the Jewish culture. Moses spoke of the Assyrian empire whose disposition was like that of Antiochus. He described their armies as a "nation of *fierce countenance*, which shall not regard the person of the old, nor shew favour to the young" (Deut. 28:50, *emphasis added*). "[The] phrase oft-repeated by Assyrian kings in their inscriptions regarding military conquests was, "I destroyed, devastated, and burned with fire those cities, towns, and regions which resisted Assyrian rule."[67] Assyrian methods of conquest were without compassion, uprooting and enslaving whole populations.

Antiochus exercised similar strategies against his own subjects, not literally sweeping whole countries away, although many individuals were sold into slavery or brutally killed, but by enforcing his will through law, policy and military force. He intended to denationalize provincial cultures and then reenforce the Hellenistic thought and culture.

The revelation states that he would also uproot the culture of the Jews by law and by policy. Gabriel informs the prophet that "through his policy also he shall cause craft to prosper in his hand" (Dan. 8:25). Antiochus's use of diplomacy, edicts and policy also proved as effective as military actions. He took advantage of the schism between the Jewish aristocracy and the more pious commoner. His craft involved the use of "dark sentences," which is often translated as riddles or a "master of intrigue" (NIV).

Some have suggested that it denotes the mark of a keen intellect or the ability to solve problems and out think opponents. This may have been true, but the meaning of dark sentences more accurately describes a crafty disposition, a tactic of pitting one group against another to gain advantage by flattery and intrigue, in this case among the squabbling Jews. Antiochus was well practiced in deceit, a consummate corrupt politician, "a master of dissimulation, able to conceal his meaning under ambiguous words and so disguise his real purposes."[68] Beginning with his own machinations to take the throne from his nephew, he became an expert in cunning and lies. He regularly used deception in his governance and negotiations and being himself full of suspicion, he could not be easily deceived.

Such characteristics are common to anti-Christs, who often do not or cannot divulge their true purposes, but rather couch their deceitful intents in cleverly crafted words and ideas. They seek their ends through guile, always looking for advantage. Contrast this strategy with the Lord's methods. Nephi taught that: "the Lord worketh not in darkness. He doeth not anything save it be for the benefit of the world; for he loveth the world, even that he layeth down his own life that he may draw all men unto him" (2 Ne. 26:23-24). The nature of the devil and those who yield themselves to him is to beguile or work in darkness [or in secret] and by force to attain their ends (Doctrine and Covenants 38:13, 28). Apparently, Antiochus was a master of the art of manipulation, both in his ascension to power, his governance of the empire and his manipulation of sympathetic Jews to attain his ends.

His ambition and personality, supported by a large military, produced the right formula to become a mighty dictator and to prosper against his foes and political enemies. Interesting is the statement "And his power shall be mighty, but not by his own power" (Dan. 8:24). He secured control, not of his own strength, for he had none, but with the help of the power of another. Without outside help he might never have attained his desire for the throne or remained in control of the empire.

Commentators have suggested a few possibilities as the source of "help." They include God, Alexander the Great, fellow collaborators, or the devil. Alexander the Great, of course, could not have helped him and God certainly took no part in his rise to power. Antiochus did elicit and receive help from the Pergamese King, Eumenes II to overthrow the usurper Heliodorus.

Once in control, maintaining the kingdom required winning internal support, which involved gaining political and military loyalty. The "wicked" leader, "a master of intrigue" (Dan. 8:23 NIV), secured loyalty through the promise of wealth, favors and station. The Book of Mormon reveals that a common method for obtaining power and position among the wicked is through evil oaths of loyalty administered in secret combinations (Ether 8). History does not portray Antiochus's rise to power in the context of secret combinations; however, it was not uncommon to secure the throne and maintain governance using cabals, oaths and combinations to secure and then maintain control. The devil is, of course, happy to reveal these technics and stir up secret combinations to place evil people in power (2 Ne. 9:9).

By all standards, he destroyed "wonderfully" and as a result, he prospered. Other translations render the verse: "He will cause a shocking amount of destruction and succeed in everything he does. He will destroy powerful leaders and devastate the holy people" (Dan. 8:24 NIV). His rise to power was bloody, especially with the murder of his nephew and likely, others. His campaigns and conquests to conquer and denationalize subdued nations were equally brutal. His treatment of the Holy People was filled with savagery and vindictiveness. And his successes brought to him a

The Punishment of Antiochus by Gustave Dore

sense of security and invincibility. While it was common for Greek and later, Roman rulers to associate themselves with pagan deity, it seems that he held a special ability to "magnify *himself* in his heart" (Dan. 8:25).

Gabriel explained that "by peace" or, in peace without warning, "shall destroy many" (Dan. 8:25). The majority of his conquests came by surprise, without notice or in the middle or overtures of peace. This was certainly true of his intrusions into Egypt. Negotiation seemed not to be an option and only the might of the Roman Empire stifled his ambition to keep Egypt in check.

His routing of the Armenians, and even his attack on the Jews, came without notice or negotiation. Finally, through the craft of flattery and deception, he seduced many to follow his designs by joining his subtle promises.

His ego, combined with the criminal oppression of the holy people became the final affront to the "Prince of princes," or Jehovah (Dan. 8.25). Antiochus was broken without hand. No mortal broke him, he did not die in battle, nor was he assassinated. The divine hand of Providence quietly brought a ignominious end to his rule in 164 B.C. Not many days after learning that the Jews had overthrown his Greek garrisons in Judea, he died of stomach worms in Tabae, Iran. His death proved to be a relatively simple execution of Divine power to bring justice to the great persecutor and desecrator of the holy temple.

The Testimony and Daniel's Reaction

26 And the vision of the evening and the morning which was told *is* true: wherefore shut thou up the vision; for it *shall be* for many days.

27 And I Daniel fainted, and was sick *certain* days; afterward I rose up, and did the king's business; and I was astonished at the vision, but none understood *it*.

The angel seals the vision with his personal witness. He testifies that what Daniel had seen and heard was true and that it should be recorded and "shut up." "This does not mean that he was necessarily to keep it secret, but that he should preserve it. 'Preserve the revelation, not because it is not yet to be understood, also not for the purpose of keeping it a secret, but that it may remain reserved for distant times.'"[69] The vision's fulfillment would span over many hundreds of years and prove a beneficial record over that time. Like any scripture, the preservation of the revelation would be a helpful resource for generations to assist them in understanding the hand of God in the affairs of both the gentiles and the holy people.

Daniel was overwhelmed by the experience, particularly the interpretation, that he fell ill. The prophet's gentle and sensitive nature was so troubled by what he had seen that he naturally reacted with disgust. What he witnessed made him physically and emotionally unwell. Only after several days could he gather himself and return to his duties in the palace. Apparently, he shared portions of the vision with friends and confidants, but none could truly appreciate what he had seen and heard.

Chapter Notes

1   Walvoord. *The Key to Prophetic Revelation*. 221
2   Young. *The Prophecy Daniel: A Commentary*. 165
3   Ibid. 167
4   Walvoord. *Daniel: The Key to Prophetic Revelation*. 223
5   Masuri. *The history of political relations between Elam and Assyria. International Research Journal of Applied and Basic Sciences*. Vol. 4. 2176-2179
6   Tavernier. Jan. "Some Thoughts in Neo-Elamite Chronology" (PDF). 27
7   Josephus. *Antiquities of the Jews* X.7. 227
8   Walvoord. *The Key to Prophetic Revelation*. 222
9   Josephus. *Antiquities of the Jews*. X:9:27-28
10   Jamieson. *Bible Commentary*. Vol. 2, 620
11   Briant. *From Cyrus to Alexander: A History of the Persian Empire*. 31–33
12   Young. *The Prophecy Daniel: A Commentary*. 168
13   Joshua. "Xerxes Ancient I." *History Encyclopedia*. 28. April 2011 http://www.ancient.eu/Xerxes_I/
14   League of Corinth or Hellenic League (Greek league) comprised of a federation of Greek states created by Philip II of Macedon in 338 BC/337 B.C. after he defeated Athens and Thebes at the Battle of Chaeronea. Its intent was to create a unified political body among all Grecian states principally to unify the Greek against the Persians (Pohlenz. *Freedom in Greek life and thought: the history of an ideal*. 20)
15   Walvoord. *Daniel: The Key to Prophetic Revelation*. 227
16   Plutarch 1919. VI. 5
17   Roisman. "*A Companion to Ancient Macedonia.* " 188
18   Phillips. *Exploring the Book of Daniel: An Expository Commentary*. 133
19   Ibid. 133
20   Josephus *Antiquities of the Jews*. Book XI. Chapter 8:5
21   Phillips. *Exploring the Book of Daniel: An Expository Commentary*. 133
22   Cartledge. *Alexander the Great*. 230. 147-49; Briant. *Alexander the Great and His Empire*. 137
23   Ibid 147-49; Ibid 51
24   Grzybeck. E.. Du calendrier macédonien au calendrier ptolémaïque. Basel. 1990. 63
25   Cartledge. *Alexander the Great*. 230. 147-49; Briant. *Alexander the Great and His Empire*. 51
26   Phillips. *Exploring the Book of Daniel: An Expository Commentary*. 134
27   Josephus *Antiquities of the Jews*. X1.8.4
28   Cartledge. *Alexander the Great*. 52. 150. 152; Briant. *Alexander the Great and His Empire*. 104
29   Walvoord. *Daniel: The Key to Prophetic Revelation*. 227
30   Briant. *Alexander the Great and His Empire*. 111-115
31   Cartledge. *Alexander the Great*. 230. 147-49; Briant. *Alexander the Great and His Empire*. 101-103. 116-117. Military 111-115
32   Phillips. *Exploring the Book of Daniel: An Expository Commentary*. 134
33   O Brian. *Alexander the Great: The Invisible Enemy: A Biography*. 95
34   Phillips. *Exploring the Book of Daniel: An Expository Commentary*. 135
35   Briant. *Alexander the Great and his Empire*. 110-11. see also 34. 106; Sachau. *The Chronology of Ancient Nations*. 484

36   Cartledge. *Alexander the Great.* 152; Briant. *Alexander the Great and His Empire.* 112-113

37   Greene. Peter. *Alexander of Macedon. 356-323 B.C.: A Historical Biography.* 200-201; Phillips. *Exploring the Book of Daniel: An Expository Commentary.* 134-35

38   Phillips. *Exploring the Book of Daniel: An Expository Commentary.* 136

39   Cartledge. *Alexander the Great.* 34. 311

40   Tarn. *Alexander the Great.* 2 Vol.. Vol. 1:145-46

41   Cartledge. *Alexander the Great.* 215

42   "Intestinal Bug Likely Killed Alexander The Great". University of Maryland Medical Center. Retrieved Aug. 21. 2011

43   Keil. *Biblical Commentary of the Old Testament. The Book of the Prophet Daniel.* 293

44   Ibid. 295

45   Volkman. "Antiochus II the Great." *Encyclopedia Britannica.* Sept. 6. 2016. https://www.britannica.com/biography/Antiochus-III-the-Great; Phillips 140

46   Ibid

47   Ibid. 140

48   The Jewish Encyclopedia. 634

49   Ironside H. A. *Lectures on Daniel the Prophet.* 202

50   Skinner, Ogden, Galbraith. *Jerusalem the Eternal City.* 142

51   Walvoord. Daniel: *The Key to Prophetic Revelation.* 234

52   Keil. *Biblical Commentary of the Old Testament. The Book of the Prophet Daniel.* Dan 8:11

53   Walvoord. *Daniel: The Key to Prophetic Revelation.* 234. Wheaton. "Antiochus" in the *New Bible Dictionary.* J. D. Douglas ed.. 41-42

54   Young. *The Prophecy Daniel: A Commentary.* 172

55   Keil. *Biblical Commentary of the Old Testament. The Book of the Prophet Daniel.* 303-04 Edited for clarity

56   Walvoord. *Daniel: The Key to Prophetic Revelation.* 235-36

57   Smith. *History of the Church.* 3:385–86 "The Priesthood was first given to Adam; he obtained the First Presidency. and held the keys of it from generation to generation. He obtained it in the Creation before the world was formed as in Gen. 1:26. 27. 28. He had dominion given him over every living creature. He is Michael the Archangel spoken of in the Scriptures. Then to Noah, who is Gabriel; he stands next in authority to Adam in the Priesthood; he was called of God to this office. and was the father of all living in his day. and to him was given the dominion. These men held keys first on earth and then in heaven." (*History of the Church.* 3:385–86.)

58   Young. *The Prophecy Daniel: A Commentary.* 177

59   "Time of the end' is the general prophetic expression for the time which, as the period of fulfillment, lies at the end of the existing prophetic horizon—in the present case the time of Antiochus." Keil. *Biblical Commentary of the Old Testament. The Book of the Prophet Daniel.* 310. Auberlen. 89

60   *Young.* Edward J.. *The Prophecy Daniel: A Commentary.* 177; Wood. Daniel. 217-19

61   *Encyclopedia Britannica.* ref: "Antiochus IV Epiphanies." Volkmann. see also 2 Macc. 9:3-37. https://www.britannica.com/biography/Antiochus-IV-Epiphanes

62   Ibid. 177

63   Driver. *Daniel.* 99

64   Young. *The Prophecy Daniel: A Commentary.* 177
65   Skinner, Ogden, Galbraith. *Jerusalem the Eternal City.* 141
66   Young. *The Prophecy Daniel: A Commentary.* 179
67   Mark. *"Assyrian Warfare." History Encyclopedia.* August 11. 2014; http://www.
     ancient.eu/Assyrian_Warfare/
68   Driver. *Young.* 179
69   Young. *The Prophecy Daniel: A Commentary.* 181. Kliefoth

Additional Notes

Efforts to Hellenize the Kingdom

Both economically and socially he [Antiochus Epiphanies] made efforts to strengthen his kingdom—inhabited in the main by Orientals (non-Greeks of Asia Minor and Persia)—by founding and fostering Greek cities. Even before he had begun his reign he had contributed to the building of the temple of Zeus in Athens and to the adornment of the theatre. He enlarged Antioch on the Orontes by adding a section to the city (named Epiphania after him). There he built an aqueduct, a council hall, a marketplace, and a temple to Jupiter Capitolinus. Babylon, which revered him as Soter (Liberator, or Saviour) of Asia, was given a Greek colony that was granted freedom of the city. Another Epiphania was founded in Armenia. Ecbatana (in Persia) was also named Epiphania and became a Greek city. Many of these cities were granted the right to coin their own municipal currency. The mint of Antioch on the Persian Gulf served the trade along the sea route between India and the district at the mouth of the great Mesopotamian rivers.

Antiochus' hellenizing policies brought him into conflict with the prosperous Oriental temple organizations, and particularly with the Jews. Since Antiochus III's reign the Jews had enjoyed extensive autonomy under their high priest. They were divided into two parties, the orthodox Hasideans (Pious Ones) and a reform party that favoured Hellenism. For financial reasons Antiochus supported the reform party and, in return for a considerable sum, permitted the high priest, Jason to build a gymnasium in Jerusalem and to introduce the Greek mode of educating young people. In 172, for an even bigger tribute, he appointed Menelausin place of Jason 169, however, while Antiochus was campaigning in Egypt, Jason conquered Jerusalem—with the exception of the citadel—and murdered many adherents of his rival Menelaus. When Antiochus returned from Egypt in 167 he took Jerusalem by storm and enforced its Hellenization. The city forfeited its privileges and was permanently garrisoned by Syrian soldiers. (Volkman, Hans, Antiochus IV Epiphanes, http://www.britannica. com/biography/Antiochus-IV-Epiphanes

Lesson of Antiochus for the Latter-days

The prophecy of Antiochus Epiphanies is commonly viewed as a foreshadowing of the Roman siege and destruction of the temple and the "little horn" or anti-Christ spoken that will come in the latter-days spoken of in chapter 7.

"The key to understand chapter 7 though 12 of Daniel's prophecies is to understand that Daniel is focusing his attention to the one great ruler and his kingdom which will rise at the end of time. And while Daniel may use historical reference and refer to events which to us may be fulfilled, Daniel is thinking of them only to give us more details about this final form of Gentile world power and its ruler who would reign on the earth...[Antiochus Epiphanies] was known as one who desolated, or "the desolator." But this passage in Daniel 8 is speaking not only of Antiochus in his desolation and his desecration of the temple; it is looking forward to the great desolator who would come, the one who is called "the little horn: in Daniel chapter 7." (Pentecost, *Prophecy for Today*, 82-83; See also: Walvoord, 240-41.)

A review of his character, motives and methods can be instructive. Pentecost provides a summary of the fact as outlined in Daniel 8:23-25: "a description of the beast in that (1) he is to appear at the latter time of Israel's history (v. 23); (2) through alliance with other nations he achieves worldwide influence; (3) a peace program helps him rise to power; (4) he is extremely intelligent and persuasive; (5) he is characterized by satanic control (v. 24); (6) he is a great adversary against Israel and the prince of princes (v 24-25) and direct judgment from God terminates his rule (v 25)" (Pentecost, *Things to Come*, 332-34. Walvoord, 241)

9

Prophecy of the Seventy Weeks

Daniel's experience in Chapter 9 occurred roughly ten years after the panoramic vision recorded in Chapter 7 and seven years after Chapter 8 (538 B.C.). At this point, he had witnessed the downfall of the Babylonian Empire and the rise and conquest of the Medo-Persian Empire. The fulfillment of the prophecies made about the local kingdoms were in full motion. In roughly two hundred years, Macedonian hoplites and cavalry would overrun the Persian Empire and so the prophetic vision would continue to unfold until the end of the world. Daniel, seeing the beginning of these things come to pass, also wondered about his own people. The Jews return to Jerusalem was a question that weighed heavily on his mind. Seventy years had passed and the hour of the fulfillment for this prophecy seemed eminent. The vision comes in answer to his reflections and prayers on this matter. It addresses the Jews return to their homelands and the restoration of Jerusalem and the mortal ministry of the Messiah. It hints of a second diaspora, the destruction of Jerusalem and scattering of the Jewish nation by the Romans.

Chapter 9 begins with Daniel's review of Jeremiah's prophecy of the desolation of Jerusalem and the seventy years in captivity that followed. Walvoord observes: "In many respects, this is the high point of the book of Daniel. Although previously Gentile history and prophecy recorded in Daniel was related to the people of Israel, the ninth chapter specifically takes up prophecies as they apply to the chosen people."[1]

Daniel Reviews the Scriptural Records

1   In the first year of Darius the son of Ahasuerus, of the seed of the Medes, which was made king over the realm of the Chaldeans;

2   In the first year of his reign I Daniel understood by books the number of the years, whereof the word of the Lord came to Jeremiah the prophet, that he would accomplish seventy years in the desolations of Jerusalem.

The name Ahasuerus is the Biblical equivalent or transliteration of the Greek name for Xerxes, both names were derived from the Old Persian language. Other than the Bible, no historical records account for him. Daniel writes that he was a royal Mede and the father of Darius who was "made king" or the governor over the Babylonian Province. Darius was certainly an appointee of Cyrus, who ruled over the entire kingdom. The circumstances surrounding his appointment and other leaders were discussed earlier in Chapter 6. This Ahasuerus, father of Darius, should not be confused with later Persian kings, Xerxes I associated with Esther (Esther 1-2).

Daniel identified the time of the vision as the "first year of Darius" (Dan. 9:1). It occurred shortly after or around the incident of the ill-advised decree banning prayer and the command to direct all matters and petitions to Darius himself (Dan. 6).

The vision is given in response to the prophet's study of "the books," specifically Jeremiah's scriptural prophecies concerning the return of the Jews to the Promised Land. The "books" included writings of many of the Old Testament prophets and he clearly had copies of the prophecies of his contemporary, Jeremiah. Years before when the Babylonians conquered Palestine, Jeremiah prophesied of the demise of Jerusalem and the exile of the children

Artist Unknown © Public Domain
Daniel in his chambers studying and writing scriptures.

of Israel for seventy years. "And this whole land shall be a desolation, *and* an astonishment; and these nations shall serve the king of Babylon seventy years" (Jer. 25:11). False prophets living at the time scoffed at Jeremiah's prediction; but Daniel, even though he was a youth, remembered his words. Throughout his life, he witnessed their complete realization, and patiently waited until the seventy years were accomplished. In a letter written to those carried into Babylon, Jeremiah encouraged the captives to settle in the land as if they were to stay:

4   Thus saith the Lord of hosts, the God of Israel, unto all that are carried away captives, whom I have caused to be carried away from Jerusalem unto Babylon;

5   Build ye houses, and dwell in them; and plant garden and eat of the fruit of them;

6   Take ye wives, and beget sons and daughters; and

take wives for your sons, and give your daughters to
husbands, that they may bear sons and daughters;
that ye may be increased there, and not diminished.

7   And seek the peace of the city whither I have caused
     you to be carried away captives, and pray unto
     the Lord for it: for in the peace thereof shall ye have
     peace.

...

10   For thus saith the Lord, That after seventy years
     be accomplished at Babylon I will visit you,
     and perform my good word toward you, in causing
     you to return to this place. (Jer. 29:4-10)

———

True to his prophetic letter, the Jews did remain in Babylon for
several generations. In the same message, Jeremiah warned against
false prophets or diviners, who would misinform the people that
their captivity would not be long, but rather, they would return to
Jerusalem after a short time. Jeremiah countered by saying, "they
prophecy falsely unto you in my name: [but] I have not sent them"
(Jer. 29:9). Jeremiah was later carried into Egypt where it is believed
that he died and was buried.

Calculating the seventy years of exile from their beginning to
end has been the fancy of many scholars. "Anderson distinguishes
the duration of the captivity from the desolations of Jerusalem [and
the temple]."[2] History records that Jerusalem's destruction occurred
in the second siege of 597 B.C. "The time of the vision recorded
in Daniel 9 was 538 B.C., about 67 years after Jerusalem had first
been [sieged and captives like] Daniel carried off to Babylon (605
B.C.)."[3] If the time of reckoning began with the first siege and not
the second, the Jewish captivity began around 606 B.C. in the third
year of the reign of Jehoiakim.[4] If we consider the "desolations and
captivity of Jerusalem" to be from between 606 B.C. to 539 B.C.,
and include 538 B.C. when Cyrus made the decree they could return
home, roughly 69 or 70 years would have passed.[5]

A review of the scriptures reveals that the desolations included
"all her waste places" (Isa. 51:3), which comprised the surrounding
cities and villages of Jerusalem. The destruction of these lands
and villages probably have predated the 606 B.C.. "The reason for

Israel's captivity was their refusal to obey the Word of the Lord from the prophets (Jer. 29:17-19) and to give their land sabbatical rest (2 Chron. 36:21). God had stated that Israel, because of their disobedience, would be removed from the land and scattered among the Gentiles until the land had enjoyed its Sabbaths (Lev. 26:33-35)."[6] The length of time pertained both to the land, and the scattering of the people as well as the destruction of the city and the temple and might reasonably be determined to be over seventy years.[7] In all the cases presented, the Lord's people remained in captivity precisely according to the words of Jeremiah, but Daniel felt that the day of their prophesied return lay ahead.

Daniel, who had access to other prophecies, was aware of the words of Isaiah. He spoke of Cyrus the Great who would decree the Jews' return to their homeland to rebuild the temple. "Thus saith the Lord, thy redeemer, and he that formed thee from the womb ... That confirmeth the word of his servant, and performeth the counsel of his messengers; that saith to Jerusalem, Thou shalt be inhabited; and to the cities of Judah, Ye shall be built, and I will raise up the decayed places thereof:...That saith of Cyrus, *He is my shepherd, and shall perform all my pleasure: even saying to Jerusalem, Thou shalt be built; and to the temple, Thy foundation shall be laid.*" (Isa. 44:24, 26, 28, emphasis added; see also Isa. 45:1-4).

One hundred forty years prior to the temple's destruction and two hundred years prior to Cyrus, Isaiah foresaw how the Lord would inspire the great Persian king to decree the return of the Jews and announce that the city and temple be rebuilt. Josephus recorded the announcement issued by the king in 538 B.C.: "And these things God did afford them; for he stirred up the mind of Cyrus, and made him write this throughout all Asia: 'Thus saith Cyrus the king: Since God Almighty hath appointed me to be king of the habitable earth, I believe that he is that God which the nation of the Israelites worship; for indeed he foretold my name by the prophets, and that I should build him a house at Jerusalem, in the country of Judea.'"[8]

The spirit of the Lord was brooding on Daniel to prepare him for the revelation to come regarding the Jews return and restoration to the Promised Land and the coming of the Messiah.

In the face of the pending fulfillment of the prophecies of Isaiah and Jeremiah, Daniel was anxious. "He took the seventy years literally and believed that there would be a literal fulfillment. Even though He was fully acquainted with the use of symbolisms in revelation and that God sometimes portrays panoramic prophetic events using symbolic numbers or signs, his interpretation of Jeremiah was literal and he expected God to fulfill his word."[9] The fact that Cyrus had arrived on the scene and decreed their return and ordered the building of the temple was reason enough to bolster his desires and faith.

Daniel's Intercessory Prayer

> 3   And I set my face unto the Lord God, to seek by prayer and supplications, with fasting, and sackcloth, and ashes:
>
> 4   And I prayed unto the Lord my God, and made my confession, and said, O Lord, the great and dreadful God, keeping the covenant and mercy to them that love him, and to them that keep his commandments;

As a Seer, Daniel held the Melchizedek Priesthood and with this authority and position his responsibilities as a prophet included that of High Priest. In this capacity, he prayed in his room as an advocate for the Jews in captivity, much as the high priest would have petitioned on behalf of the people on the Day of Atonement (Lev. 16:30, Ex. 29:36-37). In his mind the appointed captivity was approaching completion, and Daniel set "his face to the Lord God" (Dan. 9:3) to opportune for the fulfillment of the prophetic writings. Previously, he prayed to the Lord while facing towards Jerusalem (Dan. 6:10). In this important hour, all consideration was centered on petitioning the Lord, which "that he turned away from [all] other things to concentrate on his prayer."[10]

His appeal was accompanied with fasting and he clothed himself in sackcloth and ashes. He approached the Lord in a spirit of sacrifice and deep humility. "Daniel's humility, reverence and earnestness are hallmarks of effective prayer."[11] As powerful and

Illustration by Sir. Edward Poynter © Creative Commons

Daniel's intercessory Prayer on behalf of his people.

wealthy as he was, he nonetheless clothed himself in sackcloth as a token of abasing himself before the Lord. "He would assume the garb and guise of the penitent. He would show God how deeply he, at least, felt about things."[12] He obviously felt profound contrition as he reflected on the failure of his people to remain faithful to the Lord and their covenants. He responded to the prophetic writings through supplication and fasting on behalf of his people in hopes to bring about their fulfillment. No prophecy comes to fruition without the exercise of the prayer of faith expressed in harmony with the Lord's will. If God's purposes were to be fulfilled, Daniel would help bring them about through his intercessory role as a priesthood holder and a prophet to Israel.

Daniel's prayer employed the titles of both Jehovah, the God of the covenant, and Elohim, the God of creation. He addressed his prayer to "Jehovah, my Elohim. (Dan 9:4)"[13] This is the first time that Daniel uses the title Jehovah in his writings. He is addressing the God of the Covenant, Yahweh or I am, who, through Moses, established the covenant with His people on Sinai (Ex. 20, 33). "Daniel also used the name El, which described God as the Almighty—One in whom all of the divine attributes are concentrated. God, in this character was awesome and terrible."[14] He prayed to the Father the Creator and the Author of the Covenant and well understood the role of Jehovah as the Revealer of the Covenant. Jehovah fulfilled the Father's will and served as the Advocate for Israel.

His supplication focused on the relationship between God and the covenant people. Those who loved the Lord demonstrated their love by keeping the commandments (John 14:15) and, in turn, they received mercy and love. This "'steadfast love,' [is a] term [that] connotes not only forgiveness, but loyalty in keeping his covenant with Israel."[15] Israel should expect mercy and patience only when they held fast in obedience (Doctrine and Covenants 82:10).

In the years just prior to their destruction, the children of the covenant demonstrated neither loyalty nor love of God. Their rebellion resulted in the withdrawal of the Lord's protective Spirit and they were left to themselves to suffer the wrath of their enemies. Death, captivity and sorrow quickly followed. Daniel's confession served as a reminder of what befell his people; the natural consequences of just laws executed by a righteous Judge.

Daniel's Confession

5   We have sinned, and have committed iniquity, and have done wickedly, and have rebelled, even by departing from thy precepts and from thy judgments:

6   Neither have we hearkened unto thy servants the prophets, which spake in thy name to our kings, our princes, and our fathers, and to all the people of the land.

7   O Lord, righteousness belongeth unto thee, but unto us confusion of faces, as at this day; to the men of Judah, and to the inhabitants of Jerusalem, and unto all Israel, that are near, and that are far off, through all the countries whither thou hast driven them, because of their trespass that they have trespassed against thee.

8   O Lord, to us belongeth confusion of face, to our
     kings, to our princes, and to our fathers, because we
     have sinned against thee.

9   To the Lord our God belong mercies and forgivenesses,
     though we have rebelled against him;

———

This prayer exhibits a beautiful pattern of humility and self-effacement before the Lord. His offering is not for himself alone, but more a confession in behalf of his people. If, while in exile, the gravity of their sins had not penetrated deep into their souls and the hearts of their descendants, then the punishment would be in vain.

Daniel was eyewitness to their wicked works and he now offered confession in their behalf. He was not ignorant of their depraved condition at the time of their defeat. He had seen their rejection of the prophets, including Jeremiah, a friend and teacher. His confession decried the sins of "iniquity," and the perverseness of their lives. They had "bent" their course away from God and become "crooked," straying from the straight and narrow path, the "strict" and "plain road" (2 Ne. 4:32). They were immersed in pagan idolatry, driven as chaff in their pursuit of ungodly activities, and yielding themselves to their fallen natures (Mos. 3:19).[16]

Nephi described the nation's condition as being complete rebellion: "For behold, the Spirit of the Lord ceaseth soon to strive with them; for behold, they have rejected the prophets, and Jeremiah have they cast into prison. And they have sought to take away the life of my father, insomuch that they have driven him out of the land" (1 Ne. 7:14; see also Jer. 26:20-24). Among their worst sins were the perverse practices surrounding the religion of Molech, which required that they pass their children pass through the fire of human sacrifice (Jer. 7:31; 32:35; 2 Kgs. 23:10). This generation was also preoccupied with sorcery, seeking out "familiar" or evil spirits. (2 Chron. 33:6; 28:3). These were the very crimes committed by the Canaanites, that caused the Lord to sweep them from the land (1 Ne. 17:33-35, 38; 1 Sam. 15:20, 33; Lev 18-19).

Furthermore, Daniel knew that their sins and rebelliousness came from the top down. Neither the kings, nor the princes, nor their [nobles or] fathers, nor the people harkened to the prophets (Dan 9:6). The leadership sponsored the dark practices that fueled the rebellion that permeated the people. The result was a defeated nation, a broken city with burned out gates and smashed walls and a gutted temple. Those not killed in the siege and overthrow of the city, were sold into slavery and carried away captive into distant lands. A few were left to fend for themselves. Those lucky enough to be carried off remained alive to raise another generation and contemplate the possibility of a second chance.

We Have Not Walked in His Laws

10 Neither have we obeyed the voice of the Lord our God, to walk in his laws, which he set before us by his servants the prophets.

11 Yea, all Israel have transgressed thy law, even by departing, that they might not obey thy voice; therefore the curse is poured upon us, and the oath that is written in the law of Moses the servant of God, because we have sinned against him.

12 And he hath confirmed his words, which he spake against us, and against our judges that judged us, by bringing upon us a great evil: for under the whole heaven hath not been done as hath been done upon Jerusalem.

13 As it is written in the law of Moses, all this evil is come upon us: yet made we not our prayer before the Lord our God, that we might turn from our iniquities, and understand thy truth.

14 Therefore hath the Lord watched upon the evil, and brought it upon us: for the Lord our God is righteous in all his works which he doeth: for we obeyed not his voice.

15 And now, O Lord our God, that hast brought thy people forth out of the land of Egypt with a mighty hand, and hast gotten thee renown, as at this day; we have sinned, we have done wickedly.

From the days Moses led the Israelites out of Egypt, the Lord had organized, instructed and set them on a path to become a

© Used with Permission
Stain Glass depiction of Moses and the Ten Commandments

peculiar and mighty people (Deut. 14:2). Their destiny was to be a great and prosperous nation. He gave them the Law of Moses as a means to keep them on a straight path. Paul taught: "the law was our schoolmaster until Christ, that we might be justified by faith" (JST Gal. 3:24). The rites and laws were intended to bless and keep them safe. The Mosaic ordinances served to point their minds and hearts to their Lord and their obligation and to give thanks for their blessings. Yet they departed from the safety of the law.

Daniel's expression pointed to the justice of their situation. "[He] was overwhelmed by Israel's failure to keep the Godward commandments: to have no other gods, to make no graven images, to revere God's name, to sanctify His Sabbaths and to venerate parents...He thought of Israel's shocking idolatries, of a nation that was so obsessed with the adoration of graven images that God at last had seen fit to send the nation to Babylon, the capital city of idolatry, and there to have idolatry burned out of the nation's soul."[17]

Moses's Pentateuch clearly outlined the "do's" and the consequences of the "don'ts." Moses wrote: "But it shall come to pass, if thou wilt not hearken unto the voice of the Lord thy God, to observe to do all his commandments and his statutes which I command thee this day; that all these curses shall come upon thee, and overtake thee:...the Lord shall bring thee, and thy king which thou shalt set over thee, unto a nation which neither thou nor thy fathers have known; and there shalt thou serve other gods, wood and stone. And thou shalt become an astonishment, a proverb, and a byword, among all nations whither the Lord shall lead thee." (Deut. 28:15, 36-37; see also: Deut. 27:14-26; 28:15-68; 29:20-28; 30:17-19; 32:25-29). Moses had cataloged a complete list of curses to befall Israel, if they rebelled (Deut. 28:15-68).

By ignoring the warning and falling into complete rebellion, the Lord's protective hand was removed. Daniel observed that "the Lord watched upon the evil, and brought it upon us" (Dan. 9:14 NIV). Jehovah had prepared this calamity to chasten them for their rebellion. Nevertheless, Zenos' Allegory of the Olive Tree reveals how the Lord deeply sorrowed over the corruption of His people. "And it came to pass that the Lord of the vineyard wept, and said unto the servant: What could I have done more for my vineyard?... now all the trees of my vineyard are good for nothing save it be to be hewn down and cast into the fire" (Jacob 5:41-42). The covenant promises were replaced with curses and they were left to call upon their idol gods for protection. Of course, the statues of stone and wood did not, indeed could not deliver them.

Daniel emphasized how the Lord redeemed Israel from Egypt. Jerome suggests that their Deliverer had a deeper purpose in mind than simply saving them from the mud pits. "Daniel does not view the deliverance of Israel out of Egypt merely as a good deed, but as an act of salvation by which God fulfilled His promise He had given to the patriarchs; ratified the covenant He made with Abraham, and by the miracles accompanying the exodus of the tribes of Israel from the land of Egypt, glorified His name before all nations (Isa. 63:12-14)."[18] Through Israel, Jehovah established His name among all the nations in the earth.

The Bible cites examples of Israel's preeminence among the nations in the days of their obedience. They prospered under David and were admired under Solomon. The Queen of Sheba came to see the glory of Solomon and marveled at his God (1 Kgs. 10:1-4).

Naaman, a Syrian captain, declared: "I know that *there is* no God in all the earth, but in Israel" (2 Kgs. 5:15). Despite His marvelous work to prosper and elevate Israel, in the end, Israel and Judah did not glorify Him, nor give Him honor. Instead, they betrayed His trust and put Him to open shame.

Daniel held nothing back, nor did he attempt to excuse himself or the behavior of his people. His prayer serves not only as the pattern of repentance and obedience, but also as a lesson exemplifying the proper spirit of meekness needed when seeking forgiveness. He continues:

The Plea for Mercy

16 O Lord, according to all thy righteousness, I beseech thee, let thine anger and thy fury be turned away from thy city Jerusalem, thy holy mountain: because for our sins, and for the iniquities of our fathers, Jerusalem and thy people are become a reproach to all that are about us.

17 Now therefore, O our God, hear the prayer of thy servant, and his supplications, and cause thy face to shine upon thy sanctuary that is desolate, for the Lord's sake.

18 O my God, incline thine ear, and hear; open thine eyes, and behold our desolations, and the city which is called by thy name: for we do not present our supplications before thee for our righteousness, but for thy great mercies.

19 O Lord, hear; O Lord, forgive; O Lord, hearken and
do; defer not, for thine own sake, O my God: for thy
city and thy people are called by thy name.

———

Having confessed the righteousness of God's justice, Daniel
appeals to His infinite mercy and grace. Israel, once the Chosen
People, had become a reproach, "a laughingstock" before the world
(Ps. 44:14; 79:4). All the nations considered them accursed and
punished of their God. Daniel appealed to the Lord to "cause thy
face to shine upon thy sanctuary" (Dan. 9:17), the symbol of the
covenant and the gem of the holy city. If they had learned from their
experience, the prophet hoped that God would restore the covenant
by allowing their return to rebuild the city and the temple.

The Lord had already said that He would not give "His glory"
to another (Isa. 48:11; 1 Ne. 20:11). Israel had covenanted with Him
and he with them; the gentile and heathen nations had not covenanted
with Him, nor given Him glory. In the end, Daniel believed that
"God cannot let the desolation of His sanctuary continue without
doing injury to His honour."[19] He did not plead to reestablish the
covenant or his people because of their repentance alone, but he
sought the glory of his God. The raising of Jerusalem's walls and
the rebuilding of the temple would be part of the repentance process,
and also, he hoped that by doing so, the Jews would reestablish their
connection with Jehovah. This would begin the process to regain
respect and honor for their God and themselves.

Gabriel, The Messenger

———

20 And whiles I was speaking, and praying, and
confessing my sin and the sin of my people Israel,
and presenting my supplication before the Lord my
God for the holy mountain of my God;

21 Yea, whiles I was speaking in prayer, even the
man Gabriel, whom I had seen in the vision at the
beginning, being caused to fly swiftly, touched me
about the time of the evening oblation.

22 And he informed me, and talked with me, and said,
O Daniel, I am now come forth to give thee skill and
understanding.

> 23 At the beginning of thy supplications the commandment came forth, and I am come to shew thee; for thou art greatly beloved: therefore understand the matter, and consider the vision.

———

The sincerity of Daniel's petition reached the ears of the Lord. His humility and purity of motive made his petition worthy of an immediate response (Dan. 9:23; see also Doctrine and Covenants 98:2; 88:123). Gabriel was sent from the portals of heaven to bestow on Daniel "skill" and "understanding." The language suggests that as soon as Daniel began to pray, God immediately directed Gabriel to answer his prayer.[20] The swiftness of his appearance comes in part from the fact that Daniel was a man beloved of God, worthy of a response, but also because the timing was right to reveal greater knowledge in response to the petition. The combination of Daniel's faith and the Lord's timetable brought a swift answer. The question of when will the Jews be allowed to return and renew their covenant with Jehovah would be answered.

Daniel refers to Gabriel as "the man" (Dan. 9:21), signifying that he knew him. He was the same messenger that had appeared in earlier visions. Gabriel, whose name means Man of God (LDS KJV

Jorisovo at the Cathederial of Brussels, Belgium © 2018, Used with Permission

A stained glass of the angel Gabriel appearing to Daniel

BD), came at "about the time of the evening oblation" (Dan. 9:21) or the traditional time of the evening sacrifice (between 3-4 p.m.). Many decades had passed since the evening sacrifice was offered on the altars in Jerusalem. Yet Daniel still observed the sacred ordinances in his heart by praying at this very hour. The messenger's timely arrival served as a sign. He came at the prophesied time when the Messiah would be crucified and die in Jerusalem, about 3 p.m.. The Lord's atonement would be a central part of Gabriel's message, a prophecy from heaven to be recorded by the beloved prophet.

The skill and understanding brought by the messenger was *"to instruct thee in knowledge."*[21] The heavenly instructions would address the subject of his prayer, "the presenting my supplication before the Lord my God for the holy mountain of my God" (Dan. 9:20). Daniel would be shown God's purposes relative to the return of the Jews, the rebuilding of the temple and the reestablishment of the covenant. He would understand events to transpire from that very hour to the Messiah's ministry and sacrifice. "The long preamble of twenty-three verses leading up to the great revelation of the seventy weeks is, in itself, a testimony to the importance of this revelation."[22] The "skill" given would inspire him as to what to do and teach the people that would set the stage for the fulfillment of his desires.

Prophecy of Seventy Weeks

————

24 Seventy weeks are determined upon thy people and upon thy holy city, to finish the transgression, and to make an end of sins, and to make reconciliation for iniquity, and to bring in everlasting righteousness, and to seal up the vision and prophecy, and to anoint the most Holy.

25 Know therefore and understand, that from the going forth of the commandment to restore and to build Jerusalem unto the Messiah the Prince shall be seven weeks, and threescore and two weeks: the street shall be built again, and the wall, even in troublous times.

————

Gabriel's instructions are concise and powerful. The first instruction revealed that despite Daniel's perception that Judah had completed the seventy years of exile and that their return seemed imminent, there still remained a period determined in heaven "to finish the transgression, and to make an end of sins, and to make reconciliation for iniquity" (Dan. 9:24). The prophet had to be patient a short while longer before the "command" (Dan. 9:25) would be issued permitting the Jews to return and build Jerusalem and prepare for the arrival of the Messiah.[23]

The messenger directs Daniel to "listen and understand" (Dan. 9:25). From the command to rebuild Jerusalem to the coming of the Messiah will be seventy weeks, divided into seven weeks and then sixty-two weeks and then one week respectively. The angel sets forth the framework on which to measure the events. The clock begins with "the command" to return and rebuild the city. Seven weeks are then provided as the period in which the city and the walls are to be restored. Afterward, a long period of 62 weeks of growth and expansion must pass until the Messiah is anointed. A final week is then appointed wherein the Messiah will "make reconciliation for iniquity, and to bring in everlasting righteousness, and to seal up the vision and prophecy, and to anoint the most Holy" (Dan. 8:24).

The prophecy of Seventy Weeks, therefore, can be divided into the following segments:

A. *Period of Continued Exile and Preparation:* A time remaining to finish the transgression and make reconciliation — a few years remain.

B. *The period from the going forth of the command* to return to the restoration of Jerusalem with its gates and walls and the temple — 7 weeks.

C. *The period between the temple restoration and dedication* and the building up of the city to the Messiah's mortal mission – 62 weeks. The reestablishment of the covenant.

D. *The Confirmation of the Covenant,* Anointing of the Holy One, the preaching of the covenant and the Abomination of

Desolation – 1 week.

Many interpretations are offered to explain the timeframe and details of the prophecy. Some scholars express confusion and frustration at the seemingly unknowable meaning of Gabriel's words.[24] However, applying a little understanding of the Hebrew language and the use of the prophetic calendar, combined with a careful review of historical events a greater understanding of the meaning of the prophecy can be found. The result is quite remarkable.

The Meaning of the Seventy Weeks

Seventy literal weeks or 490 days provides no useful framework on which to overlay the prophecy. The period from the days of Daniel to the Messiah and on to the Abomination of Desolation spans over 500 years. Therefore, the meaning cannot be interpreted in its literal English form. It must be viewed within the context of the Hebrew writing in which it was given. The Hebrew translation for Seventy Weeks actually says seventy sevens or seventy sets of sevens and is called a *heptad*. "It is normal for lexicographical authorities in the field of Hebrew to define the time unit as 'periods of seven (days, years),' and '*heptad*, weeks.' The English word 'week' [as used] here, is misleading, since the Hebrew is actually the plural of the word for seven without specifying whether it is days months or years."[25] The interpretation should read "seventy sets of seven." But seventy sets of seven what? It cannot be seventy sets of seven days, nor of seven weeks, but to fulfill the tenets of the prophecy, it must appropriately read seventy sets of seven years, or 490 years.

> The Hebrew translation for Seventy Weeks actually says seventy sevens or seventy sets of seven, a heptad.

A number of scriptural accounts support the interpretation for changing days or weeks into years. Two accounts provide examples of the timeframe the Lord had in mind. When Joshua, Caleb and their brethren returned from Canaan, ten spies reported with dread that to take on the powerful nations in the land was folly (Num. 14:38-39). The children of Israel responded with fear, unwilling to go up against the mighty nations of Canaan. The Lord, displeased with their lack of faith and courage, warned: "After the number of the days in which ye searched the land, *even* forty days, each day for a year, shall ye bear your iniquities, *even* forty years" (Num. 14:34). The Lord interchanges a day for a year. In a similar but separate circumstance, Ezekiel also writes: "I have appointed thee each day for a year" (Ezek. 4:5-6).

By applying this pattern, that each day is equal to a year, a *heptad* is actually interpreted as seven sets of seven years in length. The first segment of the prophecy, or seven weeks equals seven heptads, which produces in 49 years. Segment two of the prophecy spans 62 *heptads,* or 434 years, and the final segment of one *heptad or* 7 years. The total duration of the prophecy spans 490 years. This interpretation satisfies both the prophetic language and fulfills the historical duration.

The Purposes of God

Gabriel then enumerates God's purposes to be accomplished in Daniel's immediate future and during the period of seventy weeks. They are: (1) to finish the transgression, (2) to make an end of sins, (3) to make reconciliation for iniquity, (4) to bring in everlasting righteousness, (5) to seal up the vision and prophecy, and (6) to anoint the most Holy.[26]

Finish the Transgression and Make an End of Sins

The first purposes concern repentance and the reconciliation of sins. The Jews are to finish their repentance for their wickedness and rebellion. "The expression '*to finish*' is derived from *piel* the verb form of the root *kálâ* (אְלַלְכ), 'to finish' in the sense of to bring to an end."[27] They had suffered much, but the appointed period of exile was still in place and the promised liberation would be brought to pass slowly in the process of time, not exactly in 70 years. God's preparations for the Jews return to the Chosen Land was already in motion, but time was still needed to prepare the hearts of the people for return, to inspire the Gentile leadership and to arrange the means to raise the temple and repair the walls of the city. Exercising patience while the Lord's preparations unfolded gave them the best chance for success in restoring them as a people and nation.

The second purpose is to "make an end of sins." This can also be interpreted to mean: "seal up sin," to be "guarded or held under lock and seal."[28] The interpretation of this goal means sealing something in a prison having removed it from society and making the environment safe and secure. God means to purge the old sins of idolatry from Israel. The disposition will "altogether be removed out of his sight. ...If the sins are sealed, they are on the one side laid under custody so that they cannot anymore be active or increase."[29] There must be a wholesale cultural change. The former sins that brought the destruction of both Israel and Judah must be removed from the culture. For the chosen people to have any chance of meeting their foreordained potential, the former sins must be locked away. Pagan idolatry, at least the worship of idols, never again plagued the Jewish nation like in her early history. This sin was indeed taken and sealed away, although other forms of idolatry like secularism, which became a problem under Greek Hellenism.

Make Reconciliation for Iniquity

The third aspect of God's redemptive purposes was to "make reconciliation for iniquity" or "atone for iniquity." The Hebrew word *kipper* (הֲפַכְלוֹ) used for atone or atonement when applied in relation to sin means to "cover" or "wipe out" or to "make as harmless, non-existent, or inoperative, or annul, (so far as God's notice or regard is concerned), to withdrawal from God's sight with the attached ideas of reinstating in His favor, freeing from sin and restoring to holiness."[30] Israel must resolve its differences with their Holy King.

Ultimately for Israel to find favor with God, to regain their confidence as a people, and to become approved under His care, there must be reconciliation. The Lord desired that they draw near unto Him (3 Ne. 27:14) through the enabling power of the Atonement. In the face of true repentance, both divine mercy and grace are extended, the relationship is mended and the two parties come together. Such tender moments are made available both individually and collectively. President Russell M. Nelson taught:

———

"Let us now ponder the deep meaning of the word atonement. In the English language, the components are at-one-ment, suggesting that a person is at one with another. Other languages employ words that connote either expiation or reconciliation. Expiation means 'to atone for.' Reconciliation comes from Latin roots *re*, meaning 'again'; *con*, meaning 'with'; and *sella*, meaning "seat." Reconciliation, therefore, literally means 'to sit again with.' Rich meaning is found in study of the word atonement in the Semitic languages of Old Testament times. In Hebrew, the basic word for atonement is *kaphar*, a verb that means 'to cover' or 'to forgive.' Closely related is the Aramaic and Arabic word *kafat*, meaning 'a close embrace'—no doubt related to the Egyptian ritual embrace. References to that embrace are evident in the Book of Mormon. One states that 'the Lord hath redeemed my soul...; I have beheld his glory, and I am encircled about eternally in the arms of his love' (2 Ne. 1:15). Another proffers the glorious hope of our being "clasped in the arms of Jesus. (Mor. 5:11; see also: Alma 5:33; Alma 34:16.) I weep for joy when I contemplate the significance of it all. To be redeemed is to be atoned—received in the close embrace of God with an expression not only of His forgiveness, but of our oneness of heart and mind. What a privilege!"[31]

———

The pre-initiation of the Seventy Weeks offers a fresh start, a new beginning, and a renewed relationship. And it did start afresh—the temple was raised and the walls and city rebuilt. History shows, however, that the Jews continued to stumble and their relationship with their Messiah at times became very strained. Eventually, it breaks again when the Jews reject and crucified Him. But in Daniel's day, they would be given a new beginning; for "behold, he who has repented of his sins, the same is forgiven, and I, the Lord, remember them no more" (Doctrine and Covenants 58:42).

In the last days, the Jews will again be reconciled to the Lord. The Doctrine and Covenants describes the most poignant moment of reconciliation between the chosen people and their God. At the end of the devastating war of Armageddon, Jesus "shall stand in that day upon the Mount of Olives, which is before Jerusalem on the east, and the mount of Olives shall cleave in the midst thereof toward the east and toward the west, and there shall be a very great valley." (Zech. 14:4)...and the surviving Jews will flee into the Mount of Olives. There they will meet the Lord: "And then shall the Jews look upon me and say: What are these wounds in thine hands and in they feet? Then shall they know that I am the Lord; for I will say unto them: These wounds are the wounds with which I was wounded in the house of my friends. I am he who was lifted up. I am Jesus that was crucified. I am the Son of God. And then shall they weep because of their iniquities; then shall they lament because they persecuted their king." (Doctrine and Covenants 45:51-53; see also Zech. 13:6). At that grand reunion, any feelings of estrangement will be washed away and they will never again leave their God. Zechariah prophecies that in that day, "they shall call on my name, and I will hear them: I will say, It is my people: and they shall say, The Lord is my God." (Zech. 13:9).

Bring Everlasting Righteousness

The fourth purpose is to "bring everlasting righteousness." Again, the messenger places emphasis on the significant event of the Lord's Atonement. The act brought everlasting righteousness and the redemption and exaltation of the men. Christ, through the atonement, provides the "righteous ground for God's justification [and ultimate salvation] of the sinner."[32] The prophecy communicates the Divine ordination, life and purpose of the Savior. It was His example, sacrifice and ultimate triumph that enabled the Plan of Salvation and fulfilled the promises made to the House of Israel.

As mentioned, the family of Israel struggled to fulfill their destiny for centuries, but just as the Jews will find reconciliation at Mt. Olivet, so too will the purposes of God be fulfilled for all of the branches of the House of Israel scattered throughout the world. The marvelous work of the latter-day Restoration will bring the kingdom of God (Dan. 2:44). Eventually, Israel will put on the beautiful garments of the priesthood and adhere to the redemptive covenants and ordinances of the temple (Isa. 52:1). Jerusalem will become again a holy city and the Kingdom of God will be established among the Jews and will extend into the eternal worlds (Rev. 22:3; Dan 2:44). The fullness of Christ's redemptive work prophesied by Gabriel will come to pass through His everlasting righteousness and power of deliverance. Isaiah queried: "*Is* it not yet a very little while, and Lebanon shall be turned into a fruitful field, and the fruitful field shall be esteemed as a forest? And in that day shall the deaf hear the words of the [Book of Mormon], and the eyes of the blind shall see out of obscurity, and out of darkness. The meek also shall increase *their* joy in the Lord, and the poor among men shall rejoice in the Holy One of Israel" (Isa. 29:17-19).

Seal up the Vision

The completion of these marvelous works "seal up the vision and prophecy" (Dan. 9:24). Every word of prophecy concerning Christ and His mission and atonement for mankind will be fulfilled (3 Ne. 12:18). "The expression indicates that no more is to be added and that what was predicted will receive divine confirmation in the form of actual fulfillment. Once the letter is sealed, its contents are irreversible."[33] Gabriel affirms that God's covenant both, uttered and written, came by the power of the Spirit and must come to pass.

Anoint the Most Holy

The final purpose was to "anoint the most Holy" (Dan. 9:24). A duel meaning is found in this action. The first meaning speaks of the anointing of Jehovah as the Messiah. The title Messiah comes from the Hebrew word *mashiach* [מָשִׁיחַ] meaning the "anointed one" or "chosen one." The title Christ is the Greek derivation of the Hebrew, Messiah, and also means Anointed One.[34] Christ was chosen in the premortal Councils of Heaven (Abr. 3:27) and received the commission to be annointed as the Savior. After the completion of

His mission and the fulfillment of all the prophecies, the Lord will again be anointed as over all the inhabitants of the earth. (Doctrine and Covenants 28:21; 3 Ne. 28:10).

The prophecy has also been interpreted to mean "to anoint the Most Holy Place" (Dan. 9:24 NIV) with reference to the rededication of the temple. The KJV omits any allusion to the temple, nevertheless, the prophecy reveals that the temple will be rebuilt and with it the most holy place, or Holy of Holies will be dedicated and sanctified unto the Lord. The rededication restores the habitation of Jehovah and provides the place for Him to come to His people. Multiple events are required for the complete fulfillment of this prophecy. The most immediate event occurred when Zerubbabel rebuilt and dedicated the temple (516 B.C.). This "second temple" remained in place even after Herod renovated the entire temple complex (mount) just prior to the ministry of the Son of God (19 B.C.) in the flesh.

The Romans destroyed Jerusalem and the temple in 70 A.D. and prophecy became again incomplete for nearly two millennia. The temple must again be restored before the Lord can come again in glory (Ezek. 40-47, Rev. 11:1).[35] In a broader context, many temples will be established in the latter-days in preparation for the Lord's coming. A temple at Jerusalem and at New Jerusalem, in Missouri, are prophesied to be built with their Holy of Holies dedicated to the God of Israel. The fruit that comes from raising the temples is a pure and righteous people. The work completed therein will prepare a holy people to meet the Lord when He comes. Jehovah will again reunite with His people and dwell with them forever (Moses 7:62-63; 3 Ne. 21:22-25).

All six of the aforementioned goals will be accomplished over the determined Seventy Week period.

Timeframe for fulfillment of the Seventy Weeks

The first set of sevens or 49 years does not begin immediately. Gabriel provides the criteria to set the starting point: "Know therefore and understand, *that* from *the going forth of the commandment to*

2018 © Public Domain
Walls and ramparts surrounding the old city of modern Jerusalem

restore and to build Jerusalem unto the Messiah the Prince *shall be* seven weeks…the street shall be built again, and the wall, even in troublous times" (Dan. 9:25, emphasis added).

Daniel probably understood the general meaning of the prophecy. He knew that the Jews should return to rebuild Jerusalem and the temple. He also knew of the prophecies concerning the coming of the Messiah into mortality. However, he could not know the details of the timeframe, nor is there any indication that he asked. Nevertheless, Gabriel's message provides sufficient clues to set the timeframe so that the conscientious might study and know with certainty the time of its fulfillment. The command to rebuild the city is the key. The clock was to begin with the "command" to "build Jerusalem" and "the wall." Other translations of these passages render the term "command" as "the word."

Scholars have debated whether "the command" or "word" comes from God, citing the subject of the command in verse 23.[36] But "it is rather obvious, however, that another subject has been introduced in verse 24 and the two commandments are quite different…here is a command of men even though it may reflect the will of God in keeping with the prophetic word."[37] The command comes from the king, but it reflects the will and promise of Jehovah to restore the Jews to their homeland. A review of the decrees issued by the kings of the day is in order.

Command 1: In 538 B.C. a decree from Cyrus, king of Persia was issued to rebuild the temple in Jerusalem (see: Ezra 1:1-4; Chron. 36:22-23). No mention, however, is made of the city or the walls, which were clearly included as criteria given by Gabriel. Text found on the ancient Cyrus Cylinder confirms that Cyrus intended that the Jews return to build the sanctuary, but again no mention was made of the city. "I returned to (these) sacred cities on the other side of the Tigris, the sanctuaries of which have been ruins for a long time the images which (used) to live therein and established for them permanent sanctuaries. I (also) gathered all their inhabitants and returned (to them) the habitations"[38]

Command 2. In 520 B.C. the Jews began rebuilding the temple. Their Samaritan neighbors to the north challenged their right to rebuild and attempted to stop the project by complaining to the authorities that they were a "troublesome people" (Ezra 5:1-7, 7-17). After an appeal by the Jews, Darius confirms Cyrus's order and commands: "Let the work of this house of God alone; let the governor of the Jews and the elders of the Jews build this house of God in his place" (Ezra 7:7). He further commanded that a portion of the tribute or treasury be given to the Jewish Elders to further the work and "that they not be hindered" (Ezra 7:8). His decree confirms again the right and commission to build the temple, but the command to rebuild the city was again not mentioned.

Command 3. 457 B.C. Artaxerxes decrees that Ezra should go to Jerusalem to review the progress of the temple. Like Darius, he ordered that gold and silver from Babylon's treasury be given to Ezra to buy rams, bullocks and lambs for their meat offerings (Ezra 7:11-26). The king also authorized all ancient "vessels" used in the worship of God be returned to the House of the God of Jerusalem (Ezra 7:19). The assumption is that "the vessels" were those taken by Nebuchadnezzar when he destroyed the city. Up to this point, all edicts from the Persian kings concerned the rebuilding of the temple and the establishment of worship rites, but nothing was "commanded" about Jerusalem itself, nor was the erecting of her walls mentioned. The rebuilding of the walls surely would have been a point of concern for rival neighbors, as Jerusalem had hither to been a very strong fortress for the Jews.

Command 4: Artaxerxes commands Nehemiah to rebuild the city. The decree that most fulfills Gabriel's prophecy comes from Artaxerxes to Nehemiah in 444 B.C. (Neh. 2:1-8). Saddened that little progress had been made to the city itself, Nehemiah laments: "The remnant that are left of the captivity there in the province *are* in great affliction and reproach: the wall of Jerusalem also *is* broken down, and the gates thereof are burned with fire" (Neh. 1:3). After fasting and prayer, Nehemiah approaches the king and petitions to "send me unto Judah, unto the city of my fathers' sepulchres, that I may build it." (Neh. 2:5).

While significant progress had been made on the temple complex, little had been done to rebuild the city itself. Nehemiah's graphic description of Jerusalem, her burned gates and the crumbled walls, were the subject of his petition. "Ye see the distress that we *are* in, how Jerusalem *lieth* waste, and the gates thereof are burned with fire: come, and let us build up the wall of Jerusalem, that we be no more a reproach" (Neh. 2:17). Nehemiah's goal was to restore Jerusalem to its former self. "The word [restore] literally means to bring back."[39]

Gabriel's prophecy confirms that Jerusalem would not only be restored, but also built up and expanded to its former stature. "To build in distinction from to restore 'denotes building after restoring and includes the constant preservation in good condition as well as carrying forward of the edifice beyond its former state.'"[40] By the time of the Messiah's ministry Jerusalem was again a fortress, a prosperous city with bustling trade, a large population and an educated people. A modern and great Jerusalem was the desired backdrop for the Savior's ministry.

All this was to be done, as Gabriel says, in times of trouble. From the time that Zerubbabel arrived in the Holy Land and began work on the temple, to Ezra's assistance, to Nehemiah's finishing of the city-fortress, there were always threats and opposition from neighboring nations who opposed the Jews. The initial construction of the wall took 53 days to complete (Neh. 6:15). After its completion, the rulers of the people moved into Jerusalem and the remaining people cast lots so that one in ten could dwell in the city, which was made habitable again (Neh. 11:1).

Having reviewed the scriptural and historical accounts, the evidence supports that "Jerusalem was not rebuilt in the sixth century B.C.—although the rebuilding of the temple was indeed the first step toward the restoration of the city and nation....accordingly, the best explanation for the *terminis ad quo* in Daniel 9:25 is the decree to [rebuild Jerusalem itself and the walls] given in Nehemiah 2:1-6 about ninety years after the first captives returned and started building the temple."[41] The command to rebuild the city and the walls is the starting point from which to calculate the prophecy of seventy-sevens.

The Calculation of the Prophecy

The scholar Anderson conducted a thorough study of the timeframe and created a framework for determining the chronology for the sixty-nine week time period. He begins with the decree given to Nehemiah to rebuild the city (445 B.C.). He specifies that the seventy sevens began on the first of Nisan (March 14), 445 B.C. and ended on the tenth of Nisan (April 6) A.D. 32. A series of computations are made converting the time into prophetic years lasting 360 days (not 365) and resulting in 173,880 days or 483 years according to biblical chronology.[42] Latter-day Saints may find this conclusion interesting as it ends on the date April 6, 32 A.D. or the day recognized as the birth of the Savior.[43] However, there remains a problem. In that year (32 A.D.) there are no apparent historical events surrounding the anointing of the "most Holy" (Dan 9:25) or His mission of Atonement and crucifixion. The Lord was in the middle of His mission, and these events happened at a later date.

Dr. Harold Hoehner validated the work of Anderson, but updated the calculations to include the prophetic model of 360 days in a year plus also accounting for actual solar years by adding five days per year (365 days) and adding leap days for every four years. He also based his revision on the beginning date of the first of Nisan (March 5) 444 B.C., which aligns with the scriptural and historical record more completely. "Know therefore and understand, *that* from the going forth of the commandment to restore and to build Jerusalem unto the Messiah the Prince *shall be* seven weeks, and threescore and two weeks" (Dan. 9:25). The results place the end date on the tenth of Nisan (or March 30) A.D. 33. See chart:

Prophetic calculation adapted by Herald Hoehner		
444	B.C.	Nisan 1, 444 B.C. = March 5
	+ A.D. 33	
	477 Years	
	-1	[1 B.C. to A.D. 1 = 1 yr. not 2]
	476	Years
x 365	days	
	=173,740	days
	+25 leap	
	173,765	Nisan 10 A.D. 33 = March 30

Seventy sevens calculation adapted by Herald Hoehner [44]

The date, March 30, 33 A.D. places the prophetic time line on or near the final week of the Lord's ministry, which begins with his triumphal entry into Jerusalem. The events of the week that follow include Jesus teaching at the temple and on Mount Olivet, the last supper, the betrayal, the trial and the crucifixion. The Passover was on a Friday (Matt. 26:2; Mark 14:1; Luke 22:1; John 18:39), and most set the date of the crucifixion on Friday, April 3rd, A.D. 33, just four days after the end of 62nd heptad is completed. If the end of the sixty-two weeks in Gabriel's prophecy came on March 30th and the day of the Lord's death was April 3rd at the very beginning of the seventieth heptad, then Gabriel's prophecy to Daniel is fulfilled with perfect accuracy. The prophetic dates are remarkably precise down to the very last week, or the 69th heptad. The prophecy now enters into the final week, or the 70th set of seven years.

It is worth noting how precisely the prophecy is fulfilled. Again and again Daniel's visions demonstrate great details with which the Lord foresees the future and plans for the outcome.

The Messiah is Cut Off

26 And after threescore and two weeks shall Messiah be cut off, but not for himself: and the people of the prince that shall come shall destroy the city and the sanctuary; and the end thereof shall be with a flood, and unto the end of the war desolations are determined.

Gabriel reveals the events to take place in the final heptad. First, the Messiah will be "cut off" from among the living (Dan. 9:26). The term cut off "signifies *to be rooted up,*...and denotes generally a violent kind of death, though not always, but only the uprooting

Carl Bloch 1834 -1890 © Used with Permission
Christ in Gethsemane blessed by an angel

from among the living."[45] Isaiah uses similar language when prophesying that the Messiah would be "cut off out of the land of the living" (Isa. 53:8). Both prophecies foretell of the violent death to come upon the Messiah, the necessary mocking, bruising and crucifixion (Isa. 53:4-5), and giving up of his life, all required to fulfill of the Atonement.

Gabriel's use of the title Messiah or the Anointed One is one of only three scriptural references in the Bible (Dan. 9:25-26; John 1:41; 4:25). As previously discussed, Messiah is "an Aramaic [title] meaning 'the anointed'... [and] denotes the King and Deliverer whose coming the Jews were eagerly expecting."[46] The fulfillment of this prophecy comes when Christ is anointed King of Israel, and the universal Savior from evil, death and hell (Rev. 1:18; 20:13). There is no record of this anointing, but the Lord did testify that "all power [was] given unto me in heaven and in earth" (Matt. 28:8). Whether the anointing took place in the pre-mortal world prior to His birth, during mortality, or after He completed His mission is not said. It is that He had the necessary lineage, power and keys to be the Messiah. He was anointed and given all the rights and privileges required to fulfill the mission of Savior. To His brethren in Nazareth, He cited from Isaiah:

18 The Spirit of the Lord is upon me, because he hath anointed me to preach the gospel to the poor; he hath sent me to heal the brokenhearted, to preach deliverance to the captives, and recovering of sight to the blind, to set at liberty them that are bruised,

19 To preach the acceptable year of the Lord...

And then He declared:

21 This day is this scripture fulfilled in your ears. (Luke 4:18-19, 21; see also Isaiah 61:1-4)

The Lord Himself testified that He had received the commission as the Savior by an anointing. And as the Son of the Father, He possessed the capacity to overcome death. He later received the keys over death and the resurrection, which were given Him only after He fulfilled the requirements of reconciliation. The "cutting off" from the land was a necessary step to bring about the Plan of Salvation and attain the miracle of Eternal Life.

The phrase "not for himself" (Dan. 9:26) might also be rendered, He shall have no help or no one who had followed Him will be able to help.[47] In those critical hours from His suffering in the Garden of Gethsemane, through the trial to the death on Calvary's Cross, the Savior remained virtually alone. He did receive help from an angel who gave Him strength to endure the infinite pains and pressures of the Atonement in the Garden of Gethsemane (Luke 22:43). But the Gospel accounts show that after the betrayal His closest associates, the Apostles, either watched from afar or abandoned the scene altogether (Matt. 26:31, 69-75; Mark 14:50, 67-72; Luke 22:55-62; John 18:25-27). On the cross, the account reads that even the Father's supportive spirit was withdrawn. He hung alone. In agony and desperation, He cried: "My God, my God, why hast thou forsaken me?" (Matt. 27:45-46; Mark 15:34; see also: Ps. 22:1).

Elder James E. Talmage provides this explanation of the Father's withdrawing of His spirit from His Son in this crucial time:

"At the ninth hour, or about three in the afternoon, a loud voice, surpassing the most anguished cry of physical suffering issued from the cross, rending the dreadful darkness. It was the voice of Christ: "My God, my God, why hast thou forsaken me?" What mind of man can fathom the significance of that awful cry? It seems that in addition to the fearful suffering incident to crucifixion, the agony of Gethsemane had recurred, intensified beyond human power to endure. In that bitterest hour the dying Christ was left alone, alone in most terrible reality. That the supreme sacrifice of the Son might be consummated in all its fullness, the *Father seems to have withdrawn the support of His immediate Presence, leaving the Savior of men the glory of complete victory over the forces of sin and death.*"[48]

The Messiah's ultimate triumph required that He meet and overcome death and hell on His own, that He might attain ultimate

Vinikitenko © Used with Permission
Arch of Titus in Rome depicting Titus's victory over the Jewish rebellion

victory (John 16:33; Doctrine and Covenants 63:47). Isaiah writes in poetic soliloquy: "I have trodden the winepress alone; and of the people there was none with me: for I will tread them in mine anger, and trample them in my fury; and their blood shall be sprinkled upon my garments, and I will stain all my raiment" (Isa. 63:3, see also: Doctrine and Covenants 76:107; 133:50-53).

A few other translations render the passage "not for himself" as "having accomplished nothing." Perhaps from secular or unbelieving eyes the act of the Atonement, the trial and crucifixion appeared to accomplish very little, if not nothing. Without the context of the Gospel, the Plan of Salvation and the witnesses' testimony of the resurrection the series of actions would be perplexing and appear for naught. Of course, the testimony of the Apostles, the scriptures and the Spirit provide the needed clarity and insight to comprehend this supreme event.

The City and Temple Destroyed (vs. 26-27)

The Jews' rejection and murder of the Son of God resulted in heaven's severe retribution (Matt. 21:33-41). Having "cut off" the Light of the world, the Jewish nation was delivered to their own strength and wisdom. They would answer for their infamous cry: "His blood *be* on us, and on our children" (Matt. 27:25). In the decades that followed, the Jews suffered from serious internal political schisms and were stirred up by false messiahs, which brought about a national rebellion against the Romans. The uprising was met with a swift response from Roman authorities. Gabriel states that "the people of the prince that shall come shall destroy the city and the sanctuary" (Dan. 9:26). While some have interpreted "the prince" to be the Messiah and others the prince of this world or the devil, the angel probably referred to the mortal political prince Titus, the son of Vespasian, a Roman prince.[49] In 67 A.D., Titus marched with three legions (45,000 troops) to put down the Jewish rebellion beginning in Galilee and eventually on to Jerusalem.[50]

After a long and tortured siege, the city was overrun by angry soldiers who cut down the majority of the citizens. The temple was set on fire and reduced to rubble. The soldiers overturned every stone looking for treasure (Matt. 24:2). Titus reportedly refused to accept a victory wreath, as he claimed not to have won the victory on his own, but was the vehicle through which their God manifested His wrath against the nation.[51] Just as Gabriel had prophesied, war came against the Jews as a consuming flood "poured upon the desolate." Desolations and misery advanced with typical Roman relentlessness until the judgments decreed in heaven were fulfilled.

The Covenant Confirmed

> 27 And he shall confirm the covenant with many for one week: and in the midst of the week he shall cause the sacrifice and the oblation to cease, and for the overspreading of abominations he shall make it desolate, even until the consummation, and that determined shall be poured upon the desolate.

The antecedent to "he" can only be interpreted as either the

Francesco Hayez 1791-1882 © Used with Permission
Painting The Destruction of the Temple of Jerusalem

prince or the Messiah. Titus made no treaty or covenant with the Jews. Even though the natural consequence of Jerusalem's destruction and the toppling of the temple ended the Mosaic sacrifices, Titus required unconditional surrender. He made no treaty.

The Lord, however, did make a covenant with the faithful Jews and Israel, through the New and Everlasting Covenant of the Gospel (Doctrine and Covenants 22:1). "The true antecedent to 'He' is the Messiah, who fulfilled the Mosaic covenant"[52] and the tenants of the Law were met, He, therefore, stopped the sacrificial worship. To the Nephites in the Promised Land, He commanded: "And ye shall offer up unto me no more the shedding of blood; yea, your sacrifices and your burnt offerings shall be done away, for I will accept none of your sacrifices and your burnt offerings. And ye shall offer for a sacrifice unto me a broken heart and a contrite spirit" (3 Ne. 9:19-20). "The fruits of the covenant had brought salvation to *many*. Therefore, a contrast is introduced between *He* and the *Many*, a contrast which appears to reflect the great Messianic passage... Isa 53:11 [my righteous servant justify many; for he shall bear their iniquities']...Although the entire nation will not receive salvation, the *many* will receive it."[52]

The Lord reaffirmed the establishment of the New and

Everlasting Covenant with the Apostles, the converted Jews, and later "many" Gentiles. Having fulfilled the requirements of the Atonement, He answered or satisfied the "ends of the law" (2 Ne. 2:27), including the purpose for which the Law of Moses was given. Its practices would be discontinued. Paul taught this same principle to the Hebrews: "…A new covenant, he hath made the first [or the Mosaic Law] old. Now that which decayeth and waxeth old *is* ready to vanish away" (Heb. 8:13; see also: 7:11; 9:25, 26). A new Gospel covenant was set in place and with it the ordinance of the Sacrament, accompanied with a broken heart and contrite spirit (3 Ne. 9:20). The transition from the Mosaic Law to the New Covenant or Testament again can be applied perfectly within the timeframe fixed for the last set of sevens.

As for the apostate Jews, the Mosaic rituals were brought to an end when the Romans destroyed the city and the temple. The holy rites were ended, and this condition remains in effect until this day.

The Overspreading of Abomination Until the End

For the faithful, the covenant was confirmed. Having been forewarned (Matt 24:16-20), the majority of the members escaped Roman destructions. The phrase "overspreading of abominations," gives a sense that the sins and abominations became universal and predicted the general apostasy (Rev. 12:14; 2 Thes. 2:3). The phrase has also been translated to mean "*upon the wings of abomination*" where the word *wing* means the "pinnacle of the temple, which became so desecrated that it could no longer be regarded as the Temple of the Lord, but as an idol temple."[54] The Jews were not idol worshipers, but they were nonetheless idolatrous having rejected the Son of God for power, position and their old traditions. The Lord, Himself, referred to the temple as "your house" (Matt. 23:38), no longer claiming it either as His Father's nor as His. By the end of His ministry, the Father had withdrawn His spirit, leaving the edifice unprotected.

The wars with the Romans brought desolations and the ultimate consummation or end of the nation. Young writes of the consummation spoken by Gabriel: "The word *end* means full end with the phase *that determined* should be regarded as the subject of *shall pour*...we might paraphrase it as follows: 'and until the full end which has been determined shall pour upon the desolate'...It is a determined [or just] end."[55] The judgments exacted upon the Jews were "determined" or fixed by heavenly justice and involved the total consummation of the city and the dispersion of the Jewish people. Young continues: "The desolate...is impersonal that which is desolate, i.e. the ruins of the Temple and city. Thus, since the Messiah has caused sacrifices and oblations to cease, there comes a desolator over the temple and devastation continues until a full, determined end pours forth upon the desolation."[56]

The total destruction of the temple and the consummation of the city symbolized the broken covenant. The judgements of the Lord could have brought a full end to the covenant people, but a very few were spared. In the discourse on Olivet, the Lord warned: "in those days, shall be great tribulation on the Jews, and upon the inhabitants of Jerusalem, such as was not before sent upon Israel, of God, since the beginning of their kingdom until this time; no, nor ever shall be sent again upon Israel... *And except those days should be shortened, there should none of their flesh be saved*; but for the elect's sake, according to the covenant, those days shall be shortened (JS-M 1:18, 20, emphasis added). Less than 10% were spared. The remaining fell into generations of apostasy. The true covenant was fulfilled through the believing Jews, who had also been rejected and were scattered among the nations.

The Seventieth Seven

The Messiah's death and the fulfillment of the Mosaic tenants of the Law can be placed comfortably within the final set of seven or seven years after His ascension. The duration of the seventieth seven, taken literally, is only seven years and the whole prophecy can not be interpreted satisfactorily within that timeframe. A review of the historical realities compared to the details of the prophecy is in order. The destruction of the city and the temple followed by the dispersion of the Jews occurred with the Abominations of Desolation of 70 A.D., some 37 years after the Son of God was "cut off." The seventieth week serves as a symbolic pause or coma in the history of Israel, a pause symbolic of the long night of apostasy that would follow (2 Thes. 2:2-5).

What marks the termination of the 70th sevens? The answer is that the prophecy does not say a word about its termination. It simply foretells of events to come. "The *terminius ad quem* of the 69 sevens is clearly stated, namely, an anointed one, a prince. No such *terminus ad quem* however, is given for the 70 sevens themselves. It would seem, therefore, that the *terminus ad quem* was not regarded as possessing particular importance or significance."[57] Gabriel states that the fulfillment of the 70th seven is set with the "consummation" or utter destruction of the city and the people. The repercussions of these events would continue for two millennia.

The Jews were scattered among the nations. There they would remain until the Lord would begin again to recover them to their home. They will rebuild again the city, the walls and the temple. Nephi saw that "it shall come to pass that the Jews which are scattered also shall begin to believe in Christ; and they shall begin to gather in upon the face of the land; and as many as shall believe in Christ shall also become a delightsome people" (2 Ne. 30:7). The Lord promises to recover His people, both the tribes of Israel and the Jews scattered across the world. He looks forward to the day when they will again "be sanctified in holiness before the Lord, to dwell in his presence day and night his, forever and ever" (Doctrine and Covenants 133:35).

Conclusion

The prophecy of the seventy weeks begins with Judah's return in Daniel's day to rebuild the temple. It continues through to the days of Nehemiah in 444 B.C. and on, until the mortal ministry of the Messiah. Daniel's prayer relative to the return of his people to their home and the restoration of the temple and the city is answered. Gabriel adds details about the setting of the Lord's ministry in mortality. The long preparation for His mortal ministry occurs over a period of sixty-two *heptads,* where the Jewish nation is nourished, strengthened, empowered and becomes great and ready for the ministry of the Messiah.

The final heptad must be viewed as a "comma" wherein the Lord introduces the New and Everlasting Covenant and then is "cut off" from among the living. "Those who seek to interpret prophecy in its normal sense find in Daniel 9 a solid chronological bridge connecting God's past covenant promises to Israel with His future fulfillment of those promises. They see consistency between the timing of the event provided by Daniel and the coming of the Messiah…chapter 9 is doing what it is claiming to do—announcing God's 490-year future plan for the Jewish people and Jerusalem."[58]

It represents a remarkable example of the planning and foresight of the Father. Gabriel predicted the mission of the Messiah almost to the very day. Future visions in Daniel demonstrate that the Lord sees all things with the same precision and plans accordingly.

Chapter Endnotes:

1   Walvoord. *Daniel: The Key to Prophetic Revelation*. 249
2   Anderson. *The Coming Prince*. iii. Walvoord. *Daniel: The Key to Prophetic Revelation*. 251
3   Ibid. 250
4   Ibid. Young. Edward J.. *The Prophecy Daniel: A Commentary*. 184
5   Walvoord. *Daniel: The Key to Prophetic Revelation*. 251
6   Hoehner. Harold W.. *Chronological Aspects of the Life of Christ*. Part 6. Daniel's Seventy Weeks and the New Testament Chronology." *Bibliotheca sacra* 132. no. 1 (January –March 1975). 47-63
7   Walvoord. *Daniel: The Key to Prophetic Revelation*. 253
8   Josephus. *Antiquities of the Jews*. Book 11. Ch. 1:1-Possible Notes Entry
9   Walvoord. *Daniel: The Key to Prophetic Revelation*. 254
10   Ibid. 255
11   Ibid. 255
12   Phillips. *Exploring the Book of Daniel: An Expository Commentary*. 155
13   Ibid. 156
14   Ibid. 156
15   Glueck. Nelson. *Hesed* in the Bible. Alfred Gottscholk. ed.; see also: R. Laird Harris. Gleason L. Archer Jr.. and Bruce K. Walkte. eds. *Theological Workbook of the Old Testament*. Chicago. Moody. 1980. 305-7. Walvoord. *Daniel: The Key to Prophetic Revelation*. 255
16   Phillips. *John Exploring the Book of Daniel: An Expository Commentary*. 157
17   Ibid. 158
18   Keil. *Biblical Commentary of the Old Testament. The Book of the Prophet Daniel*. 333
19   Keil. *Biblical Commentary of the Old Testament. The Book of the Prophet Daniel*. 334
20   Walvoord. *Daniel: The Key to Prophetic Revelation*. 265
21   Keil. *Biblical Commentary of the Old Testament. The Book of the Prophet Daniel*. 335
22   Walvoord. *Daniel: The Key to Prophetic Revelation*. 266
23   Ibid. 266
24   see: Montgomery. *A Critical and Exegetical Commentary on the Book of Daniel*. https://archive.org/details/criticalexegetic22montuoft
25   Walvoord. *Daniel: The Key to Prophetic Revelation*. 269
26   Ibid. 271
27   Ibid. 271
28   Keil._Biblical Commentary of the Old Testament. The Book of the Prophet Daniel*. 342
29   Ibid. 342
30   Driver. "*Propitiation*" in *Dictionary of the Bible*. James Hastings. ed. vol. 4. 131
31   Nelson. Russell. M.. "The Atonement." General Conference. October 1996
32   Walvoord. *Daniel: The Key to Prophetic Revelation*. 272
33   Ibid. 273
34   Talmage. *Jesus the Christ*. 34-41
35   Smith. *History of the Church* 5:337
36   Young. *The Prophecy Daniel: A Commentary*. 201
37   Walvoord. *Daniel: The Key to Prophetic Revelation*. 275

38   Prichard. *Ancient Near Eastern Text Relating to the Old Testament. 3rd. Ed.* 316
39   Young. *The Prophecy Daniel: A Commentary.* 203
40   Keil. *Biblical Commentary of the Old Testament. The Book of the Prophet Daniel.* 351; Young. *The Prophecy Daniel: A Commentary.* 203
41   Walvoord. *Daniel: The Key to Prophetic Revelation.* 277-78. see also: Phillips. E*xploring the Book of Daniel: An Expository Commentary.* 168, Expositors Bible Commentary, 114
42   Anderson. *The Coming Prince.* 128; See also Walvoord. Daniel: *The Key to Prophetic Revelation.* 279
43   Lee. in *Conference Report.* April 1973. 4; or *Ensign.* April 1973. 2
44   Adapted from Herald Hoehner. "Daniel's Seventy Weeks and New Testament Chronology. *Bibliotheca Sacra* (January—March. 1975). 65. See also Walvoord. 280)
45   Keil. *Biblical Commentary of the Old Testament. The Book of the Prophet Daniel.* 359
46   LDS Bible Dictionary. Messiah
47   Gaebelein, *Expositors Bible Commentary.* Zondervan. 1976-1992. Vol 7. 113-114
48   Talmage. *Jesus The Christ.* 661 *emphasis added*
49   Young. *The Prophecy Daniel: A Commentary.* 207
50   Josephus. *The War of the Jews* II. 19.9; III.1.2. 4.2
51   Philostratus. Flavius. *The Life of Appollonius of Tyana.* 6:29. translated by F.C. Conybeare. Loeb Classical Library. 1912; See also: Neh. 1:8
52   Young.. *The Prophecy Daniel: A Commentary.* 213
53   Ibid. 213
54   Ibid. 218
55   Ibid. 219
56   Ibid. 219
57   Young. *The Prophecy Daniel: A Commentary.* 220
58   Walvoord. *Daniel: The Key to Prophetic Revelation.* 295-96

Additional Notes

On this latter view, it is also argued that the prophecy exhibited a high degree of literary structure at an earlier stage of its development in such a way that the six infinitival clauses of v. 24 were chiastically linked to six divisions of v. 25-27 via an elaborate system of word counts, resulting in the following reconstruction of this earlier redactional stratum:

A   To withhold the rebellion.
B   To seal up sins.
C   To atone for iniquity.
D   To bring a righteous one for the ages.
E   To stop vision and prophecy.
F   To anoint the Holy One of holy ones.
F'   You will discern wisdom from the departure of a word to return and rebuild Jerusalem until an anointed one is ruler.
E'   You will return for seven weeks and sixty-two weeks, and by the distress of the times it will be rebuilt, square and moat.
D' After the sixty-two weeks he will cut off an anointed one, and the coming ruler will not save the people.
C' He will destroy the holy city and its end will be by a flood, and by the end of the determined warfare there will be desolations.
B' He will take away the sacrificial offering in the other week, and confirm a covenant for many in the middle of the week.
A' On your base will be eighty abominations, and you will pour out for desolation until a complete destruction is determined.

Waters, Benjamin Victor. (2016). "The Two Eschatological Perspectives of the Book of Daniel" *Scandinavian Journal of the Old Testament*, Rice University, 30 (1): 98-100 (91–111).

10

Daniel's Vision
of the Lord

The previous two chapters (8-9) add to the overarching vision given in Chapter 7. Chapter 8 revealed details concerning the rise of the kingdoms of Persia and Greece. Chapter 9 focused on Daniel's petition concerning the restoration of the Jews to Jerusalem. The timeframe spans from Daniel's day until a few decades after the Messiah's ministry. These final three chapters are a continuation of this pattern of revealing the future to the prophet. The Lord wished to teach Daniel great lessons to help him understand how He watches over the gentile kingdoms and will protect the destiny of the Chosen people.

Chapters 10-12 constitute the fourth and final vision. It includes a great deal of information about the period after the Jews returned to the Holy Land. It focuses on the Ptolemaic and Seleucid kingdoms, which ruled over the land for 180 years. The vision ties events of those days to similar circumstances to transpire in the latter-days. Once again, the vision brings insight to questions weighing on the prophet's mind. His concern spawned from a dream or vision, "a thing" as he calls it (Dan. 10:1) that had been shown him, a revelation not recorded as yet in this record. His reaction was to seek clarity from the Lord. Heavenly messengers again will visit the prophet to give him comfort and understanding.

The explanation of the "thing" is found in Chapters 11:2-12:4 and is divided into two sections. The first, Daniel 11:2-35, covers the immediate future, from the reign of Darius (the Persians) to the conquering of the Greeks and the reign of the Ptolemaic and Seleucid Empires. It offers unparalleled details into the Egyptian (Ptolemaic) and Syrian (Seleucid) kings (circa 305 B.C.) up to the reign of Antiochus IV Epiphanies (175–164 B.C.). The vision touches lightly on the Roman Empire. "This revelation connects itself, both as to its contents and form, so closely with Daniel 8, that it is to be viewed as a further unfolding of that prophecy."[1] The second section, Daniel 11:36-44–12:5-13, focuses specifically on the latter days and presents details about the future anti-Christ, the turbulent wars in the world and troubled events that befall the Holy People in the period just prior to the coming of the Lord.

These final two chapters (11-12) constitute Daniel's fourth recorded and final vision. "[He] received the last revelation regarding the future of his people, which gives a fuller unfolding of the hostile attitude of the world-power toward the people and the kingdom of God."[2] The visions provide a significant message. They reveal that the Chosen People will be preserved though the generations, and in the end will triumph over all their foes to establish the Kingdom of God as prophesied in Daniel's interpretation of king Nebuchadnezzar's dream (Dan. 2:44).

Daniel Receives the Visions

> 1   In the third year of Cyrus king of Persia a thing was revealed unto Daniel, whose name was called Belteshazzar; and the thing was true, but the time appointed *was* long: and he understood the thing, and had understanding of the vision.

The third year of Cyrus's reign over Babylon places the time of this vision at about 72 years since the Jews were carried away from Jerusalem (536 B.C.). By this time, Daniel was in his 80's. The first bands of exiled Jews had already left Babylon to return to their homeland, where they began laying the foundations to restore the temple. Daniel did not return with his people to Jerusalem, some argue because of his age. The records show that others had gone who were as old as the prophet and when they arrived, they wept at the site of the ruined city. They wept again when the foundations of the temple were first laid (Ezra 3:12). The prophet stayed in Babylon at his post by commission from the Lord, knowing that he could do more good for his people while in office at the king's court.[3]

He begins the record by referring to his Babylonian identity, "whose name was Belteshazzar." The statement was simply intended to make it obvious that the Daniel of the third year of Cyrus, who wrote this vision, was the same person carried away into Babylon in the first years of Nebuchadnezzar.[4] His declaration provides the needed linkage to keep the records in order and also demonstrates the continuity of his ministry from the beginnings of Israel's exile until their return.

The prophet opens with the subject of "a thing," or a vision, which he knew to be true. The nature of the vision is not evident other than he says that it spanned over a long period of time. Other translations report that the subject for "thing" was of a "great conflict" or "the future—times of war and great hardship."[5] Details about the hardship and war are not given in this chapter, but come later in the text (Dan. 11:35-45, 12:1-4). Nevertheless, wars, dissention and persecution are the subjects of the vision that caused Daniel to mourn and to worry greatly because of their impact on the Chosen People.

The details in Chapters 11 and 12 reveal that the "long period of time" spanned from his day through to the end of the world, roughly 2500 years. The record, and possibly the vision, contains significant gaps in history, but as we shall see, the messages that the Lord intends to relay are clear. The subject matter is largely about kings and kingdoms with specific focus on important conflicts and, as mentioned, on trials and persecutions inflicted on the people of God. It highlights, for example, the infighting and intrigue among the Seleucid and Ptolemaic kings and covers again the rise of a certain king, Antiochus Epiphanies IV, who sought to stamp out the Jewish religion (See also: Dan 8: 9-14, 23-25). This was addressed in Chapter 8 and will be revisited in Chapter 11 because there are parallels and lessons that are applicable for the end of times. Daniel's greatest concern centered on the events of the last days and the great conflicts to befall the world. These conflicts involve the rise of anti-Christs, the great battle of Armageddon and the persecutions of the Saints.

Daniel also seems concerned about the fate of the Jews in his days. Immediate anxieties arose in his mind, which highlight the struggles of his brethren who had newly arrived in Jerusalem. Zerubabbel and Joshua lead a small fraction of the Jewish exiles (about 40,000) back to Judea. The majority remained in Babylon or Persia with families and businesses that were by now well established. The younger generations saw Babylonia and Elam as home. Almost immediately after Zerubabbel's arrival in Israel, the exiles were met with opposition from the local nations (Ezra 4). These conflicts would prove to be the beginning of centuries of struggle. Upon hearing news of their difficulty, the prophets' first reaction was to petition the Lord on their behalf.

Daniel's Fast and Preparation

———

2   In those days I Daniel was mourning three full weeks.

3   I ate no pleasant bread, neither came flesh nor wine in my mouth, neither did I anoint myself at all, till three whole weeks were fulfilled.

4   And in the four and twentieth day of the first month, as I was by the side of the great river, which is Hiddekel;

———

His supplication began with a period of fasting and prayer, which would extend for over three weeks (24 days). The fast did not involve a complete abstinence of food and water, but of pleasant bread, flesh and wine. He refused the usual diet and delicacies afforded a person of his station. The general description of the fast is reflective of a Passover Feast of unleavened bread or "bread of affliction" (Deut. 16:3) and bitter herbs. Only the bare essentials needed to sustain life were eaten. "Daniel's fast had spanned both the Passover and the Feast of Unleavened Bread, two feasts designed to remind Israel of their bondage in Egypt and their marvelous emancipation."[6] He fasted in remembrance of these events wherein the Lord showed remarkable power unto deliverance, hoping that God would extend anew His arm of assistance for his people in Jerusalem.

Later in the chapter, we come to understand that God was aware of his petition from the time he began to pray, but the answer would be delayed in order to teach Daniel a valuable lesson. Undoubtedly, he hoped for an immediate response like that in Chapter 9 (Dan 9:19-23), but in this case the answer came only after much struggle and anxiety in the spirit.

In this period of mourning, Daniel apparently did not observe the normal preparations or duties of the day. He did not anoint himself or tend to other seemingly routine obligations, but rather remained focused in prayer to demonstrate sincerity as he petitioned for greater understanding and solicited help. His sacrifice was "as an abstaining from the better sustenance of common life, [and] was the outward sign of sorrow of soul."[7] His state of mind made it so that he either could not perform his duties, or he wanted no distractions until he could settle the matter with the Lord.

On the 24th day of Nisan, Daniel left the palace and traveled some 30 miles out of Babylon to the bank of the river Hiddekel (or the Tigris). A number of attendants and associates accompanied him. While pondering and praying at the scene, the long awaited answer came. A celestial messenger appeared; the Lord, Himself, had come to reassure His beloved servant and to reveal more about the "things" that caused him so much distress.

The Glory of the Lord

5   Then I lifted up mine eyes, and looked, and behold a certain man clothed in linen, whose loins were girded with fine gold of Uphaz:

6   His body also was like the beryl, and his face as the appearance of lightning, and his eyes as lamps of fire, and his arms and his feet like in colour to polished brass, and the voice of his words like the voice of a multitude.

7   And I Daniel alone saw the vision: for the men that were with me saw not the vision; but a great quaking

fell upon them, so that they fled to hide themselves.

8   Therefore I was left alone, and saw this great vision, and there remained no strength in me: for my comeliness was turned in me into corruption, and I retained no strength.

9   Yet heard I the voice of his words: and when I heard the voice of his words, then was I in a deep sleep on my face, and my face toward the ground.

———

When the heavenly Being appeared, his associates, struck with mortal fear, fled and immediately hid, leaving Daniel to himself. The experience draws a close parallel to Saul's vision on the road to Damascus (Acts 9:4-19), whose companions also saw a great light and heard a voice as of thunder, but could see no figures or beings. In this case, Daniel's companions quickly withdrew into secluded places abandoning the aged prophet to himself.

The Being who appeared was clothed in the white linen of the High Priesthood (JS-H 1:31), girded with fine gold sash of Uphaz. His countenance was as lightning and his body was described as the jewel "beryl," which is like a chrysolite or topaz stone. Such stones are known for their translucent and brilliant characteristics.

> The Being who appeared was clothed in the white linen of the High Priesthood... His countenance was as lightning

"The impression given to Daniel was that the man's entire body was like a gigantic transparent jewel reflecting the glory of the rest of the vision."[8] Daniel's depiction of this Being was unlike the previous angels, who were glorious, but described simply as marvelous illuminated men.

His experience mirrors those of other prophets like Ezekiel, Isaiah and John the Revelator, who also saw the Son of God. John for example described the Son of Man as: "clothed with a garment down to the foot, and girt about the paps with a golden girdle. His head and his hairs were white like wool, as white as snow; and his eyes *were* as a flame of fire. And his feet like unto fine brass, as if they burned in a furnace; and his voice as the sound of many waters" (Rev. 1:13-15). Isaiah records the glory of the Lord on His throne as "high and lifted up, and his train [of glory] filled the temple" (Isa. 6:1). Ezekiel also speaks of the great brilliance of fire (Ezek. 1:26-28).

Daniel's physical description matches that of the brother of Jared who saw the Lord as a spirit in the likeness of a man who had a physical tabernacle of flesh and blood (Ether 3:6-9). In all cases, the mortals responded by falling to the earth overwhelmed with fear. Ezekiel dropped to his face (Ezek. 1:26-28), John "fell to his feet as dead" (Rev. 1:13-17) and the Brother of Jared "fell down before the Lord, for he was struck with fear." (Ether 3:6). Isaiah's reaction was to cry because of unworthiness before the Lord, saying: "Woe is me! for I am undone; because I am a man of unclean lips" (Isa. 6:5).

It is evident that this visitation was different from previous manifestations of angelic messengers. Jehovah, Himself, came to comfort the prophet. He wished to appear personally to reassure His beloved servant that despite the challenges ahead, He would watch over Israel. The record is not clear what message, if any, the Lord relayed. It may be that He simply appeared as a testimony to His concerned servant that He would be faithful to his covenants to preserve his people. Just as Jehovah had promised to Joshua "I will be with thee: I will not fail thee, nor forsake thee" (Josh. 1:5), so too He promises Daniel the protection and eventual triumph of the Covenant People through all trials until the end of the world.

As with previous vision experiences, it is unlikely that Daniel recorded all the details of what was revealed. Other spiritual experiences show that the Lord conveyed expansive insights and intelligence to the recipient and the record provides only a small portion. John, for example, beheld the entire Plan of Salvation including a detailed panorama of the apocalyptic events of the last days (Rev. 1-22). His record contains only a fraction of what was given. Moses saw the creations of the universe and an account of this earth with great precision, showing every facet of the lives of its inhabitants (Mos. 1:1-11). Ezekiel received vivid impressions of heaven, and heavenly beings and creatures (Ezek. 1:3-15). None of these experiences could be conveyed given their limited mortal abilities. Nevertheless, even in their limited form, they provide valuable lessons and perspectives. As we will discover Daniel's record is no different

Daniel's Strength Leaves Him

———

10 And, behold, an hand touched me, which set me upon my knees and upon the palms of my hands.

11 And he said unto me, O Daniel, a man greatly beloved, understand the words that I speak unto thee, and stand upright: for unto thee am I now sent. And when he had spoken this word unto me, I stood trembling.

12 Then said he unto me, Fear not, Daniel: for from the first day that thou didst set thine heart to understand, and to chasten thyself before thy God, thy words were heard, and I am come for thy words.

13 But the prince of the kingdom of Persia withstood me one and twenty days: but, lo, Michael, one of the chief princes, came to help me; and I remained there with the kings of Persia.

14 Now I am come to make thee understand what shall befall thy people in the latter days: for yet the vision is for many days.

———

At the sight of the Lord, Daniel collapses face down to the earth. A ministering attendant lifts the aged prophet to strengthen him setting him upright and admonishing him not to be afraid. The ministering attendant then explains that he had the specific assignment to respond to his prayer. With his help, Daniel stands to receive the instructions.

This angelic watcher confirms that from the very first day of his fast the heavens had heard his prayers, but the response was delayed. He then makes a rather interesting statement as he reveals the cause of the delay. For the twenty-one days of the fast "the prince of the kingdom of Persia withstood him" (Dan. 10:13). The idea conveyed seems to be that a prince in Persia was contending with him and held his attention so that he could not come to Daniel. It is unlikely that he fought or was detained by a mortal man, who had remarkable power to restrain a heavenly being for 21 days. Even if the messenger had engaged a mortal in battle, he would have prevailed quite easily.

The heavenly angel sent against the Assyrian kings "smote in the camp of the Assyrians an hundred fourscore and five thousand: and when they arose early in the morning, behold, they *were* all dead corpses" (2 Kgs. 19:35). Sennacherib's grand army of 180,000 was no match for a single heavenly being. Similarly, the destroying angel that smote the firstborn of the Egyptians proved that any battle between mortals and the heavenly hosts would end swiftly and decisively (Ex. 12:29).

The prince, spoken of by the angel, "was not a mortal leader in Persia but was the leader of the evil forces that supported the unrighteous dominion of the kingdoms of the world."[9] The conflict within the Persian kingdom doubtless involved protecting the king and keeping the nation stable. We already know of the favorable station Cyrus held in the eyes of the Lord. The messenger was engaged in an ongoing battle with Satan and his minions who fight against every purpose of God. Moroni taught: "that which is evil cometh of the devil; for the devil is an enemy unto God, and fighteth against him continually, and inviteth and enticeth to sin, and to do that which is evil continually" (Moro. 7:12).

In his role as a "watcher" (Dan. 4: 13,17, 23), the heavenly messenger had expended great effort to thwart the designs of the adversary or the "prince" of darkness (JST Jn. 14:30; Doctrine and Covenants 127:11). He and his servants ever stir up conspiracy, trouble and insurrection in the empire to create unrest in an attempt to place his own servants in power. Paul warned the Ephesians: "For we wrestle not against flesh and blood, but against principalities, against powers, against the rulers of the darkness of this world, against spiritual wickedness in high places" (Eph. 6:12). The conflict was real and the watcher was actively engaged with the adversary. A key message is that the struggle continues through the ages on both sides of the veil, involving both mortals and immortals.

This circumstance required Michael's intervention to support and sustain the righteous messenger in his conflict with Satan. Similar accounts are found in other scriptures (Jude 1:9; Doctrine and Covenants 128:20). As the Arch or Chief Angel, Michael commands many resources including hosts of angelic beings that together with the keys of the priesthood are frequently employed to subdue the adversary and bring about the purposes of the Lord. Since man's agency is always enforced, battles where Satan tempts mankind are protracted to allow choices and circumstance to play out. These factors may have contributed to the watcher's delay in attending to Daniel and answering his concerns.

"The Hebrew word translated 'I was left there' (nótarti [נוֹתַרְתִּי], from yãtar) does not mean 'to remain behind' but rather signifies 'to remain over, to be superfluous.'"[10] The angel's assignment was to watch over the Persian kingdom and to protect God's interests and purposes. The messenger's report provided an important lesson for Daniel. His fasting and prayers were being answered, not by an immediate visitation or spiritual manifestation, but with real tangible, tactical efforts to protect Israel and those who supported God's purposes, mainly the Persians. Keil expounds on the subject: "The plural [Persian Kings] denotes, that by the subjugation of the demon of the Persian kingdom, his influence not merely over Cyrus, but over all the following kings of Persia, was brought to an end, so that the whole of the Persian kings became accessible to the influence of the spirit proceeding from God and advancing the welfare of Israel."[11] By protecting the Persian Empire, the chosen people would remain in a secure and guarded circumstance. Later, however, in the times of Esther, when troubles emerged in the Empire as Haman sought to destroy the Jews (Esther 3:8-11), further intervention was needed. The angel confirms that he would remain in defense of the Persian kings and the Jewish people for as long as was necessary. Variations of this principle would continue to play out throughout Israel's entire history.

The answer provides a comforting lesson. The Lord employs his servants, or watchers, to protect His children and interests. In contrast, His protective hand is withdrawn from the wicked who reject His council, leaving them to themselves to suffer the wrath and consequences of their actions. With this valuable lesson in mind, the messenger then tells the prophet that he had come to "make [him] understand what shall befall thy people in the latter days: for yet the vision *is* for *many* days" (Dan. 10:14, emphasis).

The war waged between Michael and the adversary, which began in the pre-mortal world (Rev. 12:7), will continue over the centuries among the kingdoms of the earth. The devil will gain successes only as he obtains power over the hearts of the kings and people. Heavenly influence and protections will be present during every turbulent time, in every circumstance throughout the history. This will be especially true during the troubled events just prior to the Coming of the Lord. This subject is specifically addressed in the end verses of chapter 11 and in the beginning of chapter 12. The promise of the vision extends for "many days," far into Daniel's future. The Lord's covenants are sure, Michael and his hosts will come in force in the latter-days to preserve and protect the Saints of God to help them prevail.

Daniel Strengthened Again

———

15 And when he had spoken such words unto me, I set my face toward the ground, and I became dumb.

16 And, behold, one like the similitude of the sons of men touched my lips: then I opened my mouth, and spake, and said unto him that stood before me, O my lord, by the vision my sorrows are turned upon me, and I have retained no strength.

17 For how can the servant of this my lord talk with this my lord? for as for me, straightway there remained no strength in me, neither is there breath left in me.

18 Then there came again and touched me one like the appearance of a man, and he strengthened me,

19 And said, O man greatly beloved, fear not: peace be unto thee, be strong, yea, be strong. And when he had spoken unto me, I was strengthened, and said, Let my lord speak; for thou hast strengthened me.

———

As the vision progressed, the aged prophet again began to falter under the strain of the experience. He fell to his face and became dumb, so that he could not speak. The prophet was weak by virtue of his age and from three weeks of fasting. These heavenly visitations and manifestations take their toll even on younger more vigorous individuals. Young Joseph Smith said, of his First Vision experience, that as soon as the "light had departed, I had no strength" (JS–H. 1:20). Other prophets remained prostrate for hours and took days to fully recover. Moses spoke of his metaphysical encounter saying: "And it came to pass that it was for the space of many hours before [I] did again receive [my] natural strength like unto man" (Moses 1:10). Daniel's expression implies that these conversations were sapping the energy of both body and spirit. He was so emotionally and physically exhausted that he could hardly breath. In response to Daniel's weakness, a heavenly being, *one* like the appearance of a man, touched his lips to give him strength to utter.

A second angel appears to minister to him, perhaps by giving a blessing. He commands that he fear not and be strong. He exhorts the prophet twice to rise and be strong (Dan. 10:19), indicating that the grace of the Lord would attend him and that he should exert every effort on his own behalf despite his aged condition. The messenger reassures the prophet of his favored status in the sight of heaven as one who was "greatly beloved" and respected. His prayers had been heard, and his desires were known and his faith would be honored. The angel bestowed a spirit of peace upon his soul. The prophet had been already greatly distressed over the troubles of his people and he needed reassurance that all would be well. The angel counseled him to be still and have faith with the assurance that the Lord's hands were over him and his people (Doctrine and Covenants 101:16). Exerting some effort, he stood for the remainder of the vision.

The Prophecies Will Be Fulfilled

20 Then said he, Knowest thou wherefore I come unto
    thee? and now will I return to fight with the prince
    of Persia: and when I am gone forth, lo, the prince
    of Grecia shall come.

> 21 But I will shew thee that which is noted in the
> scripture of truth: and there is none that holdeth with
> me in these things, but Michael your prince.
> ———

The messenger reminds Daniel of the purpose of his visit and also of his mission. Spiritual and physical battles remained ahead, continuing through the reign of the Persian Empire, the Greeks and so on. We know that eventually the Persian leadership fell into wickedness and Alexander the Great defeated Darius and swept over the kingdom. Logically, similar struggles would continue under Greek and Roman rule, into the Dark Ages, and even until the latter-days. The messenger promised to continue in his fight against the forces of evil at least through the reign of the Persians and the Greeks. For now, He would "show Daniel the terrible ceaseless conflicts that would take place on the earth in the years ahead, conflicts that would ravage the Promised Land again and again. Judah would be a pawn in the power plays of two rival kingdoms, one to the north and the other to the south. That little land would become a battleground as hostile kingdoms marched back and forth, one against the other. But behind the turmoil are unseen sinister spiritual forces. Satanic princes keep the world in upheaval."[12]

> His mission is to serve and protect the holy people, to prove that the prophecies revealed in the scriptures are true and that no power will frustrate the designs and purposes of the Lord.

But Daniel should not fear, the angel will ensure that God's covenants are fulfilled among men (Moro. 7:31). His mission is to serve and protect the holy people, to prove that the prophecies revealed in the scriptures are true and that no power will frustrate the designs and goals of the Lord. "The Speaker has already declared that the people of God must experience the opposition of Persia and

Greece. However, this opposition cannot exceed the limits of what has been decreed by God, it is inscribed in the writing of truth."[13] When the opposition arises, the Lord will frustrate such events or if necessary, use it as a means of chastening and refining His people. The messenger, together with Michael and the hosts under his command will ensure that the Lord's promises concerning the destiny of Israel are fulfilled.

We remember Elisha's revelation to the affrighted servant who trembled at the approach of a large host of Syrian chariots. This account remains a valuable lesson throughout the history of Israel. When the servant asked in terror: "Alas, my master! how shall we do? And [Elisha] answered, Fear not: for they that *be* with us *are* more than they that *be* with them. And Elisha prayed, and said, Lord, I pray thee, open his eyes, that he may see. And the Lord opened the eyes of the young man; and he saw: and, behold, the mountain *was* full of horses and chariots of fire round about Elisha" (1 Kgs. 6:15-17). Indeed, the chosen people under Michael's protection, are surrounded with his hosts of a thousand times ten thousands! (Rev. 5:11) In the final dispensation, the Lord promised: "I will go before your face. I will be on your right hand and on your left, and my Spirit shall be in your hearts, and mine angels round about you, to bear you up (Doctrine and Covenants 84:88). The Lord and His messengers came personally to convey this promise to Daniel. The prophet "probably did not understand the details [of the vision to come], he could [however] be reasonably assured that God had a plan that ended in the ultimate victory of divine power. Although the prophecies made clear that there were powerful forces at work against Israel that would inflict upon them much suffering and loss, in the end the power of God would triumph and Israel would be exalted as a nation."[14]

The angel now expressed his desire to show the prophet what was written in the "scripture of truth." It is unclear exactly what this "scripture" is, but it appears to be a record like the book that John saw in the Father's right hand that contained the will and designs of heaven for the world (Rev. 5:1; Doctrine and Covenants 77:6). This "Scripture of Truth" shows, among other things, Israel's destiny amidst the intrigue and strife of the nations of the world. Soon after the vision was given, the messenger returned to his assignment. The battle against the forces of evil continued against powers who sought to corrupt the Persians, and later the Greeks. No doubt this is true in the case of the Romans and the other kingdoms that followed.

Amidst it all, the angel says that "*there is* none that holdeth with me" (Dan. 10:21) or supports me except Michael. This statement should not be viewed in a negative light, but rather provides the assurance that Michael will render all necessary aid for him to be successful in his assignment. Though there is always intrigue, conflict and wars and the world seems to be in turmoil, the outcome is foreseen and victory guaranteed. Most of the struggles are not geopolitical or national, or even regional, but are personal. Elder Richard G. Scott has counseled: "Our Father in Heaven knew [what] would happen to us. It is all part of His perfect plan of happiness. He prepared a way through the life of His perfectly obedient Son, Jesus Christ, our Savior, for His Atonement to overcome every difficulty that we may experience in mortality....We were taught in the premortal world that our purpose in coming here is to be tested, tried, and stretched (Abr. 3:25). We knew that we would face the evil darts of the adversary. Sometimes we may feel more aware of the negative things of mortality than we are of the positive. The prophet Lehi taught, "For it must needs be, that there is an opposition in all things" (2 Ne. 2:11). Despite all of the negative challenges we have in life, we must take time to actively exercise our faith. Such exercise invites the positive, faith-filled power of the Atonement of Jesus Christ into our lives."[15] The Lord had personally visited Daniel to deliver this clear message! His purposes will prevail, both globally and individually. He has covenanted to be a protector and a guide, and all the while man's moral agency is preserved.

Chapter Notes

1 Keil. *Biblical Commentary of the Old Testament. The Book of the Prophet Daniel.* 402

2 Ibid. 402

3 Ibid. 406

4 Ibid. 406

5 *New International Version of the Bible.* The New Living Version

6 Phillips. *Exploring the Book of Daniel: An Expository Commentary.* 177

7 Keil._*Biblical Commentary of the Old Testament. The Book of the Prophet Daniel.* 408)

8 Walvoord. *Daniel: The Key to Prophetic Revelation.* 166. See also Prichard. *Near Eastern Studies.* 307

9 *Old Testament Institute Manual* Section 28-48. 307-08

10 Brown. *A Hebrew and English Lexicon of the Old Testament.* 451

11 Keil._*Biblical Commentary of the Old Testament. The Book of the Prophet Daniel.* 419

12 Phillips. *Exploring the Book of Daniel: An Expository Commentary.* 182-83

13 Young. *The Prophecy Daniel: A Commentary.* 229

14 Walvoord. *Daniel: The Key to Prophetic Revelation.* 166. See also Prichard. *Near Eastern Studies.* 31

15 Scott. "Make the Exercise of Faith Your First Priority." General Conference. October 2015

Additional Notes

Angels influence in the nations

Bad angels, called demons in the New Testament, are, without a doubt, referred to here. In the course of time, these demonic powers gained a very strong influence over certain nations and the governments of these nations. They became the controlling power. They used whatever resources they could muster to hamper God's world and to thwart His purposes....We get a rare glimpse behind the scenes of world history. There are spiritual forces at work that are far in excess of what men who disregard revelation would suppose. They struggle behind the struggles that are written on the pages of history. Leupold, *Daniel*, 457-58

11

The
Gentile Kingdoms and
the Latter-day Anti-
Christs

SECTION 1

Chapter 10 ends with the promise from the messenger to show Daniel what is written in the "scripture of truth" (Dan. 10:21). These writings reveal the true history of the world as inscribed by God. In Revelation, John the Apostle saw God sitting upon His throne with "a book written within and on the backside, sealed with seven seals." (Rev. 5:1). The book contained "the revealed will, mysteries, and the works of God; the hidden things of his economy concerning this earth during the seven thousand years of its continuance, or its temporal existence" (Doctrine and Covenants 77:6). "The 'scripture of truth' is the book in which God has designated beforehand, according to truth, the history of the world as it shall certainly be unfolded."[1] Before the foundations of the world was laid, the Lord organized the entire our mortal existence. He said: "I Am, Alpha and Omega, the beginning and the end, the same which looked upon the wide expanse of eternity, and all the seraphic hosts of heaven, before the world was made; The same which knoweth all things, for all things are present before mine eyes" (Doctrine and Covenants 38:1). With precise foreknowledge, He separated the children of Adam setting in order the kindreds and nations. He set the bounds of their dominion (Deut. 32:8), and His will is reflected in the record Daniel, John and others saw.

The vision opened in Chapter 10 and Chapter 11 continues with the fourth and final vision that spans from the reign of Darius the Mede (539 B.C.) to the last gentile ruler at the end of times.[2] As stated previously, not every detail was recorded, but only critical highlights. Chapter 11 is divided into three sections. The first section comprises verses 1-20, and gives remarkable descriptions of the major rulers of the Persian Empire, Alexander the Great and detailed accounts of conflict and intrigue between two of the subsequent Greek Kingdoms—the Seleucid and Ptolemaic Empires. Section two is a second account of the reign of terror brought by the anti-Christ, Antiochus Epiphanies (Dan. 11:21-35). The first was given in Chapter 8 (Dan. 8:9-15, 23-25). After the account of the great persecutor, the record is silent about events and kingdoms from that point until the latter-days. No mention is made of the Romans, the Moors, the Ottomans or the gentiles that ruled over of the Holy Land after World War I. The events surrounding the Messiah's ministry and the destruction of Jerusalem were covered in the vision in Chapter 9, and nothing is said directly about the Great Apostasy.

The third section begins in the latter verses of Chapter 11 (35-45); keeping in the spirit and theme of the previous verses (Dan. 11:25-34). This section transitions to the latter-days, wherein a new anti-Christ in the likeness of Antiochus Epiphanies has come to power among the gentiles. The "appointed time" is just prior to Christ's second advent (Dan. 11:35).[3] The purpose of the vision is to reveal tribulations to come upon the people of God, both in Israel and around the world. The backdrop of Antiochus's reign of terror serves as a pattern for the modern-day crisis when the Saints will again suffer under the reign of anti-Christs to come.

Chapter 12 follows as an immediate succession to the events in Chapter 11, adding details about the timeframe and a command to endure well during the turmoil just prior to the Second Coming.

The Vision's Detail

The prophetic details of Chapter 11 are remarkable, particularly the sequence outlining the reign of the Greek kings and the intrigue and conflicts between the northern (Seleucid or Syrian) and the southern (Ptolemaic or Egyptian) kingdoms. So precise are the prophetic predictions that they draw criticism from skeptics like Porphyry who claimed that Daniel's revelation was a forgery. "Porphyry established the fact that history corresponded closely to the prophetic revelation of Daniel 11:1-35, and the correspondence was so precise that he was persuaded no one could have prophesied these events into the future...the attack prompted Jerome to defend the book of Daniel and to issue his own commentary, which for over one thousand years was considered the standard commentary on Daniel."[4] The revelations teach that all things "past, present, and future,... are continually before the Lord" (Doctrine and Covenants 130:7), and revealing in great detail things that to the reader will be in the future, is easily accomplished by the Lord. It serves as yet another witness of the prophetic gift of Daniel.

The Persian Empire and Alexander the Great

----

1   Also I in the first year of Darius the Mede, even I, stood to confirm and to strengthen him.

2   And now will I shew thee the truth. Behold, there shall stand up yet three kings in Persia; and the fourth shall be far richer than they all: and by his strength through his riches he shall stir up all against the realm of Grecia.

The angel begins again by informing Daniel of his assignment to "confirm and strengthen" Darius as the Persian king over the Babylonian province. Apparently, the Lord wanted the king in that position as he was the man best suited to protect Israel and fulfill His purposes. This was true despite being duped into signing the law against praying and counseling with other gods (Dan. 6:9 (7-9). At this point in history, there seemed to be forces within the Persian Kingdom scheming to disrupt the peace or even take the prized providence of Babylon. The angel's work was intended to thwart such efforts and ensure Darius's success (Dan. 11:1).

Three successive kings of Persia are then presented in the vision. These kings are yet to gain the throne over the vast Empire. History records the three successors of Cyrus the Great were Cambyses II (529-522 B.C.), not mentioned in the Old Testament, the pseudo-Smerdis (522-521 B.C.), and Darius I Hystaspes (521-486 B.C., Ezra 5-6). The fourth king mentioned is Xerxes I (486-465 B.C.) or *Ahasuerus* as he is referred to in the Bible (Ezra 4:6, Esth. 1:1). The Jewish maiden Esther married Xerxes and became queen of Persia (Esth. 2:17). The chief characteristic mentioned of the fourth king was his riches. With each king, Persia expanded and prospered. The kingdom, and therefore the monarchy, became wealthier and grew more powerful as it expanded. A significant portion of riches was spent building infrastructure, rebuilding or expanding the capitals (Susa, Persepolis and Ecbatana) and the temples and for governance. Large portions of the treasury were also expended in creating and sustaining the armies used to maintain the peace or in efforts to expand the kingdom, such as into Greece.

Conflicts between the Persian Empire and the Greek states began under Cyrus when he took the region of Iona (Western Turkey) in 546 B.C. Later a number of skirmishes with Satrap led rebellions, encouraged by Greek colonists, forced Darius I (Hystaspes) to mount a large campaign to subdue Athens and Eretria and to establish a permanent presence in Greece. In 492 B.C. the Persians crossed Hellespont to re-subjugate Thrace and Macedonia. In the September campaign of 490 B.C., Persian ships anchored offshore at Marathon with at least 100,000 light infantries and 10,000 cavalry that landed on the southeastern shore. Athens met their force with 11,000 hoplite troops and a small contingent of cavalry.

After a four-day standoff, Darius I decided to take a portion of their forces by sea and attack the unguarded city of Athens. He loaded cavalry and troops back onto the ships and set a course

Relief of Darius I Hystapes in Persepolis

around the peninsula to the city-capital. The Athenian military took advantage of the divided Persian force that was left at Marathon and attacked, routing the Persian infantry within a few hours. Exhausted, the hoplite troops marched in haste back to Athens a distance of 22 miles to meet Darius and the fleet prior to his landing. Astonished and disappointed to see the troops on the shore, the king decided against invading the city.[5]

Ten years later in 480 B.C., Xerxes I renewed his father's effort to finish the work of taking the Grecian peninsula. This time he marched with an even larger assemblage of troops gathered from most of the provinces in the empire. Like the previous campaign, Daniel states that he stirred up "all" against the realm of Grecia (Dan. 11:2). It is believed that the Persian army amassed one of the largest forces in history. Herodotus records that there were representatives from over 40 countries and provinces in the empire.[6] He "...stirred up Phoenician Carthage against Greek colonies in Italy and Sicily. The Carthaginians, seeing a chance to plunder a rival maritime power, raised a respectable army of their own along with a naval force of two hundred ships. So, as the prophecy states, Xerxes did 'stir up all' against the realm of Greece."[7]

The Persian army won an initial, hard fought victory against 300 Spartans at Thermopylae, which allowed Xerxes to push southward and overrun much of Greece. When they marched into Athens, he ordered the city burned in retribution for the loss at Marathon. The next day, feeling that he had committed a great mistake, he ordered the city rebuilt. The retreating Greeks countered in 479 B.C. when Themistocles, leading a fleet of Trireme warships and outnumbered at almost 4 to 1, routed Xerxes's Persian navy at Salamis.[8] His navy sank or captured at least 200 ships. The Greeks then defeated the Persian army at Plataea, in the region of Boeotia.[9] Thus the Greek alliance ended the advance of the Persians into Greece. "The day would come when Greece would exact full retribution against Xerxes folly."[10] Alexander would take his revenge by invading Asia Minor. When king Darius III asked the reason for his incursion, he would remind him of the two previous invasions mounted by his father and grandfather.

No subsequent Persian king commanded so many resources or military might as Xerxes, and none of the other Persian kings were mentioned in the vision. "From the conflict of Persia with Greece, the angel (Dan. 11:3) passes immediately over to the founder of the Grecian (or Macedonian) world-kingdom. The prophecy proceeds, but not with extensive historical details. It only mentions the principle character, Alexander, and the rise of Greece and the fall of Persia. Xerxes expedition against Greece brings to the foreground the world-historical conflict between Persia and Greece, and led to the destruction of the Persian kingdom by Alexander the Great."[11] The vision record continues in the pattern of the vision, highlighting important historical points, but not addressing every detail.

A Mighty Grecian King

3   And a mighty king shall stand up, that shall rule with great dominion, and do according to his will.

4   And when he shall stand up, his kingdom shall be broken, and shall be divided towards the four winds of heaven; and not to his posterity, nor according to his dominion which he ruled: for his kingdom shall be plucked up, even for others beside those.

"A mighty king stands up" (Dan. 11:3), who doubtless was the renowned Alexander the Great. A more complete review of his rise to power and campaigns were presented in Chapter 8. Once in power over all of Greece and Macedonia, Alexander indeed "did according to his will" (Dan. 11:3). He resolved to invade Persia to take revenge for decades of intrusions from Darius and Xerxes. "Within a dozen years, he had brought Asia, [western] India, and parts of Africa and Europe under his kingdom. He never met a foe whom he could not conquer, a city he did not subdue, a people he could not subjugate."[12] He only stopped in India when his commanders and Macedonian troops would proceed no further. "Who in Daniel's day would have thought that the disunited states of the Greek Peninsula would produce a conqueror who would grind the powerful Persian Empire to pieces?"[13] His drive for conquest and empire building seemed relentless. In the end, however, he died suddenly in Nebuchadnezzar's Palace in Babylon. The Lord's stern rebuke of the rich and powerful who employ all their means to create and support earthly kingdoms applies quintessentially to this young Grecian king: "For what is a man profited, if he shall gain the whole world, and lose his own soul? or what shall a man give in exchange for his soul?" (Matt. 16:26). All of Alexander's focus and energy availed him very little in the end.

Lvova Anastasiya © Used with Permission
Alexander the Great

His death came at the height of his power, and with his sudden passing his dominion ended and the kingdom was "divided to the four winds" (Dan. 11:4). None of his family or posterity succeeded him. His half brother, Philip Arrhidaeus, an epileptic, reigned for a small season, but was deemed mentally incompetent, and was murdered in 317 B.C.[14] Philip's wife, Eurydice, was forced to commit suicide, at the instigation of Alexander's mother, Olympias. Alexander's generals did not recognize his illegitimate sons, the older of whom was Hercules. "His posthumous son Alexander Aegus, born to Roxane, was put under a guardian and then murdered by order of Olympias through the treachery of general Cassander. Within fifteen years of his own

Lysimachus   Cassander   Ptolemy   Seleucus

death, none of his family remained alive."[15] The vision foretold that Alexander's expansive kingdom would not be given to his direct posterity, nor would his reign and dominion remain intact. These words were fulfilled with remarkable precision. No heir assumed the throne and the kingdom was broken into four smaller kingdoms.

The kingdom eventually rested on four of his generals. Exercising their military and political might, they carved out major Greek kingdoms. Cassander, Ptolemy, Lysimachus and Seleucus consolidated power from their rivals into four principal kingdoms: Greece, Thrace-Phrygia, Syria-Babylon and Egypt. These rulers became known as The *Diadochi* or the "successors."[16]

| Coin of Seleucus I | Coin of Ptolemy I |

The Greek Kingdoms of the South and North

Daniel's vision now centers on the Holy Land. It focuses on the struggle between two of the four kingdoms carved from Alexander's empire. The messenger makes reference to the king or kingdom of the north (Syria) and the kingdom of the south (Egypt). The terms north and south refer to their relative locations to Palestine or the glorious land (Dan. 11:16).[17] These kingdoms became most relevant to Israel's future; its politics and stability were ever influenced because of its geographic location which sat squarely in the middle of the two powers. "In tracing the struggles between Egypt and Syria, the prophecy is selective and not all the rulers are mentioned, but usually the identification is clear."[18]

The contentions between these two kingdoms (Egyptian Ptolemy and Syrian Seleucids) came to be known as the Syrian Wars. As the prophecy is reviewed, we must be reminded of Kiel's counsel that not every historical detail was revealed, but only the major and relevant events and in many cases, with remarkable precision.

The focus on the kings of the north and the south has relevance to the Jews as they must serve as subjects to these greater powers. The grand geo-political conflict between these two empires creates much tension and intrigue in the region, and as we shall see the cultural impact and friction overflows into the Jewish state itself.

Dominion of Seleucus I Nicator and Ptolemy I Soter

5 And the king of the south shall be strong, and *one* of his princes; and he shall be strong above him, and have dominion; his dominion shall be a great dominion.

Egypt, northeastern Africa and the land of Israel came under control of general Ptolemy and was referred to as the kingdom of the south (Dan. 11:8). It is translated in the Septuagint as Egypt.[19] After Alexander's death, Ptolemy I Soter also known as Lagides, (367–283 B.C.) secured control over Egypt at the counsel of the generals or the Treaty of Triparadisus. "Convinced from the outset that the generals could not maintain the unity of Alexander's empire, he proposed during the council at Babylon…that the satrapies (the provinces of the huge empire) be divided among the generals. He became satrap of Egypt, with the adjacent Libyan and Arabian regions, and methodically took advantage of the geographic isolation of the Nile territory to make it a great Hellenistic power."[20]

Ptolemy I Soter or "savior" became the first "king of the south" spoken of in the vision. One of his most important accomplishments was the development of Alexandria, which became the principle seaport, and an intellectual and cultural center of the ancient world. It reached its zenith in importance under the Romans. Alexandria was also a central Jewish community for centuries.

Ptolemy proved to be an accomplished diplomat and a capable leader. He gained the loyalty of the people by restoring the temple of Pharaoh, which the Persians had destroyed. Because of its geographical location, Egypt was never poised to be a major military power among the Macedonian kingdoms. Ptolemy preferred securing or expanding his empire through diplomacy, alliances and marriages rather than warfare and conquest.[21] Egypt remained a fertile breadbasket providing wheat and other grains throughout the Mediterranean, making it both rich and influential.

The Prince of the King

Daniel refers to another king, which was "one of his princes" (Dan. 11:5), meaning a prince of Ptolemy. Historical accounts reveal that the prince of Ptolemy was Seleucus I Nicator, the founder of the Seleucid Empire. He was an excellent infantry general in Alexander's army, but received no land or kingdom after the king's death. In the scramble for power, he reportedly supported Perdiccas the Regent over Babylon and was given command over the

Naples Archaeological Museum. © Used with Permission
Roman bust of Seleucus I Nicator

Companions Cavalry. With the outbreak of the Wars between the Diadochi in 322 B.C., Perdiccas' military failures led to the mutiny of his troops. Perdiccas was betrayed and assassinated by Seleucus and others in 321 B.C..[22]

At the Treaty of Triparadisus (321 B.C.) the Asian satrapies were realigned, and Seleucid received Babylonia. He was forced to flee, however, because a rival Antigonus I moved to take Babylon in a power serge from Phrygia. Seleucus escaped to Egypt to join Ptolemy who appointed him a general. As a general under Ptolemy, Seleucus was a prince (sometimes translated official) of the king of the South, thus fulfilling the scriptural prophecy. Ptolemy I, Cassander and Lysimachus defeated Antigonus to retake Phrygia, Lydia, Ionax (Turkey) and Syria. Seleucus again received the province of Babylonia in 312 B.C. the date from which the era of the new Seleucid kingdom is reckoned.[23]

As the first king of the north, Seleucus subsequently secured the eastern kingdoms namely: "Parthia, Bactria, Arabia, Tapouria, Sogdia, Arachosia, Hyrcania, and the adjacent tribes as far as the Indus river. The boundaries of the newly formed Seleucid Empire became the most expansive in all Asia and Africa."[24]

The Seleucid dynasty lasted from 321 B.C. to about 63 B.C. The scripture says that the kingdom of the south [Egypt] "shall be strong," and "he," meaning the prince of the north, "shall be above him" or Ptolemy (Dan. 11:5). Seleucus's dominion spanned from Hellespont in Phrygia (Istanbul, Turkey) to India in the east and stood as a "great dominion." It became the largest of all of the kingdoms created by the Diadochi.[25] It also proved the most difficult to maintain.

Coin of Antiochus II   Coin of Ptolemy II Philadelphus

Marriage of the Daughter of Egypt to Syrian King

6   And in the end of years they shall join themselves together; for the king's daughter of the south shall come to the king of the north to make an agreement: but she shall not retain the power of the arm; neither shall he stand, nor his arm: but she shall be given up, and they that brought her, and he that begat her, and he that strengthened her in *these* times.

The dust of controversy and intrigue over the four Macedonian kingdoms never completely settled. Rival dynasties battled for naval supremacy in the Aegean Sea and armies sparred over land, treasure and property. Ptolemy II Philadelphus (308–246 B.C.) engaged Antiochus II (261–246 B.C.) and the Seleucid Empire in two separate Syrian wars (c. 274-270 and c. 260-253), which involved incursions and battles in the Promised Land. When Ptolemy's military operations proved unsuccessful, he turned to diplomacy, or rather bribery, to broker peace. The expression "in the end of years" is translated "after the laps of several years (2 Chron. 18:2; Dan. 11:8, 13 NIV)."[26] Egypt proposed to form an alliance with Syria.

Ptolemy II arranged that Antiochus II take his daughter Bernice to wife under the condition that he divorce Laodice I and declare the two sons, Seleucus and Antiochus, illegitimate.[27] Antiochus II agreed and, as a token of peace, the alliance was sealed with the marriage to Bernice. The Egyptian king paid a huge dowry. Antiochus provided land grants to his wife and dismissed her to the west. A new succession line to the throne was created.[28]

The intent of all such marriages was to build a more prosperous alliance between two kingdoms and both parties celebrated success. But no part of the union bore the desired prosperity or political fruit. When Ptolemy died a few years later, Antiochus repudiated Bernice and took back his former wife. "To gain revenge, however, [Laodice] poisoned her husband as well as his Egyptian wife, Bernice, and the infant son of Antiochus and Bernice."[29]

The scripture states that "she shall not retain the power of the arm; neither shall he stand, nor his arm" (Dan. 11:6). Bernice would be rejected and lose her political position, and both she and her son would lose their lives. The political alliance collapsed and Ptolemy's plans would not "stand" and the treaty based on expediency, treachery and dishonor imploded.[30] "He that begat her [Ptolemy]" and "brought her," did not achieve the goal in strengthening the relationship nor did he bring peace. He that "strengthened her," Antiochus, also died. The treaty conceived in iniquity resulted in the Third Syrian war with much more intrigue and bloodshed.

Bernice's brother, Ptolemy III Euergetes ("benefactor"), succeeded the throne in Egypt. Furious at the demise of his sister, he set out to avenge her murder by invading Syria.

Coin of Seleucus Callinicus   Coin of Ptolemy III Euregetes

Ptolemy III Euergetes and Seleucus Callinicus

――――

7 But out of a branch of her roots shall *one* stand up in his estate, which shall come with an army, and shall enter into the fortress of the king of the north, and shall deal against them, and shall prevail:

8 And shall also carry captives into Egypt their gods, with their princes, *and* with their precious vessels of silver and of gold; and he shall continue *more* years than the king of the north.

9 So the king of the south shall come into *his* kingdom, and shall return into his own land.

――――

The "branch of her roots" (Dan. 11:7) refers to Bernice's brother, Ptolemy III Euergetes (246–221 B.C.), who was crowned king at the death of their father. Angry at the murder of his sister, Ptolemy III waged war against the new king of the north Seleucus Callincus (246–226 B.C.). The scripture indicates, he "enter[ed] into the fortress of the king of the north" (Dan. 11:7), which meant that the Egyptians pushed upward and took the land of Seleucia and subjugated the people. At the same time Laodice supported her second son in a civil war against the first and was defeated and killed. Ptolemy pushed his way past Antioch to Babylon, Susiana and into Bactria (Afghanistan).[31] Jerome's account of Ptolemy III Euergetes war outlines the scope of the crushing conquest:

> He came up with a great army and advanced into the province the king of the North, that is Seleucus Callinicus, who together with his mother Laodice was ruling in Syria, and abused them, and not only did he seize Syria but also took Cilicia and the remoter regions beyond the Euphrates and nearly all of Asia as well. And then, when he heard that a rebellion was afoot in Egypt, he ravaged the kingdom of Seleucus and carried off as booty forty thousand talents of silver, and also precious vessels and images of the gods to the amount of two and a half thousand. Among them were the same images, which Cambyses had brought to Persia at the time when he conquered Egypt. The Egyptian people were indeed devoted to idolatry, for when he had brought back their gods to them after so many years, they called him Euergetes (Benefactor). And he himself retained possession of Syria, but he handed over Cilicia to his friend, Antiochus that he might govern it, and the provinces beyond the Euphrates he handed over to Xanthippus, another general.[32]

Ptolemy's campaign penetrated deep into the eastern regions of the Seleucid Empire and proved to be crushing to the northern kingdom. As victors, the Egyptians "brought back to Egypt four thousand talents of gold, forty thousand talents of silver, twenty-five hundred molten idols and their sacred vessel, including many that had been captured and taken from Egypt by Cambyses some three hundred years earlier."[33] Daniel's vision specifically mentions "carrying captives" to their idol gods (Dan 11:8). He also carried back to Egypt, princes and thousands of hostages and "their recovered Egyptian idols were reinstalled in their temples with great ceremony."[34]

A truce was signed and in exchange for peace in 241 B.C., Ptolemy was awarded new territories on the northern coast of Syria, including Seleucia Pieria, and the port of Antioch. The Seleucid kingdom was divided as Antiochus's younger brother, Antiochus Hierax, was given portions of Asia Minor. The truce lasted ten years.

The language in verse 9 comes across as an afterthought, giving the impression that the king of the south returned to his land of Egypt. "A better translation, however, would indicate that he, Seleucus Callincus, 'shall come to the realm of the king of the south.' This may refer to the fact that Seleucus mounted a counter attack against Egypt, but was routed and "returned to his own land."[35] In final humiliation the vision comes to a complete fulfillment as Seleucus Callincus dies prematurely from a fall from his own horse.[36] The Egyptian king lived to see the death of a much younger Syrian rival, fulfilling the words "he shall continue more years than the king of the north" (Dan. 11:8).

This portion of the prophecy provides the context for the next sequence outlined. Verses 10-19 reveal the ascendancy of the Syrian regime over Egypt. The Promised Land would swing back under the control of the Seleucids and set the stage for Antiochus IV Epiphanies war with Egypt. His misfortunes in Egypt result in severe problems for the Jews and the Abomination of Desolation against the temple.

Seleucus, Antiochus, the Great and Ptolemy IV Philopator (11:10-19)

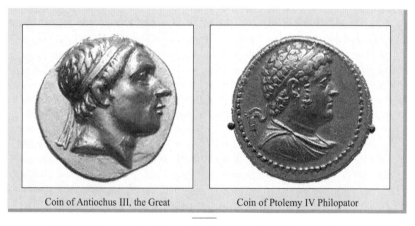

| Coin of Antiochus III, the Great | Coin of Ptolemy IV Philopator |

10 But his sons shall be stirred up, and shall assemble a multitude of great forces: and *one* shall certainly

> come, and overflow, and pass through: then shall he
> return, and be stirred up, *even* to his fortress.
>
> ———

The vision focuses on the sons who were "stirred up" from the losses suffered at the hands of Ptolemy III Euergetes. Seleucus Ceraunus (243–223 B.C.) and Anitochus III (241–187 B.C.), later known as "the Great." These sons were born of Seleucus II Callinicus and Laodice II. The poor handling of territorial challenges, military defeats and the untimely death of their father left the Seleucid Empire in disarray. Seleucus Ceraunus (Thunder) attempted to stabilize the situation by first leading an army on a campaign to reclaim Asia Minor. He was defeated by his cousin Attalus I, king of Pergamon and assassinated in Anatolia by members of his army.

Antiochus III, the Great, his younger brother, assumed the throne at the age of 18. He became the "one who would come and overflow, and pass through" (Dan. 11:10) against Ptolemy IV in Egypt. He would restore the Seleucid Empire to its previous grandeur. After securing the kingdom, his court advisor Hermeias pressured him to move immediately against Egyptian interests near Antioch,[37] but consulting his council, Antiochus felt he needed to secure the Asian provinces of Media and Persia and the far eastern territories of Bactria and Parthia.

Generals were sent to defeat the brothers Molon and Alexander, rebellious satrapies who had been given Media and Persia, but they failed in their attempts to recapture these important provinces. Antiochus marched himself with the army, which caused Molon's troops to desert. The abandoned satrapies, together with the entire leadership and their families, committed suicide rather than face the wrath of Antiochus.[38] Bactria to the east had also broken away and Parthia came under a nomad chieftain. Both rebellions would have to wait ten years (209 B.C.) before Antiochus could reassert control in that part of his kingdom.

With Persia and Media secured and "having notified his uncle Archaeus that he had not forgotten the revolt in the west,"[39] Antiochus began preparations to move against Ptolemy IV and Egypt. The first objective was to retake the port of Seleucia Pieria, which lay only 16 miles to the west of Antioch and served as a constant reminder of Egypt's intrusive occupation from the south.

Antiochus's rival in Egypt was Ptolemy IV Philopator, who turned out to be a drunken, degenerate reveler.[40] In a completely despicable act, he ordered his mother Bernice II, uncle Lysimachus and younger brother Magas murdered at his inauguration.[41] He frequently showed weakness in affairs of the kingdom and was indecisive, often seeking advice from incompetent court favorites.[42] His weak character and wavering policy made him vulnerable to the firm minded counterpart from Syria.

Antiochus's campaigns against Egypt began in 218 B.C.. He made swift work of Egyptian garrisons retaking the port of Seleucia, then moving southward to Tyre, the costal city of Ptolemais, and with an "overflowing" mass of troops and cavalry "passed through" Palestine, Dora and overran a powerful Egyptian garrison in a fortress just north of Caesarea" (Dan. 11:10). [43]

In a frantic scramble, Ptolemy and his advisors (Sosibius and Agathocles) began assembling troops and mercenaries. To buy time, they sent several embassies to negotiate a truce.[44] Antiochus halted for the winter and resided to enjoy the spoils in the port of Seleucia. The following spring, he "returned" (Dan. 11:10) and renewed the war capturing a number of cities and soundly defeated Nicolas, the Egyptian general, who retreated to Sidon.[45] The next year, he advanced further south until he captured the fortified Gaza referred to in the scripture as "his fortress" (Dan. 11:10), which was the limit of the Syrian assault set by the prophecy. Antiochus would not be able to move further south into Egypt.

Ptolemy Philopator Successfully Defends Egypt

———

11 And the king of the south shall be moved with choler, and shall come forth and fight with him, *even* with the king of the north: and he shall set forth a great multitude; but the multitude shall be given into his hand.

> **12** *And* when he hath taken away the multitude, his heart
> shall be lifted up; and he shall cast down *many* ten
> thousands: but he shall not be strengthened *by it.*
>
> ————

The vision reveals that Antiochus's march against Egypt enraged the Pharaoh. Having delayed the Syrian invasion of Egypt for two years, he met Antiochus just above the traditional Egyptian border near the modern-day city of Rafah. Prepared to defend the land of the Pharaohs, he marched forward with his sister Arsione at the head of an army of 70,000 troops.[46] Arsione rode ahead of the cavalry and proved invaluable to the battle as, in a speech, she inspired the troops to fight bravely and honorably.[47]

Antiochus stood prepared with "a great multitude" of 62,000 hoplite infantry, 5,000 cavalry and about 100 war elephants.[48] He expected a swift victory over his enemies, but was met with disappointment. In a series of miscalculations and overestimations, Antiochus was defeated and forced to retreat to Gaza.[49] The battle "was given into [Ptolemy's] hands" (Dan. 11:11). The Greek Pharaoh, however, took no advantage of his success, but was content to sign a truce and return to Egypt. After the truce was signed, Antiochus left Coele-Syria for nearly twenty years battling in Asia Minor and on the eastern frontier.[50]

The proximity of the war brought the Jews into the middle of the great conflict. A few sided with Antiochus, but many remained loyal to the Ptolemy Empire. After the great battle Ptolemy remained in the region setting in order town governments and the district leadership.[51] A Maccabean account relates that he visited Jerusalem. In a familiar royal show of arrogance, being "lifted up in pride" (Dan. 11:12), he attempted to enter the temple and the Holy of Holies (3 Mac. 2:21-24). The record states that he was severely shocked, leaving his limbs without strength and forcing those that were with him to drag him from the temple mount.

Humiliated and angered by the incident, the king returned to Egypt and began a campaign to spread rumors and levy false accusations against the Jews living in Alexandria. In a calculated ploy, he offered to elevate the Jews to become full-fledged citizens if they renounced their religion and branded themselves with the "ivy leaf sign of Dionysus. If not they were to be stripped of any privilege or status and refused entrance into their synagogues" (3 Mac 2:25-30; 3:20-24). The Jewish community protested against the demands, but at the same time endeavored to prove loyalty and demonstrate their faithfulness as citizens in the kingdom (3 Mac. 3:1-10). A number of Jews bribed local leaders not to enforce the king's edict.

Ptolemy retaliated against those who circumvented the process by issuing an edict to round up all the Jews. Tens of thousands were "cast down" (Dan. 11:12) or taken from Alexandria to be trampled by elephants in the Hippodrome. In the end, through a series of miraculous events, Ptolemy's rage was subdued and the Jews were not killed, but allowed to return to Alexandria (3 Mac 7:1-10, 17-23). As the scripture indicates, these events did not strengthen the Egyptian king (Dan. 11:12), but created a very tense situation for the Jews. The overall status of the kingdom remained the same.

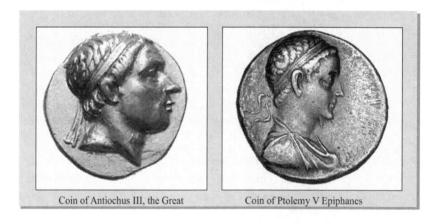

Coin of Antiochus III, the Great   Coin of Ptolemy V Epiphanes

The Fifth Syrian War

13 For the king of the north shall return, and shall set forth a multitude greater than the former, and shall certainly come after certain years with a great army and with much riches.

14 And in those times there shall many stand up against the king of the south: also the robbers of thy people

shall exalt themselves to establish the vision; but they shall fall.

15 So the king of the north shall come, and cast up a mount, and take the most fenced cities: and the arms of the south shall not withstand, neither his chosen people, neither *shall there be any* strength to withstand.

16 But he that cometh against him shall do according to his own will, and none shall stand before him: and he shall stand in the glorious land, which by his hand shall be consumed.

————

Ptolemy IV Philopater died in 204 B.C. leaving the kingdom to his young four-year-old son, Ptolemy V Epiphanies. Serious internal conflict erupted in Egypt as the chief ministers, Agothocles and Sosibius, took temporary control over the kingdom. In a miscalculation, Agothocles incited mobs in Alexandria, who rebelled and hung him amidst a riot.[52] The kingdom spiraled into a near state of anarchy, which spilled out into the provinces. Seeking to take advantage of this turmoil, Antiochus III staged a second invasion of Coele-Syria. He "set forth a multitude greater than the former" invasion (Dan. 11:13), which included the dispersion of "much riches," to win support for the campaign. He formed an agreement with Philip V of Macedon to conquer and share the Egyptian territories and isles outside of Egypt. The fertile land that he wanted as part of his kingdom, he now felt was with his grasp.

The scripture says: "many shall stand up against the king of the south" (Dan. 11:14). Fallout from the leadership vacuum in Egypt spread into the whole region. Egypt became engulfed in intrigue and turmoil, while Antiochus massed armies in Antioch, and the local nations began to turn against their current Ptolemaic masters. The Jews at Jerusalem were not immune to the political storms. The record continues: "The robbers of thy people shall exalt themselves to establish the vision" (Dan. 11:14). The translation for robbers has also been rendered "the violent among thy people" or the "sons of oppressors."[53] Hoping to capitalize from the upheavals, groups from among the Jews incited the people to side in favor of Antiochus. A new vision for the Jewish nation, abandoning the Ptolemaic masters for the Syrians was promoted. Their goal seemed to be to usurp control over the local offices by seizing an opportunity to gain favor through siding with Antiochus. Some Jews did join with the Syrians in battle against the Ptolemy's forces, but in the end, the robbers failed to take control and the Jewish leadership was preserved intact. They failed in their "vision" to rule Jerusalem (Dan. 11:14).

The invasion south into Coele-Syria began in 202 B.C. The Hebrew word for *mount* can also be translated siege-works. Tactically, Antiochus employed traditional siege-works and earthen ramps to "cast up a mount" (Dan. 11:15) to facilitate entrance into the most fortified or "fenced cities" like Gaza.[54] The Syrians gained a major victory at the Battle of Panium where they defeated the army of Scopas near the mountains at the head of the river Jordan. Using elephants and heavily armored cavalry, Antiochus's armies routed Scopas's cavalry, and then flanked his army to beat the infantry from the rear. Later, the Egyptian general surrendered at Sidon. As prophesied, the "arms of the south shall not withstand, neither his chosen people" (Dan. 11:15). Even Egypt's best (chosen) troops did not prevail "nor was their "strength to withstand" (Dan. 11:15).

The chosen people did not resist the armies from the north. The citizens of Jerusalem actually received Antiochus and his army, extending provisions and welcoming him. Appreciative of their reception, he had compassion and respected the local laws and religion, by providing money for their sacrifices and rescinding taxes for three years.[55] Local Jews followed the example of their ancestors who gave Alexander the Great a similar welcome. This gesture and the hand of the Lord quelled the scheming plans of the "robbers."

Antiochus marched past Gaza to the Egyptian border, but he had no intention of entering Egypt. He had regained the old Empire including the "glorious land" (Dan. 11:16), which would remain under Seleucid control until Rome subdued the kingdom in 63 B.C..

Intrigue with daughter (Cleopatra) of Antiochus III and Ptolemy V Epiphanies

_____

17 He shall also set his face to enter with the strength of his whole kingdom, and upright ones with him; thus shall he do: and he shall give him the daughter of women, corrupting her: but she shall not stand *on his side,* neither be for him.

18 After this shall he turn his face unto the isles, and shall take many: but a prince for his own behalf shall cause the reproach offered by him to cease; without his own reproach he shall cause *it* to turn upon him.

19 Then he shall turn his face toward the fort of his own land: but he shall stumble and fall, and not be found.

_____

Within a year (199 B.C.), Antiochus III "set his face to enter [Egypt] with the strength of his whole kingdom" (Dan 11:17). The "idiom to 'set ones face' means to 'be determined' or resolved.[56] However, Roman emissaries came to Antiochus demanding that they refrain from moving further south. The Romans would suffer no disruption of the import of grain from Egypt, key to supporting the massive population in Italy.[57] The Syrian king, together with the "upright ones" (Dan. 17:17), or his personal council, decided against an invasion. He turned west and north to attack the Ptolemaic possessions in Cilicia and Lycia. "It was no secret that Antiochus wanted to conquer Pergamum, a constant thorn in his flesh; he also wanted to conquer Greece and become a second Alexander."[58] Within the previous decade, however, the Romans had beaten Hannibal to subdue Carthage and were victorious against the Greeks. Knowing of their military power and fearing Roman determination to keep Egypt free, Antiochus held his ground on the border.

Unable to secure Egypt through military force and under great pressure from Rome, Antiochus purposed diplomacy by proposing an alliance with Egypt through marriage to his daughter Cleopatra I Syra (204–177/176 B.C.). She would marry the young king of the south after a season of five years. They were married in 193 B.C. near Raphia. At the time Ptolemy was 16 and she was 10.[59] She apparently grew to be a very attractive woman, but at the time was a "daughter of women" (Dan. 17:17) a lovely young damsel, but not quite a mature woman.

The scripture indicates that Antiochus's intent was to "corrupt" (Dan. 17:17) his young daughter to favor his designs to take over the kingdom. She did not, however, "side" with the interests of her father. Having been sent to Egypt at such a young age, she remained very impressionable and essentially became an Egyptian and very loyal to her husband. As testimony to this fact, later in life she sent an "envoy to congratulate the Romans on their victories over her father" in a battle in Asia Minor.[60]

With the Egyptian conquest in stalemate, and Antiochus, unable to be content and enjoy his empire, he turned his attention to other campaigns. The scripture specifically mentions the isles. His latter military campaigns were fought in Asia Minor, which included the isles in the Mediterranean and skirmishes in the Aegean Seas. He assembled a fleet of over 300 ships to seize control of the eastern Mediterranean and the Aegean Sea. Again, the Romans sent ambassadors to meet with the king at Lysimachia demanding that he return the conquered isles to the Egyptians and the Greeks. Since the Romans had conquered the Greeks, they saw the isles as their property.[61]

Enraged at the request, Antiochus replied: "that he wondered what the Roman people had to do with Asia or why they should seek to know what Antiochus was doing in Asia…and why they should prescribe limits."[62] He concluded by stating that he was "no vassal of theirs" and that they he had the right to retake what was formerly Alexander's dominion.[63]

The Romans response came by force rather than words. In 191 B.C., a Roman army led by consul Manius Acilius Glabrio confronted Antiochus at Thermopolis, where the Greeks had famously defeated the Persians. Acilius routed Antiochus's army killing or capturing 10,000 troops and forcing him to abandon any desire to conquer Greece. The Romans under the command of Scipio Asiaticus followed Antiochus's retreat across the Aegean. Fifty-eight Roman ships combined with twenty-two of the Rhodian fleet,[64] defeated the Seleucid navy commanded by Hannibal, of

Carthage fame, in two battles one near Eurymedon and other on the sea at Myonessus.[65] The naval victories permitted the Romans to cross at Hellespont into Asia Minor.

A final confrontation was fought on the plains of Lydia at Magnesia and Sipylum. Antiochus approached with 80,000 troops and confronted consul Lucius Cornelius Scipio and his brother General Scipio Africanus, who arrived with a local ally Eumenes II of the Pergamese Kingdom. While the Seleucid army won initial advantages by scoring breeches on the Roman flanks, eventually the Romans routed the infantry with the help of the Pergamese army. Antiochus was defeated. Those who were not killed surrendered.[66]

The battle proved disastrous for the Seleucids, and Antiochus was forced to surrender under humiliating circumstances. Among the terms of the Treaty of Apamea, Antiochus was forced to pay 15,000 talents (or 900,000 pounds) of silver as a war indemnity. He gave up all but 10 ships and the Romans required him to abandon all territory west of the Taurus Mountains. His son, Antiochus IV, was carried off to Rome along with other hostages to ensure good behavior.[67] This colossal defeat so weakened the Seleucid kingdom, that they were completely removed as a power of influence in Europe and paved the way for Roman expansion. The scripture prophesied that "a prince ... shall cause the reproach offered by him to cease... [and that] his own reproach he shall cause *it to turn upon him*." (Dan. 11:18). This phrase can also be rendered: "a commander from another land will put an end to his insolence and cause him to retreat in shame."[68] The prince spoken of was the Roman general who repelled the king and sent him shamefully back to his own kingdom.

If Antiochus had left Egyptian interests and Greece alone, he might have been considered one of the greatest conquers in world history. Like his predecessor, Alexander, he aspired to nothing but war and conquest, which eventually brought about his demise. He died while on an expedition in Susa of Elam where he was killed attempting to loot the treasury at the temple of Bel.[69] The money might have paid for more conquests or the bounty exacted by the Romans. "His end is ignominious. He stumbles and falls and he is found no more a fallen king (Dan. 17:19).[70]

Seleucus IV Philopator – The Taxer

20 Then shall stand up in his estate a raiser of taxes *in* the glory of the kingdom: but within few days he shall be destroyed, neither in anger, nor in battle.

Coin of Selecus IV Philopater

The death of Antiochus the Great brought his eldest living son Seleucus IV Philopator (218-175 B.C.) to the throne. In consequence of his father's failures against the Romans, Seleucus inherited the heavy war debt. His first priority was to pursue an ambitious policy to rebuild the treasury, and therefore restored prestige and might to the empire. The scripture says that he shall "stand up in his estate a raiser of taxes *in the glory of the kingdom.*" (Dan. 11:20).

Seleucus levied substantial taxes on his entire domain over twelve years. One very controversial event occurred when Heliodorus, the principle tax collector, went to Jerusalem to retrieve gold from the people and raided the temple treasury. Simon, the temple overseer, who was angry with the high priest, Onias, informed the minister of a great treasure in the temple.[71] Tradition holds that upon attempting to enter temple, he was prevented by three angels (2 Mac. 3:22-27) and returned unsuccessful in his endeavor to retrieve the wealth.

It is generally accepted that upon his return, Heliodorus poisoned Seleucus, and seized the throne for himself. As the scripture states: "he [Seleucus, the taxer] shall be destroyed, neither in anger, nor in battle" (Dan. 11:20). At the time of his murder the rightful heir, Demetrius, son of Seleucus, was on his way to Rome as a hostage in exchanged for Antiochus IV. The treachery of Heliodorus opened the door for Antiochus IV to take the dynasty by intrigue and retain the kingdom for himself.

SECTION 2

Antiochus IV Epiphanies, The Vile

This portion of the prophesy certainly applies to Antiochus Epiphanies But the ancient scholar Jerome (347 A.D.) and several other researchers of Daniel ascribe a double meaning to the vision. Young argues that with respect to the writings of Daniel, the prophecy becomes, over the course of the verses "confusingly difficult…and cannot be entirely applied to Antiochus."[72] His reasoning is that the record, especially the last ten verses, portrays events that differ from the reality of Antiochus's life.

While the record reflects the life of the ancient Seleucid king, it also provides a pattern or type for the latter-day anti-Christ. History is replete with characters that reveal the very nature of the evil one, but Antiochus's opposition to the Jews, their God, His laws and religion demonstrates a pure form of devilish enmity. Similar characteristics are found in the Caesars: Caligula, Nero, Domitian, Decius or Diocletian or modern figures like Hitler, Stalin or Mao. They all demonstrated personality traits akin to Antiochus. His attempt to destroy the Jews and their religion is also a haunting foreshadowing of latter-day events. Just prior to the advent of the Lord, anti-Christ figures will come into prominent positions of power with the same spirit of enmity Antiochus had for the people of God. They will stir up opposition against the latter-day the Kingdom of God and the Saints. The duel nature of this prophecy, therefore, refers both to Antiochus as well as the latter-day anti-Christ, or little horn (Dan. 7:25) and his associates. This section discusses the events relative to the ancient king, while at the same time reveals the nature of a future figure to come.

Antiochus's Rise to Power

> 21   And in his estate shall stand up a vile person, to whom they shall not give the honour of the kingdom: but he shall come in peaceably, and obtain the kingdom by flatteries.

22 And with the arms of a flood shall they be overflown from before him, and shall be broken; yea, also the prince of the covenant.

23 And after the league *made* with him he shall work deceitfully: for he shall come up, and shall become strong with a small people.

24 He shall enter peaceably even upon the fattest places of the province; and he shall do *that* which his fathers have not done, nor his fathers' fathers; he shall scatter among them the prey, and spoil, and riches: *yea,* and he shall forecast his devices against the strong holds, even for a time.

———

The messenger describes the next Syrian ruler as a "vile" or contemptible person. Considering the works of his predecessors, this statement is quite revealing. Compared to the Greek aristocracy, this ruler will exceed all others in the art of crafty guile, volatile temperament, and contemptible policy. He will become one of the most reprehensible characters exhibited on the pages of antiquity. Historians note that he demonstrated both avaricious and prodigal tendencies, excessive in his indulgences and prone to violent passions, a compound of follies and strength of character that would manifest itself many times during his reign. He also showed great cunning and dexterity in the use of flattery and self-preservation. Antiochus was politically and socially very astute. The following estimate by Stuart provides an excellent background of his character: "Records show that his extravagances and follies and cruelties were so great, that his contemporaries, gave him the nickname 'epimanes' (madman), instead of the title which he assumed, viz,. 'Epiphanies' (Illustrious)."[73] At one period of his reign, the prospect of his becoming quite powerful was very real. But, in the end, the reverse came upon him and he died, in ignominy, as his father before him had done and under similar circumstances.

A Brief History of Antiochus Epiphanies

Antiochus IV Epiphanies (215 B.C.-164 B.C.) was the younger son of Antiochus III. As previously stated, after the defeat at Magnesia, Antiochus IV was taken to Rome with other hostages, where he remained for 14 years until the death of his father.

Seleucus IV, his brother seeing a need for him in the kingdom, sent an embassy to exchange him for his son Demetrius. In route from Rome (at Athens), Antiochus learned of his brother's murder at the hand of Heliodorus. Employing all of his skills of flattery, he formed alliances with King Eumenes II of Pergamum and his brother Attalus, and together they secured an army to assist Antiochus in restoring the family kingdom of his father. He also sought to "secure his good-will; for, by reason of certain bickerings, they had already grown suspicious of the Romans."[74] The Syrians in Antioch conceded quickly, Heliodorus was executed and Antiochus took the throne "peacefully," (Dan 11:21) which has also been translated *unexpectedly*. His unexpected rise in the kingdom certainly held true for Heliodorus, but perhaps the entire kingdom as well. He immediately proclaimed himself co-regent with the infant son of his late brother, Seleucus.

The phrase "they shall not give the honour of the kingdom" (Dan. 11:21) refers to the fact that Antiochus IV was not the lawful heir to the throne. The honor of royalty remained with Demetrius, who was under house arrest in Rome. The infant son was killed a few years after Antiochus's coronation. The scriptural account says that he "obtained" and then held control of the kingdom through the art of "flatteries" and intrigue (Dan. 11:21). While his flatteries surely included lofty words, corruption, and bribes, secret promises and alliances were the primary means to obtain and keep power. The Book of Mormon portrays how Gadianton wooed his followers with the promises of position and reward: "Therefore he did flatter them, and also Kishkumen, that if they would place him in the judgment-seat he would grant unto those who belonged to his band that they should be placed in power and authority among the people" (Hel. 2:5; See also 3 Ne. 1:29, 7:12). Such tactics for power were not uncommon among the Greek rulers of the day.

The vision speaks of a flood, or an overwhelming force used to overthrow or "sweep away" before him. It also states that: "he shall become strong with a small people" (Dan. 11:23). When Antiochus marched into Antioch his supporters were few. With the help of Eumenes II, he took the kingdom from Heliodorus. The Pergamum king and his army assisted for a time, but Antiochus needed to win the hearts of the Syrians and obtain his own power base. Again, he would employ all skill and craft of diplomacy and plot to entice the aristocracy and people. Historical records reveal that his behavior was often erratic. Historians write that he reveled at bathhouses with the "common folk," engaging in bazar conversations and strange performances. He gave money and presents to strangers on the street. He frequently engaged in excesses such as furnishing cities with sacrifices to the gods in quantities that far surpassed his predecessors.[75] The messenger confirmed that "he shall scatter among them the prey, and spoil, and riches" (Dan. 11:24). All these efforts were attempts to persuade the local officials and the public.

The vision states that after he made a "league," he "worked deceitfully," recruiting and winning loyalty over time. Any objectors were converted or quietly "swept away" by force (Dan. 11:22). His cunning plans were supported through riches that he obtained from the "fattest" or wealthiest places in the province (Dan. 11:24). As the king, he engendered loyalty, not as his fathers, who were rightful heirs to the kingdom, but through enticement and corruption. He would distribute among loyal followers the spoils and wealth of the rich—something his predecessors had done far more sparingly. Apparently, the distribution of wealth became so reckless and egregious that it proved harmful to areas of the kingdom. "The contest decidedly refers to conduct which injured the fat provinces. This can only consist in squandering and dissipating the wealth of this province which he had plundered to its injury"[76]

He "forecasted devices" (Dan. 11:24) or plotted to overthrow greater strongholds to obtain more riches in order to expand the kingdom and maintain power, but only for a short while. While such extravagant behavior was not unique among the Seleucid kings, apparently his excesses deserved special note.

The political corruption impacted directly the covenant people in Jerusalem. The "prince of the covenant" (Dan. 11:22) referred to the Jewish religious leader or the high priest, Onias III. He was pious and loyal to the Mosaic practices and did not advocate the pagan elements of Hellenism (2 Mac. 3:5). As mentioned, he resisted Simon's petition to be market commissioner (*Agoranomos*), who in revenge went to the Syrian officials informing them about the treasure in the temple. Heliodorus's failure to retrieve the treasure placed Onias III out of favor with the Seleucid authorities. "When Antiochus IV ascended the throne (175 B.C.), "[Onias] was summoned to Antioch, and his brother Jason was appointed high priest in his place, having apparently promised a large sum of money for the appointment" (2 Mac 4:7-8).[77] Jason, a strong proponent of Hellenism, built a Gymnasium in Jerusalem (2 Mac. 4:9). Three years later Menelaus, not a descendant of Aaron (2 Mac. 4:26), obtained the appointment by paying a larger sum of money. He was also a staunch advocate of Hellenism and continued the transformation of Jewish society away from their Mosaic roots. Menelaus, aided by the royal governor Andronicus, secretly had Onias assassinated in defiance of his oath of office (2 Mac 4:29-39). He represented a "break" in the ancestral line of Aaron and the religious leadership of Judah.

The scripture states that all these combinations of wickedness, will last "even for a time" or a short while during the initial years as Antiochus IV settled in as king over the Empire (Dan. 11:24).

Syrian War with Egypt

25 And he shall stir up his power and his courage against the king of the south with a great army; and the king of the south shall be stirred up to battle with a very great and mighty army; but he shall not stand: for they shall forecast devices against him.

26 Yea, they that feed of the portion of his meat shall destroy him, and his army shall overflow: and many shall fall down slain.

With the kingdom in hand, Antiochus "stirred his power" and "courage" (Dan 11:25) against the king of the south. The fulfillment of this prophecy refers to the war with Ptolemy VI (180-164 B.C.), who rose to the Egyptian throne at the age of 6 and ruled jointly with his mother, Cleopatra I, until her death in 176 B.C.. His guardians, Eulaeus the chief eunuch, and Lenaeus, a native of Coele-Syria,

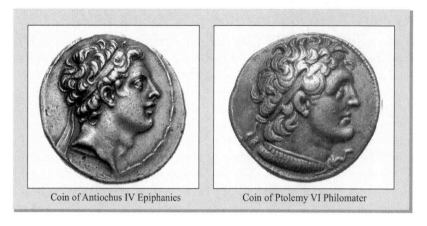

| Coin of Antiochus IV Epiphanies | Coin of Ptolemy VI Philomater |

came to Antiochus demanding the return of Coele-Syria, which had been taken by his father, but was to be returned to Egypt as part of Cleopatra's marriage dowry.[78] The land was never returned. The Egyptians assembled a "great and mighty army" and set off from Alexandria to retake the disputed territories.[79] Hearing of the threat, Antiochus preemptively launched a campaign against Egypt and the two armies met at the frontier-fortress of Pelusium. The battle that ensued was "a crushing defeat for the generals of Ptolemy."[80] In the meantime, the young Egyptian king was hurriedly packed onboard a ship to escape to the sacred island of Samothrace. It proved to be a foolish step. Ptolemy was intercepted by Syrian vessels and fell into the hands of Antiochus.[81]

The Egyptian forces could not "stand" (Dan. 11:25). Thousands were cut down in the battle and the capital Alexandria fell into panic. Antiochus quickly advanced south to occupy Memphis and then formed up his armies to lay siege against Alexandria. The Alexandrians, feeling betrayed by Ptolemy transferred allegiance to his younger brother, Physcon (Eurgetes), a boy of about fifteen years. Seleucid warships defeated the Egyptian navy sent from Alexandria andâ then reinforced the fortress of Pelusium. The series of victories opened the entire lower delta of Egypt to the Syrians.

Antiochus won by "forecasting devices," or employing secret plan (Dan. 11:25) that some believe were successful because he bribed internal elements within Ptolemy's government. The nature of the plot is described in the scripture: "they that feed of the portion of his meat shall destroy him (meaning the Egyptian king)" (Dan. 11:26). His own household, advisors and countrymen conspired with Antiochus to betray him and cause his capture. It is believed that his advisors, Eulaeus and Lenaen, actually informed the Syrians of his escape and location, thus facilitating his capture.[82]

The young Physcon Eurgete rallied the local army in Alexandria, who successfully staved off Antiochus's advance and greatly increased his prestige.[83] Unable to take the capital, the Syrian king began negotiations from Memphis. With Ptolemy in hand and the capital well defended, he turned to a very devious stroke of flattery. Representing himself as the champion or guardian of the legitimate king against the usurper brother, "[he] fixed the seat of the rival government, for which Ptolemy Philometor was to serve as figure-head, at Memphis."[84] It should be remembered that Cleopatra, the mother of Philometor, was Antiochus's sister and his declaration, while hollow, could be interpreted by some as legitimate. His claim provided a plausible explanation to the Romans for the unrest in Alexandria and Egypt.

The Negotiations Over the Kingdom

----

27 And both these kings' hearts *shall be* to do mischief, and they shall speak lies at one table; but it shall not prosper: for yet the end *shall be* at the time appointed.

28 Then shall he return into his land with great riches; and his heart *shall be* against the holy covenant; and he shall do exploits, and return to his own land.

Across the conference table Antiochus was gracious to the ambassadors from Alexandria. The Alexandrian court "fully admitted that Egypt had been in the wrong in opening war, but the blame for that wrong lay with the party, now fallen, of Eulaeus."[85] Pressures from outside kingdoms like Rhodes were made to remove the siege around Alexandria, which had become a vital commercial center. While Ptolemy outwardly complied with Antiochus, his only goal was to get him to leave Egypt. In the mean time, they "will sit at the same table and lie to each other" (Dan. 11:27 NIV). Later, he would play no part of being a puppet to his uncle. From the outset any agreement between the two kingdoms was fraught with "mischief"— hollow promises and false commitments to each other.

In reality, Antiochus wished to take Egypt, but that was impossible. He feared an internal revolution and the objections of the Romans. Without explanation, he abruptly "left... leaving the kingdom in a state of civil war with Ptolemy Philometor reigning at Memphis in opposition to his brother at Alexandria. Antiochus also took the precaution of keeping the door unbolted against his return by leaving a strong garrison in Pelusium."[86]

Ptolemy did not or could not assume sole custody of the kingdom, as the Alexandrians would not abandon Eurgetes. He was received back as joint king. Despite the conflict and negotiations neither side gained advantage and the status between Syria and Egypt essentially remained the same. The prophecy states that the "end *shall be* at the time appointed," (Dan. 11:27) meaning Antiochus would return to try and finish what he had started. The war would continue at a future time. Antiochus left Egypt packing a tremendous bounty of riches.

A very unfortunate occurrence for the Jews took place towards the end of the war. Rumors circulated in Jerusalem that Antiochus had died in battle. Jason, of the Hasmonean Dynasty and the ousted high priest family, immediately raised an army of a thousand men and retook his position at the temple. Menelaus, initially held up in his castle, escaped and fled to Antiochus to report the uprising at Jerusalem. Many of the remaining Jews believed the city had been liberated. Celebrations broke out among a portion of the population. When the king heard the news, he was enraged.

Two phrases give insight to the prophecy: "his heart *shall be* against the holy covenant" and "he shall do exploits" (Dan. 11:28). If the Jews were not already viewed as a peculiar thorn in his side, their rebellion would turn his prejudice fully against them. The "unHellenized" barbarians were already inferior, but rebellion was too much for the king and, given his struggles in

© Used with Permission

The Desecration of the Temple by Antiochus Epiphanies

Egypt, he was in no mood for internal insurrections. The phrase "he shall do *exploits*" can be translated "he shall take action or act decisively" against the Jewish rebellion. "He fell on Jerusalem with his seasoned veterans, killed forty thousand of its inhabitants, sold another forty thousand into slavery, and plundered the temple carrying off treasure valued at eighteen hundred talents."[87] Jason fled and the Seleucids reinstalled Menelaus as the high priest, propping up again the faction of Judah most sympathetic to their secular culture and loyal to the Greeks. He set about desecrating the temple by sacrificing on the altar a sow. His heart was clearly "set against the holy covenant" (Dan. 11:28). He despised the holy people, some of whom had erroneously celebrated his death, and their backward religion. From that point on, he schemed how they might be changed, modernized, and Hellenized. But laden with Egyptian and Jewish bounty, he was forced to return to Antioch.

Antiochus's Last Invasion of Egypt

> **29** At the time appointed he shall return, and come toward the south; but it shall not be as the former, or as the latter.

30 For the ships of Chittim shall come against him: therefore he shall be grieved, and return, and have indignation against the holy covenant: so shall he do; he shall even return, and have intelligence with them that forsake the holy covenant.

Almost from the moment Antiochus left Egypt, his nephew did not remain loyal to him or the treaty. Rather, he decided to join with his brother and the Alexandrians. "[Antiochus] was in an awkward position for retaining his hold on Egypt. He had proclaimed to the whole Greek world that his interference in Egypt had been solely in order to support the legitimate king."[88] In anger and out of political necessity, in 168 B.C., Antiochus again thought it necessary to intervene. The Syrian fleet was sent to Cyprus and he gathered his troops against Egypt demanding that both the island province and Pelusium be ceded to him permanently. "Pelusium in Seleucid occupation would lock the door against any attack by land, whilst Cyprus could be the base for a naval attack on Syria."[89] Having made his demands, he then moved the army south to invade Egypt a second time. But as the scripture warns "this war shall not be as the former, or as the latter" (Dan. 11:29).

At the onset of this second incursion, the Egyptians petitioned Rome for help, renouncing Antiochus's claim as guardian and asking for aid against a second occupation. The Romans did not respond and all seemed lost, when in June 168 B.C., word came that Rome had defeated Perseus in a third war against Macedonia. Having settled affairs in Greece, they immediately turned attention to the Syrian-Egyptian problem. The reference to the "ships of Chittim" (Dan. 11:30) is translated in the Septuagint as Romans. The wood used to make many of their ships came from the western forests of the isle Cyprus at a place called Kittim. The reference came to mean the whole island.

The Romans sent an ambassador and a small contingent of centurions to intervene on behalf of Egypt. "In Eleusis, a suburb of Alexandria, the Roman ambassador, Gaius Popillius Laenas, presented Antiochus with the ultimatum that he evacuate Egypt and Cyprus immediately. Antiochus, taken by surprise, asked to consider the matter with his counsel. Popillius drew a circle in the earth around the king with his walking stick and demanded an unequivocal answer before Antiochus left the circle."[90] The Syrian king responded. "If it so please the senate, we must depart."[91] Antiochus's ambitions were stopped and he felt humiliated, but fearing war with Rome, or more importantly Roman soldiers, he withdrew his designs and vacated the country and the isle of Cyprus.

On his return to Antioch, Antiochus became weighed down with depression and anger. Unable to vent his fury on Egypt, he would turn his displeasure against Jerusalem and Judah. In a blatant display of unbridled resentment and knowing there would be no outward retribution, Antiochus moved his army into the holy land. Fueled by the humiliating events at Alexandria, he lost all patience with the Jews and their religion. He vowed revenge because of their previous insolence. He and his army stopped at Jerusalem to "have intelligence, [or gain alliances] with them that forsake the holy covenant" (Dan. 11:30). With the help of Jewish secularists, favorable to Hellenism, he entered the city in an act of reprisal and opened a period of severe persecution against those who would be true to Jehovah and the Mosaic religion.

The Abomination of Desolation

----

31 And arms shall stand on his part, and they shall pollute the sanctuary of strength, and shall take away the daily *sacrifice,* and they shall place the abomination that maketh desolate.

32 And such as do wickedly against the covenant shall he corrupt by flatteries: but the people that do know their God shall be strong, and do *exploits.*

33 And they that understand among the people shall instruct many: yet they shall fall by the sword, and by flame, by captivity, and by spoil, *many* days.

34 Now when they shall fall, they shall be holpen with a little help: but many shall cleave to them with flatteries.

35 And *some* of them of understanding shall fall, to try them, and to purge, and to make *them* white, *even* to the time of the end: because *it is* yet for a time appointed.

"When it became obvious to Antiochus that he had the support of the Hellenizers in Jerusalem but that the policy of Hellenization was violently opposed by most of the Jewish people, he determined to wipe out the Jewish religion altogether."[92] Josephus records the nature of the assault: "[he] took their city by force, and slew a great multitude of those that favored Ptolemy, and sent out his soldiers to plunder them without mercy. He also spoiled the temple, and put a stop to the constant practice of offering a daily sacrifice."[93]

Antiochus's "reformations" began with an assault on the Temple with his own siege troops. The phrase "arms shall stand on his part" is frequently interpreted to be "with the help of his army," (Dan. 11:31 NLT). Using soldiers and siege equipment he stormed the temple complex and raided the sanctuary. The Syrian troops broke through the gates defending the temple. The altar would after be thrown down and a Greek altar constructed in its place, thus halting all Mosaic practices. Later, a statue of Zeus was "placed" in the temple, thus "polluting [or desecrating] the sanctuary" by setting "the abomination," or Zeus made in the image of Antiochus, in the temple (Dan 11:31). The desecration resulted in the cessation of the worship of Jehovah and the placing, or setting up of the abomination of desolation–the idol-altar–in Jehovah's house.[94]

Antiochus followed the desecration of the temple with a series of decrees outlawing the practice of the Jewish rites and commandments. "The king also sent edicts by messenger to Jerusalem and the towns of Judah, directing them to adopt customs foreign to the country... they should forget the Law and revoke all observance of it" (1 Macc. 1:44, 49). Jews were not only to stop the worship practices, but also to renounce their culture and the religion altogether. Josephus writes: "Being overcome with his violent passions, and remembering what he had suffered during the siege [of Alexandria], he compelled the Jews to dissolve the laws of their country, and to keep their infants uncircumcised, and to sacrifice swine's flesh upon the altar."[95]

The new policies prohibited any religious freedoms: the rites of the mosaic sacrifices, circumcision, Sabbath observance, feasts and festivals, scriptural recitations, and other general observances.

All these traditions and commandments were now outlawed and became offenses against laws and statutes of the state.[96]

Many of the population rejected the mandate and left Jerusalem (1 Macc. 1:38), but the majority were forced to remain and deal with the vexing circumstances. Antiochus reinforced his will under the strength of his military and by employing local "inspectors" to ensure compliance to the decrees (1 Macc. 1:51). Citizens found not to be in submission to the civil law and embracing the Greek culture could be imprisoned or put to death using cruel and brutal methods.

The vision speaks of native Jews who "did wickedly" (Dan. 11:32). These were men and women who had violated their covenants in support of Antiochus's campaign to Hellenize Jerusalem (Isa. 24:5).[97] The "wicked Jews sympathized with the Greeks by supporting the reforms of 'the wicked' [an epithet used by the pious Jews to describe Antiochus]. 'They were attracted by the sophistries and brilliance of [heathen] Greek rationalism.'"[98] The scripture states that they were "corrupted by his flatteries," the smooth and crafty promises of the king (Dan. 11:32). We have already discussed how a portion of the population had broken away from the Mosaic Law and traditions. Jason and Menelaus both led a segment of reformists sympathetic to Greek ideology. At the core of the flatteries, however, were the lures of riches and station, and the gratification of pride by vying for positions of power.

These Hellenized Jews participated whole heartedly in the Greek festivals. They supported the pagan feasts and sacrifices, competed in the philosophical debates and in the games of the gymnasium. They accepted the doctrines of secular reason, which in and of itself was not wrong, but when combined with pagan mysticism, humanism or Greek sophistry, they were lead away from the truth down apostate paths. As sympathizers to the Greek leadership, they collaborated in efforts to find and punish those not compliant with the oppressive laws.

The Faithful Who Know God

The prophecy contrasts "the wicked" with those who "knew their God" (Dan. 11:32). Among the Jews were the strong and loyal, who stood firm in the face of the extreme opposition. The unjust laws did not sway them, nor did the cultural pressures. The scriptures states that they too did "exploits" (Dan. 11:32). The faithful acted with resolve and ministered to one to another to strengthen and preserve the faith. Just as Antiochus was decisive "to do exploits" in punishing the Jews for their rebellion (Dan. 11:28), so too the faithful remained resolute in their response to the crisis. Despite the disruption in the formal worship, they stood firm in their religious convictions. "Such people united to God, by a living faith, [and would] not succumb to the subtle brandishments of a man of the character of Antiochus, but exhibited consistency and firmness, refusing to yield to temptations."[99] The "exploits" of the wise were centered on what could be done to keep the faith, practice worship and trust in God despite being banished from the temple and the attempts to purge them culturally. They supported and kept each other safe under the severe pressures placed by the authorities.

> Gabriel emphasized that in the face of tribulation, the response of the wise was to provide comfort, direction, and instruction through ministering efforts

The prophecy places a spotlight on those described as having "understanding" (Dan. 11:33). Other translations confirm this idea of faithful "who had insight among the people" or were "endowed with spiritual understanding."[100] They served as pillars of strength and examples.

Gabriel emphasized that in the face of tribulation, they applied their wisdom to the circumstances and extend comfort, direction and instruction through ministering and teaching. Not only were their testimonies firm in the Lord, but they conveyed strength and built unity and faith. The sum of their life's experiences gave them the means to endure the trials. Modern scriptures ascribe similar qualities to the latter-day wise men and women, who "…have received the truth, and have taken the Holy Spirit for their guide, and have not been deceived" (Doctrine and Covenants 45:57). The Lord visited them with His strengthening grace, with spiritual power to deal with the difficulties.[101] He often intervened unawares to mitigate dire and complex circumstances. "They performed no heroic deeds on the battlefield. They read the scriptures, loved them, understood them, looked beyond the tribulation of their day, and, with sure and certain hope, looked for the [redemption] of Christ."[102] Jehovah consecrated their afflictions for their gain (2 Ne. 2:2).

The messenger tells Daniel that the Lord allowed the tribulations and used them for the purpose of sanctifying the righteous. The crisis would serve "to try them, to purge wickedness, and to make *them* white" (Dan. 11:33). Fidelity in the heat of persecution yielded purity, humility and meekness and steeled the resolve of their faith. While a number of the "wise" did "fall" victim to the treachery and brutality of traitors and the Greeks, the majority of the faithful would benefit and become refined as silver (Mal. 3:2-3). A generation of the devout and worthy Jews emerged from the fires of Antiochus's rage. With the specter of life threatening situations looming, many of the wise moved underground, worshiping together privately and in secret groups. If they were discovered the consequences proved dire, and for some, fatal, as a number were executed, burned, jailed or plundered.

False Jews, or "the wicked," sought surreptitiously to join the clandestine congregations (Dan 11:34). The intent was to uncover their hidden assemblies and expose their worship practices. They then turned treacherously against the faithful exposing them to the authorities for punishment. The record states that during the critical years of tribulation, the "wise" received little outside support, but acted independently as guided by the Spirit: "they shall [need] help," [and] little help will be given" (Dan. 11:24). The vision suggests that when they were turned over to the officials (Dan. 11:34), the captives would received little or no political or judicial help. They relied in the merits of the Lord to faithfully endure the trial.

His campaign against the Jews brought about the Maccabean rebellion, which eventually threw off the power of the reformist Jews and Greek oppressors.

Antiochus met his end following a major campaign against the Parthians who threatened the empire on the eastern borders. After subduing the Parthians, he set out on an expedition to Persia and the Arabian coast. While returning from Persia to Babylon, he died of an illness at Tabae in Persis (B.C.). Many saw his death as a punishment, because, like his father, he was attempting to loot the shrine of Nanaia in Elam.[103] A few weeks prior to his death, he was informed that his garrisons in Judea had been defeated and that his campaign to subjugate the Jews was overthrown. There were no further incursions into Judea or against Jerusalem.

SECTION 3

As we have observed, "the amazingly detailed prophecies of Daniel 11:1–35 contain approximately 135 prophetic statements that have all been fulfilled" with great precision.[104] But from this point very little in Antiochus's history accounts for the next several verses of the chapter. The vision moves forward to focus on the "time of the end" (Dan. 11:25). It is important to note the timing of the break. It comes at the end of the great period of persecutions that were brought on under Antiochus "the vile," which sets the stage for similar events to transpire in the last days. These events will be discussed in the subsequent verses and in Chapter 12.

Antiochus - A Type of anti-Christ (vs. 36-39)

Most scholars believe that Daniel's vision changes and involves events that were never realized during Antiochus's reign over Syria. These verses have fulfillment in another context.[105] Keil argues: "the statements made in Daniel 11:36-39 *incl.* regarding the king of the north, now fall, in accordance with the context, into the period which shall expire *at that time of the end* are then to be prophesied."[106] The prophetic account refers to a future king and the prophecies herein come to pass at the *end of time* or in the latter-days (Dan. 11:40).

A sensible approach to these verses (36-39) would be to apply the relevant characteristics to Antiochus, but also to assign a duel interpretation to a future person forecast to be in the likeness of the

Seleucid tyrant. It is not uncommon to find similar attributes among notable despotic figures. Therefore, we can look for these traits in latter-day figures.

In reality, corrupt and tyrannical figures are and will be frequent in the last days. The pattern of a well-spoken, deft, yet corrupt character in the likeness of Antiochus is quite commonplace. Like the ancient king, they will reveal themselves in character and deed, in policy and ultimately in conflict. A hallmark feature will be to "raise [oneself] above every god, not merely 'subjectively in his lofty imagination,' but also by his actions."[107] As for the latter-day despotic anti-Christ prophesied to come, the messenger to Daniel begins the description of him in verses 35-45. He refers to him as the king of the north. The characteristics and events prophesied in these verses will serve to identify the individual and his intentions when he arrives on the world scene.

___

36 And the king shall do according to his will; and he shall exalt himself, and magnify himself above every god, and shall speak marvellous things against the God of gods, and shall prosper till the indignation be accomplished: for that that is determined shall be done.

37 Neither shall he regard the God of his fathers, nor the desire of women, nor regard any god: for he shall magnify himself above all.

38 But in his estate shall he honour the God of forces: and a god whom his fathers knew not shall he honour with gold, and silver, and with precious stones, and pleasant things.

39 Thus shall he do in the most strong holds with a strange god, whom he shall acknowledge *and* increase with glory: and he shall cause them to rule over many, and shall divide the land for gain.

___

This vision begins with a quintessential description of a megalomaniac personality. By definition, the anti-Christ suffers from "a delusional mental illness that is marked by feelings of personal omnipotence and grandeur."[108] He is obsessed with his own persona and power. Such a description would certainly be applicable to Antiochus, but not unique. The tyrant will exalt himself above all around him. He glories in power, opulence, position and control. In the ancient eastern cultures the deification of rulers or warriors was commonplace.[109] Alexander the Great professed to be "ordained by divine forces. He called himself the son of Zeus, and so claimed the status of a demi-god, linking his blood-line to his two favorite heroes of antiquity, Achilles and Herakles, and modeling his behavior after theirs."[110] Emperors and kings grew accustomed to their exalted and magnified positions. Antiochus proclaimed himself *Epiphanies,* signifying the divine manifestation of the gods.

In many respects, they were treated as gods and often received more respect than the idol gods themselves. When they spoke, the generals, councils, courts and the people responded. While they may not have openly spoken against the true and living God, their attitude reflected self-willed supreme authority. In most cases, they were a law unto themselves—even when encumbered with bureaucratic systems—they viewed their decrees as final. In an epistle to his kingdom, Antiochus wrote that under him: "all should be one people, and everyone should have his laws, [as the law]" (1 Macc. 1:4). Such a perception of omnipotence cultivates the fertile ground wherein the pride of tyranny flourishes and the attitude of anti-Christ blossoms.

Antiochus's governance practices certainly ran contrary to the God of Heaven. The expression *marvelous things,* is more accurately rendered monstrous things.[111] His distaste for the Jewish religion and efforts to stamp out religious freedom generally, with the exception of his own Hellenism, were manifestations of his open disregard for Jehovah, His people, and the revealed laws of the Covenant. It was an affront to freedom and agency generally. His "monstrous," but flattering words espoused the virtues of his "higher" and "enlightened" cultural station. Undoubtedly, it was sprinkled with snide criticisms against the backward Mosaic sect and their God. The unfortunate reality was that the God of heaven had inspired much of the Greek culture. Inspiration's light sprinkled down on their classical arts, philosophical reason, logical sciences, architecture and reformed democratic views. But Greek mysticism and cultural cynicism along with their pagan traditions perverted aspects of their enlightened culture so that it was very worldly. Inspiration often gave way to sophisticated thought that sprang from the minds of men and devils. Greek culture certainly collided with the simple spiritual truths revealed by Jehovah. Such contradictive world-views would inevitably clash, and the anti-Christ exercised his power to put down the backward cultures who oppose him.

The vision's language parallels the prophecy written in Chapter 7, which speaks of the little horn who will speak great and equally monstrous things (Dan 7:8, 20, 25). Like Antiochus, this horn makes war with the Saints (Dan. 7:21). He intends to change the times (culture) and impose his own laws (Dan. 7:25). The latter-day anti-Christ will mirror this same hedonistic attitudes possessed by Antiochus, that of his own supreme position and his disgust for religion, especially Christianity. The changing of times and laws will, as we shall see, bring strife to devoted and religious persons. A real effort to subvert, even extinguish religion in favor of modern secularist views will be pursued with vigor.

The record says that he "shall prosper till the indignation be accomplished" (Dan. 11:36). The indignation spoken of here is God's indignation, not that of the king. If we remember, in the great campaign against the Jews, Antiochus served as a means of sifting the "hypocrites" from the true believers in Israel. Antiochus was permitted to prosper until the determined purposes of the Lord were "accomplished" and then the trial came to an end. Similar patterns will emerge in the last days. Trials will arise designed to purge the tares from the wheat and seal the wicked against the day of vengeance (Isa. 13:9; Doctrine and Covenants 63:6, 54; 109:38, 46). The Lord has warned: "Therefore, let the wheat and the tares grow together until the harvest is fully ripe; then ye shall first gather out the wheat from among the tares, and after the gathering of the wheat, behold and lo, the tares are bound in bundles, and the field remaineth to be burned." (Doctrine and Covenants 86:7).

No Regard for gods of Fathers

The vision provides further insight into the demeanor of the anti-Christ (Dan. 11:36). He has no regard for his father's gods or the gods of women, which is also interpreted "the one beloved of women." Anciently, these gods included idols such as: Adonis, Aphrodite or any gods favored by the women.[112] Again, the text reinforces an overall attitude of defiance against outside influences. He regards neither the traditions of his fathers, nor the passions of men, neither do the gods of his allies or foes influence his will. Keil suggests: "'he shall not regard the desire of women, or the love of women,' which agrees perfectly with the connection. After it has been said in the first clause: he shall set himself free from all religious reverence transmitted from his fathers, from all piety toward the gods in which he had been trained, it is then added in the second clause: not merely so, but generally from all piety toward men and God, from all the tender affections of the love of men and of God. The 'love of women' is named as an example selected from the sphere of human piety, as that affection of human love and attachment for which even the most selfish and most savage of men feel some sensibility."[113]

Nephi referred to this condition as becoming "past feeling" (1 Ne. 17:45). Mormon laments that his people had become so depraved that they were without affection: "I fear lest the Spirit of the Lord hath ceased striving with them. For so exceedingly do they anger that it seemeth me that they have no fear of death; and *they have lost their love, one towards another*; and they thirst after blood and revenge continually" (Mor. 9:4, emphasis added). Moroni recorded the condition of the anti-Christ, Shiz and his people who were also completely devoid of the Spirit. He states: "the Spirit of the Lord had ceased striving with them, and Satan had full power over the hearts of the people; for they were given up unto the hardness of their hearts, and the blindness of their minds." (Ether 15:19). The anti-Christ lives without the familiar feelings or passions common in men. Even his carnal passions are hollow and without efficacy. He holds little regard for culture, tradition or the religions of the people, although he may feign words of fondness towards other gods or national traditions in the craftiness of his speech. This was certainly not the case of Antiochus as he favored the Greek religion and pagan gods immensely. But what does he worship? "He shall magnify himself above all" (Dan. 11:27).

In this "estate" or in this disposition, he gives honor only to the god of forces or fortresses. According to the passage, his fathers did not know this god. Again, there is no application to Antiochus here, as he did worship Zeus, Hades and Apollo, which were also known and worshiped by his fathers. This passage applies more fully to the latter-day anti-Christ, who, in addition to worshiping himself, revers the god of forces or fortresses. For him the wielding of raw power is his god. Pure strength, the might of coercion, and the manipulation of policy through force and military dominance are what he venerates. Kiel notes that "the 'god of fortresses' is the personification of war, and in light of this fact, he will regard no other god, but only power through war; the taking of fortresses he will make his god."[114] Like the ancient anti-Christ, Cain, he will personify the art of gaining power by murder, and employ the "great secret" that through murder and war, he can obtain kingdoms and get gain (Moses 5:31). He will honor this god of forces and glory in his successes as he gains the prizes of victory. His rewards will be dominion, control and his enemies will fear him. He will obtain much "gold, and silver, and precious stones, and pleasant things" (Dan. 11:38). The spoils of conquest will make him powerful, revered and influential among the nations.

The scriptures relate that with massive military might (god of forces) and with "the help of a foreign god," he lays siege to the mightiest fortresses and cities of the day (Dan. 11:39). His alliances will include those from another religion who worship a "foreign god." This statement agrees with John's vision, who foresees a union between the political "beast" and a latter-day "false prophet" (Rev 16:13; 13:10-11). Although he holds no true regard for their religion, the anti-Christ is willing to use their resources and armies in his ambitious campaigns. And apparently, he will obtain a great alliance by which he will confront even "the most strong holds" or the mightiest nations of the day. Through the campaigns of political manipulation and conventional and asymmetric warfare a number of kingdoms, strong fortresses, cities, and nations are brought low and subdued. More will be spoken of this later. The coveted spoils of victory will then be bestowed upon his associates and allies as reward. Praise and acknowledgement are given to favor those who supported him. He will divide the land and spoils to his subjects. With each victory his glory and power increases. No practice, no belief system, no endeavor is more indicative of anti-Christ than the corruption and abuses that arise from raw conquest.

In many respects these verses could apply to Antiochus, and his fathers, as they were consummate warriors and kingdom builders. It could be argued that they worshiped the "god of forces." But they also reverenced their Greek heritage and traditions of their culture. The latter-day anti-Christ apparently holds no deep predilection to past ancestry, religion or traditions. He worships and exalts only himself and that which upholds his kingdom. And it is clear that his principle religion is the worship of power, which serves to help him obtain what he wishes to achieve.

The Time of the End

These final verses reflect only the latter-day anti-Christ. "Daniel 11:40-45 do not apply to Antiochus Epiphanies, but, with most ancient interpreters, they refer only to the final enemy of the people of God, the Antichrist."[115]

Daniel's vision culminates in events brought about at the end of times, the final days of the Gentile's power (2 Ne. 27:1), when the nations of the earth will be thrown down and the saints be given the kingdom (Dan. 7:11-14, 22). His prophecy has similarities with other scriptural accounts like John's Revelation (11,13,17), Ezekiel's prophecy of Gog and Magog (Ezek. 38, 39) and Zechariah's depiction of the latter-day in the battles of Armageddon (Zech. 13-14). In addition, we can draw upon sources like the Lord's Sermon on Mt. Olivet (Matt. 24; JS-M 1; Doctrine and Covenants 45) and other latter-day revelations (Doctrine and Covenants 29, 86, 133). Finally, we can apply important prophecies in the Book of Mormon (2 Ne. 22; 3 Ne. 16, 20-21). As we review all these recourses, we begin to piece together many clues pertaining to the end of times. There are a few references unique to Daniel's vision, which have caused some confusion as expositors seek to interpret his prophecies independent from all others. A number of them predict the rise of an anti-Christ who gains worldwide power and control in events seemingly separate from the prophesied battle of Armageddon spoken of by Ezekiel and John (Rev 16:16). They predict that he will establish a worldwide government and hold up the light of his own universal religion and kingdom.[116] Other scriptures support the idea of a coalition of nations rather than a single kingdom. Whether the latter-day events come about through a worldwide government or coalition regional conflicts remains to be seen.

In truth, Daniel's prophecy adds yet another perspective and must be viewed harmoniously with all of the revelations, each contributing their portion and perspective. We must, as the Lord counsels, treasure up the word and continually observe (Matt. 24:32, 40-42) as geopolitical affairs unfold. The final latter-day events will come about naturally, or as a natural sequence of geopolitical events that are in motion today. Nations and characters, policies and perplexities currently in play will coalesce to bring about the final outcome. Only by applying this practical approach will the reader be able to make sense of the scriptural records. Daniel's prophecy must be placed in context with the prophecies of Ezekiel (38-39), Revelations (11, 13-14), Zechariah (14), Isaiah, the Lord and others, all of which were revealed by God who sees the end from the beginning.

With this in mind, Daniel's vision is set in events at the "time of end" or the latter-days just before the coming of the Lord. It is a period of war, when all nations are gathered against Jerusalem to battle (Zech. 14:1). The great war of Armageddon will have commenced against Israel. Ezekiel provides the ancient names of those who will come with arms against the Jewish people.

---

2   Son of man, set thy face against Gog, the land of Magog, the chief prince of Meshech and Tubal, and prophesy against him,

3   And say, Thus saith the Lord God; Behold, I am against
     thee, O Gog, the chief prince of Meshech and Tubal:

4   And I will turn thee back, and put hooks into thy
     jaws, and I will bring thee forth, and all thine army,
     horses and horsemen, all of them clothed with all
     sorts of armour, even a great company with bucklers
     and shields, all of them handling swords:

5   Persia, Ethiopia, and Libya with them; all of them
     with shield and helmet:

6   Gomer, and all his bands; the house of Togarmah of
     the north quarters, and all his bands: and many
     people with thee. (Ezek. 28:2-6)

Gog, the prince of Meshech or Tubal, is mentioned as the leader or the king of the ancient land of Magog (Ezek. 38:1-2). The lands of Magog were found near the Black Sea and are generally accepted today to be modern Russia. Persia translates to modern day Iran, but may also include other nations that anciently were part of the Persian Empire: Turkey, Syria, Iraq (Babylon), Armenia, Afghanistan, etc. (Ezek. 38:5). Gomer represents modern Europe with all its bands and tribes (Gen. 10:2-3), including the house of Togarmah, or northeastern Europe (Ezek. 38:6). It is interesting to note that from among the list of ancient lands, Moab and Ammon (Jordan, see Jer. 25:21), and Arabia (Saudi Arabia) are missing. This does not mean they are not participants in the war, but it is important to remember these facts as future verses of Daniel's prophecy are reviewed.

The Kings of the North and the South

Armies assembled from the alliance of nations have come primarily from the north to Armageddon or the land of Mt. Meggido in Israel. This provides the setting for the verses outlined in Daniel 11:41-45, which speaks of war brought by the king of the north.

The scope of the vision has expanded to accommodate the latter-days, and so too must the geographic interpretation change to coincide with this increased scale and relevance. At this point "the north, from which the angry king comes in his fury against the king of the south, reached far beyond Syria. The king of the north is thought of as the ruler of the distant north."[117] It should follow that the king of the south refers to the area controlled anciently by the Ptolemaic kings in which the Holy Land was, for much of the history, a protectorate. The reference of southern king refers to the Jewish nation represented by the reference to the "glorious land" or modern day Israel (Dan. 11:16. 41, 45). It is not literally Egypt as in the days of the Seleucid and Ptolemy kingdoms.

> **40** And at the time of the end shall the king of the south push at him: and the king of the north shall come against him like a whirlwind, with chariots, and with horsemen, and with many ships; and he shall enter into the countries, and shall overflow and pass over.
>
> **41** He shall enter also into the glorious land, and many *countries* shall be overthrown: but these shall escape out of his hand, *even* Edom, and Moab, and the chief of the children of Ammon.

According to the prophecy the kingdom of the south will "push" or engage the king of the north in battle. The language is difficult to interpret, but the pronoun "*him*" refers to the king of the north, or Gog, the latter-day anti-Christ (Dan. 11:35-39; Ezek. 38:2-6). Since the narrative changes from Antiochus's days to events of the latter-days, the pronoun *him* must also change to mean the latter-day figure. All references to *him* or *he* found in the remaining verses (40-45) represent the king of the north who executes all actions against the king of the south, or Israel.

In a series of political and possibly military engagements, the king of the south contends with the king of the north. The contentions result in war. The king of the north responds by storming down against the southern kingdom into the "glorious land" (Dan. 11:41). The armies of the northern king advance with chariots, cavalry and a great fleet of ships. Chariots and cavalry were ancient equivalents of modern tanks and trucks filled with troops. A naval fleet accompanies the invasion force sent to attack the southern kingdom by sea. The collection of weapons "is an oratorical exemplification of the powerful war-host which the king of the north displayed; for the further statement, he presses into the countries, overflows and passes over."[118] The army represents the gods of force personified. Ezekiel's description of the army is very similar to that of Daniel: "Thou shalt ascend and come like a storm, thou shalt be like a cloud to cover the land, thou, and all thy bands, and many people with thee…thou shalt come from thy place out of the north parts, thou, and many people with thee, all of them riding upon horses, a great company, and a mighty army" (Ezek. 38:9, 15-16). John's Revelation places the number of troops at the command of the king of the north at two hundred million troops or myriads of myriads (Rev. 9:16).

Daniel's prophecy further states that prior to obtaining the border of the "glorious land," the northern king must "overthrow" or pass through many countries (Dan. 11:41). A sizable army cannot reach Israel from the Black Sea region, unless it travels by sea or over countries such as: Georgia, Armenia, Turkey, Iraq and Syria. The inferior nations opposed to Gog are compelled to submit, while the allied nations join his force as it marches to the borders of Israel.[119] It seems that "the countries [and] all their treasures fall into the possession of the conqueror."[120]

The prophecy continues by stating that other countries, ancient Edom, Moab and Ammon escape the terrors of the massive army. Modern Jordan constitutes the ancient lands immediately to the east of Israel. "These enemies escape the overthrow when the other nations sink under the power of the Antichrist."[121] Apparently, they are at least neutral, and likely sympathetic to the king of the north.

The anti-Christ Moves to take the "land of Egypt"

42 He shall stretch forth his hand also upon the countries: and the land of Egypt shall not escape.

43 But he shall have power over the treasures of gold and of silver, and over all the precious things of Egypt: and the Libyans and the Ethiopians *shall be* at his steps.

44 But tidings out of the east and out of the north shall trouble him: therefore he shall go forth with great fury to destroy, and utterly to make away many.

45 And he shall plant the tabernacles of his palace
between the seas in the glorious holy mountain; yet
he shall come to his end, and none shall help him.

———

The anti-Christ extends his power over many countries; and the land of Egypt will not escape. The language in these verses would suggest that the northern king's reach extends beyond Israel into modern Egypt. Again, the prophecy speaks of the land controlled by the ancient Polemic kingdom, which extended from Libya and Somalia to Alexandria and at times north to Antioch or modern-day Lebanon. Much of that kingdom would include modern Israel. The vision already indicates that the armies of Gog will enter into the "glorious land." Therefore, the angel's reference to Egypt means in part the ancient Ptolemaic kingdom of which Israel was included.

All latter-day indications point to the fact that modern Egypt would ally with the king of the north in a contest against Israel. A prophecy from Joel affirms that Egypt will suffer much because of atrocities they commit in the war: "Egypt shall be a desolation, and Edom shall be a desolate wilderness, for the violence *against* the children of Judah, because they have shed innocent blood in their land" (Joel 3:19). Modern Egypt must, therefore, be included as part of the forces of Africa who follow in "step" with the king of the north (Dan. 11:43).

The primary goal of the king and his false prophet ally is Israel's total annihilation. But both Daniel's and Ezekiel's prophecies reveal another motivating objective of the campaign is to gain treasures or to take possession of the land (Dan. 11:43). Gog will stir up the nations "to take a spoil, and to take a prey; to turn thine hand upon the desolate places *that are now* inhabited" (Ezek. 38:12, 13). Just as Antiochus pillaged ancient Egypt and carried away much treasure and looted Jerusalem taking many slaves, so too, Gog and his forces will sweep the glorious land of its precious riches as they overtake the people and move towards Jerusalem. Both goals are served in the conquest of the land.

In the middle of the campaign disturbing reports come from the east and the north that alarm the king (Dan. 11:44). We know nothing of the fulfillment of this very specific prophecy. There may be disturbances or threats on the other fronts; reports of defeats or of insurrection or rebellion in other campaigns or among previously conquered lands. The reports apparently represent a major setback, which deserve his personal attention. His responds by turning to deal with the setback in great rage to "destroy and annihilate many" (Dan. 11:44 NIV). The exact fulfillment of the prophecy remains unclear and will be played out in the events of this great conflict.

Upon his return, he "pitches his royal tents" (Dan. 11:45), or establishes his headquarters, in the land between the seas. The "seas" refer to the Mediterranean Sea and the Dead Sea on the "glorious holy mountain" of Jerusalem (Dan. 11:45). The mountain refers to the temple mount, where Gog and his allies wish to set-up a new kingdom. The false prophets or religious leaders (Rev. 13:10-15, 16:13), his allies from Persia and other countries are highly motivated to destroy Israel and set-up a new Caliphate with Jerusalem as a principle capital.

At that location, near the end of the war, the king of the north and his army come to an abrupt demise. Ezekiel confirms that the anti-Christ dies in the valleys of Ephraim, just between Tel Aviv and Jerusalem. "And it shall come to pass in that day, *that* I will give unto Gog a place there of graves in Israel, the valley of the passengers on the east of the sea: and it shall stop the *noses* of the passengers: and there shall they bury Gog and all his multitude: and they shall call *it* the valley of Hamon-gog." (Ezek. 29:11). No one comes to his rescue or redeems his army (Dan. 11:45), but the question must be asked, what happens to him and the army?

Daniel's prophecy does not provide the factors surrounding his destruction. Other revelations, however, give the important details. John's Revelation speaks of his massive army that surrounds Jerusalem, and describes the final battleground in the war (Rev. 11:2, 8; Zech. 14:1-2). He sees that two prophets of God have come to Israel to bear witness of the Messiah and defend the nation against an overwhelming foe (Rev. 11:3-7). The prophets are doubtless a major cause of the ills that plague the king of the north and cause him so much trouble. Elder Bruce R. McConkie has revealed that these prophets are members of the First Presidency or the Quorum of the Twelve of the Church.[122] Their priesthood authority is sufficient to put to flight the massive armies, for "these are the two anointed ones that stand by the Lord of the whole earth" (Zech. 4:14). They hold the Melchizedek Priesthood with the keys to seal the heavens, as did Elijah; or to turn the waters to blood, or smite the earth with plagues, as did Moses (Rev 11:5-6). Those "after this order and calling should have power, by faith, to break mountains, to divide the seas, to dry up waters, to turn them out of their course; To put at defiance the armies of nations, to divide the earth, to break every band, to stand in the presence of God; to do all things according to his will, according to his command, subdue principalities and powers" (JST Gen. 14:30-31). Such powers are vested in them by virtue of their divine ordination as Apostles, who act according to the "will of the Son of God" (JST Gen. 14:31). These Apostles and their authority will certainly be on display in defense of the righteous in Israel.

By virtue of their Apostleship, they are seers, possessing the keys to open the doors to proclaim the Gospel to the nations and preach to the entire world. They are witnesses of Christ and exercise keys to gather in all the tribes of Israel, of which Judah is an essential member (Doctrine and Covenant 107:35; 112:21). The sum of all these powers will be exercised to preach, to seal, to protect, to destroy and to bless in the course of their ministry.[123] Endowed with Priesthood power, they put at defiance the armies of Gog and his allied nations (JST Gen. 14:31); and like Moses and Enoch, they bring plagues and destruction on the advancing foe. The two servants of Jehovah create real trouble for the northern king and his overwhelming force, but John sees that Gog (the Beast), will make war with and overcome the prophets, who are killed in Jerusalem. Their bodies lay dead in the streets for three days (Rev. 11:11-12).

After their death, Zechariah foresees that "the city shall be taken, and the houses rifled, and the women ravished; and half of the city shall go forth into captivity, and the residue of the people shall not be cut off from the city" (Zech. 14:2). Tanks and troops swarm over Jerusalem, looting and ravaging as they go. They surround the temple mount and come into the Kidron Valley east of the holy mount (Joel 3:14), known as the valley of Jehoshaphat or the valley of decision (Joel 3:2).

At this dire moment, Zechariah foresees a sudden turn of events that reverse the situation and save the remaining Jews. "Then shall the Lord go forth, and fight against those nations, as when he fought in the day of battle" (Zech. 14:3). The martyrdom of the Apostles seals the fate of Gog, his army and the nations that joined with him. Miraculously, after three days the two Apostles rise to their feet and at the command of God, and they are taken up into heaven. (Rev. 11:11-12). The Lord then sets his foot on the Mount of Olives, which cleaves open "*and there shall be* a very great valley; and half of the mountain shall remove toward the north, and half of it toward the south. (Zech. 14:4). A "great earthquake" is initiated and violently shakes the city and it is "divided into three parts" (Rev. 16:19). Gog, together with the majority of his army are destroyed. (Rev 11:13; Zech. 14:5). The earthquake reverberates across the world, "and the cities of the nations fall" (Rev 16:19).

Ezekiel again provides important details of this event: "For in my jealousy *and* in the fire of my wrath have I spoken, Surely in that day there shall be a *great shaking* in the land of Israel; So that the fishes of the sea, and the fowls of the heaven, and the beasts of the field, and all creeping things that creep upon the earth, and all the men that *are* upon the face of the earth, shall shake at my presence, and the mountains shall be thrown down, and the steep places shall fall, and every wall shall fall to the ground. And I will call for a sword against him throughout all my mountains, saith the Lord GOD: every man's sword shall be against his brother. And I will plead against him with pestilence and with blood; and I will rain upon him, and upon his bands, and upon the many people that *are* with him, an overflowing rain, and great hailstones, fire, and brimstone." (Ezek. 38: 19-22).

This earthquake has worldwide scope. Coastlines, mountains, valleys and deserts are all impacted. And the earthquake will be accompanied by natural disasters that lay waste the cities of the wicked across the globe. Modern Babylon or the world is thrown into disarray and anarchy engulfs every nation and region (Rev. 17:16; 18:8). Zechariah foresees the horrors of nuclear conflict sweep away the wicked who once allied to destroy the people of God. "And this shall be the plague wherewith the Lord will smite all the people that have fought against Jerusalem; Their flesh shall consume away while they stand upon their feet, and their eyes shall consume away in their holes, and their tongue shall consume away in their mouth. And it shall come to pass in that day, that a great tumult from the Lord shall be among them; and they shall lay hold every one on the hand of his neighbour, and his hand shall rise up against the hand of his neighbour" (Zech. 14:12-13).

Total anarchy erupts where the wicked turn on each other. Nephi prophesied: "And the blood of that great and abominable church, which is the whore of all the earth, shall turn upon their own heads; for they shall war among themselves, and the sword of their own hands shall fall upon their own heads, and they shall be drunken with their own blood. And every nation which shall war against thee, O house of Israel, shall be turned one against another, and they shall fall into the pit which they digged to ensnare the people of the Lord. And all that fight against Zion shall be destroyed, and that great whore, who hath perverted the right ways of the Lord, yea, that great and abominable church, shall tumble to the dust and great shall be the fall of it" (2 Ne. 22:13-14).

The surviving Jews, those who harkened to the prophecies of the two Apostles, "shall flee *to* the valley of the mountains" (Zech. 14:5) or Mount Olivet for safety. There, the Savior will be waiting to meet them. In a tender scene of reconciliation and love (Zech. 12:10, Doctrine and Covenants 45:51-53), they meet their Redeemer. He will show them the wounds in His hands and feet and they will come to understand that their ancestors had rejected the Messiah, and their people had followed in their traditions for centuries. In mercy and tenderness, He came to redeem and receive them. This reunion opens the door for the reconciliation of the Jews to the true Messiah, even Jesus Christ.

The faithful survivors will then build Jerusalem and the temple in preparation for the return of the Lord in glory and His millennial reign. Zechariah concludes: "In that day shall there be upon the bells of the horses, HOLINESS UNTO THE LORD; and the pots in the Lord's house shall be like the bowls before the altar. Yea, every pot in Jerusalem and in Judah shall be holiness unto the Lord of hosts: and all they that sacrifice shall come and take of them, and seethe therein: and in that day there shall be no more the Canaanite in the house of the Lord of hosts" (Zech. 14:20-21).

The king of the north is defeated and his tremendous alliance is brought into chaos. An thus comes the end of the little horn, the false prophet as Daniel and the prophets foresaw.

Chapter Notes

1   Keil. *Biblical Commentary of the Old Testament, The Book of the Prophet Daniel.* 423

2   Walvoord. *Daniel: The Key to Prophetic Revelation.* 166; See also Prichard. *Near Eastern Studies.* 319

3   Ibid. 319

4   Ibid. 319-20

5   Roisman and Worthington. *A Companion to Ancient Macedonia.* 135-138

6   Herodotus VII. 66-75

7   Phillips. *Exploring the Book of Daniel: An Expository Commentary.* 190

8   Cartwright. "Salamis." *Ancient History Encyclopedia.* 05 May 2013 http://www.ancient.eu/salamis/

9   Herodotus. VIII. 89

10 Phillips. *Exploring the Book of Daniel: An Expository Commentary.* 191

11 Keil. *Biblical Commentary of the Old Testament, The Book of the Prophet Daniel.* 431

12 Phillips. *Exploring the Book of Daniel: An Expository Commentary.* 191

13 Ibid. 190

14 Seleucus I. *Encyclopedia of World Biography.* The Gale Group 2004. http://www.encyclopedia.com/topic/Seleucus_I.aspx#1

15 Phillips. *Exploring the Book of Daniel: An Expository Commentary.* 191

16 Mark. Alexander the Great. *Ancient History Encyclopedia.* Nov. 2013; http://www.ancient.eu/Alexander_the_Great/

17 Young. *The Prophecy Daniel: A Commentary.* 234

18 Walvoord. *Daniel: The Key to Prophetic Revelation.* 166, See also Prichard. *Near Eastern Studies.* 331. Price. An extensive discussion is found: Walter. *In the Final Days.* 33-163

19 Walvoord. *Daniel: The Key to Prophetic Revelation.* 166, See also Prichard. *Near Eastern Studies.* 331

20 Werner. Ptolemy I Soter. *Macedonian King of Egypt. Encyclopedia Britannica* 2015. http://www.britannica.com/biography/Ptolemy-I-Soter

21 Werner. Ibid

22 Seibert. *Encyclopedia Britannica.* 3-23-15. References https://www.britannica.com/biography/Seleucus-I-Nicator

23 Young. *The Prophecy Daniel: A Commentary.* 234

24 Appian. *History of Rome.* The Syrian Wars. 55

25 Young. *The Prophecy Daniel: A Commentary.* 234

26 Walvoord. *Daniel: The Key to Prophetic Revelation.* 166, See also Prichard. *Near Eastern Studies.* 332

27 Bromiley. *International Standard Bible Encyclopedia: A-D* 144, Phillips. *Exploring the Book of Daniel: An Expository Commentary.* 193

28 Heinen. Heinz. Ptolemy II Philadelphus. Macedonian King of Egypt. Encyclopedia Britannica. 2015). http://www.britannica.com/biography/Ptolemy-II-Philadelphus

29 Walvoord. *Daniel: The Key to Prophetic Revelation.* 166; See also Prichard. Near Eastern Studies. 333

30 Phillips. *Exploring the Book of Daniel: An Expository Commentary.* 193

31 Driver. *Hebrew and English Lexicon of the Old Testament.* 615

32 Jerome. *Commentary of the Book of Daniel.* 123

33   Phillips. *Exploring the Book of Daniel: An Expository Commentary.* 194
34   Ibid
35   Zeockler. *The Book of the Prophet Daniel.* Theologically and Homiletically Expounded (Part of Lang's Bible) Translated. enlarged and edited by James Long. New York. 1976. 242
36   Josephus. *Against Apion* **1.206-207;** Justin. *Epitome* **27.1-3;** Appian. *History of Rome: Syrian Wars* **11.66**
37   Phillips. *Exploring the Book of Daniel: An Expository Commentary.* 195
38   Polybius; *The Histories.* V. 40-41. 43. 54
39   Phillips. *Exploring the Book of Daniel: An Expository Commentary.* 195
40   Polybius. *The Histories* 5:85
41   Polybius. *The Histories* 5.83-85. 89; 15.25-34; Justin. *Epitome* 30.1-2; Josephus. *Antiquities* 12.130-31
42   Ibid
43   Phillips. *Exploring the Book of Daniel: An Expository Commentary.* 195
44   Polybius. *The Histories* 5:40-41; Phillips. *Exploring the Book of Daniel: An Expository Commentary.* 195
45   Phillips. *Exploring the Book of Daniel: An Expository Commentary.* 195
46   Polybius. *The Histories V*: 194-198
47   Ibid
48   Ibid
49   Ibid 201-207
50   Ibid 214-217
51   Ibid V 87
52   Phillips. *Exploring the Book of Daniel: An Expository Commentary.* 197
53   Ibid. 197
54   Young. *The Prophecy Daniel: A Commentary.* 241
55   Josephus. *Antiquities.* VII:III. 252
56   Young. *The Prophecy Daniel: A Commentary.* 240
57   *Ancient Egypt: From Prehistory to the Islamic Conquest.* Britannica Educational Publishing. 102
58   Phillips. *Exploring the Book of Daniel: An Expository Commentary.* 198
59   Polybius 28.20.9; Livy 33.40.3 and 35.13.4; Appian. *Syriaca* 3.13 and 5.18
60   Phillips. *Exploring the Book of Daniel: An Expository Commentary.* 199
61   "Antiochus." *The Biographical Dictionary Vol 3 Issue 1.* 35-36
62   Ibid
63   Phillips. *Exploring the Book of Daniel: An Expository Commentary.* 199
64   Venning. *A Chronology of Ancient Greece.* 258
65   Livy 37.23-24 as quoted by Appian. *The Syrian Wars.* V. 27. English translation from: Appian. *The Foreign Wars*
66   Grainger. *The Roman War of Antiochos the Great.* 307-25
67   Phillips. *Exploring the Book of Daniel: An Expository Commentary.* 199
68   Phillips. *Exploring the Book of Daniel: An Expository Commentary.* 199; Walvoord. *Daniel: The Key to Prophetic Revelation.* 166. See also Prichard. *Near Eastern Studies.* 337-338
69   Gleason. *Jerome's Commentary on Daniel.* 134; Walvoord. *Daniel: The Key to Prophetic Revelation.* 338
70   Young. *The Prophecy Daniel: A Commentary.* 240
71   Phillips. *Exploring the Book of Daniel: An Expository Commentary.* 200
72   Young. *The Prophecy Daniel: A Commentary.* 241

73   Ibid. 241
74   Appian. The Syrian Wars 9:45; Phillips. *Exploring the Book of Daniel: An Expository Commentary.* 201
75   Polybius 26:1. 483
76   Keil. *Biblical Commentary of the Old Testament, The Book of the Prophet Daniel.* 11:23-24
77   "Onias III." *Encyclopaedia Judaica.* ©2008 The G. 403-04. https://www.jewishvirtuallibrary.org/jsource/judaica/ejud_0002_0015_0_15109.html
78   Keil. *Biblical Commentary of the Old Testament, The Book of the Prophet Daniel.* 11:20
79   Bevan. *The House of Ptolemy: A History of Egypt Under the Ptolemaic Dynasty.* 284
80   Bevan. *The House of Seleucus.* 136; Volkmann. Hans. *Antiochus IV Epiphanies.* Encyclopedia Britannica
81   Bevan. *The House of Ptolemy: A History of Egypt Under the Ptolemaic Dynasty.* 284
82   Phillips. *Exploring the Book of Daniel: An Expository Commentary.* 203
83   Ibid. 203
84   Bevan. Edwin Robert. *The House of Ptolemy: A History of Egypt Under the Ptolemaic Dynasty.* 1927. 284-85
85   Ibid
86   Bevan. *The House of Seleucus.* 144
87   Phillips. *Exploring the Book of Daniel: An Expository Commentary.* 204
88   Bevan. *The House of Seleucus.* 144 Bevan. *The House of Ptolemy: A History of Egypt Under the Ptolemaic Dynasty.* 136
89   Keil. *Biblical Commentary of the Old Testament. The Book of the Prophet Daniel.* 11:38
90   Volkmann. "Antiochus Epiphanies." Encyclopedia Britannica. *Encyclopædia Britannica Online.*
91   Phillips. *Exploring the Book of Daniel: An Expository Commentary.* 205
92   Skinner. Ogden. and Galbraith. *Jerusalem. The Eternal City.* 142
93   Josephus. *Wars of the Jews.* 1:2
94   Keil. *Biblical Commentary of the Old Testament. The Book of the Prophet Daniel.* 11:31
95   Josephus *Wars of the Jews.* 1:3
96   Skinner. Ogden and Galbraith. *Jerusalem. The Eternal City.* 142
     "In 168 B.C. Antiochus IV set about to destroy every distinctive feature of the Jewish faith. Sacrifices were forbidden. Sabbath and feasts days were no longer to be observed. The rite of circumcision was abolished. Books of the Torah were desecrated or destroyed. Jews were forced to eat swine flesh and perform sacrifices at idolatrous altars set up throughout the land. Disobedience to any aspect of his decree was punishable by death."
97   Keil. *Biblical Commentary of the Old Testament. The Book of the Prophet Daniel.* 11:31
98   Phillips. *Exploring the Book of Daniel: An Expository Commentary.* 207
99   Young. *The Prophecy Daniel: A Commentary.* 245
100 NASB (New American Standard Bible. 1971). Dan. 11:33
101 Young. *The Prophecy Daniel: A Commentary.* 245
102 Phillips. *Exploring the Book of Daniel: An Expository Commentary.* 207
103 Volkmann. Encyclopedia Britannica

104 Walvoord. *Daniel: The Key to Prophetic Revelation.* 166. See also Prichard. *Near Eastern Studies.* 345-46

105 Ibid. 346

106 Keil. *Biblical Commentary of the Old Testament. The Book of the Prophet Daniel.* 11:35. emphasis added. Kranichfield

107 Ibid 11:36

108 Megalomania." *Merriam-Webster.* Merriam-Webster. George and Charles Merriam. G & C Merriam Co. in Springfield. Massachusetts. www.merriam-webster.com/dictionary/megalomania

109 Brisch. "Of Gods and Kings: Divine Kingship in Ancient Mesopotamia." 37-43

110 Mark. "Alexander the Great" *Ancient History Encyclopedia.* 14. November 2013

111 Phillips. *Exploring the Book of Daniel: An Expository Commentary.* 209

112 Walvoord. *Daniel: The Key to Prophetic Revelation.* 166. See also Prichard. *Near Eastern Studies.* 251

113 Keil. *Biblical Commentary of the Old Testament, The Book of the Prophet Daniel.* 11 37)

114 Ibid. 11:38

115 Keil. *Biblical Commentary of the Old Testament, The Book of the Prophet Daniel.* 40-43

116 Walvoord. *Daniel: The Key to Prophetic Revelation.* 166. See also Prichard. Near Eastern Studies. 353-56; Phillips. *Exploring the Book of Daniel: An Expository Commentary.* 211 (211-13)

117 Keil. *Biblical Commentary of the Old Testament, The Book of the Prophet Daniel.* 11:40

118 Ibid 11:40

119 Ibid 11:43

120 Ibid 11:43

121 Ibid 11:41

122 McConkie. *Doctrinal New Testament Commentary.* 3:509–10

123 Ibid

Persia (or Persians) Invade Greece

Second invasion, in the battle of Thermopylae a Greek force of approximately 7,000 men marched north to block the pass in the summer of 480 BC. The Persian army, alleged by the ancient sources to have numbered over one million but today considered to have been much smaller (various figures are given by scholars ranging between about 100,000 and 150,000) Cassin-Scott, Jack (1977). The Greek and Persian Wars 500-323 B.C. Osprey. 11.

Modern Christianity and Islam - Elder Orson Pratt taught that "so great will be the darkness resting upon Christendom, and so great the bonds of priestcraft with which they will be bound, that they will not understand, and they will be given up to the hardness of their hearts. Then will be fulfilled that saying, That the day shall come when the Lord shall have power over his Saints, and the Devil shall have power over his own dominion. He will give them up to the power of the Devil, and he will have power over them, and he will carry them about as chaff before a whirlwind. He will gather up millions upon millions of people into the valleys around about Jerusalem in order to destroy the Jews after they have gathered. How will the Devil do this? He will perform miracles to do it. The Bible says the kings of the earth and the great ones will be deceived by these false miracles. It says there shall be three unclean spirits that shall go forth working miracles, and they are spirits of devils. Where do they go? To the kings of the earth; and what will they do? Gather them up to battle unto the great day of God Almighty. Where? Into the valley of Armageddon." (In Journal of Discourses, 7:189.)

Hitzig Ferdinand Das Buch, Daniel Berklard, Leipzig 1850

The historic scene which followed was one which Roman pride never allowed to be forgotten. Antiochus was prepared to receive Popillius-whom he had known in Rome-with that easy familiarity which belonged to him. As soon as he saw the ambassadors approaching he greeted Popillius in a loud glad voice and held out his hand as to an old friend. But the Roman came on with a grim and stony irresponsiveness. He reached the King a little tablet, which he carried in his hand, and curtly bade him first read that through. Antiochus looked at it; it was a formal resolution of the Senate that King Antiochus should be required to evacuate Egypt. Then there sprang to his lips one of those diplomatic phrases which came so readily to him, something as to laying the matter before his Friends. But the Roman was determined he should not wriggle free. To the amazement of the courtiers, he drew with his walking-stick a circle in the sand all round the King: Yes or No before he stepped outside of it. Such methods were certainly a new sort of diplomacy, and Antiochus collapsed. When he got his voice, it was to say that he would agree to anything. The next minute he found the Romans shaking his hand and inquiring cheerfully how he did. (Bevan, Edwin Robert, The House of Seleucus, 144)

Kings of the Kingdoms of the North and South

Syrian Kings	(from b.c.)	Egyptian Kings	(from b.c.)
Seleucus Nicator	310	Ptolemy Lagus	323
Antiochus Sidetes	280	Ptolemy Philadelphus	284
Antiochus Theus	260		
Seleucus Callinicus	245	Ptolemy Euergetes	246
Seleucis Ceraunus	225		
Antiochus the Great	223	Ptolemy Philopator	221
Seleucis Philopator	186	Ptolemy Epiphanes	204
Antiochus Epiphanies	175	Ptolemy Philometor	180

Map of the kingdoms allied with Gog that will war against Israel

Modern tanks typifying great armies that enable up the god of Fortresses or war.

A harmony of key events from several prophets relative the Second Coming.

Event Sequence	Daniel	Ezekiel	Revelation, Zechariah, Others
Massive hosts of armies	40 King of the north shall come against him like a whirlwind, with chariots, and with horsemen, and with many ships; and he shall enter into the countries, and shall overflow and pass over.	**Ezek. 38:15** And thou shalt come from thy place out of the north parts, thou, and many people with thee, all of them riding upon horses, a great company, and a mighty army: **16** And thou shalt come up against my people of Israel, as a cloud to cover the land; it shall be in the latter days, and I will bring thee against my land, that the heathen may know me, when I shall be sanctified in thee, O Gog, before their eyes. **38:4** I will bring thee forth, and all thine army, horses and horsemen, all of them clothed with all sorts *of armour, even* a great company with bucklers and shields, all of them handling swords. **38:9** Thou shalt ascend and come like a storm, thou shalt be like a cloud to cover the land, thou, and all thy bands, and many people with thee. **Ezek. 39:2-3** **2** And I will turn thee back, and leave but the sixth part of thee, and will cause thee to come up from the north parts, and will bring thee upon the mountains of Israel: **3** And I will smite thy bow out of thy left hand, and will cause thine arrows to fall out of thy right hand.	**Rev 16:16 16** And he gathered them together into a place called in the Hebrew tongue Armageddon. **Rev. 9:17** And thus I saw the horses in the vision, and them that sat on them, having breastplates of fire, and of jacinth, and brimstone: and the heads of the horses *were* as the heads of lions; and out of their mouths issued fire and smoke and brimstone.

Anti-Christ enter into the promised land of Israel	**41** He shall enter also into the glorious land, and many countries shall be overthrown:	**28:8** After many days thou shalt be visited: in the latter years thou shalt come into the land that is brought back from the sword, and is gathered out of many people, against the mountains of Israel, which have been always waste: but it is brought forth out of the nations, and they shall dwell safely all of them.	**Rev. 11:8** And their dead bodies shall lie in the street of the great city, which spiritually is called Sodom and Egypt, where also our Lord was crucified. (Jerusalem)
They come rob and plunder	**43** But he shall have power over the treasures of gold and of silver, and over all the precious things of Egypt:	**38:12** To take a spoil, and to take a prey; to turn thine hand upon the desolate places that are now inhabited, and upon the people that are gathered out of the nations, which have gotten cattle and goods, that dwell in the midst of the land. **13** Sheba, and Dedan, and the merchants of Tarshish, with all the young lions thereof, shall say unto thee, Art thou come to take a spoil? hast thou gathered thy company to take a prey? to carry away silver and gold, to take away cattle and goods, to take a great spoil?	**Zech 14:2** For I will gather all nations against Jerusalem to battle; and the city shall be taken, and the houses rifled, and the women ravished; and half of the city shall go forth into captivity, and the residue of the people shall not be cut off from the city.
Kingdoms of Ethiopia and Libya allied with Gog	**Dan 11:43** and the Libyans and the Ethiopians shall be at his steps (March with him as allies)	**38:5**…Ethiopia, and Libya with them; all of them with shield and helmet:	
Problem with the campaign	**44** But tidings out of the east and out of the north shall trouble him: therefore he shall go forth with great fury to destroy, and utterly to make away many.		

Judgments of God destroy king of north a and massive army, and judgments poured out upon nations A great earthquake		**19** For in my jealousy and in the fire of my wrath have I spoken, Surely in that day there shall be a great shaking in the land of Israel; **20** So that the fishes of the sea, and the fowls of the heaven, and the beasts of the field, and all creeping things that creep upon the earth, and all the men that are upon the face of the earth, shall shake at my presence, and the mountains shall be thrown down, and the steep places shall fall, and every wall shall fall to the ground. **21** And I will call for a sword against him throughout all my mountains, saith the Lord God: every man's sword shall be against his brother. **22** And I will plead against him with pestilence and with blood; and I will rain upon him, and upon his bands, and upon the many people that are with him, an overflowing rain, and great hailstones, fire, and brimstone.	**Rev. 11:13** And the same hour was there a great earthquake, and the tenth part of the city fell, and in the earthquake were slain of men seven thousand: and the remnant were affrighted, and gave glory to the God of heaven. **Rev 16:18-21** **18** And there were voices, and thunders, and lightnings; and there was a great earthquake, such as was not since men were upon the earth, so mighty an earthquake, and so great. **19** And the great city was divided into three parts, and the cities of the nations fell: and great Babylon came in remembrance before God, to give unto her the cup of the wine of the fierceness of his wrath. **20** And every island fled away, and the mountains were not found. **21** And there fell upon men a great hail out of heaven, every stone about the weight of a talent: and men blasphemed God because of the plague of the hail; for the plague thereof was exceeding great.

Gog meets his end in "valley of passengers," between sea and holy mountains (Jerusalem)	**45** And he shall plant the tabernacles of his palace between the seas in the glorious holy mountain; yet he shall come to his end, and none shall help him	**Ezek. 39:5-6, 11** Thou shalt fall upon the open field: for I have spoken it, saith the Lord God. And I will send a fire on Magog, and among them that dwell carelessly in the isles: and they shall know that I am the Lord. **11** it shall come to pass in that day, that I will give unto Gog a place there of graves in Israel, the valley of the passengers on the east of the sea: and it shall stop th e noses of the passengers: and there shall they bury Gog and all his multitude: and they shall call it The valley of Hamon-gog.	

12

Epilogue

Chapter 12 serves as an appendix to the vision that began in Chapter 10, the vision of "the scripture of truth" (Dan 10:21). This section gives greater insights into the promises of protection that will be extended to the faithful in the latter-days. God's oversight of the Chosen People is a theme in all of Daniels's visions, but especially in this chapter. At the beginning of the vision, the messenger revealed his mission to defend the holy people against the forces of darkness and the conspiracies pervasive in the Persian and Grecian empires (Dan. 10:20-21). While it is not explicitly detailed in the events of the previous chapter, we can infer that heaven's protective hand remained active in all the ages. Angels were given charge to keep and defend the covenant people and preserve the purposes of the Lord throughout the sweep of history (Doctrine and Covenants 84:88). His watchcare and protection over the House of Israel comes full circle in the last days. This chapter reaffirms the covenant to defend the faithful in the turbulent times preceding the Lord's coming.

Michael Defends the Covenant People in the Last Days

1   And at that time shall Michael stand up, the great prince which standeth for the children of thy people: and there shall be a time of trouble, such as never was since there

> was a nation *even* to that same time: and at that time
> thy people shall be delivered, every one that shall be
> found written in the book.
>
> ———

Chapter 12 is set "at that time" (Dan 12:1), meaning the time when the anti-Christ, or evil men and women reign in many parts of the world. As Chapter 7 teaches, these rulers "shall speak great words against the most High, and shall wear out the saints of the most High" (Dan. 7:25). It is a time like the days of Antiochus, when secularism, religious radicalism and general wickedness abound. Society seeks opportunity to punish discipleship and stamp out the worship of the true and living God. Both the prevailing political apparatus and radical religious forces will join in a crusade against the followers of Christ in the world.

It is a time of social contention and war. The great battle outlined in Daniel 11:40-45 continues in full motion and the entire world is distressed as a result of conflicts and political upheavals (Doctrine and Covenants 45:26; 88:91). In this epic struggle, Michael "stands up" with his angelic hosts to defend the "children of thy people" (Dan. 12:1). Two main groups comprise the "children of thy people" or descendants of the House of Israel; the Jews gathered in Israel and the Saints in the Church of Jesus Christ. Other righteous and honourable people around the world are also in peril.

As described in Chapter 11, the situation that surrounds the Jews in the war of Armageddon (in the Middle East) put them in a pitch battle for their very survival. Israel remains alone against the alliance of nations backed by the king from north (Zech. 14:2; see also Ezek. 38-39; Rev. 9, 11,16). The situation around the world place the Saints and honorable men everywhere in perilous circumstances. Evil combinations in government and other organizations combine in campaigns of oppression, much as Antiochus brought fierce punishments against the Jews. Wicked cultures are hostile to the doctrines of Christ and many in society back the evil plans and rage against righteousness.

All these latter-day events are characterized as the "time of trouble, such as never was since there was a nation *even* to that same time" (Dan. 12:1). Jeremiah referred to Israel's war as "Jacob's distress or trouble" (Jer. 30:7). Throughout the sweep of history, no people or nation will have encountered such perilous odds as Israel will face when the king of the north pushes down with his armies. Young reinforces that "no nation has ever witnessed distress such as this" since nations existed.[1] This declaration is remarkable when we consider other terrible events such as the destruction of Jerusalem by the Babylonians or the carnage brought by the Romans under Titus or the holocaust under Hitler. Speaking specifically of the great conflict of Armageddon, the Lord warned: "And except those days should be shortened, there should no flesh be saved: but for the elect's sake those days shall be shortened" (JS-M 1:20).

Zechariah wrote that in the last great battle roughly two parts or two-thirds of the Jewish people will fall victim in the conflict. But the Lord promises that "I will bring the third part through the fire, and will refine them as silver is refined, and will try them as gold is tried: they shall call on my name, and I will hear them: I will say, It *is* my people: and they shall say, The Lord *is* my God" (Zech. 13:9). Note that Zechariah's language is similar to the message given by Gabriel in Chapter 11. He stated that the purpose of Antiochus's persecutions was to "try them, and to purge, and to make them white" (Dan. 11:35). Those who have remained true to their covenants are preserved through the afflictions. The process serves to make them purer and prepared to meet their Lord. We should be careful not to take the number 1/3 too literally, but it seems clear a majority of the Jews will be lost.

World conditions will be so adverse against the righteous that discipleship to Christ will appear, in the world's eyes, to be a liability. "The people of God need such powerful help for their deliverance, because that time shall be one of oppression without any parallel."[2]

The angel states that those delivered from the latter-day calamities have their names written in the Book of Life (Dan. 12:1; Rev. 13:8). John's Revelation teaches that to have ones name written in the book means to place the protective seal of the Father on their foreheads (Rev. 7:2). This sealing power comes by faith in the Lord, Jesus Christ, repentance and the ordinances of the Gospel. The temple ordinances bestow the promise "that no combination of wickedness shall have power to rise up and prevail over thy people upon whom thy name shall be put in this house" and that Jehovah will "fight for thy people as thou didst in the day of battle, that they may be delivered from the hands of all their enemies" (Doctrine and Covenants 109:26, 28). Michael will cause "the heavens to shake" (Doctrine and Covenants 35:24; 21:6) and send down angelic hosts (unseen watchers) to provide protection and safety. This heavenly help combined with the power of worthy mortal priesthood holders will be required to defend the people of Zion amid the persecutions, calamities and judgements of the Lord. Nephi "beheld the power of the Lamb of God, that it descended upon the saints of the church of the Lamb, and upon the covenant people of the Lord, who were scattered upon all the face of the earth; and they were armed with righteousness and with the power of God in great glory." (1 Ne. 141:14). Among the Jews, the two Apostles will declare the message of the Messiah, but also use their authority to preserve Israel according to the Covenant (Rev. 11:4; 2 Ne. 25:16).

Those who qualify for heaven's protective power have kept their covenants and remained true to their testimonies. They have fastened their faith and devotion to the latter-day prophets. They remained diligent in the work of the Gospel and true to their commitments. These will be like the "wise Jews" in the persecutions of Antiochus. They will have prepared themselves for the tests to come. President Spencer W. Kimball taught that now is the time to gather the oil in preparation for the trials: "Attendance at sacrament meetings adds oil to our lamps, drop by drop over the years. Fasting, family prayer, home teaching, control of bodily appetites, preaching the gospel, studying the scriptures—each act of dedication and obedience is a drop added to our store. Deeds of kindness, payment of offerings and tithes, chaste thoughts and actions, marriage in the covenant for eternity—these, too, contribute importantly to the oil with which we can at midnight refuel our exhausted lamps."[3] The cumulative effect of their spiritual development, faithful works and devoted ministering will bear valuable fruit in this dark period of world history.

Firmness and mastery of Christ-like attributes also proves essential in retaining one's name brightly written in the Book of Life (Doctrine and Covenants 109:24). Again, the lessons of the "wise" in Chapter 11 are evident (Dan. 11:32-33). Those with "understanding," are guided by the Spirit in their actions. President Russell M. Nelson has warned: "But in coming days, it will not be possible to survive spiritually without the guiding, directing, comforting, and constant influence of the Holy Ghost. My beloved brothers and sisters, I plead with you to increase your spiritual capacity to receive revelation."[4]

> "But in coming days, it will not be possible to survive spiritually without the guiding, directing, comforting, and constant influence of the Holy Ghost."
>
> President Russell M Nelson

They will be strengthened and confront the trials of the day with a spirit of confidence, assurance and firmness. They will endure the turbulent times with the gift of resolute joy despite outward pressures and adverse circumstances. President Russell M. Nelson also taught that "[joy] is key to our spiritual survival. It is a principle that will only become more important as the tragedies and travesties around us increase."[5]

John taught the necessity of having one's name written in the Book of Life. He declared that the names of the followers of the anti-Christ (the beast), those deceived by the world, will not be "written in the book of life" (Rev. 13:8; 17:8, see also Rev. 3:5; 22:19). These "are bound in bundles, and the field (or the world) remaineth to be burned" (Doctrine and Covenants 86:7, 101:66, 88:94, Matt. 13:30). The "wise" will not only be preserved themselves, but prove to be of great value and strength to others of less understanding as they provide guidance and counsel to many who are also required to traverse the turbulent waters of the last days.

The Resurrection and Redemption of Israel

———

2   And many of them that sleep in the dust of the earth shall awake, some to everlasting life, and some to shame *and* everlasting contempt.

3   And they that be wise shall shine as the brightness of the firmament; and they that turn many to righteousness as the stars for ever and ever.

———

Daniel is shown the fulfillment of promised rewards given the faithful in the eternities, the resurrection and the crowning of the righteous with the glory of Eternal Life (Doctrine and Covenants 14:7). The Savior has promised: "But blessed are they who are faithful and endure, whether in life or in death, for they shall inherit eternal life" (Doctrine and Covenants 50:5). While the latter-day troubles will place virtually everyone in both alarming and perilous circumstances, the angel reaffirms that the "wise" will "shine as the brightness of the firmament" (Dan. 12:3). A number will suffer a martyr's death, standing firm until the very end, but all the just have the promise to receive greater blessings when they rise in the Morning of the First Resurrection (Doctrine and Covenants 76:50-63). Their obedience and fidelity will provide the inner confidence and protection to weather the calamites. The hope is of greater rewards, a crown and entrance into the kingdom of God, will instill upon the faithful as they prove themselves worthy in the trials.

The angel declares that not only do the wise secure protection for themselves, but they will help "turn many to righteousness." (Dan 12:3). Amidst the chaos, there will be "many" searching for direction and refuge. The faithful will shine as examples to help gather in multitudes to be preserved from the storms and conflicts (Doctrine and Covenants 115:6). The prophet Joseph Smith foresaw the day when the people and government in the united States would rely on the Latter-day Saints, leaning on them as a "staff" for their very survival. "Even this nation will be on the verge of crumbling to pieces and tumbling to the ground and when the Constitution is on the brink of ruin this people will be the staff upon which the nation shall lean and they shall bear the Constitution away from the very verge of destruction."⁶ This prophecy foresees the influence of those endowed with the gifts of God, who will "shine" forth and provide strength, direction and exercise power to uphold the nation to prevent its total collapse. Other poignant examples will emerge as Saints all over the world act in meaningful ways under the inspiration of the Spirit to preserve life and bring order.

In the resurrection, these wise shall shine "like the stars forever and ever" (Dan. 12:4). The vision of the three degrees of glory reveals how the just will come forth in the first resurrection to inherit the highest kingdom and attain a glory, which brightness "is that of the sun, even the glory of God, the highest of all, whose glory the sun of the firmament is written of as being typical" (Doctrine and Covenants 76:70; 1 Cor. 15:41).

In contrast to the great blessings and security promised the faithful, the record also makes it clear that others will not remain true, but be overcome by the world and fall into wickedness. These will rise to a lesser resurrection of "shame *and* everlasting contempt" (Dan. 12:2). They reap the rewards of a kingdom of inferior glory. Their reward is tainted with regret of not having chosen the better part and remained true. These must come forth in humiliation to great Judgement bar of Jehovah to face the fruits of their unbelief and iniquity and receive a lesser portion of the possible inheritance.

Shut and Seal the Word of the Vision

---

4   But thou, O Daniel, shut up the words, and seal the book, *even* to the time of the end: many shall run to and fro, and knowledge shall be increased.

The vision concludes and Daniel is commanded to write and then "shut up the words" or seal the book. The charge to "shut up" or "roll up the scroll" was a commandment to ensure the preservation of its prophetic contents. "The statement can be interpreted in two ways: It can refer to the idea that the text was being sealed or preserved in a way that would prevent it from being 'tampered with or changed.' And it can be understood in the sense that the interpretation of the revelation would not be fully revealed until a time close to its fulfillment."[7] The charge was an immediate assignment to record and preserve the prophecy from destruction or loss. He was to take the necessary steps to ensure its preservation through the ages. Anciently, the process for persevering parchments was to meticulously copy and recopy their contents, and then distribute the work to local synagogues. The protected scrolls were kept in the cabinets or vaults where they would be stored, used and recopied over time. Some of the ancient records among the Jews and many of the Nephite records were kept on metal plates such as: brass, gold or other ores (1 Ne. 3:3, 5;18-19; 12; 4:16, 24, 38; Mos. 28:11), thus preserving them for centuries.

The charge also meant that much of its contents would remain unclear or obscure until the time of its fulfillment. Daniel's prophecies were to be preserved, reviewed and pondered from the pages of parchment. They were to be read and taught many times throughout history. The meaning of the visions would unfold and the knowledge of the prophecy would become clearer as their each prophecy drew nigh. The record would serve as an ongoing witness of God's foreknowledge and His hand in the preservation of the Holy People through the ages.

The messenger stated that the latter-day portions of this vision would be understood in a time when "many shall run to and fro, and knowledge shall be increased" (Dan. 12:4). The angel foretells of the modern age, a time of industrial and technical innovation where people move to and fro in cars, trains and airplanes, and where the combination of the printing press, computers and the Internet bring information to our fingertips which greatly increases knowledge in the world. These marvelous discoveries pave the way for the advancement of the Gospel. President Dallin H. Oaks has taught:

> The significance of our increased discretionary time has been magnified many times by modern data-retrieval technology. For good or for evil, devices like the Internet and the compact disc have put at our fingertips an incredible inventory of information, insights, and images. Along with fast food, we have fast communications and fast facts. The effect of these

> resources on some of us seems to fulfill the prophet
> Daniel's prophecy that in the last days 'knowledge
> shall be increased' and 'many shall run to and fro'
> (Dan. 12:4).[8]
>
> ————

These innovations and advancements are necessary as the Lord makes preparations for His final coming. They serve as instruments to be used and catalysts that create an environment where the dissemination of the restored Gospel is facilitated. Elder Deiter F. Uchtdorf added this meaningful insight:

> ————
>
> Sometimes we think of the Restoration of the gospel
> as something that is complete, already behind us—
> Joseph Smith translated the Book of Mormon, he
> received priesthood keys, the Church was organized.
> In reality, the Restoration is an ongoing process; we
> are living in it right now. It includes "all that God
> has revealed, all that He does now reveal," and the
> "many great and important things" that "He will yet
> reveal." Brethren, the exciting developments of today
> are part of that long-foretold period of preparation
> that will culminate in the glorious Second Coming
> of our Savior, Jesus Christ.[9]
>
> ————

It is also important to note that the angel referred specifically to the "word's of Daniel's prophecy, meaning this vision which foretells of 'the end.' "The Hebrew for the 'word' is $had\cdot d\bar{a}\cdot$ 'at, (תַעֲדָה:) which means literally, 'the knowledge,' that is, the understanding of this long prophecy."[10] Young provides an important explanation to the phrase that the word will go "to and fro" to increase knowledge: "Preserve the book until the end, for it contains the truth as to the future. Many shall go to and fro in search of knowledge, but they shall not find it."[11] Through the ages many will expend great energy to understand it, but they will struggle to find meaning and clarity. Only near the "time of the end" will this become clear and then only to the wise (Dan. 12:4).

The prophet Amos spoke of a great famine "of hearing the words of the Lord," a day when "they shall wander from sea to sea, and from the north even to the east, they shall run to and fro to seek the word of the Lord, and shall not find it" (Amos 8:11–12). Amos's words apply to periods of individual, national or even global apostasy. The famine of the word was especially severe during the Great Apostasy, which swept across the earth after the death of the Lord and the Apostles. But the angel is also saying that attempts to interpret "the knowledge of the end" from Daniel's immediate future and through the ages will yield little understanding. The time for its fulfillment was still far off. Without the context of the events of the day, the true meaning will remain unknown.

The Restoration, with all of its facets, has brought an outpouring of light, innovation, advancement and the means to more fully comprehend the vision. As world events coalesce towards their foreseen fulfillment, the lessons and warnings of the vision will become more poignant. The wise will discern what is coming and focus on the needed preparations. At the same time the spiritual famine in large measure continues until, for many, it will be too late. Unfortunately, the world will be largely disinterested in the message of the prophecy. The modern, secular age is consumed in other pursuits, distracted by worldly concerns and entertainment or busy with other "important things." Ironically, there is always much speculative interest surrounding the latter day events, but most people do not turn to the prophecies of the Lord. Rather, they tune to other sources or "prophets" that predict or foretell the future. They also "run to and fro," "ever learning, and never able to come to the knowledge of the truth" (2 Tim. 3:7). The knowledge and wisdom of this prophecy remains largely unknown today.

How Long Will the Times of Tribulation Last?

5   Then I Daniel looked, and, behold, there stood other two, the one on this side of the bank of the river, and the other on that side of the bank of the river.

6   And one said to the man clothed in linen, which was upon the waters of the river, How long shall it be to the end of these wonders?

7   And I heard the man clothed in linen, which was upon the waters of the river, when he held up his right hand and his left hand unto heaven,

> and sware by him that liveth for ever that it shall
> be for a time, times, and an half; and when he shall
> have accomplished to scatter the power of the holy
> people, all these things shall be finished.

———

Daniel observes that additional personages now attend him. One angel stands near him on his side of the Tigris River (Dan 10:4) and another on the far side, while the third stands in the middle on the waters. The angel closest to him, presumably the deliverer of the vision, directs a question to the one on the river clothed in priesthood "linen." The reference to linen signifies that the angel that stands upon the water is in greater Priesthood seniority than him. The question is asked: "how long to the end of these wonders?" We might initially believe that he was asking how long until these events occur. But the messenger, sensing that the prophet is more concerned about the content of the vision than its timing, was in fact inquiring, "how long will these trying times last?" He desires to give Daniel additional clarity as to the duration of the days of crisis. If we remember in the trial of Antiochus, Daniel expressed the same concern and the Lord set a time limit to those events (Dan. 11:26). The trials and persecutions of the Abomination of Desolation were allowed only for the prescribed period, long enough to fulfill His purposes. Likewise, a limit will be placed on the dominion of the wicked and their evil works in the latter-day events.

To answer the question, the angel Michael raises both hands to the square and in the authority of the priesthood swears with an oath declaring that the duration will last no longer than time (1), and times (2) and half a time (½). (Compare this oath to that of the mighty angel referred to in a similar context in Revelation 10:2-3). The number 3½ is symbolic of a critical period, a time of trial, but it also represents the relative number in years.[12] The Hebrew verse in Dan. 12:7 is an equivalent to the Aramaic phrase found in Dan. 7:25, a time and times and the dividing of time, which confirms the appointed time when the anti-Christs are allowed dominance and great influence in the world. "Ordinarily, when an oath was taken, only one hand was raised, cf: Gen. 14:22; Deut. 32:40. The solemnity of this oath, therefore, is emphasized by the fact that both hands are raised. The man clothed in fine linen swears by Him [or speaking in the authority of Him] who lives forever, the true God"[13] that the trial will not be one day longer than is necessary. Jehovah, through his authorized servant, seals this promise with an oath (Dan. 11:35). The other angels serve as witnesses to establish the veracity and binding nature of the oath.[14]

While the end of days will surely bring instability and conflict at a scale more than at any other time in history, the Lord still places limits, both in terms of timeframe and also scope. For the righteous who will be required to pass through the trials, this may not appear to be the case, but the Lord will control both micro and macro events. He sets the bounds to suit His purposes and has promised:

---

13   And he that fighteth against Zion shall perish, saith God.

14   For he that raiseth up a king against me shall perish, for I, the Lord, the king of heaven, will be their king, and I will be a light unto them forever, that hear my words.

15   Wherefore, for this cause, that my covenants may be fulfilled which I have made unto the children of men, that I will do unto them while they are in the flesh, I must needs destroy the secret works of darkness, and of murders, and of abominations.

16   Wherefore, he that fighteth against Zion, both Jew and Gentile, both bond and free, both male and female, shall perish; for they are they who are the whore of all the earth; for they who are not for me are against me, saith our God.

17   For I will fulfil my promises which I have made unto the children of men, that I will do unto them while they are in the flesh—(2 Ne. 10:13-17, emphasis added)

Michael takes action with a similar oath in John's Revelation that demonstrates the promise first given to Daniel will be kept. He stands with one foot on the land and the other on the sea and lifts his hands to heaven to "sware [in the name of Him] that liveth for ever and ever…that there should be time no longer." (Rev 10:1, 6). Here, at the zenith of the trials and persecutions, the Archangel declares the end and there will be no more delay in the fulfillment of God's covenant. In the authority of the Almighty, the verdict reached at the council recorded in chapter 7 (Dan. 7:9-14) is brought to fruition. He signals that all subsequent actions will lead to the destruction of the anti-Christs and their dominions. The cup of their iniquity is full and in preparation of the Lord's advent, they will be swept from the earth (Doctrine and Covenants 101:11; 77:12; 103:3).

The Scattering of the People of God

The three and a half years will be the necessary period for events to play out according to the Lord's purposes. The three and one half years will serve as a time of sifting and separating the wicked from the righteous and to prove and purify the faithful. At the same time, the Lord will bind up the law and the testimony against the wicked (Dan 12:10). During the trial, the enmity of the wicked will manifest itself in many forms. The wicked one will have full sway in stirring up society and the culture against the righteous. The crude and fowl environment remains a persistent force constantly vexing the humble with all manner of evil deeds and actions.

The cultural and political pressures will be immense. The anti-Christ and the wicked in society will combine in an attempt to force a wholesale cultural change to bend the commitment and fidelity of the faithful. The cumulative burdens described by the angel have the effect of "[scattering] the power of the holy people" (Dan. 12:7). The verb *scatter* [נפץ] is commonly rendered "shattering" and gives the idea of breaking something into pieces like pottery is shattered.[15] "The phase can be translated when (they) finish shattering the hand (or the power) of the holy people."[16] Keil provides this helpful interpretation: "breaking to pieces of the might of the people is identical with their scattering, but it has the meaning *to make perfect, to accomplish*, so that nothing more remains to be done. *Hand*, is the emblem of active power; the shattering of the hand is thus the complete destruction of power to work, the placing in a helpless and powerless condition."[17] It seems an odd statement, but the same idea is also found in Daniel 7:25, which speaks of efforts to "wear out the saints of the most High" (Dan. 7:25).

The implication is that the people of God are placed in a situation where they are seemingly powerless to throw off the circumstances of the trial. The hostile environment appears overwhelming and the righteous at times feel alone. They will be placed in situations where they become totally dependent on the Lord for their protection and survival as was the case with Alma and his people under the persecutions of Amulon (Alma 23-24). The adversary intends to grind down the Saints by making it appear that they are helpless or powerless. With the assistance of the ungodly and the deceived, he will methodically place a combination of social, political and legal burdens upon the righteous. Social ostracization, pointed accusations, general ridicule, the denial of the right to worship, the destruction of property, murder and other strifes will all be used in the intent to get them to abandon their convictions. The Revelation of John speaks of the day when "no man might buy or sell, save he that had the mark, of the name of the beast, or the number of his name. (Rev 13: 17). Certainly, economic pressures will be added to the overall climate where the wicked will rage with indignation and malice against that which is good.

Speaking specifically of the Jews in Israel, the crisis means that they will literally be surrounded at Jerusalem with numberless hosts of troops intent on their annihilation. There will be no room for compromise, no quarter for treaty. It will be a mortal struggle for survival. When the two prophets are killed, it will appear that they too stand helpless (Rev. 11:7). Only the intervention of Jehovah on Olivet will save them from destruction (Zech. 14:4).

In addition to outward pressures, there will arise internal strife within the Church. The Book of Mormon records a time of great tribulation that erupted among the members just prior to the Lord's coming to the Americas. Mormon's account describes the contention as a period of great separation and sifting, where internal schisms rent the Church. "Some were lifted up in pride, and others were exceedingly humble; some did return railing for railing, while others would receive railing and persecution and all manner of afflictions, and would not turn and revile again, but were humble and penitent before God" (3 Ne. 6:13). The strife resulted in that "...there became a great inequality in all the land, *insomuch that the church began to be broken up*; yea, insomuch that in the thirtieth year the *church was broken up* in all the land save it were among a few" (3 Ne. 6:14).

The most poignant tests will arise from contention and strife among family and friends and brothers and sisters in the Gospel. And if the latter-day events mirror the persecutions when the "transgressors" allied with Antiochus, similar contentious and treacherous conditions will reemerge. Real turmoil will swirl within the Church. Heber C. Kimball, who was one of the original Twelve Apostles and First Counselor to President Brigham Young, warned:

> Internal strife combined with the outward political and social forces will be at the root of the "TEST" sent to try the Church.
>
> Heber C. Kimball

"The time is coming when ... it will be difficult to tell the face of a Saint from the face of an enemy to the people of God. Then ... look out for the great sieve, for there will be a great sifting time, and many will fall." He concluded that there is "a TEST coming."[18] Internal strife combined with the outward political and social forces will form the root of the "TEST" that will try the Church and its members. Elder Neal Maxwell confirms both positive and negative effects of such a test. "For the Church, the scriptures suggest both an accelerated sifting and accelerated spiritual and numerical growth—with all this preceding the time when the people of God will be 'armed with righteousness'—not weapons—and when the Lord's glory will be poured out upon them (1 Ne. 14:14; see also 1 Pet. 4:17; Doctrine and Covenants 112:25). The Lord is determined to have a tried, pure, and proven people (see Doctrine and Covenants 100:16; 101:4; 136:31), and 'there is nothing that the Lord thy God shall take in his heart to do but what he will do it'" (Abr. 3:17)."[19]

As Kiel suggests, all this will bring about the means to "make perfect" the people of the Lord. He will consecrate all these trials, pressures and chaos to the good of the Saints (2 Ne 32:9). The heat of trial cleanses the soul, which yields the fruit of purity and resilience. All of the unimportant dross of the world falls away. The strengthening and sanctifying power of the Spirit combines with the grace of the Atonement help make perfect those who will not yield to the world. God has promised: "Keep all the commandments and covenants by which ye are bound; and I will cause the heavens to shake for your good, and Satan shall tremble and Zion shall rejoice upon the hills and flourish" (Doctrine and Covenants 35:24; 21:6). At the beginning of the chapter, the promise is made that Michael and his hosts will come in defense of the Lord's people (Dan. 12:1). In accordance with the oath made by the angel, in the eleventh hour (or the fourth watch, Matt. 14:25), when the power of the people of God seems "shattered," the Lord will be with and support them and in due time, He will liberate the saints. Judgments and plagues will be poured out to sweep the earth of wickedness (Doctrine and Covenants 109:30, 70; 121:15; 77:12). In the end, the events will have served to prepare a people that will "shine in brightness of the firmament" of the sun. This highly valuable fruit of prepared saints will spring from the furnace of the trial. The valiant will have gained the ability to endure the glory of the Lord at His coming and receive the blessings of everlasting life (Dan. 12:2-3, 10; see also Doctrine and Covenants 76:70).

How Will the Final Events End?

------

8   And I heard, but I understood not: then said I, O my Lord, what shall be the end of these end things?

9   And he said, Go thy way, Daniel: for the words are closed up and sealed till the time of the end.

10 Many shall be purified, and made white, and tried; but the wicked shall do wickedly: and none of the wicked shall understand; but the wise shall understand.

While Daniel saw the trial and heard the explanation, he still does not fully comprehend or at least he desires more information. He apparently doesn't witness how redemption comes and the process by which it will end. He inquires about these broader questions wishing to know more about the conclusion by asking:

"Oh Lord, what shall be the outcome of these things or how does it all end?" (Dan. 12:8 NIV). The angel's response comes almost as a rebuke. "Go thy way!" The words are closed, meaning that which was given is the official word and I will not reveal any more. "God wishes some of His predictions to be partially understood, and the rest to remain concealed until the full period of complete revelation should arrive."[20] Faith and agency must be preserved. The meaning of the prophecy will remain partially cloaked so that it is securely guarded against tampering or destruction and that it may be read and discerned at the time of its fulfillment.

In his inquiry, the prophet may have wondered: "what is the purpose for these very difficult trials?" Or in other words, "does it have to be so involved or so painful?" The angel reaffirms again the objective of the great tribulation. "Many shall be purified, and made white, and tried" (Dan. 12:10). The pressures and "heat" brought upon by the difficult trials bring much needed sanctification. Those who endure the process and remain steadfast become more unified and are "cleansed" and "refined." They become as white in the furnace of affliction. The Spirit of the Lord together with ministering angels (watchers) will support and defend the faithful, despite their seemingly helpless circumstances. Focus and fidelity, together with the Spirit will purge out any impurities. In the end, they are brought through as pure gold and silver, pure and brilliant. Malachi challenged: "But who may abide the day of his coming? And who shall stand when he appeareth? For he *is* like a refiner's fire, and like fullers' soap: And he shall sit as a refiner and purifier of silver: and he shall purify the sons of Levi, and purge them as gold and silver, that they may offer unto the Lord an offering in righteousness" (Mal. 3:2-3). The answer to Malachi's question is the "wise" men and women of the kingdom who had long since covenanted to be faithful and endure just as the ancient wise bolstered and ministered each other during the terrible days of Antiochus's rage.

"The wicked shall do wickedly," the messenger continues: "and none of the wicked shall understand; but the wise shall understand" (Dan. 12:10). The anti-Christs together with the wicked populations of the world will not understand the Lord's purposes. They will be

blinded in their own goals and led captive by the devil. The wicked
will rage against the truth and fight against righteousness and the
followers of Christ (2 Ne. 28.20). Among the wicked persecutors
will be those who have fallen away from the truth and broken the
Everlasting Covenant (Isa. 24:5; Doctrine and Covenants 1:15;
78:11). These "hypocrites," as the Lord calls them, (Matt. 24:51;
JS-M 1:54) will abandon the kingdom in favor of other causes
or paths, thinking they know more than the prophets. They are
blinded by the political, social and economic distractions of the
day. The Lord has warned that until the final hours "there will be
foolish virgins among the wise; and at that hour cometh an entire
separation of the righteous and the wicked; and in that day will
I send mine angels to pluck out the wicked and cast them into
unquenchable fire" (Doctrine and Covenants 63:54).

Those who remain standing will have proven their metal. They
will be readied to receive white robes of righteousness and crowns
of glory in the first resurrection as stated in the beginning of this
chapter (Dan. 12:2).

Daily Sacrifice Taken Away

------

11 And from the time *that* the daily *sacrifice* shall be
taken away, and the abomination that maketh
desolate set up, *there shall be* a thousand two
hundred and ninety days.

12 Blessed *is* he that waiteth, and cometh to the
thousand three hundred and five and thirty days.

13 But go thou thy way till the end *be:* for thou shalt rest,
and stand in thy lot at the end of the days.

The angel then declares the specific nature of the trial. A major
focus of the persecutions surrounds a "time *that* the daily sacrifices
shall be taken away" (Dan. 12:11). Religious freedoms are under
attack today, but as wickedness increases so too will pressures build
until the freedom of worship will be penalized, if not "taken away,"
as stated in Daniel (Dan. 7:25). The Saints will not only suffer under
serious political, social and legal stresses, but the privilege of regular

Sabbath worship and the closing or desecration of the temples, as was the case in the days of Antiochus's persecutions, will also be imposed upon the Saints. Culturally, Christian conviction will not only be unpopular, but scorned by the majority. The modern anti-Christs will seek to change the "times and laws" as a means to enforce their own cultural standards. The new policies and laws will by their very nature, penalize righteousness as not just old fashioned nonsense, but bigotry and crimes of hate (Dan. 7:25). The vision suggests that the penalties will result in the taking a way of religious freedoms and the right to openly worship.

The angel provides additional clues to clarify these critical events surrounding the end of times and the meaning of the sign or oath pronounced in verse 7. From the days that the daily sacrifices are taken away to the time when the anti-Christs are thrown down will be 1290 days. "The time that the daily sacrifice is taken away is equated with the setting up of the abomination that makes desolate."[21] Anciently, when Antiochus sacrificed a pig on the altar at the temple and later placed Zeus in the Holy of Holies, this signified the setting-up of the abomination and the beginning of the pagan oppressions.

> The modern anti-Christs will seek to change the "times and laws" as a means to enforce their culture, standards and policies, by law.

"The time *that* the daily *sacrifice* shall be taken" and setting of the "abomination that maketh desolate" will come about in modern times under similar circumstances. As we have reviewed, the persecutions and desecrations will stem from a combination of anti-Christ officials and leaders, false prophets, apostate transgressors and the willing support of a wicked generation. The political secularists may not place a pagan idol in the temple, as did the Greeks, but rather, they will set themselves up as the highest authority, pitting their moral values against the doctrines of Christ and the practices of His kingdo as the standard to be followed.

These disingenuous leaders will seek to enforce their own "righteousness" in an attempt to halt the practice of what they will declare to be "backward and racist religion." They will not only assert that Christian doctrines are uninformed, but practices that constitute blatant prejudice and in some cases are deemed illegal. Traditional religion will be subverted in favor of a new "social justice" a modern "enlightened" belief system, which is "set up" as progressively better and they will seek to enforce it by law. As mentioned, modern "transgressors," those who have broken the everlasting covenants (Isa. 24:5), will also play a pivotal part in the litigation of fellow members and their condemnation.

In the war against the Jews, modern secular governments will join with unprecedented irony the radical religionists of the false prophet, to fight against the State of Israel in an effort to "setup" the new totalitarian Caliphate. A major portion of this goal will be facilitated in the campaign to annihilate the Jews. Their total destruction will be a motivating call to join the cause.

Daniel is given the number 1290 days, which matches the coded language (time=1, times=2, and half time=½) or three and a half years. Revelations provides a similar code of 1260 days (Rev. 12:6; see also Rev. 12:6 JST version), which is given to represent the long night of apostasy. As Seiss states, the symbols given in each of the revelations essentially have the same meaning.

Nor shall the state of things be only for a few days, weeks or months, but for a full three and a half years, In no less than six different places, and in almost as many different ways, is this declared in the prophecies, including both Testaments. It is for 'a time, times, and half a time' (Dan. 7:25)—'a time, times and half a time' (12:7) —'they will trample the holy city for forty-two months' (Rev 11:2) —'and the woman fled into the wilderness, where she has a place prepared by God, in which she is to be nourished for 1260 days'—for 'she is to be

> nourished for a time, and times and half a time' (Rev
> 12:6, 14)—'and it was allowed to exercise authority
> for forty-two months' (Rev. 13:5).All these passages
> refer to one and the same period representing the
> oppression and trouble under the Antichrist. In each
> instance the measure is three and a half years, dating
> from the breaking of the league and the suspension
> of the daily offering to the destruction of the monster
> [beast] by the revelation of Jesus Christ. Our Lord
> ministered on earth three and a half years, and the
> Antichrist shall enact his Satanic ministry for the
> same length of time."[22]

As has been stated, the numerical symbols represent the
days when abominations reign or days of crisis. Each reference
approximates the duration of the trial (3 1/2 years), after which
the Lord promises that "the great and abominable church, which
is the whore of all the earth, shall be cast down by devouring fire,
according as it is spoken by the mouth of Ezekiel the prophet, who
spoke of these things, which have not come to pass but surely must,
as I live, for abominations shall not reign" (Doctrine and Covenants
29:21).

The messenger then adds that blessed are the faithful who wait
upon the Lord with patience and endure until the end. This time
period is symbolized by 1,335 days or roughly 45 days longer than
the period of the trial (Dan 12:12). Those who remain true must
pass through the full duration of the trial plus the small additional
time to reap the blessing of seeing the Lord return and His reign in
the Millennium.

Daniel Commanded to be Faithful

Anticipating the end of the prophecy, the angel commands
Daniel to "go thou thy way till the end *be*" (Dan. 12:13). He does
not speak of the end of the world, but counsels that he must continue
faithful until his life's mission is completed. The prophet will die
and find rest in the Lord. The angel's command is also given as
an injunction applied to all of Israel. Stand in thy lot, which is to
say: "rise unto your destiny" and receive his great portion or an
inheritance in the day of resurrection.

Conclusion

John Walvoord wrote of the prophetic writings of Daniel: "The concluding revelation of Daniel's Prophecy, acting as a capstone to all the tremendous preceding revelations, establishes the book of Daniel as the greatest and most comprehensive prophetic revelation of the Old Testament."[23] His prophecies are insightful in their details affirm the powerful message that God watches over and protects the covenant people and His children generally with remarkable care and precision.

The lessons contained in Daniel's writings remain as relevant today as when he was alive. His stories of fidelity to God and the kings have been read and re-read for millennia. They rank among the most inspirational in scripture. Daniel held the admiration and trust of the kings and the respect of both friend and foe. Most of all, he was beloved and trusted of the Lord. Having been tested and proven again and again, God placed him in positions of influence, not only to serve the king and the kingdom, but also to watch over the displaced captives of Israel. The welfare of his people was ever a concern on his mind. Doubtless other stories could be told of his influence in their preservation and for their benefit. His personal experiences and visions demonstrate how one man can be a powerful servant in the hand of the Lord.

Daniel's visions are also as impressive as any in scripture. They demonstrate again and again the Divine influence of a conerned Parent for His children in this moral estate. They summarize how He cares for them. The prophet Nephi admonished: "He doeth not anything save it be for the benefit of the world; for he loveth the world, even that he layeth down his own life that he may draw all men unto him. Wherefore, he commandeth none that they shall not partake of his salvation." (2 Ne. 26:24). Despite His care and long-suffering, Daniel's visions also reveal the great conflict that is constantly waged by the forces of evil against good in the world. The histories of worldly kingdoms are turbulent and fraught with intrigue, strife and bloodshed.

Daniel is shown how the angels of heaven, "the watchers," contend with the forces of darkness to influence and protect the children of men. While the purposes of the Lord will eventually come to pass, the devil fights with fierce opposition and enjoys much success. Agency and choice must be preserved in the process. The revelations make it clear that these battles will continue to rage through history until the coming of the Son of Man.

Among the important messages given to Daniel is the Lord's watchcare over the covenant children of Israel. The destiny and protection of the Chosen People was of constant concern to Daniel. Those portions of the visions that revealed future strife and hardship among the children of the Covenant caused him much distress. The message from attending angels was consistently clear, the Lord will manage these critical events and preserve the covenant. Despite the hardships, they will be preserved and protected. His covenants and purposes would be fulfilled and the destiny of Israel would be brought to pass. The messengers, themselves, revealed that they had filled assignments to protect and defend the interests of the Lord with respect to Israel scattered among the nations of the world.

While the majority of Daniel's prophetic record has already been fulfilled, yet there still remain a few very critical prophecies to be accomplished in these last days. All these events will come to pass with the same precision and completeness as the previous revelations. "For verily I say unto you, Till heaven and earth pass, one jot nor one tittle shall in no wise pass from the law, till all be fulfilled" (Matt. 5:18; 24:34).

As these pivotal days draw closer when the final prophecies must finally be fulfilled. The wise disciple must have etched in their heart the lessons taught by the testimony of Daniel.

First, God honors those who honor Him. Just as Daniel determined not to defile himself, but remain true to his covenants, so too must the wise resolve in their hearts that despite dangers and threats of the evil one, they must also be true to the Lord. They can stand confident with the promise that He will be with and protect them through every trial

Second, the Lord holds the destiny of the nations in His hand. Evil will be allowed to flourish and prosper for a season, but the scope of the wicked is limited by the Lord. Sufficient space will be given for the wicked to cause much pain, damage and chaos, but their ultimate purposes will be thwarted.

Finally, the Lord has covenanted to establish His people and bring forth Zion. No other power under heaven will impede this promised goal. Joseph Smith declared: "the Standard of Truth has been erected; no unhallowed hand can stop the work from progressing; persecutions may rage, mobs may combine, armies may assemble, calumny may defame, but the truth of God will go forth boldly, nobly, and independent, till it has penetrated every continent, visited every clime, swept every country, and sounded in every ear; till the purposes of God shall be accomplished, and the Great Jehovah shall say the work is done." [24]

The message of Daniel is to remain true and trust in the Lord's ability to guide, prepare and preserve the Saints for the great things to come. In a Revelation given to the Latter-day Saints the Lord admonished: "Wherefore, be faithful, praying always, having your lamps trimmed [or full] and burning, and oil with you, that you may be ready at the coming of the Bridegroom— For behold, verily, verily, I say unto you, that I come quickly. Even so. Amen (Doctrine and Covenants 33:17-18).

Chapter Endnotes

1   Young. *The Prophecy Daniel: A Commentary*. 255

2   Keil *Biblical Commentary of the Old Testament, The Book of the Prophet Daniel.* XII 1, 474-475

3   Kimball. *Faith Precedes the Miracle*. 256

4   Nelson, "Revelation for the Church Revelation for Our Lives," General Conference, The Church of Jesus Christ of Latter-day Saints, General Conference April 2018, https://www.lds.org/general-conference/2018/04/revelation-for-the-church-revelation-for-our-lives?lang=eng

5   Nelson, "Joy and Spiritual Survival." *By President Russell M. Nelson*, The Church of Jesus Christ of Latter-Day Saints, 2 Oct. 2016, www.lds.org/general-conference/2016/10/joy-and-spiritual-survival?lang=eng.

6   *Joseph Smith Papers* (Website), LDS Church Historical Archives, Box 1, March 10, 1844
"It has been prophesied that the Constitution of the United States will hang by a thread and that the elders of Israel will step forth to save it (Brigham Young, Journal History, 4 July 1854; Church News, 15 December 1948). In my mind that does not require a few heroes in public office steering some saving legislation through the halls of Congress, neither some brilliant military leaders rallying our defense against an invading army. In my mind, it could well be brought about by the rank and file of men and women of faith who revere the Constitution and believe that the strength of democracy rests in the ordinary family and in each member of it." (Packer, Let Not Your Heart Be Troubled. 68 [Address given at American Freedom Festival, Provo, Utah, 25 June 1989].)

7   Walvoord. *Daniel: The Key to Prophetic Revelation*, 375; Miller, Daniel, The New American Commentary. 320; Pentecost, J Dwight, *Daniel The Bible Knowledge Commentary: Old Testament*. 1:373

8   Oaks, "*Focus and Priorities*," General Conference, April 2001

9   Uchtdorf. "*Are You Sleeping through the Restoration?,*" General Conference, April 2001. https://www.lds.org/general-conference/2014/04/are-you-sleeping-through-the-restoration?lang=eng

10   Walvoord. *Daniel: The Key to Prophetic Revelation*, 376

11   Young. *The Prophecy Daniel: A Commentary*. 258

12   Gaskill, Alonzo, *The Lost language of Symbolism*, Deseret Book Company, Salt lake City, UT, 2003, 117-119

13   Young. *The Prophecy Daniel: A Commentary*. 259

14   Walvoord. *Daniel: The Key to Prophetic Revelation*, 377-78; Young. *The Prophecy Daniel: A Commentary*. 259

15   Harris, Archer, Waltke, *Theological Workbook*, 587

16   Brown, and others. *The Hebrew and English Lexicon of the Old Testament*. 658

17   Keil. *Biblical Commentary of the Old Testament, The Book of the Prophet Daniel*. XII 6-7 490-91

18   Whitney. *Life of Heber C. Kimball*. 446

19   Maxwell, "For I will Lead You Along," General Conference, April 1988, https://www.lds.org/general-conference/1988/04/for-i-will-lead-you-along?lang=eng

20   Cites Calvin, Young. *The Prophecy Daniel: A Commentary*. 260

21   Walvoord. *Daniel: The Key to Prophetic Revelation*, 380

22   Seiss. *Voices from Babylon, Or the Record of Daniel the Prophet*. 310-11

23   Walvoord. *Daniel: The Key to Prophetic Revelation.* 382
24   Smith. "The Wentworth Letter," *History of the Church*, 4:535–41, https://www.
     lds.org/ensign/2002/07/the-wentworth-letter?lang=eng

Additional Notes:

There will also be "a great division among the people" (2 Ne. 30:10; see also D&C
63:54). This stressful polarization will, ironically, help in the final shaking of that
strange confederacy, the "kingdom of the devil," in order that the honest in heart, even
therein, may receive the truth (2 Ne. 28:19).

This "great division" is what President Brigham Young also saw, saying: "It
was revealed to me in the commencement of this Church, that the Church would
spread, prosper, grow and extend, and that in proportion to the spread of the Gospel
among the nations of the earth, so would the power of Satan rise" (in Journal of
Discourses, 13:280). (Maxwell, "For I will lead You Along," General Conference
April 1988, https://www.lds.org/general-conference/1988/04/for-i-will-lead-you-
along?lang=eng)

Works Cited
and References Consulted

Abbott, Frank Frost. *A History and Description of Roman Political Institutions.* Elibron Classics, Ginn & Company Publishers, The Athenaeum Press, 1901

Acta Theologica, University of Free State, Bloemfontein, South Africa

Andersen, Neil L. "A Witness of God." General Conference Report, October 4, 2016. Accessed December 20, 2017. https://www.lds.org/general-conference/2016/10/a-witness-of-god?lang=eng.

Anderson, Robert, *The Coming Prince, 14th Edition.* Kregel, Grand Rapids, MI, 1954

Appian, *History of Rome: Syrian Wars*

——— The Foreign Wars, Horace White ed., New York, The Mcmillan Company, 1899

Benson, Ezra Taft. "In His Steps: Wisdom, Stature, and Favor." BYU Speeches, Brigham Young University, Mar. 4, 1979, speeches.byu.edu/talks/ezra-taft-benson_in-christs-steps/.

——— "Civic Standard for faithful Saints," Conference Report April 1972.

——— "The Book of Mormon Warns America" BYU Speeches, May 21, 1968

Bevan, Anthony Ashley, *Short Commentary on the Book of Daniel*, Cambridge University Press, Cambridge, United Kingdom, 1892

Bevan, Edwin Robert, *The House of Seleucus.* Barnes and Noble Inc., New York, NY, (First published 1902), 1966

——— *The House of Ptolemy: A History of Egypt Under the Ptolemaic Dynasty*, Argonaut, Chicago, 1927

The Biographical Dictionary Vol 3 Issue 1, Longmand, Brown, Green and

Longmans, Paternoster-Row, 1843

Briant, Pierre, *Alexander the Great and His Empire*, Translated by Amélie Kuhrt Princeton University Press, Princeton, New Jersey, 2010

——— *From Cyrus to Alexander: A History of the Persian Empire*, Eisenbrauns, Warsaw, IN, 2002

Brandt, Edward J., "The Exile and First Return of Judah," Ensign, July 1974

Brisch, Nicole, "Of Gods and Kings: Divine Kingship in Ancient Mesopotamia," University of Cambridge, Religion Compass Journal, 2013

Bromiley, Geoffrey W., *International Standard Bible Encyclopedia: 4 Vol.*, Eerdmans, Grand Rapids, MI. 1979

Brown, Francis, Driver, S.R. and Briggs, Charles A, *A Hebrew and English Lexicon of the Old Testament*, Oxford, Clarendon, Oxford University, United Kingdom 1955

Brown, Victor L., "Where Are You Going." BYU Speeches, June 04, 1978,m Accessed on July 15, 2016, https://speeches.byu.edu/talks/victor-l-brown_going/

Bullock C. Hassell, *An Introduction to the Old Testament Prophetic Books*, Moody Books, Chicago, IL. May 1, 2007

Butler, J. Glentworth, *The Bible-work*, vol ix, New York, 1894

Carey, Brian Todd, *Hannibal's Last Battle: Zama and the Fall of Carthage*, Westholme Publishing, Yardley, PA, 2007

Cartledge, Paul, *Alexander, the Great*. Vintage Books, Random House, New York, NY, 2004

Cartwright. Mark. "Salamis." *Ancient History Encyclopedia*. 05 May 2013 http://www.ancient.eu/salamis/

Charles, Robert Henry, *A Critical and Exegetical Commentary on the Book of Daniel*, Oxford, Clarendon, United Kingdom, 1929

Chisholm, Hugh, Encyclopedia Britannica 11th Ed. Charles Scribner's Sons, New York, NY. 1911

Christofferson, D. Todd, "Why the Church," General Conference, October 2015. https://www.lds.org/general-conference/2015/10/why-the-church?lang=eng

——— "Reflections on a Consecrated Life," General Conference, October 2010, https://www.lds.org/general-conference/2010/10/reflections-on-a-consecrated-life?lang=eng

Clark, Adam, *Commentary on the Whole Bible*, Vol. IV. Hunt and Eaton, New York, NY, 1832

Cornell Tim. J., Article in A Comparative Study of Thirty City-state Cultures: An Investigation, Volume 21, edited by Mogens Herman Hansen, Study conducted by the Copenhagen Polis Centre (Historisk-filosofiske Skrifter 21, 2000, 209 (Cornell says the form was used by the fetiales for declaring war and cites Livy 1.32.11-13)

Dawisha, Karen, *Putin's Kleptocracy: Who Owns Russia?*. Simon and Schuster, New, York, NY, 2014,

Derrick, Royden G. "Valiance in the Drama of Life." General Conference, April 1983

Driver, Samuel Rolles, *The Book of Daniel, with Introduction and Notes*, Cambridge University Press, Cambridge, United Kingdom, 1900

———— *Hebrew and English Lexicon of the Old Testament*, Oxford, Clarendon, 1955

Dyre, Charles, H., "Musical Instruments, Associate Professor of Bible Exposition, Dean of Enrollment Management," Bibliotheca Sacra, BSAC 147:588 (Oct 1990), http://www.galaxie.com/journals/1

Encyclopedia of World Biography, The Gale Group 2004, http://www.encyclopedia.com/topic/Seleucus_I.aspx#1

Encyclopedia Britannica "Ancient Egypt: From Prehistory to the Islamic Conquest." Britannica Educational Publishing, New York, 2011

Encyclopaedia Judaica. https://www.jewishvirtuallibrary.org/jsource/judaica/ejud_0002_0015_0_15109.html

Faust, James E. "Where Is the Church?," BYU Speeches, Mar. 1 2005 and Ensign, Aug. 1990

Featherstone, Vaugh J., *Incomparable Christ: Our Master and Model*, Deseret Book Company, September, 1995

Fields, Nic. *The Roman Army of the Punic Wars 264–146 B.C.* (Battle Orders), Osprey Publishing, United Kingdom, 2007

Fuller, John Fredrick Charles ,*The Generalship of Alexander the Great*. Da Carpo Press, Perseus Book Group, Cambridge, MA, 2004

Gaskill, Alonzo, *The Lost Language of Symbolism: An Essential Guide for Recognizing and Interpreting Symbols of the Gospel*, Deseret Book Company, Salt Lake City, Utah 2012

Gibbon, Edward *The Decline and Fall of the Roman Empire*, Chapter XXXVI

Gleason L. Archer, Jr. *The Expositor's Bible Commentary, vol. 7*, Frank E Gaebelein, ed. Grand Rapids, Zondervan, 1967

———— *Jerome's Commentary on Daniel*, Baker Book House, Grand Rapid MI, 1958

Glueck, Nelson, *Hesed in the Bible*, Alfred Gottscholk, ed., Gerald A. Lasruc, translation, Cincinnati, Hebrew Union College, Cincinnati, OH, 1967

Goldinggay, John E., *Daniel, Word Biblical Commentary Vol. 30*, David A. Hubbard and Glenn W. Barker, eds. Dallas: Word, 1989

Grainger, John D., *The Roman War of Antiochus the Great*, (Mnemosyne, Bibliotheca Classica Batava Supplementum), Brill Academic Pub. Netherlands, 2002

Grayson, A. Kirk, *Assyrian and Babylonian Chronicles*, repr, Winona Lake, IN, Eisenbrauns, 2000, 109-10

Greene, Peter, *Alexander of Macedon, 356-323 B.C.: A Historical Biography*, University of California Press, Berkley, CA. 1970

Grzybeck, E., *Du calendrier macédonien au calendrier ptolémaïque*, Basel, 1990

Guinness Book of World Record, "Largest Empire by Percentage of World Population." *Guinness World Records.* Retrieved 11 March 2015, Published by the Jim Pattison Group, Vancouver, BC, Entry: "Largest empire by percentage of world population." Guinness World Records. Retrieved 11 March 2015

Harris, Murray J., Harrison, Everett J., Bauman, Louis, *Expositors Bible Commentary 12 Vol*, Zondervan-Harper Collins, Nashville, TN,. June 2966

Harris, R. Laird, Archer Jr., Gleason L, and Walkte, Bruce K. , eds. *Theological Workbook of the Old Testament*, Chicago, Moody, Chicago, IL. 2003

Hastings, James. *"Propitiation", in A Dictionary of the Bible ed.* vol. 4, Edinburg T&T Clark, Edinburg, Scotland, 1902

Heinen, Heinz. "Ptolemy II Philadelphus, Macedonian King of Egypt." *Encyclopedia Britannica*, 2015), http://www.britannica.com/biography/Ptolemy-II-Philadelphus

Henrichsen, Kirk B. "Golden Plates Look Like?" *New Era* July 2007 - new-era. July 31, 2007 The Church of Jesus Christ of Latter-day Saints, Accessed October 26, 2017. https://www.lds.org/new-era/2007/07/what-did-the-golden-plates-look-like?lang=eng

Herodotus The Histories IV, V VII

Hochner, Herold, "Between the Testaments in *The Expositor's Bible Commentary*, Vol. 1, Frank E. Gabelein, ed, Zondervan, Grand Rapid, MI, 1985

——— *Chronological Aspects of the Life of Christ, Part 6*, "Daniel's Seventy Weeks and the New Testament Chronology," Zondervan, Grand Rapids, MI, 1973

Hunter, Howard W. "Standing As Witnesses of God." *Ensign*, The Church of Jesus Christ of Latter-day Saints, Salt Lake City, UT, May 1990

Hirsch, Emil G, Pick, Bernard, Schechter, Solomon, Ginzberg, Louis. "JewishEncyclopedia.com." JEHOIAKIM - JewishEncyclopedia. com, Jewish Encyclopedia, www.jewishencyclopedia.com/articles/8562-jehoiakim.

——— and Konig Edward. JewishEncyclopedia.com." BOOK OF DANIEL - JewishEncyclopedia.com, Jewish Encyclopedia

Ironside Henry Allen, *Lectures on Daniel the Prophet*, Loizeaux Brothers, Neptune, NJ. 1911

The Jewish Encyclopedia. Funk and Wagnalls, New York, NY, 1901-06

Jamieson, Robert, Brown, David. *Jamieson-Fausset-Brown A Commentary critical and explanatory on the whole Bible*, Zondervan, Grand Rapids, MI, 1871

Joshua, Marl J. "*Xerxes Ancient I*," History Encyclopedia, 28, April 2011 http://www.ancient.eu/Xerxes_I/

Josephus, *Antiquities of the Jews*

Journal of Discourses Vol. 1. The Church of Jesus Christ of Latter-day Saints , Salt Lake City. Utah. 1886

——— *Journal of Discourses* Vol. 22. The Church of Jesus Christ of Latter-day Saints. Salt Lake City. Utah. 1886

Jerome. *Commentary of the Book of Daniel, Trans. Gleason L Archer Jr. Ed.* Zondervan. Grand Rapids, MI. 1958

Justin, *Epitome*

Katz, Josh. "Drug Deaths in America Are Rising Faster Than Ever." The New York Times, The New York Times, 5 June 2017, www.nytimes. com/interactive/2017/06/05/upshot/opioid-epidemic-drug-overdose-deaths-are-rising-faster-than-ever.html.

Kindy, Kimberly, and Dan Keating. "For Women, Heavy Drinking Has Been Normalized. That's Dangerous." T*he Washington Post,* WP Company, 23 Dec. 2016, www.washingtonpost.com/national/for-women-heavy-drinking-has-been-normalized-thats-dangerous/2016/12/23/0e701120-c381-11e6-9578-0054287507db_story.html?utm_term=.773e75077249.

Keil, Carl Friedrich, and Franz Delitzsch. *Commentary on the Old Testament.*

Peabody, MA: Hendrickson Publishers, 2011.

Kimball Spencer W., "The Stone Cut Without Hands." General Conference, April 1976. https://www.lds.org/general-conference/1976/04/the-stone-cut-without-hands?lang=eng

———— "Why Call Me Lord, Lord and Do Not the Things Which I Say", General Conference April 1975

———— *Conference Report*, The Church of Jesus Christ of Latter-day Saints, Salt Lake City, UT, Apr. 1976

———— "Church Growth and Lamanite Involvement," BYU Speeches November 7, 1971. https://speeches.byu.edu/talks/spencer-w-kimball_church-growth-lamanite-involvement/

———— *Faith Precedes the Miracle*. Deseret Book, Salt Lake City, UT. 1972

Le Glay, Marcel, Voisin, Jean-Louism Le Bohec, Yann, *A History of Rome*, Blackwell Publishers, Oxford, U.K., 1996,

Lee, Harold B., in *Church News*, Deseret News, Salt Lake City, Utah, 15 Aug. 1970

———— in *Conference Report*, Apr. 1973; or *Ensign*, The Church of Jesus Christ of Latter-day Saints, Salt Lake City, UT, Apr. 1973

Lendering, Jona, Phalanx and Hoplites, Livius.org July 27, 2013. http://www.livius.org/pha-phd/phalanx/phalanx.html

Leupold, Herbert C., *Exposition of Daniel* (Seven Volumes), Minneapolis, Augburg, 1949 or Baker Book House, Grand Rapids, MI, 1969

Livy, *The History of Rome*, Penguin Classics, London, United Kingdom, 1946

Lonsdale, David J., *Alexander the Great: Lessons in strategy*. Routledge, Taylor and Francis Group, Abingdon, United Kingdom, 2007

Mallowan, M.E.L., "Nimrud", in *Archeology and Old Testament Study*, D. Winton Thomas ed., Oxford, Clarendon, 1967

"Intestinal Bug Likely Killed Alexander The Great". University of Maryland Medical Center. Retrieved Aug 21, 2011

Mark, Joshua J., "The Greek Phalanx" *History Encyclopedia*, 181, January, 2012, http://www.ancient.eu/article/110/

———— "Assyrian Warfare," *History Encyclopedia,* August 11, 2014; http://www.ancient.eu/Assyrian_Warfare/

———— "Alexander the Great," *Ancient History Encyclopedia*, Nov. 2013; http://www.ancient.eu/Alexander_the_Great/

Masuri, Behroozi, Majdabadi. *The history of political relations between Elam and Assyria, International Research Journal of Applied and Basic*

Sciences, Vol 4, 2176-2179

Maxwell, Neal A., "Endure It Well" General Conference, April 1990. Accessed May 24, 2016. https://www.lds.org/general-conference/1990/04/endure-it-well?lang=eng

———— *All These Thing Will Give Thee Experience*. Deseret Book Company, Salt Lake City, 1979.

———— "But for a Small Moment" BYU Devotionals. Brigham Young University Press. September 1, 1974. https://speeches.byu.edu/talks/neal-a-maxwell_small-moment/

———— "For I Will Lead You Along," General Conference, April 1988, ,The Church of Jesus Christ of Latter-day Saints, https://www.lds.org/general-conference/1988/04/for-i-will-lead-you-along?lang=eng

———— Insights from My Life, *Ensign*,The Church of Jesus Christ of Latter-day Saints, Salt Lake City, Utah. August 2000. https://www.lds.org/ensign/2000/08/insights-from-my-bernsonlife?lang=eng

———— Interview with Janet Peterson, Liahona June 1984, https://www.lds.org/liahona/1984/06/friend-to-friend?lang=eng

Maynes, Richard J. "The Truth Restored" Worldwide Devotional for Young Adults, May 1, 2016. https://www.lds.org/broadcasts/article/worldwide-devotionals/2016/01/the-truth-restored?lang=eng

McConkie, Bruce R. "*Understanding the Book of Revelation*." Ensign Sept. 1975, The Church of Jesus Christ of Latter-day Saints, Accessed on website October 26, 2017. https://www.lds.org/ensign/1975/09/understanding-the-book-of-revelation?lang=eng

McConkie, Bruce R., *Mormon Doctrine*, Bookcraft, Salt Lake City, UT. 1972

McConkie, Bruce R., *The Millennial Messiah: The Second Coming of the Son of Man*, Deseret Book, Salt Lake City, UT, 1982

McKay, David O., General Conference Address, Priesthood Session, The Church of Jesus Christ of Latter-day Saints, Salt Lake City, UT., April 9, 1966

Meissner 1, 122

Merriam-Webster, Merriam-Webster, George and Charles Merriam, G & C Merriam Co. in Springfield, MA, Ref: megalomania

Miller, Daniel, *The New American Commentary*, Broadman & Holman, Nashville, TN. 2001

Montgomery, James A., *A Critical and Exegetical Commentary on the Book of Daniel*, T&T Clark, Edinburgh Scotland, New York, NY, Scribner, 1927

National Institute on Drug. "Overdose Death Rates." NIDA, U.S. Department of Health and Human Services, 15 Sept. 2017, www.drugabuse. gov/related-topics/trends-statistics/overdose-death-rates.

Nelson, President Russell M. "Joy and Spiritual Survival." General Conference, October 2016. The Church of Jesus Christ of Latter-Day Saints, 2 Oct. 2016, www.lds.org/general-conference/2016/10/ joy-and-spiritual-survival?lang=eng.

—— "Revelation for the Church, Revelation for Our lives," General Conference   April   2018,   https://www.lds.org/general-conference/2018/04/revelation-for-the-church-revelation-for-our-lives?lang=eng

New American Standard Bible, Lockman Foundation, La Habra, CA, 1995 (1963, 1971)

New York Times Staff. "The Numbers Behind America's Heroin Epidemic." The New York Times, The New York Times, 30 Oct. 2015,   www.nytimes.com/interactive/2015/10/30/us/31heroin-deaths.html.

Oats, Harry, "The Great Jewish Revolt of 66 CE." *Ancient History Encyclopedia*, published on 28 August 2015. http://www.ancient. eu/article/823/

O Brian, John Maxwell., *Alexander the Great: The Invisible Enemy: A Biography*, Routledge, London and New York, 1992

Old Testament Institute Manual Vol. 2, Third Edition, The Church of Jesus Christ of Latter-day Saints, Salt Lake City, UT, 1981, 1982, 2003

Olmstead, A. T., History of the Persian Empire, University of Chicago Press, 1948

Oppert, *Expedition Scientifique on Mesopotamie* 1:238 ff

Packer, Boyd K., *Let Not Your Heart Be Troubled*. Deseret Book Company, Salt Lake City, Utah 1991. Ref. Address given at American Freedom Festival, Provo, Utah, 25 June 1989

Pentecost, J. Dwight, *Prophecy for Today*, Zondervan, Grand Rapids, MI, 1961

——— *Daniel The Bible Knowledge Commentary: Old Testament* Vol. I, John, Zuck Roy B., eds., Victor Books, Wheaton, Il. 1985

Perry, L. Tom, "I Confer the Priesthood of Aaron," General Conference, October 1985

Phillips, John, *Exploring the Book of Daniel: An Expository Commentary*,

Kregel Publications, Grand Rapids, MI, 2004

Philostratus, Flavius, *The Life of Appollonius of Tyana*, 6:29, translated by F.C. Conybeare, Loeb Classical Library, 1912; See also: Neh. 1:8

Plutarch Vol. VI

Pohlenz, Max. *Freedom in Greek life and thought: the history of an ideal*, Springer, New York, NY, 1966

Polybius; *The Histories*, Evelyn S. Shuckburgh (translator); McMillian, London - New York, 1889, reprint Bloomington 1962

Pratt Orson, *Journal of Discourses*. Vol. 18 and "Theocracy" Vol. [7.] The Church of Jesus Christ of Latter-day Saints , Salt Lake City, Utah

Pratt Parley, P., *Autobiography of Parley Parker Pratt*, Deseret Book Company, Salt Lake City, Utah, 1938

Pusey, Edward B., *Daniel the Prophet*. Funk & Wagnalls, New York, NY. 1885

Prichard, James B., *Ancient Near Eastern Texts Relating to the Old Testament*, Princeton 3rd. ed. , Princeton University Press, Princeton, NJ, 1969

Ramirez-Faria, Carlos, *Concise Encyclopedia of World History*, New Delhi: Atlantic Publishers & Distributors, New Delhi, India 2007

Rojas, Nicole. "Iran's Ayatollah Ali Khamenei publishes book to destroy Israel and deceive US." *International Business Times,* United Kingdom. August 02, 2015. Accessed December 20, 2017. http://www.ibtimes.co.uk/irans-ayatollah-ali-khamenei-publishes-book-destroy-israel-deceive-us-1513761.

Romney, Marion G., "We Need Men of Courage," General Conference, April 1975. The Church of Jesus Christ of Latter-day Saints, Salt Lake City, Utah

Roisman, Joseph and Worthington, Ian; A *Companion to Ancient Macedonia*. Jon Wiley and Sons, Hoboken, N.J., 2010

Sachau, C. Edward. *The Chronology of Ancient Nations*. Kessinger Publishing., Whitefish, MT, 2004

Scott, Richard G. "*Make the Exercise of Faith Your First Priority*," General Conference, October 2015

Seibert, Jakob. *Encyclopedia Britannica*, 3-23-15, References https://www.britannica.com/biography/Seleucus-I-Nicator

Seiss, Joseph A., *Voices from Babylon, Or the Record of Daniel the Prophet*, Porter and Coates, Philadelphia, PA.1879

Shea, William H., Daniel's Extra-Biblical Text and the Convocation on the Plains of Dura, Andrews University Seminary Studies 20, (Spring, 1982), Andrews University Press, Berrien Springs, MI, 1982

Simmons, Dennis E. "But If Not…" General Conference, April 2004, Accessed March 24, 2014. https://www.lds.org/general-conference/2004/04/but-if-not?lang=eng

Skinner, Andrew C., Ogden, Daniel Kelly, and Galbraith, David B. *Jerusalem, The Eternal City*. Deseret Book, Salt Lake City, UT, 1996

Smith, Joseph, The History of the Church, The Church of Jesus Christ of Latter-day Saints, Salt Lake City, UT, 2010

Smith, Joseph Fielding, *Seek Ye Earnestly*, Deseret Book Company, Salt Lake City, 1970

———— *Teachings of the Prophet Joseph Smith,* Deseret Book Company, Salt Lake City, Utah, 1976

———— *The Progress of Man*, 3rd ed. [1944], Deseret Book, Salt Lake City, 1973

———— Scriptural Enhancement by Galbraith, Richard, C *Scriptural Teachings of the Prophet Joseph Smith*, Deseret Book Company, Salt Lake City, Utah, 1993

———— *Way to Perfection,* Deseret Book Company, Salt Lake City, Utah, 1978 (17th Printing)

Smith, William, *A Dictionary of the Bible: Comprising Its Antiquities, Biography, Geography, and Natural History*. Cambridge University Press, Cambridge, United Kingdom, 1893

Smith, William (1813-1893), *A Dictionary of the Bible*, s.v. "Shinar."

Steinman, Andrew E., *Daniel* - Concordia Commentary, Concodia Publishing House, St. Louis, MO, 2008

Stone, David R., "Zion in the Midst of Babylon, " General Conference, April 2006, https://www.lds.org/general-conference/2006/04/zion-in-the-midst-of-babylon?lang=eng

Stuart, Moses, *A Commentary of the Book of Daniel*, Boston: Crocker & Brewster, 1850

Tanner, J Paul, "Ancient Babylon: From Gradual Demise To Archaeological Rediscovery," APP. P.1 http://paultanner.org/English%20Docs/Daniel/Introductory/App%20P%20-%20Archaeological%20Backgrd.pdf

Tarn, William W. *Alexander the Great, 2 Vol.*, Cambridge University Press, Cambridge, United Kingdom, 1948

Teachings of Presidents of the Church: George Albert Smith, The Church of Jesus Christ of Latter-day Saints, Salt Lake City, UT, 2010, Chapter 17, Strengthening Power of Faith

Trapp, John, *A Commentary on the Old and New Testaments* Vol X, London, 1660

Uchtdorf, Deiter, F., "Be Not Afraid,." Only Believe, General Conference Report, October 3, 2015. Accessed December 17, 2016. https://www.lds.org/general-conference/2015/10/be-not-afraid-only-believe?lang=eng

———— "Are You Sleeping through the Restoration?" General Conference, April 2001. https://www.lds.org/general-conference/2014/04/are-you-sleeping-through-the-restoration?lang=eng

Venning, Timothy. *A Chronology of Ancient Greece*. Pen and Sword, Barnsley, United Kingdom. 2016

Volkmann, Hans. "Antiochus IV Epiphanies." Encyclopedia Britannica, Encyclopædia Britannica, Inc., 5 May 2014, www.britannica.com/biography/Antiochus-IV-Epiphanes

Walvoord, John F. Daniel: *The Key to Prophetic Revelation*, Moody Publishers, Chicago IL, 2012

Walter K., *In the Final Days*, Moody, Chicago, IL. 1977

Waters, Benjamin Victor. "The Two Eschatological Perspectives of the Book of Daniel" *Scandinavian Journal of the Old Testament*, Rice University, Tx. 2016

Watrall, Ethan. >. "ANP203-History-of-Archaeology-Lecture-2". Anthropology.msu.edu. Retrieved 7 April 2014

Werner, Robert, "Ptolemy I Soter, Macedonian King of Egypt," *Encyclopedia Britannica 2015*, http://www.britannica.com/biography/Ptolemy-I-Soter

Wheaton, D. H. "Antiochus" in *New Bible Dictionary*, J. D. Douglas ed., Eerdmans, Grand Rapids, MI, 1965

Whitney, Orson F., *Life of Heber C. Kimball*, Juvenile Instructor Office, 1988, Published by Kessinger Publishing, Whitefish, MT

Widstoe, John ., *Discourses of Brigham Young,* Deseret Book Company, Salt Lake City, Utah, *1924*

Wilford Woodruff, *Conference Report*, April 1898, The Church of Jesus Christ of Latter-day Saints, Salt Lake City, UT, 1898

Wiseman, D.J., "Belshazzar, in the *New Bible Dictionary*, J.D., Douglas, ed. Grand Rapids. Eerdmans, 1965

Woodruff, Wilford, *Conference Report* 1898. The Church of Jesus Christ of Latter-day Saints, Salt Lake City, Utah, 1998

Wood, Leon J., *A Commentary on Daniel,* Zondervan, Grand Rapids, MI, June 1, 1975 or Zondervan, 1973

Xenophon, *Cyropaedia,* 194-95

Yarshater, *Iranian Encyclopedia,* 1996

Young, Brigham, In *Journal of Discourses,* The Church of Jesus Christ of Latter-day Saints , Salt Lake City, Utah, 1886

——— Journal History, 4 July 1854; Church News, 15 December 1948

Young, Edward J., *The Prophecy Daniel: A Commentary,* Eerdmans Publishing Company, Grand Rapids, MI, 1977

Young, T. Cuyler, Jr. (1988), "The early history of the Medes and the Persians and the Achaemenid empire to the death of Cambyses", in Boardman, John; Hammond, N. G. L.; Lewis, D. M.; Oswald, M., The Cambridge Ancient History 4, Cambridge University Press, Cambridge, United Kingdom

Youngblood, Ronald F., Bruce, F.F, and Harrison, R. K. ed. *Unlock the Bible: Keys to Exploring the Culture and Times.* Harper Collins Christian Publishing, Thomas Nelson, Nashville, TN, 2012

Zeockler, Otto, *The Book of the Prophet Daniel, Theologically and Homiletically Expounded* (Part of Lang's Bible) Translated, enlarged and edited by James Long, New York, 1976

Index

Symbols

3 1/2 (three and one half), Daniel is given the number 1290 days, which matches the coded language (time=1, times=2, and half time=½ 400, number 3½ is symbolic of a critical period, a time of crisis 391

A

Abed-nego (Azariah) 38, 72, 74

Abomination of Desolation cast the "truth" and the hosts of chosen to the ground 233, Overspreading of Abomination until the End 286, of 70 A.D 287, sacrificed a pig on the altar and ordered the worship of the Olympian Zeus 231, temple participated in celebrations with drinking and the sacrificing of forbidden animals 231, 234, How long shall be the vision concerning the daily sacrifice, and the transgression of desolation 234, 389

Achaemenid Empire 169, 195, flag of Achaemenid Empire 142

Adam, (see also; Michael, the archangel): Adam as a glorious being of majesty and beauty to whom thousands and tens of thousands attend 186-187, he will make his report, as the one holding the keys for this earth, to his Superior Officer, Jesus Christ 190

Adam-ondi-Ahman The Great Council at Adam-ondi-Ahman 189, ruins of three altars built of stone 189, gathering of the children at Adam-ondi-Ahman will involve thousands of participants 191

Agothocles and Sosibius (Egyptian Counselors) 331

Ahasuerus 252, is the Biblical equivalent or transliteration of the Greek name for Xerxes 252, as he is referred to in the Bible 314

Alexander the Great, led swift campaigns from Greece to Hellespont on the tip of Lydia all the way to Babylon and on to India 172, was Greek, a student of Aristotle 174, He died abruptly from illness and over drinking 174, His juggernaut forces captured the Persian empire in just twelve years 174, successfully subdued rebellions from Thrace and other uprisings from competitive city-states 219, inherited his father's kingdom and maintained the rule over Greece 219, obtained the kingdom at the age of 20 220, his passion as pathos, or an insatiable drive for battle 220, he sacrificed a bull to Poseidon and made libation with a golden vessel 221, both as a liberator and a new Pharaoh, a son of the gods 223, expeditions extended from Greece into India 223, general routed the king in a pitch battle at Gaugamela 223, recruited and trained troops from among the Persian ranks 224, wanted a bloodless victory and promised to honor the gods of Babylon 224, the great horn was broken 226, would exact his revenge by invading Asia Minor 316, A mighty king stands up, who doubtless was the renowned Alexander the Great 317, he died suddenly in Nebuchadnezzar's Palace in Babylon 317, His half brother, Philip Arrhidaeus, an epileptic 318, used this power to expand the Grecian Empire from Athens to India 239, He called himself the son of Zeus 354

Amel-Merodach (Evil-Merodach) 5, 113

Ancient of Days (see also Adam or Michael), The title means "one of advanced days or the oldest man 186, Daniel records that Christ, the Son of Man, comes to the Ancient of Days at this council 187

Anderson, conducted a thorough study of the timeframe and created a framework 278

Angel (see also Watcher), One angel stands near him on his side of the Tigris River 388

Anoint, Anointed, or "chosen one 273, the Most Holy 273 anointed'… [and] denotes the King and Deliverer whose coming the Jews were eagerly expecting 281

anti-Christ (see also Little Horn, Beast or Gog), anti-Christ speaks great words 200, ever promote major cultural transformations that move society 201, in the likeness of Antiochus Epiphanies has come to power 312, a future king and the prophecies come to pass at the end of time or in the latter-days 352, He refers to him as the king of the north 353, He has no regard for his father's gods or the gods of women 356, the pronoun "him" refers to the king of the north, or Gog, the latter-day anti-Christ 361, dies on the mountains of Ephraim, just between Tel Aviv and Jerusalem 364, anti-Christs together with the wicked populations of the world will not understand the Lord's purposes 395, modern secularist governments will join with unprecedented

B

D

X

Z

49725053R00252

Made in the USA
Columbia, SC
27 January 2019